Taking Sides: Clashing Views
on Psychological Issues, 20/e

Edwin E. Gantt

http://create.mheducation.com

ISBN-10: 1259910741   ISBN-13: 9781259910746

Contents

Detailed Table of Contents

Gerald J. Haeffel and his colleagues believe that psychological studies of American people often generalize to people of other cultures, especially when basic processes are being studied. Jeffrey Jensen Arnett, a psychological research professor, argues that culture is central to the functioning of humans and thus to psychological findings.

Issue: Are Traditional Empirical Methods Sufficient to Provide Evidence for Psychological Practice?
YES: APA President Task Force on Evidence-Based Practice, from "Report of the 2005 Presidential Task Force on Evidence-Based Practice," *American Psychological Association* (2006)
NO: Brent D. Slife and Dennis C. Wendt, from "The Next Step in the Evidence-Based Practice Movement," *Speech or Remarks* (2006)

The APA Presidential Task Force on Evidence-based Practice assumes that a variety of traditional empirical methods is sufficient to provide evidence for psychological practices. Psychologist Brent D. Slife and researcher Dennis C. Wendt contend that traditional empirical methods are guided by a single philosophy that limits the diversity of methods.

Issue: Is Psychology a Science?
YES: Robert E. Silverman, from "Is Psychology a Science?" *Skeptic Magazine* (2011)
NO: Peter Rickman, from "Is Psychology Science?" *Philosophy Now* (2009)

Robert E. Silverman, an academic psychologist writing in Skeptic Magazine, presents a brief history of psychology and a few of its main figures while addressing the role of science in psychology. He argues that over time psychology has become more scientific (i.e., more objective in observations and measurement). He concludes that as the current partnership of psychology and neuroscience grows stronger, there will be no question that psychology is indeed a science. Peter Rickman, formerly professor of philosophy at City University in London, argues that psychology is not a science like physics and other natural sciences because although it shares certain aspects of the scientific method, it must and does rely on the methods of hermeneutics. He argues that because observable facts are not the data being studied in psychology, but rather meaningful communication, psychology must always consider context and background in its research. The scientific method is not sufficient for psychology to accomplish this task.

Unit 3: Development Issues

Issue: Are Violent Video Games Harmful to Children and Adolescents?
YES: Steven F. Gruel, from "Brief of *Amicus Curiae* in Case of *Brown v. Entertainment Merchants Association*," *U.S. Supreme Court* (2010)
NO: Patricia A. Millett, from "Brief of *Amici Curiae* in Case of *Brown v. Entertainment Merchants Association*," *U.S. Supreme Court* (2010)

Prosecutor Steven F. Gruel, in arguing before the Supreme Court, cites what he says is an overwhelming amount of research support to conclude that viewing violence causes children to act more violently. Defense attorney Patricia A. Millett argues before the Supreme Court that psychological research about the effects of media violence on children is inconclusive, with these researchers making claims about causation that cannot be substantiated.

Issue: Does Parent Sexual Orientation Affect Child Development?
YES: Peter Sprigg, from "New Study on Homosexual Parents Tops All Previous Research: Children of Homosexuals Fare Worse on Most Outcomes," *Family Research Council* (2012)
NO: Carmine D. Boccuzzi, Jr. et al., from "Brief of Amicus Curiae of the American Sociological Association on Behalf of Appellants," *American Sociological Association* (2013)

Peter Sprigg of the Family Research Council recapitulates the arguments and findings of Mark Regnerus, concluding that the idea that children of homosexual parents are no different than children of heterosexual parents and, thus, are unharmed by the gender of their parents is a myth. Attorney Carmine Boccuzzi and colleagues, critiquing that the methods and findings of the Regnerus's study and other similar studies, argue that children of homosexual parents are just as well off as children of heterosexual parents in most aspects of life.

Unit 4: Cognitive-Emotional Issues

Issue : Can Positive Psychology Make Us Happier?
YES: Stephen M. Schueller and Acacia C. Parks, from "The Science of Self-Help: Translating Positive Psychology Research into Increased Individual Happiness," *European Psychologist* (2014)
NO: Laurel C. Newman and Randy J. Larsen, from "How Much of Our Happiness Is Within Our Control?" *Original Essay* (2009)

Positive psychologists Stephen M. Schueller and Acacia C. Parks present a summary of the current state of positive psychological interventions as they pertain to self-help, interventions   that have been shown to lead to increases in individual happiness. Psychologists Laurel C. Newman and Randy J. Larsen challenge the external validity and sustainability of the effects of these strategies, arguing that most of what influences our long-term happiness is outside our control.

Psychologists John D. Mayer, Peter Salovey, and David R. Caruso maintain that some individuals have a greater emotional intelligence, a greater capacity than others to carry out sophisticated   information processing about emotions. Psychologists Gerald Matthew, Moshe Zeidner, and Richard D. Roberts contend that the concept of emotional intelligence, as currently understood, is fundamentally flawed, having no reliable foundation in biological, cognitive, coping, or personality models of human behavior.

Unit 5: Mental Health Issues

The National Institute of Mental Health asserts that ADHD is a real disorder that merits special   consideration and treatment. Sami Timimi and Nick Radcliffe insist that ADHD is not a medical disorder as it has no demonstrable biological cause; rather, it is not a disorder at all, but an agenda-driven,   socially constructed entity invented by Western society.

The National Institute on Drug Abuse describes drug abuse and addiction as a disease of the brain. Although initial drug use may be voluntary, the resulting physical changes to brain circuits explain the compulsive and self-destructive behaviors of addiction. Environmental and genetic factors explain why some become addicted more readily than others. Journalist and author Peter Hitchens argues that because the disease model of addiction is deterministic, it fundamentally misunderstands human nature and the ability people have to make meaningful choices regarding how they are going to live their lives.

Robert H. Howland argues that although medications may be dangerous in some situations, the history of psychiatric pharmacology has demonstrated the actual benefits from the medications outweigh the potential harm. Gary G. Kohls, a retired physician, argues that many of the "facts" about psychiatric medications are myths, questioning the effectiveness and safety of their use.

Unit 6: Psychotherapy Issues

Psychologists Mark A. Hubble, Barry L. Duncan, and Scott D. Miller argue that all effective therapies are essentially alike, while all ineffective therapies are ineffective in their own way. In addition,   while many different psychotherapies are effective in relieving the suffering of patients, all of these therapies are effective because of the factors they all possess in common, not for any unique belief or procedure a therapy may possess. Psychologists Jedidiah Siev, Jonathan D . Huppert, and Dianne L. Chambless assert that outcomes among the various psychotherapies differ primarily because one technique or therapy is better than another.

Issue: Should Therapists Be Eclectic?
YES: Jean A. Carter, from "Theoretical Pluralism and Technical Eclecticism," *American Psychological Association* (2006)
NO: Don MacDonald and Marcia Webb, from "Toward Conceptual Clarity with Psychotherapeutic Theories," *Journal of Psychology and Christianity* (2006)

Counseling psychologist Jean A. Carter insists that the continued improvement and effectiveness of psychotherapy requires that techniques and theories include the different approaches of psychological theory and practice through an eclectic approach. Professors of psychotherapy Don MacDonald and Marcia Webb contend that eclecticism creates an unsystematic theoretical center for psychological ideas and methods that ultimately limits overall therapeutic effectiveness.

Unit 7: Social Issues

Issue: Can Psychotherapy Change Sexual Orientation?
YES: Joseph Nicolosi, A. Dean Byrd, and Richard W. Potts, from "Retrospective Self-Reports of Changes in Homosexual Orientation: A Consumer Survey of Conversion Therapy Clients," *Psychological Reports* (2000)
NO: Pan American Health Organization, from "'Cures' for an Illness That Does Not Exist," PAHO (2012)

Joseph Nicolosi, A. Dean Byrd, and Richard W. Potts surveyed a large number of individuals who self-identified as homosexual—both before and after receiving conversion therapy—to determine whether the therapy was an effective means of changing sexual orientation. PAHO asserts that there is no scientific evidence for the effectiveness of sexual reorientation efforts, and that efforts aimed at changing non-heterosexual orientations lack medical justification. The PAHO statement views "conversion therapies" as threats to personal autonomy and to personal integrity.

Issue: Is Gender Identity Biological?
YES: Aruna Saraswat, Jamie D. Weinand, and Joshua D. Safer, from "Evidence Supporting the Biological Nature of Gender Identity," *Endocrine Practice* (2015)
NO: Michael J. Carter, from "Gender Socialization and Identity Theory," *Social Sciences* (2014)

Aruna Saraswat, Jamie D. Weinand, and Joshua D. Safer review empirical studies that suggest gender as biologically caused. They discuss congenital adrenal hyperplasia, gray and white matter studies, and twin case studies as evidence for their argument is that gender has a biological basis. Michael J. Carter explores a review of the literature that emphasizes gender identity as being based in learned roles. He discusses how gender is learned over time in the family environment and how gender can be a person identity, role identity, or social identity in gender identity theory. He argues that gender comes from learned roles in society.

Issue: Is Marriage Uniquely Important?
YES: Galena Rhoades, from "Sliding versus Deciding: How Cohabitation Changes Marriage," *The Family in America* (2016)
NO: Brienna Perelli-Harris and Marta Styrc, from "Re-evaluating the Link between Marriage and Mental Well-being: How Do Early Life Conditions Attenuate Differences between Cohabitation and Marriage?" *ESRC Center for Population Change, Working Paper 75* (2016)

Galena Rhoades summarizes research findings that indicate that stronger and more enduring marital relationships, and better mental health outcomes, occur when people make conscious decisions to commit to another person in a marital relationship rather than "sliding into" a marriage as the result of a progressive development of cohabiting. Brienna Perelli-Harris and Marta Styrc argue that marriage affords no benefits over cohabitation in most circumstances. Their results indicate that when controlling for childhood characteristics, living with a partner increases well-being, but the type of relationship (marriage vs. cohabitation) does not matter.

Issue: Is Excessive Use of Social Media a Form of Narcissism?
YES: Soraya Mehdizadeh, from "Self-Presentation 2.0: Narcissism and Self-Esteem on Facebook," *Cyberpsychology, Behavior, and Social Networking* (2010)
NO: Alex Lambert, from "Discovering Intimacy on Facebook," *Macmillan* (2013)

Soraya Mehdizadeh examines how narcissism and self-esteem are manifest on Facebook. Her study reveals that individuals who rate higher in narcissism and lower in self-esteem tend to use Facebook significantly more than those who score lower in narcissism and higher in self-esteem. Alex Lambert, a researcher of new media at University of Melbourne, reviews the arguments against the narcissism hypothesis. He claims that Facebook use is primarily about seeking intimacy with other people and not about fulfilling narcissistic desires.

Preface

Critical-thinking skills are essential to a meaningful education in psychological science, and so this book is specifically designed to help develop critical thinking abilities by stimulating lively and informed dialogue on psychological issues. In this book, we present 36 selections, arranged in pro and con pairs and addressing a total of 20 different controversial issues in contemporary psychology. One of the main things that these opposing views clearly demonstrate is that even experts can derive conflicting conclusions and opinions even when drawing on the same body of information and research.

A back-and-forth, dialogue-centered approach to learning is certainly not new. Ancient Greek philosophers such as Socrates and Aristotle engaged in it with their students some 2,400 years ago. The point–counterpoint procedure they employed was termed a *dialectic*. Although these ancient philosophers hoped to eventually arrive at and know the "truth" by this method, they did not see the dialectic as necessarily having a predetermined end. That is, they acknowledged that there was usually no one right answer to know or arrive at that had been determined in advance. The emphasis in a dialectical learning approach is not so much on memorizing facts or deriving the only correct answer to a puzzle, as it is on learning how to evaluate information and developing critical and careful reasoning skills.

It is in this dialectical spirit that *Taking Sides: Clashing Views on Psychological Issues* was originally compiled, and which has guided work on this edition as well. To encourage and stimulate discussion and to focus the debates in this volume, each issue is expressed in terms of a single question that is answered with two different points of view. However, the reader should never feel confined to adopt only one or the other of the positions presented. Rather, readers are encouraged to work through the various issues at hand and fashion their own conclusions. In so doing, it would not be surprising to find that readers' positions may fall in a variety of places between the views expressed in these pages or even totally outside them.

Some of the questions raised in this volume go to the very heart of what psychology as an intellectual discipline is all about—its most basic aims and assumptions and its accepted methods and practices, not to mention the manner in which psychologists go about their work. Other questions address newly emerging social, moral, and political concerns. In choosing readings for this volume, the following criteria have been of central concern: the readings have to be understandable to newcomers to psychology, they must have academic substance, and they must express markedly different points of view.

Plan of the Book

Each issue in this volume has an issue *introduction*, which defines each author's position and sets the stage for debate. Also provided is a set of possible learning outcomes and critical thinking/reflection questions that pertain to the issue and help to get the dialogue off the ground. Each issue concludes by exploring whether there may be some common ground between the differing perspectives that might warrant further consideration and discussion. The introduction and critical thinking questions are designed to assist the reader in achieving a critical and informed view on important psychological issues. Also, at the end of each issue is a list of Internet References that will prove useful as starting points for further research.

A Word to the Instructor

An online guidebook, *Using Taking Sides in the Classroom*, which discusses methods and techniques for integrating the pro–con approach into any classroom setting, is available for the instructor using *Taking Sides*. *Using Taking Sides in the Classroom* and a correspondence service for *Taking Sides* adopters can be found at www.mhhe.com/createcentral.

Taking Sides: Clashing Views in Psychological Issues is only one title in the *Taking Sides* series. If you are interested in seeing the table of contents for any of the other titles, please visit the *Taking Sides* website at www.mhhe.com/cls.

Edwin E. Gantt, PhD
Brigham Young University

Editor of This Volume

EDWIN E. GANTT is currently an associate professor of psychology at Brigham Young University, where he is a member of the applied social psychology faculty. He is also an associate graduate faculty at the University of Nevada, Las Vegas and a visiting fellow of the

Wheatley Institution. He has been honored with several awards for his scholarship and teaching, including the Sigmund Koch Award for Early Career Contributions to Theoretical and Philosophical Psychology, Teacher of Honor Award (BYU Student Honor Association), and Teacher of the Year by the BYU chapter of Psi Chi, the psychology student honor society.

Gantt received his doctoral degree in clinical psychology from Duquesne University, where he focused his studies on existential phenomenology and qualitative research methods. While there he was recognized for excellence in scholarship by a graduate student. He has been active in several professional organizations, including the American Psychological Association (APA) and the Society of Theoretical and Philosophical Psychology. He has served as a membership chair and as conference program chair for Division 24 (Theoretical and Philosophical Psychology) of the APA. He has served on the editorial boards and as a reviewer for a variety of academic journals, including Journal of Mind and Behavior, Journal of Theoretical and Philosophical Psychology, Theory and Psychology, Journal of Humanistic Psychology, Psychological Methods, Journal of Family Theory and Review, Journal of Contemporary Psychotherapy, Philosophy of the Social Sciences, and Issues in Religion and Psychotherapy.

He has authored over 50 articles and book chapters, as well as coedited the book Psychology-for-the-Other: Levinas, Ethics, and the Practice of Psychotherapy. He is currently working on a book about the history of scientism in psychology. His work has appeared in such journal as Theory and Psychology, Journal of Theoretical and Philosophical Psychology, Journal of Phenomenological Psychology, Journal of Clinical Psychology, American Journal of Medical Quality Journal of Moral Education, and Journal of Humanistic Psychology, as well as in such books as Meaning in Existential and Positive Psychology (2014, Springer), Self-Observation in the Human Sciences (2012, Transaction Publishers), Taking Sides: Clashing Views on Psychological Issues (2009, McGraw-Hill), and Critical Thinking About Psychology: Hidden Assumptions and Plausible Alternatives (2005, APA Books).

Acknowledgments

In working on this revision, I have received many useful suggestions from the users of the previous edition and have incorporated a number of their recommendations for new issues and new readings. Of particular assistance in preparing this new edition have been the tireless and careful efforts of our editorial research assistants: David Top, Thomas Bown, Daniel Davies, Caitlyn Mack, and Kaitlyn Wright. In addition, special thanks to the McGraw-Hill staff for their support and perspective.

Academic Advisory Board Members

Members of the Academic Advisory Board are instrumental in the final selection of articles for each edition of Taking Sides. Their review of articles for content, level, and appropriateness provides critical direction to the editor and staff. We think that you will find their careful consideration well reflected in this volume.

Gary Forde
St. Louis Community College—Forest Park

William Fry
Youngstown State University

John Gamble II
Georgia Piedmont Technical College

Ericka Goerling
Portland Community College—Cascade

Evan Gorelck
Germanna Community College

Jerry Green
Tarrant County College—Northwest Campus

Jennifer Grewe
Utah State University—Logan

Nancy Gup
Georgia Perimeter College

Carmon Hicks
Ivy Tech Community College

Debra Hollister
Valencia College

Martha Hubertz
Florida Atlantic University

Alisha Janowsky
University of Central Florida

Jason Jarvis
University of Michigan—Flint

Staci Simmelink Johnson
Walla Walla Community College

Richard Kensinger
Mount Aloysius College

Sandra Kerr
West Chester University

Shelley Kilpatrick
Southwest Baptist University

Richard Klene
Central Wyoming College—Jackson Campus

Romney Landis
Weatherford College

Barbara LaRue
Baker College, Port Huron

Sandra Lee
LA Southwest College

Linda Lockwood
Metropolitan State University of Denver

Donald Lynch
Unity College

Frank Machovec
Stetson University

Christopher McNally
John Carroll University

Charles Meeker
St. Clair County Community College

Megan Meyer
Holy Family University

Dennis Miller
University of Missouri

Scott Mirabile
St. Mary's College of MD

Kathy O'Brien
Grand View University

Natasha Otto
Morgan State University

Brian Parry
Colorado Mesa University

David Payne
Wallace Community College

Tracey Powell
Western Oregon University

Harvey Richman
Columbus State University

Robert Ridge
Brigham Young University

Sheldon H. Rifkin
Kennesaw State University

Vicki Ritts
St. Louis Community College, Meramec

Lisa Routh
Pikes Peak Community College

Clayton Ryan
Bunker Hill Community College

Josephine Salloway
Curry College

David Schwartz
Kennesaw State University

Jin Shin
Hofstra University

Weylin Sternglanz
Nova Southeastern University

Monica Sylvia
Le Moyne College

Kim Taylor
Spokane Falls Community College

Melissa Terlecki
Cabrini College

Barbara Toner
Troy University

Leasa Tucker
Indiana University Southeast

Anna Tyrell
Lake Erie College

EA Vasquez
Los Angeles City College

Jason Warnick
Arkansas Tech University

Glenda Warren
University of the Cumberlands

Kittie Weber
New England College

Jane Whitaker
University of the Cumberlands

Lois J. Willoughby
Miami Dade College

Paul Wills
Kilgore College

Troy University

Karen Wolford
SUNY Oswego

Introduction: Clashing Views and Critical Thinking

A persistent topic of discussion in higher education, and particularly in psychology, is the need to develop more and better critical thinking skills among both psychology students and the larger public. Unfortunately, what exactly the term "critical thinking" means, or how best to develop critical thinking skills in others, is not always clearly articulated or understood. What is clear, however, is that despite some serious disagreements and confusions about what critical thinking might actually look like and how we might teach it most effectively, almost everyone agrees that we would all benefit if there were more of it taking place.

While this textbook is not specifically a primer on critical thinking, per se, it does aim to contribute to the development of some basic and necessary critical thinking skills in students of psychology. Before we can appreciate exactly how this textbook might successfully achieve that lofty goal, however, it is vital that we take some time to discuss briefly (and, necessarily, incompletely) some of the essential features of critical, analytical thinking. Indeed, taking time to clarify concepts, provide definite meanings to them, and get clear about what it is exactly one is doing is one hallmark feature of critical thinking.

Ironically, perhaps the best way to begin such a discussion is to clarify what exactly critical thinking is NOT. For many people, the "critical" part of "critical thinking" means just being dismissive of, or cynical about, what other people have said or think solely for the sake of criticizing it. A continuously dismissive or negative attitude toward ideas, however, does not serve to advance the pursuit of truth and knowledge. Rather, it can be quite limiting insofar as always greeting others' ideas or perspectives with negative dismissal, in the mistaken belief that one is being a sophisticated critical thinker, can blind you to opportunities to understand the world in new and fruitful ways.

Being unduly negative is not the only way in which some have misunderstood the nature of critical thinking. Some people assume that critical thinking is really just another term for unbridled skepticism; that is, thinking critically means doubting everything anyone ever says and never accepting anything as true or reliable. Such an extreme approach, however, ought never be confused with the type of healthy (but moderated) skepticism that is vital to careful critical thought. Unbridled skepticism can often seem like a sophisticated form of reasoning, but in the end is really just self-indulgent question raising; an approach to knowledge that is never satisfied with any answer—no matter how good or valid the answer might be. Interestingly, the one thing that such skeptics are never really fully skeptical of is their own skepticism. In other words, the one thing that the most committed skeptic never doubts is the value of doubting everything. (Perhaps, engaging in a little more careful, critical thinking would help such people to see the problem inherent in unbridled skepticism.)

So, what then is critical thinking? As we noted above, the answer to that question is a hotly contested one that would require far more space than we have here to even begin to answer. Nonetheless, there are some things that we can safely say about the nature of critical thinking in order to help make clear how this text can facilitate greater critical thinking in psychology. First, critical thinking is a way of thinking about problems that requires the systematic and careful use of a number of important intellectual skills. Brookfield (2012) notes that the basic process of critical thinking entails:

> (1) Identifying the assumptions that frame our thinking and determine our actions, (2) checking out the degree to which these assumptions are accurate and valid, (3) looking at our ideas and decisions (intellectual, organizational, and personal) from several different perspectives, and (4) on the basis of all this, taking informed actions. (p. 1)

Other examples of careful critical thought often involve evaluating the rational coherence and logical persuasiveness of opposing arguments, attending to possible logical fallacies, assessing the relevance and viability of evidence offered, and contextualizing and synthesizing information in meaningful ways. Ultimately, then, the skills of critical thinking are those we deploy in the service of determining "whether arguments are sound, i.e., whether they have true premises and logical strength" (Hughes & Lavery, 2008, p. 22).

Of course, genuinely critical thinking requires not only that we systematically interrogate the assumptions, biases, and logic of others but also that we just as systematically and carefully reflect upon our own assumptions, biases, and intentions. In other words, critical thinking is very much self-critical thinking. That is, the genuinely *critical* critical thinker is someone who, in thinking about problems, claims, and questions, strives to be as aware of possible of their own prejudices (intellectual, moral, social, cultural, and otherwise) and perspective, rather than just assuming that only others have biases or make assumptions.

For example, it is not unusual to see some psychologists employing a variety of critical thinking skills to analyze and debunk some of the irrational ways in which ordinary people sometimes explain their own and other people's behavior by means of "common sense" or "received folk wisdom" (see, e.g., Borgida & Fiske, 2008; Coon & Mitterer, 2013; Ratcliffe, 2007). Much of the work such psychologists do is well thought-out and sophisticated, furthering the cause of a psychological understanding of the nature and reasons for various human behaviors. However, despite the rigorous and systematic way in which such psychologists go about studying human behavior and critiquing common sense explanations of it, these same psychologists seldom critically reflect on their own methods, assumptions, and biases. For example, the assumption commonly held by scientific psychologists that the scientific method—when properly employed—generates objective and value-neutral knowledge is seldom ever acknowledged or held up to rigorous critical scrutiny. Likewise, the widely accepted view that human behavior is solely caused by impersonal natural forces (i.e., naturalism) is one that is almost never questioned in mainstream psychological research. Indeed, despite the critical work of many scholars (see, e.g., Bishop, 2007; Goetz & Taliaferro, 2008; Slife, Reber, & Richardson, 2005; Slife & Williams, 1995), most textbooks and research articles in psychology rarely acknowledge their assumptions about objectivity, the scientific method, and/or naturalistic determinism, nor do they often admit that viable alternative perspectives exist.

Unfortunately, far too often, critical thinking in psychology is understood simply as "rigorous thinking"—that is, the type of thinking that is usually identified with scientific analytic reasoning, and which focuses almost entirely on "methodological concerns such as quality of research design, appropriateness of statistical analyses, and rigor of general reasoning" (Slife, Yanchar, & Reber, 2005, p. 4). Indeed, as Slife, Yanchar, and Reber (2005) note, "psychologists are well-known to engage skillfully in this type of thinking" (p. 4). While the methodological

and statistical forms of reasoning in which psychologists are so well trained clearly do provide benefit to the scholarly study of human behavior, overly relying on such forms of thinking often results in psychologists being blind to the limitations and hidden values of an exclusively experimental and quantitative approach to psychological investigation. Genuinely, critical thinking requires more than just a mastery of the norms and practices of statistical reasoning, experimental design, operational definition, and naturalistic explanation.

To this end, then, it is perhaps important to distinguish between critical thinking *in psychology* and critical thinking *about psychology* (Kirschner, 2011). While critical thinking *in* psychology is, as we have stated, primarily concerned with matters of methodological precision, experimental design, and careful measurement, critical thinking *about* psychology seeks to articulate the larger context within which various empirical and theoretical claims are made and justified by psychological researchers. The end result of much training in psychology these days is that students are often taught to think only in a way that is "concerned with fostering the capacities that help students become better producers and consumers of the kinds of psychological research most commonly encountered" (Kirschner, 2011, p. 175). And, as such, they become insufficiently attuned to the historical, philosophical, political, and moral context of their own thinking, as well as blind to some of the important practical and conceptual implications (often unintended) of their research and theorizing. The central aims of critical thinking *in* psychology revolve around identifying research design flaws that might threaten the internal validity of one's research program, formulating specific operational definitions so as to ensure construct validity, choosing appropriate analytic instruments so as to ensure statistical validity, and discern the generalizability of ones findings so as to preserve external validity of the larger theoretical claims attendant to one's research findings. However, as a number of scholarly have pointed out, this form of critical thinking, if taken to be identical with critical thinking *as such* is ultimately far too limited and limiting to provide the sole basis for scientific investigation and theorizing (see, e.g., Bishop, 2007; Richardson & Slife, 2011; Williams, 2005).

Critical thinking *about* psychology, on the other hand, is less interested in determining whether certain statistically based inferences can be legitimately made regarding particular data sets and more interested in carefully reflecting on whether the larger conceptual, moral, and philosophical questions psychologists seek to resolve can even be legitimately answered by such means. This is not to say, however, that critical thinking *about* psychology involves a rejection of careful scientific reasoning or empirical forms of investigation. Rather, it is to say that scientific research that focuses only on methodological matters will always be insufficiently self-reflective and, therefore, inherently limited, guided by hidden assumptions that may or may not actually be justified or helpful.

In short, then, a richer and more broadly informed approach to critical thinking—one that is informed by a variety of perspectives, evidences, arguments, and critical analyses—is vital to the progress of scientific psychology. This is especially important to understand given that not all of the important questions relevant to psychology can be answered solely in experimental or quantitative terms. Genuinely, scientific critical thinking in psychology would therefore seem to require not only methodological innovation but also a "continual critical examination of the assumptions that undergird methods and other research resources" (Yanchar, Gantt, & Clay, 2005, p. 27). Indeed, as noted historian of psychology, Daniel N. Robinson (2000) has pointed out, "Progress in science is won by the application of an informed imagination to a problem of genuine consequence; not by the habitual application of some formulaic mode of inquiry to a set of quasi-problems chosen chiefly because of their compatibility with the adopted method" (p. 41).

Among the various practical benefits that might flow out expanding our understanding of the nature and scope of genuine critical thinking is that it can assist us in not only assessing the coherence and viability of major psychological theories and claims, but it can also help us to evaluate the utility of those theories for productively addressing real-world concerns. Much time and effort spent reinventing the wheel or heading down conceptual dead-ends could be saved if psychologists were trained more fully to critically reflect on their theories, research questions, and methods from a variety of intellectual perspectives and other traditions of inquiry. In addition, carefully and critically reflecting on the assumptions, biases, and values inherent in our research methods, as well as the logical implications of those assumptions and values, can be an invaluable tool in appreciating the moral and social impact of our research and theories. As a science that is heavily oriented toward application and intervention, and which has tremendous cultural and political clout in the modern world, it is vital that psychology exhibit great diligence in sensitively gauging the various ways in which its findings and claims influence how people come to see and understand themselves, their families, and their communities. Finally, dialogue informed by careful critical thinking can help us to

navigate our way through often difficult and contentious intellectual, political, and social issues—issues that often cannot be settled by appeals to the empirical findings of scientists alone. This is not to say, of course, that empirical science in psychology has no role to play in navigating our way through such complex issues or that it only plays a secondary role. Rather, it is to say that complex and multi-faceted issues demand complex and multifaceted responses if such issues are to be truly taken seriously, or any real consensus or resolution is to be achieved.

Taking this broader approach to critical thinking about important issues in psychology can not only deepen and mature the way in which we investigate and consider those issues but can also alert us to important issues that might otherwise have gone entirely unnoticed or unappreciated for their relevance to psychological understanding. Indeed, expanding our perspective on the nature of critical thinking, both *in* psychology and *about* it, can lead to the raising of important new research questions and novel research methods for engaging those questions (Yanchar, Slife, & Warne, 2008), and, thereby, help the discipline avoid growing stale or getting bogged down in unproductive or overly narrow research agendas. At the very least, encouraging the development of the necessary skills for critical thinking both in and about psychology will help preserve a "democratic spirit" in the discipline, wherein a variety of viewpoints and lines of analysis are not only acknowledged but are also genuinely appreciated and relied upon. Such a democratic spirit of free, critical inquiry is, in fact, the very lifeblood of truly scientific inquiry and serves to ensure that the so-called "marketplace of ideas" is always a vibrant and stimulating place for serious intellectual exchange.

Ultimately, it is in the spirit of wishing to encourage greater and more informed dialogue in psychology, as well as deeper and more productive critical thinking, that this book has been prepared. Clearly, sophisticated critical-thinking skills are essential to a meaningful education in psychological science, and so this book is specifically designed to help students develop such skills by stimulating lively and informed dialogue on a variety of complex and controversial psychological issues. Thus, the issues presented in this book offer a wide assortment of both empirical questions, which are primarily decided by research, and more philosophical or conceptual questions, which are decided by discussion, logic, and consensus. The intent is, therefore, to invite students to identify what precisely is at stake in a given issue, what the assumptions of the various authors are, what the internal logic of the arguments presented are, what the various evidence are that the authors provide for the positions they take, and whether such evidences are genuinely convincing or relevant. Additionally, students are encouraged to explore the various intellectual, social, and moral implications of the arguments presented in order to weigh not only their content but their likely impact if taken seriously by other psychologists, policy makers, and the general public. Finally, by virtue of the dialectical approach inherent in examining rival perspectives on particular issues, students are also invited to reflect on their own perspectives, biases, and values, to explore their own thinking by encountering and intimately engaging other points of view. It is sincerely hoped that as students wrestle with the various articles and issues in this book, they will come to experience a deepened sense of not only what some of the more pressing and contentious issues in contemporary psychology are, but, perhaps most importantly, they will learn how to think more productively and insightfully about them.

References

Bishop, R. C. (2007). *The philosophy of the social sciences*. London, UK: Continuum.

Borgida, E., & Fiske, S. T. (Eds.) (2008). *Beyond common sense: Psychological science in the courtroom*. Malden, MA: Blackwell.

Brookfield, S. D. (2012). *Teaching for critical thinking: Tools and techniques to help students question their assumptions*. San Francisco, CA: Jossey-Bass.

Coon, D., & Mitterer, J. O. (2013). *Introduction to psychology: Gateways to mind and behavior* (13th Ed.). Belmont, CA: Wadsworth.

Goetz, S., & Taliaferro, C. (2008). *Naturalism*. Grand Rapids, MI: William B. Eerdmans.

Hughes, W., & Lavery, J. (2008). *Critical thinking: An introduction to the basic skills* (5th Ed.). Buffalo, NY: Broadview Press.

Kirschner, S. R. (2011). Critical thinking and the end(s) of psychology. *Journal of Theoretical and Philosophical Psychology, 31*(3), 173–183.

Ratcliffe, M. (2007). *Rethinking common sense psychology: A critique of folk psychology, theory of mind and simulation*. New York, NY: Palgrave Macmillan.

Richardson, F. C., & Slife, B. D. (2011). Critical thinking in social and psychological inquiry. *Journal of Theoretical and Philosophical Psychology, 31*(3), 165–172.

Robinson, D. N. (2000). Paradigms and "the myth of framework": How science progresses. *Theory and Psychology, 10*(1), 39–47.

Slife, B. D., Reber, J. S., & Richardson, F. C. (Eds.) (2005). *Critical thinking about psychology: Hidden assumptions and plausible alternatives*. Washington, DC: APA Press.

Slife, B. D., & Williams, R. N. (1995). *What's behind the research? Discovering hidden assumptions in the behavioral sciences*. Thousand Oaks, CA: Sage.

Slife, B. D., Yanchar, S. C., & Reber, J. S. (2005). Introduction: Thinking critically about critical thinking. In B. D. Slife, J. S. Reber, and F. C. Richardson (Eds.), *Critical thinking about psychology: Hidden assumptions and plausible alternatives* (pp. 3–14). Washington, DC: APA Press.

Williams, R. N. (2005). The language and methods of science: Common assumptions and uncommon conclusions. In B. D. Slife, J. S. Reber, and F. C. Richardson (Eds.), *Critical thinking about psychology: Hidden assumptions and plausible alternatives* (pp. 235–250). Washington, DC: APA Press.

Yanchar, S. C., Gantt, E. E., & Clay, S. L. (2005). On the nature of a critical methodology. *Theory and Psychology, 15*(1), 27–50.

Yanchar, S. C., Slife, B. D., & Warne, R. (2008). Critical thinking as disciplinary practice. *Review of General Psychology, 12*(3), 265–281.

Edwin E. Gantt
David N. Top
Brigham Young University

Unit 1

UNIT

Biological Issues

*O*ur biology is obviously a fundamental influence on behavior, one of the most important subject matters of psychology. But can we take biology's influence too far? Is it the basis or determinant for all behaviors, or is there room for personal decision making that is not completely forced by our biology? These are just some of the questions that arise in trying to understand behaviors such as addiction and homosexuality. Do people have a choice about their homosexual or addictive behaviors, or are they forced by their brain chemistry or genes to behave the way they do? Evolutionary theory is a prominent biological approach to explaining not only species changes but also social changes. Could it be another valid approach to understanding the biological influences in such behaviors as addiction and homosexuality?

Selected, Edited, and with Issue Framing Material by:
Edwin E. Gantt, *Brigham Young University*

ISSUE

Are Evolutionary Explanations a Good Foundation for Understanding Morality?

YES: Patricia S. Churchland, from "The Neurobiological Platform for Moral Values," *Behaviour* (2014)

NO: Edwin E. Gantt, from "Morality, Red in Tooth and Claw: How Evolutionary Psychology Renders Morality Meaningless," *Original Essay* (2017)

Learning Outcomes

After reading this issue, you will be able to:

- Understand how mechanisms involving vasopressin and oxytocin can explain other care between members of a species.
- Understand how social behavior may have evolved into morality.
- Identify some of the underlying assumptions of evolutionary psychological theory.

ISSUE SUMMARY

YES: Patricia S. Churchland argues that morality can best be explained in terms of evolutionary theory. She asserts that brain chemicals such as oxytocin and vasopressin are responsible for social bonding in mammalian species. These nonapeptides cause individuals to treat others in various ways such as protecting them from pain and desiring to keep them healthy. Churchland calls these sorts of feelings and behaviors "other care." Because human beings learn sociability through observation and problem-solving, Churchland claims that morality is based on a group's understanding of sociability. Many cultures have the same moral and ethical principles (e.g., don't kill) due to the human race's evolutionary roots.

NO: Prepared specifically for this edition of *Taking Sides: Clashing Views on Psychological Issues*, Edwin E. Gantt refutes the notion that evolutionary psychology is the best way to explain the development of morality. He argues that if this way of accounting for behavior is true, then every action we take is determined by our biology and its interactions with the environment, and, thus, our moral sense becomes only the experience of an illusion. He states that evolutionary psychology itself rests on a self-nullifying argument, as our moral desires and sensibilities would be based only on reproductive success and not on the rational search for truth. Gantt describes previous research that shows how an individual's views on morality and free will affect their choices and argues that the way we view our world and the essence of morality affects how we act toward others.

We all experience our world and the choices we make in terms of morality. We cheer for the hero and boo the villain. We each have our own views regarding what we think is right and wrong, and we experience guilt when we do something we feel is immoral. But where does this moral sense come from? Today questions of morality are being pursued by some of the brightest minds in the fields of philosophy, psychology, neuroscience, and cognition. The two proceeding articles attempt to explain how evolutionary psychology gives either an adequate or an inadequate account of why we have a moral sense.

Darwin changed the world when he proposed the theory of natural selection-based evolution. This theory has been expanded in the century and a half since his findings to explain more than just the hereditary nature of physiological traits. Evolutionary psychology has grown over the past decades to become a large and controversial branch of psychology. Founded in neo-Darwinism, evolutionary psychology asserts that not only biological traits but also psychological traits have been passed down through the ages. Since many people have fears of snakes or spiders, it seems natural to think that these fears (which could have kept early hominids from being bitten and killed, and thus have survival value) were passed on through their genes along with their bone structure and hair color. But can evolutionary psychology explain something as abstract as morality?

Most agree that murder is wrong. While you and your neighbor might give differing responses as to why it is wrong, deep down you will both feel its wrongness. Whether inborn or due to what our society teaches us, the belief that certain things are wrong is deeply rooted in our very beings and if we break this moral code, we tend to feel guilt. While different cultures have different customs in regard to ethical codes, certain behaviors such as rape, murder, and dishonesty are considered wrong in almost every society around the globe.

The two articles presented here explore the adequacy of evolutionary psychology in explaining the roots of human morality. In the first article, Patricia S. Churchland, a philosopher of mind and brain, proposes that morality is biologically based and has been passed down from our hominid ancestors to us today via natural selection. She alleges that mechanisms involving the nonapeptides vasopressin and oxytocin lead to positive sociality between members of a species and that this social bonding evolved into morality for the human race.

Edwin E. Gantt contradicts Churchland in the second article. Gantt asserts that evolutionary psychology is founded on flawed premises that, if followed to their logical conclusions, leave no room for either free will or genuine meaning in our lives. Mechanisms of nonapeptides are not a sufficient explanation for the intricacies of morality, he argues, because they only allow for a deterministic view—a view in which genuine morality becomes hardly recognizable.

YES ↵

Patricia S. Churchland

The Neurobiological Platform for Moral Values

The evolution of the mammalian brain marks the emergence of social values of the kind we associate with morality. Sociality appears to have evolved many times, but the flexibility associated with mammalian sociality is strikingly different from the sociality of insects. The evolution of the mammalian brain saw the emergence of a brand new strategy for having babies: the young grow inside the warm, nourishing womb of the female. When mammalian offspring are born, they depend for survival on the mother. So the mammalian brain has to be organized to do something completely new: take care of others in much the way she takes care of herself. So just as I keep myself warm, fed, and safe, I keep my babies warm, fed, and safe.

Bit by evolutionary bit, over some 70 million years, the self-care system was modified so that care was extended to babies. Now, genes built brains that felt pain when the babies fell out of the nest. Also new, when the babies felt pain owing to cold or separation or hunger, they vocalized. This too caused the mother pain and made her respond to diminish the pain. These new mammalian brains felt pleasure when they were together with their babies, and the babies felt pleasure when they were cuddled up with their mother. They liked being together; they disliked being separated. The pleasure and pain systems were extended to respond to social stimuli.

Social Bonding

Why do mammalian mothers typically go to great lengths to feed and care for their babies? After all, such care can be demanding, it interferes with feeding, and it can be dangerous. Two central characters in the neurobiological explanation of mammalian other care are the simple nonapeptides, *oxytocin* and *vasopressin*. The hypothalamus regulates many basic life functions, including feeding, drinking, and sexual behavior. In mammals, the

hypothalamus secretes oxytocin, which triggers a cascade of events with the end result that the mother is powerfully attached to her offspring; she wants to have the offspring close, warm, and fed. The hypothalamus also secretes vasopressin, which triggers a different cascade of events so that the mother protects offspring, defending them against predators, for example.

The lineage of oxytocin and vasopressin goes back about 500 million years, long before mammals began to appear. In reptiles, these nonapeptides play various roles in fluid regulation and in reproductive processes such as egg laying, sperm ejection, and spawning stimulation. In mammalian males, oxytocin is still secreted in the testes and still aids sperm ejaculation. In females, it is secreted in the ovaries and plays a role in the release of eggs. In mammals, the roles of oxytocin and vasopressin in both the body and the brain were expanded and modified, along with circuitry changes in the hypothalamus to implement postnatal maternal behavior, including suckling and care.

During pregnancy, genes in the fetus and in the placenta make hormones that are released into the mother's blood (e.g., progesterone, prolactin, and estrogen). This leads to a sequestering of oxytocin in neurons in the mother's hypothalamus. Just prior to parturition, progesterone levels drop sharply, the density of oxytocin receptors in the hypothalamus increases, and a flood of oxytocin is released from the hypothalamus.

The brain is not the only target of oxytocin, however. It is also released in the body during birth, facilitating the contractions. During lactation, oxytocin is needed for milk ejection, but is also released in the brain of both mother and infant with a calming influence. Assuming the typical background neural circuitry and assuming the typical suite of other resident neurochemicals, oxytocin facilitates attachment of mother to baby and of baby to mother.

Physical pain is a "protect myself" signal, and these signals lead to corrective behavior organized by self-preservation circuitry. In mammals, the pain system is expanded and modified, protect myself and protect my babies. In addition to a pathway that identifies the kind of pain and locates the site of a painful stimulus, there are pathways responsible for emotional pain, prominently associated with the cingulate cortex, but also subcortical structures such as the amygdala. So when the infant cries in distress, the mother's emotional pain system responds and she takes corrective action. Another cortical area, the insula, monitors the physiological state of the entire body. When you are gently and lovingly stroked, this area sends out "emotionally-safe" signals (*doing-very-well-now*). The same emotionally-safe signal emerges when the baby is safe and content. And of course, the infant responds likewise to gentle and loving touches: *ahhhhh, all is well, I am safe, I am fed*. Safety signals downregulate vigilance signals such as cortisol. When anxiety and fear are downregulated, contentment and peacefulness can take their place.

The expression of maternal behavior also depends on the endogenous opioids. This means that during suckling and other kinds of infant care, the opioids downregulate anxiety, allowing for peaceful responses. If opioid receptors are experimentally blocked, maternal behavior is blocked. This has been observed, for example, in rats, sheep, and rhesus monkeys.

Here is where we are in the values story: that anything has value *at all* and is motivating *at all* ultimately depends on the very ancient neural organization serving survival and well-being. With the evolution of mammals, the rudimentary "self-caring organization" is modified to extend the basic values of being alive and well to selected others—to *Me and Mine*. Depending on the evolutionary pressures to which a species is subject, caring may extend to mates, kin, and to friends. Social mammals do tend to show attachment and caring behavior to others besides their own offspring. Exactly which others come within the ambit of caring depends, as always, on the species, how it makes its living, and whether it is thriving. The pain of another's distress and the motivation to care seems to fall off with social distance. By and large, motivation to care seems to be stronger for offspring than for affiliates, for friends than for strangers, for mates than for friends, and so on.

How exactly do oxytocin and vasopressin regulate other care? A proper answer would involve the details of all the relevant circuitry and how the neurons in the circuits behave. Unfortunately, these details are not yet known. What is known is that in rodents, oxytocin downregulates the activity of neurons in the amygdala, a structure mediating fear responses and avoidance learning, among other things. When animals are in high alert against danger,

when they are preparing to fight or flee, stress hormones are high and oxytocin levels are low. When the threat has passed and the animals [are] among friends, hugging and chatting, stress hormones back off and oxytocin levels surge. So not only are the amygdala-dependent fear responses downregulated, but the brain stem switches from fight-and-flight preparation to rest-and-digest mode.

Is oxytocin the love molecule or the cuddle molecule, as has sometimes been suggested? No. The serious research on oxytocin reveals how very complicated is its action and how complicated is the circuitry underlying social attachment. Some remarkable claims about correlations between strength of love and blood levels of oxytocin are so astonishing as to raise a flag regarding experimental procedures. Caution is in order.

Morality in Humans

The foregoing constitutes a very brief overview of what is known about how oxytocin and vasopressin operate in the brain to create a platform for sociality and, hence, for morality. But how do we get from a general disposition to care about others, to specific moral actions, such as telling the truth, respecting the goods of others, and keeping promises? How do we get from familial caring to broader community-wide values such as honesty, loyalty, and courage? The answer has two intertwined parts: learning by the young and problem-solving by everyone.

In group-living species such as humans, lemurs, and baboons, learning the local conventions and the personality traits of individuals, knowing who is related to whom, and avoiding blackening one's own reputation become increasingly important. Learning, especially by imitation, is the mammalian trick that gets us both flexibility and well-grooved skills. Problem-solving, in the context of learning by trial and error, is the complementary trick that leads to stable social practices for avoiding such problems as conflict.

Children observe, sometimes quite automatically and implicitly, sometimes explicitly and with reflection, the advantages of cooperation. Two children rowing a boat gets them across the lake much faster; two turning the long skipping rope allows doubles skipping, turn-taking means everyone gets a chance so the games do not break down. Men working together can raise a barn in one day. Women working together feed all the men and the children. Singing in a group with parts makes beautiful music. Pitching a tent is easier with two people, and hiking together provides safety. A child quickly comes to recognize the value of cooperation.

This does not mean that there is a gene "for cooperation." If you are sociable and you want to achieve some goal, then a cooperative tactic can seem a fairly obvious solution to a practical problem. As philosopher David Hume observed, a crucial part of your socialization as a child is that you come to recognize the value of social practices such as cooperation and keeping promises. This means you are then willing to sacrifice something when it is necessary to keep those practices stable in the long run. You may not actually articulate the value of such social practices. Your knowledge of their value may even be largely unconscious, but the value shapes your behavior nonetheless.

In this context, it is important to remember that although all mammals are born immature and learn a great deal during development, the period of human immaturity is especially long and the amount of learning is prodigious. For example, about 50 percent of a human brain's connections emerge after birth, and the human adult brain weighs about five times that of the infant brain.

Moreover, in the period leading up to puberty, the human brain undergoes substantial pruning and therewith a decrease in connectivity, whereas rodent brains and monkey brains do not show the same degree of prepubertal pruning. Jean-Pierre Changeux (1985) has argued that these particular epigenetic features of human brain development—extended immaturity and prepubertal pruning—enable learning of complex social and cultural organization. More succinctly, Changeux proposes that the unique developmental profile is what has made human culture, including its moral institutions, possible.

What I call problem-solving is part of a general capacity to do smart things and to respond flexibly and productively to new circumstances. Social problem-solving is directed toward finding suitable ways to cope with challenges such as instability, conflict, cheating, catastrophe, and resource scarcity. It is probably an extension to the social domain of a broader capacity for problem-solving in the physical world. Depending on what you pay most attention to, you may be more skilled in the social domain or in the nonsocial domain, or vice versa. From this perspective, moral problem-solving is, in its turn, a special instance of social problem-solving more broadly.

Although evaluating how to proceed with a particular case is frequently the most pressing concern, the more fundamental problem concerns general principles and institutional structures that undergird well-being and stability.

The development of certain practices as normative—as the *right* way to handle *this* problem—is critical in a group's cultural evolution. These norms are established principles enjoining group members against such behavior as embezzlement and other specific forms of cheating. Motivated to belong, and recognizing the benefits of belonging, humans and other highly social animals find ways to get along, despite tension, irritation, and annoyance. Social practices may differ from one group to another, especially when ecological conditions are different. The Inuit of the Arctic will have solved some social problems differently from the Piranhã of the Amazonian basin in Brazil, if only because social problems are not isolated from the physical constraints such as climate and food resources.

Similarities in social practices are not uncommon, as different cultures hit upon similar solutions to particular problems. Subtle and not so subtle differences may also obtain. This is akin to common themes in other practices, such as boat building or animal husbandry. Particular cultures developed skills for building particular styles of boats—dugout canoes, birch bark canoes, skin-backed kayaks, rafts with sails, junks for fishing on the rivers, and so forth. After many generations, the boats made by separate groups are exquisitely suited to the particular nature of the waters to be traveled on and the materials available. Notice too that many different cultures learned to use the stars for navigation. Some picked up the trick from travelers, others figured it out independently, just as conventions for private property occurred in different groups as their size expanded as agricultural practices became widespread. I am reasonably confident that there is no gene for navigating by the stars.

Although expressions of moral values can vary across cultures, they are not arbitrary, in the way that the conventions for funerals or weddings tend to be. Matters of etiquette, although important for smoothing social interactions, are not serious and momentous as moral values are. Truth-telling and promise-keeping are socially desirable in all cultures and hence exhibit less dramatic variability than customs at weddings. Is there a gene for these behaviors? Although that hypothesis cannot be ruled out, there is so far no evidence for a truth-telling or a promise-keeping gene. More likely, practices for truth-telling and promise-keeping developed in much the same way as practices for boat building. They reflected the local ecology and are a fairly obvious solution to a common social problem.

Being reminded of the variability in what counts as morally acceptable helps us acknowledge that standards of morality are not universal. More generally, it reminds us that moral truths and laws do not reside in Plato's heaven to be accessed by pure reason. It reminds us that perorations about morality are often mixed with a whole range of emotions, including fear, resentment, empathy, and compassion.

Concluding Remarks

The capacity for moral behavior is rooted in the neurobiology of sociality, and in mammals depends on nonapeptides oxytocin and vasopressin, as well as on elaborated cortical structures that interface with the more ancient structures mediating motivation, reward, and emotion. The neural mechanisms supporting social behavior are tuned up epigenetically by social interactions and by learning the social practices of the group and by figuring out how to best deal with new social problems. Emerging after the advent of agriculture and the growth of large groups, organized religions would have built upon existing social practices, perhaps augmenting them in ways relevant to new social demands. Although it is known that oxytocin and vasopressin are critical in social behavior, much about their roles as well as the circuitry with which they interact remains unknown.

References

Changeux, J.-P. (1985). *Neuronal man.* New York, NY: Pantheon Books.

PATRICIA S. CHURCHLAND is an analytical philosopher known for her contributions to neurophilosophy and the philosophy of mind. After completing a BA degree at the University of British Columbia, she received an MA at the University of Pittsburgh in 1966 and a bachelor's of philosophy from Oxford in 1969. She is the University of California, San Diego (UCSD) President's professor of philosophy Emerita where she has taught since 1984. She is also a fellow of the American Academy of Arts and Sciences, an adjunct professor at the Salk Institute, and a member of the Board of Advisors, Swartz Center for Computational Neuroscience at UCSD.

Edwin E. Gantt

 **NO**

Morality, Red in Tooth and Claw: How Evolutionary Psychology Renders Morality Meaningless

Recent years have witnessed a veritable explosion of interest in evolutionary psychology (EP) and the attempt to explain all manner of human experience and behavior in fundamentally evolutionary terms. Drawing their theoretical inspiration from neo-Darwinian accounts of natural selection, many evolutionary psychologists argue that "all behavior owes its existence to underlying psychological mechanisms" and, thus, the central task of an evolutionarily informed psychology is to "discover, describe, and explain the nature of those mechanisms" (Buss, 1995, 6). Indeed, as Crawford and Krebs (2008) note, "The modern field of EP is sometimes characterized as the study of the evolved cognitive structure of the mind," and, as such, the primary focus of researchers in the field is on "the workings of the mental mechanisms that evolved in ancestral populations to solve the problems faced in those environments" (p. 13). Consequently, evolutionary psychologists have diligently worked to identify the various "evolved psychological mechanisms" that would presumably account for the wide range of human cognitive, emotional, and social behavior. Indeed, Geher (2006) asserts that EP is "a basic intellectual framework for understanding all psychological phenomena," and, as such, is a "perspective that has the potential to serve as an underlying metatheory to guide all the behavioral sciences in the future" (p. 184).

One particular area of human experience that evolutionary psychologists have been particularly keen to explain is morality. In most EP accounts, morality typically refers both to a system of ideas about what constitutes right and wrong conduct and to our more basic capacity (moral sense) to distinguish between right and wrong. Evolutionary psychologists are deeply invested in providing a naturalistic account of the origins of this basic moral capacity. Most EP accounts of morality begin by attempting to identify the evolutionarily conditioned mechanisms by which our moral sense originally developed. Rather than locating the source of morality in some transcendent or supernatural realm (e.g., God), evolutionary psychologists seek to explain our moral sense in terms of certain basic biological processes and the resultant psychological mechanisms that facilitated early hominid social life. As Churchland (2014) puts it, "A more appealing hypothesis is that moral values are not other-worldly; rather they are social worldly" (p. 283). Ultimately, for the evolutionary psychologist, morality is a complex product of both biological adaptation and social evolution—where the latter is itself a direct product of the former.

By way of a quick conceptual overview to set the stage for the analysis that follows, there appear to be at least six basic theoretical assumptions undergirding the work of most contemporary evolutionary psychologists, irrespective of their areas of particular research focus. These basic assumptions are:

1. Human behavior can (and should) be explained at both a proximate and ultimate level of analysis.

2. Domain specificity that adaptive problems are solved through specific designated physical and behavioral structures or mental modules.

3. These mental mechanisms are innate. There is no genetic variation in them between people (except for those differences between the sexes related to differences in the ancestral problems they faced).

4. Human nature is explained best as the product of genes and environment.

5. The workings of most mental mechanisms are not available to consciousness.

6. There are differences between the current and ancestral environment that may influenced the functioning or outcome of evolved mechanisms (some Darwinian anthropologists discount this difference; Crawford & Krebs, 2008, p. 13).

Each of these theoretical assumptions, in turn, rests upon an even more basic set of philosophical assumptions regarding the nature of reality, the source and character of its various operations, and the proper means by which we might discover the particularities of those operations. At minimum, these deeper philosophical assumptions include reductive naturalism, material mechanism, and necessary determinism.

Consistent with this conceptual grounding, then, a number of evolutionary psychologists have sought to articulate a suitably evolutionary account of morality. Krebs (2008) notes that, for the evolutionary psychologist, "The key to understanding what a sense of morality is and how people acquire it lies in explaining how the mechanisms that produce it evolved, which entails identifying the adaptive functions that they evolved to serve" (p. 168). Thus, the bulk of the work being done by evolutionary psychologists in this area has been in the service of explaining the origins of morality in terms of its (1) possible evolutionary functions and (2) the particular mechanisms by which moral behavior presumably arises and is maintained. In brief, EP accounts of morality commonly assert that:

> Morality originated in deferential, cooperative, and altruistic "social instincts," or decision-making strategies, that enabled early humans to maximize their gains from social living and resolve their conflicts of interest in adaptive ways. Moral judgments, moral norms, and conscience originated from strategic interactions among members of groups who experienced confluences and conflicts of interest. . . . Moral beliefs and standards are products of automatic and controlled information-processing and decision-making mechanisms. (Krebs, 2008, p. 149)

In other words, our current moral sentiments, forms of moral reasoning, and moral actions are held to be explicable primarily—if not solely—in terms of the reproductive advantages and social functionality that certain behaviors conferred in our ancestral past. Such behaviors, it is argued, gave rise to the evolved psychological mechanisms that now guide—in automatic and determinative fashion—the emotional and behavioral processes of everyday moral life.

Although somewhat more complex and nuanced than the sociobiological thinking of a few decades ago, when morality was said to be "just something that helped our ancestors make babies" (Joyce, 2006, p. 2) and, thus, "a collective illusion foisted upon us by our genes" (Ruse, 1986, p. 253), the contemporary EP account of morality nonetheless entails the same basic conclusions that sociobiological accounts reached. That is, human moral sentiments and actions are ultimately founded on illusion, possessing no genuine meaning or viable rational justification in and of themselves. On the EP account, not only are our moral sentiments and actions nothing more than the automated products of causal mechanisms operating outside of our awareness, originative, or participative control, but these causal mechanisms arose to serve (and are still only serving) fundamentally nonrational and nonmoral ends, that is, reproductive success. As Krebs (2005) asserts, "The constellation of thoughts and feelings that constitute a sense of morality evolved to enable individuals to uphold cooperative social relations that maximized their biological benefits" (p. 168). Miller (2007) concurs by stating "In evolutionary theory, a moral person is simply one who pursues their ultimate genetic self-interest through psychological adaptations that embody a genuine, proximate concern for others" (p. 103). Thus, as Churchland (2014) trenchantly summarizes, for the evolutionary psychologist, "that anything has value *at all* and is motivating *at all* ultimately depends on the very ancient neural organization serving survival and well-being" (p. 288; emphasis in the original).

If the EP account is correct, then, our moral beliefs and behaviors are in reality without genuine moral or agentic foundation—despite the fact most people believe they do have such foundation and commonly experience their lives and choices as being freighted with moral significance. In short, even though our moral intuitions, sensibilities, and beliefs—and the actions which both rest upon and found them—are experienced as profoundly real and binding, they are, nonetheless, profoundly unreal and nonbinding; that is to say, they are illusions. This seems to be precisely Joyce's (2006) point when he argues that in evolutionary psychological accounts of morality, we have "an empirically confirmed hypothesis of how this belief-formation mechanism works which does not require that the beliefs be even approximately true," and, in fact, we would be forced "to conclude that any such innate beliefs (e.g., moral beliefs) are products of an *unreliable* process" (p. 215; clarification added). Furthermore, what this highlights, Joyce (2006) contends is that our moral "beliefs might seem to be justified when they are not. The fact that morality may seem justified and that we are deeply reluctant to admit otherwise, does not make it so, and in fact is itself a phenomenon predicted by the genealogical hypothesis" (p. 218).

The difficulty here is that once this sort of evolutionary account is accepted as true, all of the "bite" (so to speak) of our moral life disappears. That is to say, once we accept that morality is really an illusion, that our experiences of moral worth are really just the product of programmed responses to the survival and reproduction problems faced by our distant hominid ancestors, and that whatever particular moral sensibilities we happen to have now are entirely contingent accidents of natural history, then it becomes all but impossible to either seriously encourage or oppose any particular moral actions or sentiments whatsoever.

For example, if in a given moral situation I "knew" (by means of my prior study of evolutionary psychological theory) that my "moral sense" of the situation was, in fact, something over which I had no control because its real origin lay eons in the past, and that its real purpose was facilitate reproductive and survival interests that may have nothing whatsoever to do with my current situation, then I would almost certainly be less inclined to take that "moral sense" at face value, to treat it as truly mattering, and as possessing any genuine moral substance. I would also be inclined to understand the situation itself in the very terms in which EP has explained it, that is, as essentially a functional matter in which underlying genetic and reproductive self-interest via the manipulation of others for those ends is what is of real importance. Indeed, "knowing" that other persons' moral responses toward me are also not what they appear to be, but are rather merely a sort of culturally conditioned "cover story" underneath which the evolved psychological mechanisms they happen to possess—and of which they are likely unaware and in whose activating processes they do not genuinely participate—govern their actions and sentiments cannot help but drain their actions (or inactions) of any real moral significance for me.

Joyce (2006) employs a thought-experimental approach when he invites us to pretend that there are such things as "belief pills" and that "taking one would inevitably lead to the forming of a certain particular belief (while at the same time invoking amnesia about the existence of the taking of the pill and, to be on the safe side, amnesia about the existence of such pills in general" (p. 179). Further, he asks us to suppose that there is not only a belief pill that will make us believe that Napoleon was victorious at the Battle of Waterloo and one that will make us believe that he lost that battle, but also an antidote that can be

taken to counteract the effects of either of those two pills. Joyce (2006) next asks us to imagine that we are:

. . . proceeding through life happily believing that Napolean lost Waterloo (as, indeed, you are), and then you discover that at some point in your past someone slipped you a "Napoleon lost Waterloo" belief pill. It is not a matter of your learning of the existence of such pills and having no way of knowing whether you have ever taken one; rather, we are imagining that you somehow discover beyond any shred of doubt that your belief is the product of such a pill. Should this undermine your faith in your belief that Napolean lost Waterloo? Of course it should. It doesn't show that the belief is *false*—for though the fictional scenario described is not our world, it still might well have contained Napolean, the Battle of Waterloo, and the event of his losing the battle—but this knowledge is certainly sufficient to place your belief on the dubious list. . . . In our imaginary case, knowledge that your belief is the product of a belief pill renders the belief unjustified (or perhaps shows that it was never justified in the first place, depending on one's epistemological tastes), demanding that unless you can find some concrete evidence either in favor or against the belief you should cease to belief this thing—that is, you should take the antidote. (pp. 179–180)

In short, the point here seems to be that because the origins of our moral intuitions, judgments, reasonings, and beliefs are not what we think they are—that is, they neither originate with us nor do we in any real way actively participate in them—such things are unjustifiable, uncertain, and cannot be taken seriously or at face value. As Joyce clearly notes, this does not mean that our moral beliefs are necessarily false, only that we cannot know whether they are true or false, only that we happen to have them and that we have them for reasons that have nothing to do with their truth or falsity. Ultimately, then, all moral beliefs are profoundly relativized, vitiated, and rendered impotent by virtue of their origins in impersonal and nonrational naturalistic processes that are mechanical and deterministic in character.

Thus, in the same way that it makes no sense to be morally offended by the actions of an acorn that happens to fall from a high tree branch and conk you on the head, it also makes no sense to be morally offended by the behavior of another person whose actions are simply the result of certain evolved psychological mechanisms of which they are unaware and in whose emotion or behavior generating processes they do not participate. After all, the acorn was simply acting as it was determined by the laws of nature and the conditions of the physical world to act, quite unaware of the origins of its behavior and in no way actively participating in or assenting to its own behavior. Obviously, ascribing genuine moral substance or meaning to the "falling behavior" of an acorn is simply not rationally defensible. Likewise, if the moral relations and interactions of human beings are governed in a similarly deterministic fashion, then they too have no genuine moral substance or meaning, and ascribing meaning to them is also not rationally defensible. Therefore, any approach to understanding human moral life that takes morality is to be illusory because it is nothing more than the necessitated and derivative product of fundamentally nonmoral, determinative and mechanical processes is, in the final analysis, a thoroughly self-nullifying and pointless one. The EP approach is self-nullifying because although researchers presumably feel that they "ought to" study morality from an evolutionary perspective—perhaps in the cause of truth—they have to admit that if their theory is true, then their moral desires are not at all what they appear to be, no matter how high-minded the rhetoric they might want to use to frame them. If the evolutionary account is true, then no one is pursuing truth. We are all only pursuing reproductive success and survival—and we seldom if ever actually realize it, and we are most certainly never the one in charge of it. Ultimately, on the EP account, reproduction is the only real point behind anything we do or anything we might happen to value.

Such implications should give us serious pause, especially in light of established research that shows clearly that human behavior reflects human beliefs and that the theories that social scientists espouse (and belief systems often entailed in those theories) do impact and can alter human behavior. For example, it is well established that invoking a sense of personal responsibility leads to individuals often modifying their behavior to better align with their attitudes. Similarly, being told that individual outcomes are based on inborn traits, as opposed to individual effort, has been shown to significantly influence behavior. Mueller and Dweck (1998), for example, demonstrated that ten-year-old children who were informed that their earlier success on a particular task was the result of native intelligence rather than hard work put forth less effort and reported lower levels of enjoyment on later tasks than those who had been told that their earlier successes were tied to the quality of their individual efforts. More recently, Vohs and Schooler (2008) reported that increases in cheating behavior were mediated by decreases in belief in free will following exposure to arguments that encouraged belief in determinism. Likewise, Baumeister, Masicampo,

and DeWall (2009) reported that participants who were induced to disbelieve in free will were less willing to help others and more likely to act aggressively toward others.

Of course, none of this should come as any great surprise, given that most contemporary forms of psychotherapy are premised on the notion that changing client beliefs (about themselves, their situation, others, their past and future, etc.) is fundamental to effecting real therapeutic change. The impact that beliefs have on behavior is also something whose importance has not been lost on Madison Avenue advertising firms. The central concern here is that if the claims of evolutionary psychologists studying morality are true, then it is difficult to sustain the claim that persons are genuinely moral agents, responsible for their choices and actions, or possess any inherent dignity or moral worth. Indeed, the very claim that individuals possess inherent dignity and worth is a moral judgment; one whose epistemological validity and rational sensibility EP rejects outright—or, at the very least, brings into serious question. In this context, one cannot help but recall Daniel Dennett's (1995) claim that neo-Darwinianism—the intellectual foundation for all of contemporary EP—constitutes the intellectual equivalent of a universal acid, one that "eats through just about every traditional concept, and leaves in its wake a revolutionized world-view, with most of the old landscape still recognizable, but transformed in fundamental ways" (p. 63). Following Dennett's lead, Stanovich notes that "full acceptance of Darwin's insights will necessitate revisions in the classical view of personhood, individuality, self, meaning, human significance, and soul . . . radical restructuring will be required" (p. 7). In the end, such a radical restructuring, Stanovich (2004) confirms, means "that there are no inherently 'higher' or 'lower' forms of life. Put simply, one form of life [or moral sentiment or judgment] is as good as another" (p. 7, comments added). In essence, then, while some of the moral terminology, traditions, and social practices of the past may remain in place as institutionalized features of daily life, the traditional meaning of such things can no longer be taken seriously or at face value because they have been profoundly altered by the "truth" of the neo-Darwinian worldview, most especially as it is articulated in contemporary evolutionary psychological theories of morality.

Of course, at this point, an evolutionary psychologist might respond that progress of science often entails challenging received wisdom and the deeply entrenched assumptions that found such wisdom. After all, just because a scientific truth is uncomfortable that does not mean that we ought to suppress or reject it. As Wallace (2010) has noted, "'It makes me feel bad, therefore it's false' is not an argument" (p. 4). Indeed, one might ask, "where would we be today if not for the relentless march of scientific discovery showing us that the world simply is not as we once believed it to be, or even as we might want it to be?" While we might want our moral sentiments and actions to have more significance than they in fact do, the evolutionary psychologist might argue, if the science clearly indicates that no such significance attends to our moral life, that our moral intuitions and sensibilities are merely illusions whose actual purpose in reality has nothing to do with morality, per se, then so be it. On with the data! The illusory nature of our moral sentiments and sensibilities is simply one more thing to be added to a long list of uncomfortable truths of science that civilization must learn to accommodate if real intellectual and social progress is to be made. Indeed, it is just such confidence in the objective and scientific status of EP leads Stanovich (2004) to claim that "We have no choice but to accept Darwin's insights because there is no way we can enjoy the products of science without accepting the destabilizing views of humans in the universe that science brings in its wake" (p. 7).

Such arguments would, of course, be more compelling were the scientific legitimacy—as well as theoretical and philosophical coherence—of EP not so heavily contested. The scientific and philosophical literature critical of EP accounts of human behavior is large and varied and growing, and, as such, far too expansive to be adequately summarized here. A small sample of some of the critiques frequently leveled at EP are that it is in fact a pseudoscience (Tattersall, 2001) that represents "one of the most pervasive of present-day intellectual myths" (Rose & Rose, 2000, p. 1), employs a far too narrow (and often inaccurate) understanding of the nature of both genetics (Lloyd & Feldman, 2002) and natural selection (Gould, 2000), has confused its descriptive metaphors for explanatory causal mechanisms (Gantt, Melling, & Reber, 2012), is beset by insurmountable methodological problems and confusions (Buller, 2005), relies on fanciful and unverifiable reconstructions of the social and physical conditions of human prehistory (Herrnstein-Smith, 2000), is ultimately self-refuting because it undercuts its own claims to epistemological validity and calls into question the reliability of human reason (Gantt & Melling, 2009; Plantinga, 2011), explains complex processes by invoking yet other complex processes (Gantt & Williams, 2014), and rests on numerous logical fallacies, such as the Mereological Fallacy, the Fallacy of Composition, the *post hoc ergo propter hoc* Fallacy or Fallacy of Coincidental Correlation, and the Fallacy of Affirming the Consequent (see, e.g., Bennett & Hacker, 2003; Cunningham, 2010; Tallis, 2011).

Suffice it to say that a great many important questions—both epistemological and metaphysical—remain to be answered before we can even begin to comfortably entertain the possibility that EP accounts of morality are genuinely scientific and adequately explanatory in nature. Indeed, as Tallis (2011) has rather convincingly shown, just accounting for such mundane daily activities as picking out a can of beans at the supermarket or using the toilet seems to require far more intellectual depth and sophistication than EP explanations have yet been able to muster or may ever be able to muster. Thus, if EP struggles so mightily to make adequate sense of even "homely things such as defecating and buying beans" (p. 150), how skeptical ought we to be when it undertakes to provide explanations of things as nuanced, complex, interpersonal, and culturally situated as moral judgment and moral action? AS evolutionary biologist, and noted EP skeptic, Ian Tattersall (2001) has thoughtfully cautioned:

> Mistake how evolution proceeds and the constraints under which this process works, and you are forever condemned to misinterpret its results. (p. 658)

Certainly, there would seem to be more than sufficient reason to exercise scholarly caution and due scientific skepticism before concluding that EP's many fascinating hypotheses are in fact explanatory truths. To borrow from a recent observation by Shariff, Schooler, and Vohs (2008) on the importance of free will in psychological theories of behavior, our understanding of morality matters—and it "matters not only to scientists in labs and philosophers in armchairs, but to the way that people live their lives" (p. 182). Ultimately, again borrowing from Shariff, Schooler, and Vohs (2008), "if science is to be used as foundation upon which to promote claims that may have social impact, then the soundness of those claims deserves particular scrutiny" (p. 182). The potential costs of failing to do so may be quite severe—indeed, it may ultimately be the intellectual and moral equivalent of disciplinary and cultural self-immolation.

References

Baumeister, R. F., Masicampo, E. J., & DeWall, C. N. (2009). Prosocial benefits of feeling free: Disbelief in free will increases aggression and reduces helpfulness. *Personality and Social Psychology Bulletin, 35*(2), 260–268.

Bennett, M. R., & Hacker, P. M. S. (2003). *The philosophical foundations of neuroscience*. Malden, MA: Blackwell.

Buller, D. J. (2005). *Adapting minds: Evolutionary psychology and the persistent quest for human nature*. Cambridge, MA: The MIT Press.

Buss, D. M. (1995). Evolutionary psychology: A new paradigm for psychological science. *Psychological Inquiry, 6(1)*, 1–30.

Churchland, P. S. (2014). The neurobiological platform for moral values. *Behavior, 151*, 283–296.

Crawford, C., & Krebs, D. (Eds.) (2008). *Foundations of evolutionary psychology*. New York: Lawrence Erlbaum.

Cunningham, C. (2010). *Darwin's pious idea: Why the ultra-Darwinists and creationists both get it wrong*. Grand Rapids, MI: William B. Eerdmans.

Dennett, D. C. (1995). *Darwin's dangerous idea: Evolution and the meaning of life*. New York: Simon and Schuster.

Gantt, E. E. & Melling, B. S. (2009). Evolutionary psychology ain't Evil, it's just not any Good. In B. D. Slife (Ed.), *Taking sides: Clashing views on psychological issues* (Vol. 16, pp. 122–130). Dubuque, IA: McGraw-Hill.

Gantt, E. E., Melling, B. S., & Reber, J. S. (2012). Mechanisms or metaphors: The emptiness of evolutionary psychological explanations. *Theory and Psychology, 22(6)*, 823–841.

Gantt, E. E., & Williams, R. N. (2014). Psychology and the legacy of Newtonianism: Motivation, intentionality, and the ontological gap. *Journal of Theoretical and Philosophical Psychology, 34(2)*, 83–100.

Geher, G. (2006). Evolutionary psychology is not evil! (. . . and here's why . . .). *Psychological Topics, 15(2)*, 181–202.

Gould, S. J. (2000). More things in heaven and earth. In H. Rose and S. Rose (Eds.), *Alas, poor Darwin: Arguments against evolutionary psychology* (pp. 101–126). New York, NY: Harmony Books.

Herrnstein-Smith, B. (2000). Sewing up the mind: The claims of evolutionary psychology. In H. Rose and S. Rose (Eds.) *Alas, poor Darwin: Arguments against evolutionary psychology* (pp. 155–1720). New York, NY: Harmony Books.

Joyce, R. (2006). *The evolution of morality*. Cambridge, MA: The MIT Press.

Krebs, D. (2005). The evolution of morality. In D. Buss (Ed.), *The handbook of evolutionary psychology* (pp. 747–775). Hoboken, NJ: John Wiley and Sons.

Krebs, D. L. (2008). Morality: An evolutionary account. *Perspectives on Psychological Science, 3(3)*, 149–172.

Lloyd, E. A., & Feldman, M. W. (2002). Evolutionary psychology: A view from evolutionary biology. *Psychological Inquiry, 13(2)*, 150–156.

Miller, G. F. (2007). The sexual selection of moral virtues. *Quarterly Review of Biology, 82*, 97–125.

Mueller, C. M., & Dweck, C. S. (1998). Intelligence praise can undermine motivation and performance. *Journal of Personality and Social Psychology, 75*, 33–52.

Plantinga, A. (2011). *Where the conflict really lies: Science, religion, and naturalism*. Oxford, UK: Oxford University Press.

Rose, H., & Rose, S. (Eds.) (2000). *Alas, poor Darwin: Arguments against evolutionary psychology*. New York, NY: Harmony Books.

Ruse, M. (1986). *Taking Darwin seriously: A naturalistic approach to philosophy*. Oxford, UK: Blackwell.

Shariff, A. F., Schooler, J., & Vohs, K. D. (2008). The hazards of claiming to have solved the hard problem of free will. In J. Baer, J. C. Kaufman, and R. F. Baumeister (Eds.), *Are we free? Psychology and free will* (pp. 181–204). Oxford, UK: Oxford University Press.

Stanovich, K. E. (2004). *The robot's rebellion: Finding meaning in the age of Darwin*. Chicago, IL: The University of Chicago Press.

Tallis, R. (2011). *Aping mankind: Neuromania, Darwinitis, and the misrepresentation of humanity*. Durham, UK: Acumen.

Tattersall, I. (2001). Evolution, genes, and behavior. *Zygon, 36(4)*, 657–666.

Vohs, K. D., & Schooler, J. W. (2008). Encouraging a belief in determinism increases cheating. *Psychological Science, 19(1)*, 49–54.

Wallace, B. (2010). *Getting Darwin wrong: Why evolutionary psychology won't work*. Exeter, UK: Imprint Academic.

Edwin E. Gantt is an associate professor at Brigham Young University. He teaches courses in the history and philosophy of psychology, as well as the psychology of religion and personality. He has published theoretical critiques of a variety of psychological theories and practices, including in the areas of clinical psychology, empathy and altruism research, religion and spirituality, psychological research methods, and critical thinking. He is an associate editor for the *Journal of Theoretical and Philosophical Psychology* and for *Issues in Religion and Psychotherapy*. He completed his BA in psychology teaching at Brigham Young University and received his MA and PhD in clinical psychology (with an emphasis on existential-phenomenological psychology) from Duquesne University in 1998.

EXPLORING THE ISSUE

Are Evolutionary Explanations a Good Foundation for Understanding Morality?

Critical Thinking and Reflection

1. Is there sufficient evidence that mechanisms of the nonapeptides, oxytocin and vasopressin, explain other care between individuals of a species?
2. If morality stems from evolution, does that mean morality is only an illusion or accident as Gantt asserts? How might this idea change the way we view our experiences with morality?
3. What does Churchland mean when she says that moral problem-solving is social problem-solving?
4. If reproduction is truly "the only real point behind everything we do," what does this say about your personal goals and accomplishments as a student?
5. How might Churchland's argument give an adequate explanation for why morals are similar and different in various cultures throughout the world?

Is There Common Ground?

We all experience the world in terms of morality. We all make important distinctions between what we take to be good and evil, right and wrong, and praiseworthy or blameworthy. Morality influences not only the choices we make but also how we feel about those choices once we have made them. Most importantly, however, our sense of morality has a profound impact on how we treat other people. Both Gantt and Churchland recognize the importance of morality in day-to-day living, both individually and as members of a social group (e.g., the human race). While both authors disagree as the origins of morality, neither can give a full explanation as to where our moral sensibility comes from. Both writers agree with the existence of natural selection-based evolution, but they differ as to what extent evolutionary psychology is valuable as a science, particularly in explaining the etiology of morality. An important question that you might ask of both authors is whether the origins of our moral sensibilities need to be known in order for individuals to live meaningful, moral lives.

One additional area in which some common ground can be found between the two articles is in the commitment to careful scientific study of morality. It was once thought that human morality and other similar phenomena (e.g., spirituality) were off-limits to deliberate scientific inquiry. While Gantt is clear that he does not think an evolutionary psychological approach to the study of morality is credible or sufficiently careful, he would seem to agree with Churchland that studying morality from a scientific and psychological perspective is worthwhile and valid. Of course, what exactly might constitute a genuinely "scientific" approach to the study of human morality (and related phenomena) is likely to be very much open to debate by these two authors, but it also seems to be the case that both would agree that scientific psychology has a stake in furthering our understanding of human moral experience.

Additional Resources

Carter C. S., Williams, J. R., Witt, D. M. & Insel T. R. (1992), Oxytocin and social bonding. *Annals of the New York Academy of Sciences, 652,* 204–211. doi:10.1111/j.1749-6632.1992.tb34356.x

Geher, G., Gantt, E. E., & Melling, B. S. (2010). Is evolution a good explanation for psychological concepts?. In B. Slife (Ed.), *Clashing views on psychological issues, 16th ed* (pp. 109–131). New York, NY: McGraw-Hill.

Hamilton, R., (2008). The Darwinian cage: Evolutionary psychology as moral science. *Theory, Culture and Society, 25*(2), 105–125. doi:10.1177/0263276407086793

Midgley, M. (2014). *The solitary self: Darwin and the selfish gene.* London, UK: Routledge.

Walter, N. T., Montag, C., Markett, S., Felten, A., Voigt, G., & Reuter, M. (2012). Ignorance is no excuse: Moral judgments are influenced by a genetic variation on the oxytocin receptor gene. *Brain and Cognition, 78*(3), 268–273. doi:10.1016/j.bandc.2012.01.003

Internet References . . .

Morality and Cognitive Science

http://www.iep.utm.edu/m-cog-sc/

The New Science of Morality

https://www.edge.org/event/the-new-science-of-morality

The Two Steves (Part I): A Debate

https://www.edge.org/conversation/steven_rose-steven_pinker-the-two-steves-part-i

Morality and Evolutionary Biology (Stanford Encyclopedia of Philosophy)

https://plato.stanford.edu/entries/morality-biology/

Selected, Edited, and with Issue Framing Material by:
Edwin E. Gantt, *Brigham Young University*

ISSUE

Is Homosexuality Biologically Based?

YES: Jacques Balthazart, from "Minireview: Hormones and Human Sexual Orientation," *Endocrinology* (2011)

NO: Stanton L. Jones and Alex W. Kwee, from "Scientific Research, Homosexuality, and the Church's Moral Debate: An Update," *Journal of Psychology and Christianity* (2005)

Learning Outcomes

After reading this issue, you will be able to:

- Discuss whether current research supports the theory of biological determination of homosexual orientation.
- Describe what evidence exists to support the learning model of homosexual orientation.
- Identify both significant research findings and conceptual arguments that are marshalled on behalf of both biological and learning theories of homosexual orientation.

ISSUE SUMMARY

YES: Neuroendocrinologist Jacques Balthazart argues that the prenatal endocrine environment has a significant influence on human sexual orientation, and that genetic differences affecting behavior, either in a direct manner or by changing embryonic hormone secretion or action, may also be involved in determining life-long sexual orientation.

NO: Professor of psychology Stanton L. Jones and clinical psychologist Alex W. Kwee claim the current research on the biology of homosexuality provides no firm evidence for biological causation and leaves room for learning models of sexual orientation.

Much of the so-called recent culture wars in the United States have been fought over the issue of homosexuality, its origins, and nature. On one side of these "wars" are those who claim that homosexuality is a fundamentally moral issue, perhaps even a "sin." Yet, for this to be a moral issue, homosexuals would have to have some measure of control over or even a choice of their sexual orientation. Do they have such control? If this orientation is biologically determined, whether at birth or later, the control or choice necessary for sexual preference to be a "moral issue" would seem to be unavailable. If, on the other hand, homosexuals have made choices that lead them learn to "prefer" (i.e., choose) a certain type of sexual orientation, then a moral understanding of homosexuality could be justified.

Only relatively recently have psychologists and neuroscientists begun to conduct scientific research to address these issues. One of the earliest and most influential of these researchers, neuroscientist Simon LeVay, a self-declared gay person, found dramatic brain differences between gay and straight men. This investigation led many to speculate that sexual orientation was completely biological. Indeed, other scientific findings have been reported, especially as sensationalized by the media, that would seem to have confirmed this speculation. Do we now have enough evidence to conclude that homosexuality is completely biologically based? Can we omit the role of learning factors in homosexuality altogether?

One of the foremost researchers in this area, Jacques Balthazart, answers these questions in the first article by reviewing research on the hormonal development of human and animal sexual orientation. He claims the research supports the proposal that homosexuality is biologically determined, even before birth. In support of his claim, he cites evidence from hormonal studies, twin studies, genetic scanning, brain structure studies, and clinical studies. From such research he claims there is overwhelming evidence for the biological basis of homosexuality.

In the second selection, noted psychologists Stanton Jones and Alex Kwee review much of the research cited by Balthazart on the biology of homosexuality but come to very different conclusions. In discussing relevant twin studies, for example, they point to various methodological weaknesses, siding with one of the original studies' researchers that there is "no statistically significant indication of genetic influence on sexual orientation." While they agree that the research points to a correlation between biology and homosexuality, they contend that there is still no evidence of the cause of this correlation, whether learning from the environment or "hard-wiring" of the brain. They argue that there is still plenty of room for a learning model in the development of homosexuality by citing a recent study about the influence of parental socialization on homosexuality.

POINT

- Evidence from twin studies points to a genetically heritable homosexuality.
- Genetic scanning shows that homosexuality is correlated with several genes.
- The maternal immune theory is well established because it relies on the very reliable fraternal birth order effect.
- The fraternal birth order effect is accounted for in the prenatal environment.
- Brain structures differ between homosexual and heterosexual men.
- Research shows that learning plays no appreciable role in the development of sexual orientation.

COUNTERPOINT

- Twin studies suffer from methodological weaknesses that call into question the genetic influence on sexual orientation.
- Findings based on genetic scanning are ambiguous.
- The maternal immune theory relies on disputed findings regarding the fraternal birth order effect.
- The fraternal birth order effect can be accounted for in the postnatal social environment.
- Brain structure difference could be the effect rather than the cause of homosexuality.
- Research shows that learning plays a role in the development of sexual orientation.

YES

Jacques Balthazart

Minireview: Hormones and Human Sexual Orientation

Most people are sexually attracted to individuals of the opposite sex; they are heterosexual. There is, however, a significant minority (3–10% according to many estimates) of men and women who are exclusively attracted to individuals of their own sex; they are homosexual. Intermediate forms of attraction also exist, and as early as in 1948, Kinsey *et al.* (1) were classifying sexual orientation in seven distinct categories ranging from completely heterosexual to completely homosexual. Sexual orientation (heterosexual *vs.* homosexual) is a behavioral trait that displays one of the largest degrees of sexual differentiation, given that 90–97% of individuals of one sex display an attraction that is different from that of the other sex.

The mechanisms that determine human sexual orientation have been the subject of heated controversies. These discussions often focused on homosexuality proper, because this orientation is less common and thus sometimes considered wrongly as "abnormal." It must be noted, however, that trying to understand the origins of homosexuality or heterosexuality essentially represents the same question.

. . .

Sexual Differentiation of Sex and Courtship Behaviors in Animals

Many behaviors in animals are sexually differentiated and produced preferentially or exclusively by one sex. Estrogens are often unable to activate female-typical behaviors (*e.g.* receptivity) in males, and vice versa, testosterone does not reliably activate male-typical copulatory behavior in females even after its conversion to estradiol (2). It was originally believed that these sex differences resulted from the presence of different hormones in the two sexes: testosterone in males and estradiol (plus progesterone) in females (3). The seminal work of Young and co-workers (4) demonstrated that, to a large extent, these differences result from the early exposure of embryos to a different endocrine milieu: a high concentration of testosterone for male embryos in mammals and a much lower (lack of?) exposure to sex steroids in females (Fig. 1). These differentiating (organizing) effects usually occur early in life, during the embryonic period or just after birth and are irreversible.

It is not the type of adult hormone (androgens or estrogens) that determines the behavior that will be expressed (male or female typical), it is the nature of the neural substrate on which this hormone acts (the sex of the animal and associated embryonic exposure to sex steroids). Recent studies also show that genetic mechanisms called "direct," because they are not mediated through the action of sex hormones, influence some behavioral differences between males and females (5).

These organizing actions of sex steroids on behavior are paralleled by irreversible changes in brain structure. Embryonic sex steroids differentiate the size of several brain structures (see Ref. 6 for a general review on this topic), including the sexually dimorphic nucleus of the preoptic area (SDN-POA). This group of cells is five to six times larger in male rats than in females, and this difference results almost exclusively from the action of testosterone during

Abbreviations: CAH, Congenital adrenal hyperplasia; 2D:4D, ratio of the lengths of the second (index) to the fourth (ring) fingers; DES, diethylstilbestrol; FoR, female-oriented ram; INAH3, interstitial nucleus of the anterior hypothalamus number 3; MoR, male-oriented ram; OAE, oto-acoustic emission; oSDN, sexually dimorphic nucleus of the ovine preoptic area; SDN-POA, sexually dimorphic nucleus of the preoptic area.

Jacques Balthazart, "Minireview: Hormones and Human Sexual Orientation," *Endocrinology*, vol. 152, August 2011, pp. 2937–2947. Copyright © 2011 by The Endocrine Society. All rights reserved. Used with permission.

Fig. 1.

In mammals, early exposure to testosterone produces a male phenotype: the behavioral characteristics of the male are strengthened (masculinization) and the ability of males to show behavior typical of females is reduced or lost (defeminization). The female phenotype develops in the apparent absence of hormone action (or in the presence of very low estrogen concentrations). These spontaneous differentiation processes occurring during early development of animals can be entirely reproduced by experimental manipulations (via castration, injections of agonists or antagonists) of steroid concentrations in embryonic or newborn animals. The figure shows that after such treatments, neonatally castrated (CX) males behave like females, whereas females treated early in life with testosterone (T) or its aromatized metabolite estradiol (E_2) behave like males. Experimental animals considered are those shaded in *blue* (genetic males) or *red* (genetic females). Other subjects represent only the test stimuli.

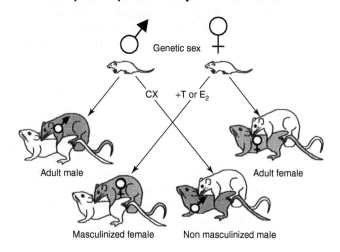

late embryonic life and the first days of postnatal life. Once acquired, the sex-typical size of the SDN-POA cannot be altered in adulthood by steroid hormones (7, 8).

Partner Preference and Its Control in Animals

These organizing effects of embryonic sex steroids specifically concern the type of behaviors that will be displayed by adults. More recent studies demonstrate that similar

principles also contribute to determine the sex of the partner that will be the target of these behaviors. Unlike other aspects of human sexuality that have no equivalent in animals (*e.g.* gender identity), sexual orientation can be studied in nonhuman animals by offering them a choice between a male or female sexual partner. Recording the time spent with each partner and the type of behavior displayed toward them will provide a measure of a behavioral phenotype (sexual partner preference) that represents a reasonable (although imperfect) model of human sexual orientation.

The sexual preference of a male for a female is controlled, like the expression of male-typical sexual behavior, by the medial part of the POA. Experimental lesion of this brain region causes a reversal of the males' preference in rats and ferrets: after surgery, they prefer to spend time with other males rather than with sexually receptive females (9, 10).

This preference for a partner of the same or the opposite sex is also determined by prenatal hormones and can be reversed by hormonal treatments during early development (weeks preceding or immediately after birth depending on the species) (11–15). The preference determined at that time subsequently appears to be a stable characteristic of the individual. Like the type (male or female typical) of sexual behavior displayed in adulthood, sexual partner preference seems to be determined by sex steroids during embryonic or early postnatal life. Exposure to testosterone (or its metabolite estradiol) induces male-typical partner preference (preference for a female over a male sex partner), whereas in the absence of high concentrations of these steroids, a female pattern of mate preference will develop (preference for male partner).

Sexual interactions between same sex partners (male mounting another male or female mounting another female) are observed quite frequently in a broad variety of animal species (16, 17). Often, these behaviors are expressed only when a suitable partner of the opposite sex is not available due to captivity (zoo or other captive populations), or when a skewed sex ratio in the population, or the presence of dominant males is preventing access to females. These behaviors do not represent a true same sex preference but serve as an outlet for sexual motivation in the absence of suitable partners of the opposite sex.

A case of spontaneous same sex preference has, however, been described and studied in detail. It concerns a sheep population in the western part of the United States. A significant fraction of rams in this population (8%) mate exclusively with other males when given a choice between a male or female partner. Various factors that could explain this male-directed sexual behavior, such as rearing in single sex groups, which is common in sheep, were ruled out (see Ref. 18 for review), and studies then focused on endocrine and neural aspects of this preference for males.

The SDN of the ovine POA (oSDN), a structure that is approximately three times larger in males than in females and contains about four times more neurons, was shown to be significantly smaller in male-oriented rams (MoR) than in female-oriented rams (FoR). The oSDN also contained fewer neurons and expressed aromatase at reduced levels in MoR compared with FoR (19). The features of this nucleus therefore correlate with sexual partner preference: subjects attracted to males (females and MoR) are similar and distinguished from subjects attracted to females (FoR).

Roselli *et al.* (20) demonstrated that the volume of the oSDN is already larger in males than in females around the end of embryonic life (around d 135) and differentiates under the influence of testosterone in males. Embryonic treatment of females with testosterone between 30 and 90 d of gestation results in a masculinized oSDN in females (18, 20). Furthermore, the size of this nucleus is no longer modified in adulthood by castration or treatment with testosterone (21). If the small size of oSDN in MoR is determined like in females by a relative lack of early exposure to testosterone, it might represent (one of) the cause(s), and not a consequence, of their atypical sexual attraction. This nucleus is indeed located in the center of the POA, a region involved in the control of sexual behavior and male-typical partner preferences, and it would in this scenario differentiate before subjects had an opportunity to express their sexual partner preference. This unfortunately remains impossible to prove with the current technology, because it is not possible to measure the volume of the oSDN in a male embryo and to know at the same time what would have been his later partner preference.

In conclusion, these studies demonstrate that sexual orientation in animals is a sexually differentiated feature like other sexually differentiated behaviors or morphological characteristics. Male-typical sexual orientation is controlled at least in part by the POA (like sexual behavior), and it differentiates under the influence of pre-/perinatal sex steroids.

Many Sex Differences in Humans Are Organized by Embryonic Sex Steroids

Do these endocrine mechanisms demonstrated in animals have any significance in humans? The answer to this question should be considered in two steps. 1) Do we have any evidence that sex steroids are, in humans like in animals, implicated in the sexual differentiation of morphology (*e.g.* genital structures) but also of brain (*e.g.* SDN-POA) and sexual behavior? And 2) are there any data indicating that embryonic sex steroids have, like in animals, organizational effects on sexual orientation in humans? The answer to the first of these questions is clearly yes, and there is probably no need to elaborate on the arguments supporting this conclusion especially in an endocrine journal. To just briefly restate the obvious:

1. Sex steroids (testosterone, estradiol, progesterone) are present in the human plasma in concentrations similar to those observed in other mammals.
2. Receptors for these steroids are present in humans, and their brain distribution is similar and even nearly identical to the general pattern observed in vertebrates.
3. Testosterone action during embryonic life clearly controls the differentiation of male-typical external and internal genital structures.
4. Sex differences in brain structures have been identified, although their control by embryonic steroids is usually not established at this time.
5. Physiological or behavioral differences between men and women are too numerous to be summarized here (22). These differences are complex in nature, and their origin is more difficult to determine than for differences in genital morphology. Learning, education, and expectations of society clearly play an important role in the genesis of behavioral and even sometimes physiological differences. Nevertheless, quite often, these environmental factors build on and amplify smaller, sometimes minor, differences caused by biological factors that were already present at birth. Many physiological and behavioral differences are thus rooted in biology. This is quite obviously the case for many sexually differentiated diseases related to brain function (*e.g.* anorexia nervosa affects 93 women for every seven men; Gilles de la Tourette syndrome affects 90 men for every 10 women) (see Refs. 22–24 for an extensive list of such differences). How would education or society induce such differences? But many behavioral differences also probably depend to some extent on biological mechanisms often already acting during prenatal life (*e.g.* increased aggressivity and greater interest in male-typical activities in girls prenatally exposed to high androgen concentration due to congenital adrenal hyperplasia (CAH) (see Refs. 25, 26).

A Hormonal Theory of Homosexuality

The second question (do embryonic sex steroids affect sexual orientation in human?) is obviously more difficult to answer for a variety of reasons, such as the intrinsic difficulties in assessing in a reliable manner the sexual orientation of a subject, the long latency between embryonic endocrine events potentially controlling sexual orientation and its overt manifestation in adulthood, and finally, the complete impossibility for ethical reasons of manipulating the process.

Many studies have analyzed the potential influence of steroids on human sexual orientation. They have clearly established that sexual orientation is not affected by activational effects of steroids in adulthood. Gonadectomy does not influence orientation nor does adult treatment with androgens and estrogens. Furthermore, numerous studies have clearly established that plasma concentrations of sex steroids are perfectly "normal" (typical of the gonadal sex) in both gay men and lesbians (27).

Organizational effects of steroids are by contrast more likely to be implicated. Sexual orientation is a sexually differentiated function that might depend, like many other behavioral characteristics, on variations in the early (fetal) exposure to sex steroids (androgens and also possibly their estrogenic metabolites). Exposure to a high concentration of testosterone during a critical phase of development would lead to a male-typical orientation (attraction to women), whereas a lower embryonic exposure to steroids would lead to a female-typical orientation (attraction to men). There would be a critical concentration of testosterone required to masculinize this feature like other aspects of behavior in animals and humans (see Fig. 2).

On average, male embryos are exposed to higher concentrations of testosterone than female embryos, but these concentrations vary around a mean value for various reasons (environmental, genetic, *etc.*). Male subjects at the lower end of this sex-specific distribution could thus acquire a female-typical orientation (and be gay), whereas females at the high end of the concentration curve would acquire a male-typical sexual attraction and be lesbian. Even if they are not attracted by the same specific individuals, females and gay men share an attraction for men, whereas males and lesbians share an attraction for women.

. . .

Although this theory remains speculative (and is likely to remain unproven due to the logistic difficulties

Fig. 2.

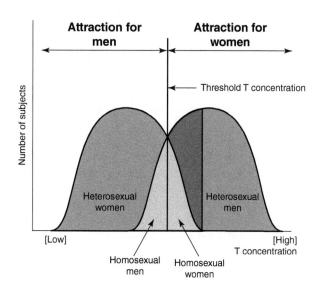

Theoretical model illustrating how fluctuations around an average concentration of testosterone (T) during embryonic life could lead to a homosexual or heterosexual orientation.

mentioned before), two types of evidence suggest that it contributes substantially to the control of sexual orientation in humans.

Atypical Sexually Differentiated Characteristics in Gays and Lesbians

Practical reasons make it nearly impossible to determine the hormonal milieu to which an individual was exposed during his/her embryonic life. We must therefore rely on indirect evidence. A number of sexually differentiated morphological, physiological, and behavioral characteristics seem to be irreversibly influenced by embryonic hormones in humans like in animals. Many studies have quantified these features comparatively in homosexual and heterosexual populations to research whether homosexual subjects had been exposed to atypical hormonal conditions during their development. Positive results were obtained in a number of these studies.

The sexually differentiated characteristics that have been studied in this context include variables that could be secondarily affected by homosexuality [*e.g.* performance in cognitive tests (see Ref. 28) or physiological responses to the smell of androgenic or estrogenic steroids produced by males or females (29, 30)]. These traits were shown to be significantly different in homosexual and heterosexual men and/or women, but we shall not review them here in detail, because they do not represent conclusive evidence for exposure to an atypical endocrine milieu during embryonic life (see Refs. 31–33 for detail).

In contrast, other morphological and physiological features are clearly influenced by prenatal testosterone, and it is difficult to conceive how they could possibly be affected secondarily by adult sexual orientation. We briefly discuss three of these traits that are significantly modified in gays or lesbians.

The ratio of the lengths of the second (index) to the fourth (ring) fingers (2D:4D)

The 2D:4D is significantly smaller in men than in women. This ratio was shown by two out of three studies to be masculinized in CAH women exposed to an excess of androgens *in utero* and also masculinized in females of a variety of mammalian and even avian species by injection of androgens during embryonic life. This ratio has therefore been used as a biomarker for embryonic exposure to testosterone in the human fetus (34), although a nume ber of studies have questioned its reliability (*e.g.* Ref. 35). Multiple studies in humans have shown that this ratio is masculinized (smaller) in lesbians compared with heterosexual women. Although there have been occasional failures to replicate this effect, and its significance has been questioned (*e.g.* Is the effect size meaningful? Does it reflect differences in bone length or in fat accumulation) (36), it has been confirmed by several meta-analyses of available data (*e.g.* Refs. 34, 37), suggesting that lesbians have, on average, been exposed to higher than typical concentrations of androgens during development. Interestingly, most studies have failed to detect a corresponding feminization of this feature in gay men, and surprisingly, some studies have even reported a lower (hypermasculinized) 2D:4D ratio in some gay men (38). A modification of the length of long bones (arms and legs), a feature also supposed to be influenced by early exposure to sex steroids, has been reported in gay men (39).

. . .

Brain structures

Several brain structures have also been shown to be different between homosexual and heterosexual subjects, and in this case, studies focused almost exclusively on males. The first of these differences concerns the suprachiasmatic nucleus, the central clock of the organism, that was shown to be significantly larger in gay men than in heterosexual subjects (40). However, this nucleus is not sexually differentiated in a control heterosexual population, and its links to reproduction are only indirect. The significance of this difference and potential relation with sexual orientation are thus difficult to assess.

The size of the anterior commissure, measured in the midsagital plane, was reported to be larger in gay men than in heterosexual control subjects (41). This difference is more interesting for the purpose of the present discussion, because the size of this commissure is known to be larger in women than in men. However the size of this commissure has no obvious relationship to sexual orientation (it could relate to functional lateralization), so the meaning of the difference between homosexual and heterosexual men remains difficult to interpret.

Finally, researchers from the laboratory of Roger Gorski (who had identified the SDN-POA of rats) at the University of California, Los Angeles (Los Angeles, CA) discovered in the human POA a nucleus they called interstitial nucleus of the anterior hypothalamus number 3 (INAH3) (a member of four cellular condensations of the POA) that was significantly larger in men than in women (42). Subsequent studies showed that INAH3 is significantly smaller in homosexual men than heterosexual men, so that its size is essentially equal to what is observed in women (43). An independent study based on different brains confirmed the reduced size of INAH3 in male homosexuals compared with heterosexuals, although the magnitude of the difference observed in this replication was lower than in the original study and not statistically significant (44). In this study, homosexual men also had a greater cell density (more cells per unit volume) but a similar total number of neurons in INAH3 than heterosexual men: neurons were more densely packed, potentially because they formed fewer synapses (during development?).

The mechanisms that control the development of this nucleus in humans are unknown, but INAH3 volume does not seem to depend significantly on hormonal status in adulthood (45). In rats and sheep, the size of a potentially homologous nucleus located in the same part of the POA (SDN-POA in rat, oSDN in sheep) is irreversibly determined by embryonic sex steroids. Moreover, lesions of this nucleus in adult male rats or ferrets modifies sexual partner preference, an animal model of sexual orientation. If the same mechanisms control the development of INAH3 in humans, the smaller INAH3 of gay men could then be a marker of deficient exposure to androgens during ontogeny and even be a cause of the modified sexual orientation. Alternatively, the small INAH3 of gay men could also be a consequence of their sexual orientation.

Clinical Studies

A potential implication of the embryonic hormonal environment in the control of sexual orientation is also supported by studies of various clinical disorders that affect the endocrine system during fetal life. In some cases, these early endocrine disruptions lead to a complete sex reversal, so that, postnatally, subjects are raised assuming a sex (gender) that is opposite to their genetic sex. For example XY subjects with complete androgen insensitivity syndrome are born with female genitalia and are typically raised as girls at least until puberty, when the absence of menstruation leads to medical examination and diagnosis. These subjects usually have a female gender identity and a female-typical sexual orientation (they are sexually attracted to men) (46). These cases demonstrate that sexual orientation is not necessarily associated with the genetic sex but tell us little about the role of prenatal hormones *vs.* postnatal environment, because both concur to produce a female-typical orientation.

The same confusion is potentially associated with the 5α-reductase deficiency affecting XY men who are born with genital structures that are not masculinized and are often raised as daughters. The rise in plasma testosterone associated with puberty later masculinizes (at least in part) the genital structures, and these individuals usually conform to a male gender and male-typical sexual orientation. It has been argued that the relative ease with which these subjects apparently change gender and (presumably) sexual orientation at puberty despite having been raised as females was related to their exposure to androgens during embryonic life (testosterone secretion is apparently normal in these subjects, it is only its 5α-reduction that is deficient) (47, 48). However, the condition of these subjects is usually known from birth, so that their sex of rearing was not necessarily unequivocally female. Furthermore the obvious social advantages related to adopting a male gender identity in the societies where this 5α-reductase deficiency frequently occurs and was studied raise additional questions about the reasons underlying the rapid and easy postpubertal change in gender orientation, identity, and role.

In other clinical conditions, however, the prenatal endocrine environment may push sexual orientation in a direction opposite to the effects of postnatal social environment. These cases therefore provide a more useful test of the role of either type of factor. Three such clinical conditions are important to mention here, because they are associated with a significantly increased incidence of homosexual orientation.

Congenital Adrenal Hyperplasia

Girls exposed *in utero* to abnormally high levels of androgens not only show masculinization of genital structures and of a variety of behavioral traits (*e.g.* aggressive play), but they also display a markedly increased probability of interest or participation in homosexual relationships in comparison with control females or to unaffected sisters (49–51). Some studies reported up to 30–40% of CAH girls having some form of homosexual attraction compared with 10% or less in control populations. Because the endocrine defect was corrected soon after birth, genital structures were surgically feminized, and these girls were presumably raised as girls, these data therefore suggest that prenatal androgens are involved in the determination of sexual orientation in women. This effect of prenatal androgens could be mediated through a direct action on the brain as well as through an indirect action on the genitalia that would secondarily induce an overall reduction of sexual activity and interest in sex in general, or more specifically of heterosexual activity. Although genitalia are surgically feminized at birth, they still do not have an ideal structure in some women and therefore allow little or no penetrative heterosexual relationships. These modified genitalia could also induce a general aversion toward sexual activity (see Ref. 26 for a more detailed discussion of this issue).

Treatment of Pregnant Mothers with Diethylstilbestrol (DES)

Between 1939 and 1960, about 2 million pregnant women were treated with DES in Europe and the United States to prevent spontaneous miscarriages. This treatment turned out to be ineffective and also to have detrimental long-term consequences, but one of the unexpected outcomes was that girls born from these treated mothers showed a significant increase in nonheterosexual (bisexual or homosexual) fantasies or sexual activity, whereas the socialization of these subjects was fundamentally consistent with their genetic female sex (52, 53). The reproducibility of this effect has been questioned, but if the effect of DES is real, which will be difficult to confirm given that this treatment has been abandoned for a long time, it would indicate that estrogens as well as androgens (testosterone) are able to masculinize sexual orientation. This would fit with rodent data, where many effects of testosterone on sexual differentiation are produced after conversion into estradiol by aromatase in the brain, but would be in conflict with other data from humans that assign a prominent role to androgens in sexual differentiation. Note, however, that in rhesus monkeys, fetal exposure to DES was shown to increase adult mounting behavior although not to the male-typical level (54).

Cloacal Exstrophy

Complex genito-urinary malformations occasionally occur during embryonic development resulting in the birth of XY males who, in addition to various malformations of the pelvis, have no penis. These subjects have normal testes and were thus presumably exposed to a male-typical pattern of androgen secretions before birth. Typically, in the past, these subjects were assigned a female sex, submitted to vaginoplasty, and raised as girls. Follow-up studies have demonstrated that in a significant number of cases (about half), when adults, these subjects chose to adopt a male identity, gender role, and male-typical sexual orientation that presumably relate to their embryonic exposure to androgens (55, 56).

Altogether, these clinical cases are consistent with the idea that embryonic hormones play a substantial role in determining adult sexual orientation. It should be noted, however, that these changes in sexual orientation as a result of embryonic endocrine disruption always only concern a fraction of affected individuals (usually a maximum of 30–40%), so that at least 60–70% of subjects in these conditions retain the heterosexual orientation consistent with their gender assignment at birth.

Genetic and Immunological Factors?

If embryonic hormones affect adult sexual orientation, then what is the cause of the endocrine changes that result in an atypical orientation in some subjects? Based on retrospective analysis of men born in Berlin during World War II (with all the problems that are potentially associated with such an approach), it has been suggested that exposure to chronic stress might be a critical determinant (57–59), but to our knowledge, these data have never been replicated and are considered unreliable by some authors.

Individual genetic differences could affect the synthesis of steroid hormones or their activity in the brain of the embryo, although to date, no evidence for such a mechanism has been obtained despite active research (60–62). Alternatively, studies in mice indicate that genes located on the sex chromosomes contribute in a direct manner to the sexual differentiation of brain and behavior (5). Various arguments suggest a significant genetic contribution to sexual orientation. Whether this partial genetic control is mediated by alterations of steroid action or more directly by a sexually differentiated expression of specific genes has not been determined.

Multiple epidemiological studies have demonstrated a correlation between concordance of sexual orientation and genetic relatedness. For example, if a boy is gay, between 20 and 25% of his brothers will share this sexual orientation, compared with 4–6% in a control population. Similarly, lesbian women have a greater probability than heterosexual women of having a homosexual sister.

Twins studies indicate that this correspondence in sexual orientation probably does not reflect a communality of postnatal experiences (psychosocial factors) but rather genetic similarity. Several studies indeed demonstrated that there is a better agreement of sexual orientation in monozygotic (identical) twins than in dizygotic twins (fraternal twins conceived from different ova and sperm) (63). If a dizygotic gay twin has a brother, there is on average a 15% probability that the brother will also be homosexual, but this probability rises to 65% in monozygotic twins (64). Overall, these studies suggest that in social conditions typical of Western societies, 50–60% of the variance in sexual orientation in humans has a genetic origin.

Although this genetic contribution was identified many years ago, the responsible gene(s) remain(s) unknown. Sexual orientation in men tends to be transmitted through the matriarchal lineage: a gay man has a higher probability of having gay men among his ancestors on the maternal side (uncles, cousins), than on the paternal side. This was originally interpreted as a sign of inheritance through gene(s) located on the X chromosome, and one study identified a linkage with markers located in the subtelomeric region of the long arm of the X chromosome, a region called Xq28 (65). This association with Xq28 was replicated in one subsequent study (66) and in another set of data that were not published in a peer-reviewed journal (see Ref. 67) but not in a fourth one (68). A meta-analysis of all these data strongly supports ($P < 0.0001$) the existence of this linkage (69). More recent studies have suggested that the differential heritage through the matriarchal lineage could also be the result of epigenetic modifications of the expression of genes located on several other chromosomes (69, 70).

In summary, the existence of a genetic contribution to the control of sexual orientation is now firmly established, but the specific gene(s) that are implicated in this process have not been identified so far. Whether or not this (these) gene(s) affect sexual orientation by modifying steroid secretion or action during ontogeny has also not been determined.

Finally, to complete the picture of biological factors affecting sexual orientation, it should be noted that the factor most reliably associated with homosexuality in males is the presence in the family of older brothers born of the same mother. The incidence of homosexuality increases by 33% for each older brother and is accompanied by a small but statistically significant decrease in weight at birth. These effects do not appear to be explained by differences in education or family background and may be the result of accumulation of antibodies in the mother during successive pregnancies against one or more proteins expressed specifically by the male brain. This interpretation currently remains an untested hypothesis and the specific antigenic proteins underlying this phenomenon have not been identified. Candidate proteins have, however, been suggested as potential target(s) for this immune reaction based on their distribution and properties (71). Whether this effect involves hormone actions is unknown.

Conclusions

There is thus substantial evidence suggesting that sexual orientation, and homosexuality in particular, is influenced before birth by a set of biological mechanisms. These mechanisms include genes that affect sexual orientation by currently unidentified mechanisms and hormonal actions classically mediating sexual differentiation. Our current understanding of these prenatal factors admittedly suffers many limitations. For example, all embryonic endocrine disorders that have been associated with an increased incidence of homosexuality have a limited effect size and never affect more than 30–40% of subjects. Furthermore, all identified correlates of homosexuality that suggest exposure to an atypical endocrine environment during ontogeny in gays and/or lesbians are only weakly associated with sexual orientation and often are modified in a reliable manner in one sex only (2D:4D ratio, OAE in women) or have been studied only in one sex (INAH3 volume in men). They are statistically correlated with sexual orientation but are unable to predict it accurately due to the large variance in this relationship.

The limitations of the results probably relate not only to the complexity of the behavioral trait under consideration but also to methodological difficulties specific to their study, such as the long latency between putative hormone actions and their effects, the absence for ethical reasons of truly experimental studies, and the taboos associated with human sexuality. One should also consider that gays and lesbians probably do not constitute homogeneous populations. In addition to the obvious gradation between heterosexuality and homosexuality that was already recognized by Kinsey *et al.* (1, 72), some lesbians display obvious male characteristics ("butch"), whereas others do not ("femme"), and the same dichotomy exists in gay men. These differences are unfortunately rarely taken into account in experimental studies.

Despite these limitations, I believe that biological studies suggest a significant contribution of genetic and hormonal factors in the control of sexual orientation. In contrast, alternative explanations based on features of the postnatal environment, such as relationships with parents, social interactions, or early sexual experiences, although they are widely accepted in the public, are not usually supported by quantitative experimental studies. It is clear, however, that none of the biological factors identified so far is able to explain by itself the incidence of homosexuality in all individuals. Three possibilities can be contemplated to explain this failure.

Either there are different types of homosexuality. Some forms could be determined by genetic effects, others by hormones, and yet others by the older brothers effect and the associated immunological modifications.

Or the effects of different biological factors interact to varying degrees in each individual, and it is only when several of these predisposing factors are combined that an homosexual orientation is observed.

Or finally, all biological factors that have been associated with homosexuality only become effective in conjunction with exposure to a given (as yet unspecified) psychosocial postnatal environment. The postnatal environment would in this scenario play an important permissive role, but it is then surprising that no quantitative study has been able so far to formally identify aspects of this environment that play this limiting role in the control of sexual orientation. It has, however, been suggested that embryonic hormones may directly affect aspects of juvenile behavior (*e.g.* play behavior) and that this in turn could condition the development of sexual orientation (73–74).

Current knowledge does not allow discriminating between these interpretations (see Ref. 33 for a more detailed discussion). It is clear, however, that biological factors acting during prenatal life play a significant role in the control of sexual orientation and that homosexuality is not, for most people, the result only of postnatal experiences or a free choice. It is often an awareness that presents itself to the individual during their adolescence or early adult life. The acceptance of a nonheterosexual orientation in a minority of subjects is often the cause of significant psychological distress and social isolation. In contrast, heterosexual orientation emerges with the individual often being unaware of the underlying process. There is no question of choice here. Data presented in this review strongly suggest that most human beings do not choose to be heterosexual or homosexual. What they choose is to assume or not their orientation and eventually reveal it openly. Sexual orientation represents a highly complex behavioral trait under multifactorial control that includes genetic, hormonal, and presumably immunological determinants potentially acting in concert with the social postnatal environment. More interdisciplinary research is needed to better understand this fascinating aspect of human behavior.

References

1. Kinsey AC, Pomeroy WR, Martin CE. 1948. Sexual behavior in the human male. Philadelphia: W.B. Saunders Co.

2. Goy RW, McEwen BS. 1980. Sexual differentiation of the brain. Cambridge, MA: The MIT Press.

3. Beach FA. 1948. Hormones and behavior. New York: Paul B. Hoeber, Inc.

4. Phoenix CH, Goy RW, Gerall AA, Young WC. 1959. Organizational action of prenatally administered testosterone propionate on the tissues mediating behavior in the female guinea pig. Endocrinology 65:369–382.

5. Arnold AP, Chen X. 2009. What does the "four core genotypes" mouse model tell us about sex differences in the brain and other tissues? Front Neuroendocrinol 30:1–9.

6. McCarthy MM, De Vries GJ, Forger NG. 2009. Sexual diferentiation of the brain: mode, mechanisms, and meaning. In: Pfaff DW, Arnold AP, Etgen AM, Fahrbach SE, Rubin RT, editors. eds. Hormones, brain and behavior. San Diego: Academic Press; 1708–1744.

7. Jacobson CD, Csernus VJ, Shryne JE, Gorski RA. 1981. The influence of gonadectomy, androgen exposure, or a gonadal graft in the neonatal rat on the volume of the sexually dimorphic nucleus of the preoptic area. J Neurosci 1:1142–1147.

8. Jacobson CD, Shryne JE, Shapiro F, Gorski RA. 1980. Ontogeny of the sexually dimorphic nucleus of the preoptic area. J Comp Neurol 193:541–548.

9. Paredes RG, Baum MJ. 1995. Altered sexual partner preference in male ferrets given excitotoxic lesions of the preoptic area anterior hypothalamus. J Neurosci 15:6619–6630.

10. Paredes RG, Tzschentke T, Nakach N. 1998. Lesions of the medial preoptic area anterior hypothalamus (MPOA/AH) modify partner preference in male rats. Brain Res 813:1–8.

11. Bakker J, Brand T, van Ophemert J, Slob AK. 1993. Hormonal regulation of adult partner preference behavior in neonatally ATD-treated male rats. Behav Neurosci 107:480–487.

12. Bakker J, van Ophemert J, Slob AK. 1993. Organization of partner preference and sexual behavior and its nocturnal rhythmicity in male rats. Behav Neurosci 107:1049–1058.

13. Bakker J, Van Ophemert J, Slob AK. 1996. Sexual differentiation of odor and partner preference in the rat. Physiol Behav 60:489–494.

14. Henley CL, Nunez AA, Clemens LG. 2009. Estrogen treatment during development alters adult partner preference and reproductive behavior in female laboratory rats. Horm Behav 55:68–75.

15. Henley CL, Nunez AA, Clemens LG. 2011. Hormones of choice: the neuroendocrinology of sexual orientation in animals. Front Neuroendocrinol 32:146–154.

16. Bagemihl B. 1999. Biological exuberance. Animal homosexuality and natural diversity. New York: St. Martin's Press.

17. Poianni A. 2010. Animal homosexuality. A biological perspective. Cambridge, UK: Cambridge University Press.

18. Roselli CE, Reddy RC, Kaufman KR. 2011. The development of male-oriented behavior in rams. Front Neuroendocrinol 32:164–169.

19. Roselli CE, Larkin K, Resko JA, Stellflug JN, Stormshak F. 2004. The volume of a sexually dimorphic nucleus in the ovine medial preoptic area/anterior hypothalamus varies with sexual partner preference. Endocrinology 145:478–483.

20. Roselli CE, Stadelman H, Reeve R, Bishop CV, Stormshak F. 2007. The ovine sexually dimorphic nucleus of the medial preoptic area is organized prenatally by testosterone. Endocrinology 148:4450–4457.

21. Roselli CE, Estill CT, Stadelman HL, Stormshak F. 2009. The volume of the ovine sexually dimorphic nucleus of the preoptic area is independent of adult testosterone concentrations. Brain Res 1249:113–117.

22. Ellis L, Hershberger S, Field E, Wersinger S, Pelis S, Geary D, Palmer C, Hoyenga K, Hetsroni A, Karadi K. 2008. Sex differences: summarizing more than a century of scientific research. New York: Psychology Press.

23. Becker JB, Berkley KJ, Geary N, Hampson E, Herman JP, Young EA. 2008. Sex differences in the brain. From Genes to behavior. Oxford: Oxford University Press.

24. Bao AM, Swaab DF. 2011. Sexual differentiation of the human brain: relation to gender identity, sexual orientation and neuropsychiatric disorders. Front Neuroendocrinol 32:214–226.

25. Hines M. 2004. Brain gender. Oxford: Oxford University Press.

26. Hines M. 2011. Prenatal endocrine influences on sexual orientation and on sexually differentiated childhood behavior. Front Neuroendocrinol 32:170–182.

27. Meyer-Bahlburg HF. 1984. Psychoendocrine research on sexual orientation. Current status and future options. Prog Brain Res 61:375–398.

28. Baron-Cohen S. 2004. The essential difference: men, women and the extreme male brain. London: Penguin Press Science.

29. Savic I, Berglund H, Lindström P. 2005. Brain response to putative pheromones in homosexual men. Proc Natl Acad Sci USA 102:7356–7361.

30. Berglund H, Lindström P, Savic I. 2006. Brain response to putative pheromones in lesbian women. Proc Natl Acad Sci USA 103:8269–8274.

31. LeVay S, Valente SM. 2006. Human sexuality. Sunderland, MA: Sinauer Associates, Inc.

32. LeVay S. 2010. Gay, straight, and the reason why. The science of sexual orientation. New York: Oxford University Press.

33. Balthazart J. 2011. Biology of homosexuality. New York: Oxford University Press, in press.

34. Breedlove SM. 2010. Minireview: organizational hypothesis: instances of the fingerpost. Endocrinology 151:4116–4122.

35. Berenbaum SA, Bryk KK, Nowak N, Quigley CA, Moffat S. 2009. Fingers as a marker of prenatal androgen exposure. Endocrinology 150:5119–5124.

36. Wallen K. 2009. Does finger fat produce sex differences in second to fourth digit ratios? Endocrinology 150:4819–4822.

37. Grimbos T, Dawood K, Burriss RP, Zucker KJ, Puts DA. 2010. Sexual orientation and the second to fourth finger length ratio: a meta-analysis in men and women. Behav Neurosci 124:278–287.

38. Williams TJ, Pepitone ME, Christensen SE, Cooke BM, Huberman AD, Breedlove NJ, Breedlove TJ, Jordan CL, Breedlove SM. 2000. Finger-length ratios and sexual orientation. Nature 404:455–456.

39. Martin JT, Nguyen DH. 2004. Anthropometric analysis of homosexuals and heterosexuals: implications for early hormone exposure. Horm Behav 45:31–39.

40. Swaab DF, Hofman MA. 1990. An enlarged suprachiasmatic nucleus in homosexual men. Brain Res 537:141–148.

41. Allen LS, Gorski RA. 1992. Sexual orientation and the size of the anterior commissure in the human brain. Proc Natl Acad Sci USA 89:7199–7202.

42. Allen LS, Hines M, Shryne JE, Gorski RA. 1989. Two sexually dimorphic cell groups in the human brain. J Neurosci 9:497–506.

43. LeVay S. 1991. A difference in hypothalamic structure between heterosexual and homosexual men. Science 253:1034–1037.

44. Byne W, Tobet S, Mattiace LA, Lasco MS, Kemether E, Edgar MA, Morgello S, Buchsbaum MS, Jones LB. 2001. The interstitial nuclei of the human anterior hypothalamus: an investigation of variation with sex, sexual orientation, and HIV status. Horm Behav 40:86–92.

45. Garcia-Falgueras A, Swaab DF. 2008. A sex difference in the hypothalamic uncinate nucleus: relationship to gender identity. Brain 131:3132–3146.

46. Wisniewski AB, Migeon CJ, Meyer-Bahlburg HF, Gearhart JP, Berkovitz GD, Brown TR, Money J. 2000. Complete androgen insensitivity syndrome: long-term medical, surgical, and psychosexual outcome. J Clin Endocrinol Metab 85:2664–2669.

47. Imperato-McGinley J, Miller M, Wilson JD, Peterson RE, Shackleton C, Gajdusek DC. 1991. A cluster of male pseudohermaphrodites with 5α-reductase deficiency in Papua New Guinea. Clin Endocrinol 34:293–298.

48. Imperato-McGinley J, Zhu YS. 2002. Androgens and male physiology the syndrome of 5α-reductase-2 deficiency. Mol Cell Endocrinol 198:51–59.

49. Money J, Schwartz M, Lewis VG. 1984. Adult erotosexual status and fetal hormonal masculinization and demasculinization: 46, XX congenital virilizing adrenal hyperplasia and 46, XY androgen-insensitivity syndrome compared. Psychoneuroendocrinology 9:405–414.

50. Dittmann RW, Kappes ME, Kappes MH. 1992. Sexual behavior in adolescent and adult females with congenital adrenal hyperplasia. Psychoneuroendocrinology 17:153–170.

51. Zucker KJ, Bradley SJ, Oliver G, Blake J, Fleming S, Hood J. 1996. Psychosexual development of women with congenital adrenal hyperplasia. Horm Behav 30:300–318.

52. Ehrhardt AA, Meyer-Bahlburg HF, Rosen LR, Feldman JF, Veridiano NP, Zimmerman I, McEwen BS. 1985. Sexual orientation after prenatal exposure to exogenous estrogen. Arch Sex Behav 14:57–77.

53. Meyer-Bahlburg HF, Ehrhardt AA, Rosen LR. 1995. Prenatal estrogens and the development of homosexual orientation. Dev Psychol 31:12–21.

54. Goy RW, Deputte BL. 1996. The effects of diethylstilbestrol (DES) before birth on the development of masculine behavior in juvenile female rhesus monkeys. Horm Behav 30:379–386.

55. Reiner WG, Gearhart JP. 2004. Discordant sexual identity in some genetic males with cloacal exstrophy assigned to female sex at birth. N Engl J Med 350:333–341.

56. Meyer-Bahlburg HF. 2005. Gender identity outcome in female-raised 46, XY persons with penile agenesis, cloacal exstrophy of the bladder, or penile ablation. Arch Sex Behav 34:423–438.

57. Dörner G, Geier T, Ahrens L, Krell L, Münx G, Sieler H, Kittner E, Müller H. 1980. Prenatal stress as possible aetiogenetic factor of homosexuality in human males. Endokrinologie 75:365–368.

58. Dörner G, Schenk B, Schmiedel B, Ahrens L. 1983. Stressful events in prenatal life of bi- and homosexual men. Exp Clin Endocrinol 81:83–87.

59. Dörner G. 1980. Sexual differentiation of the brain. In: Vitamins and hormones. New York: Academic Press, Inc.; 325–381.

60. Macke JP, Hu N, Hu S, Bailey M, King VL, Brown T, Hamer D, Nathans J. 1993. Sequence variation in the androgen receptor gene is not a common determinant of male sexual orientation. Am J Hum Genet 53:844–852.

61. DuPree MG, Mustanski BS, Bocklandt S, Nievergelt C, Hamer DH. 2004. A candidate gene study of CYP19 (aromatase) and male sexual orientation. Behav Genet 34:243–250.

62. Mustanski BS, Dupree MG, Nievergelt CM, Bocklandt S, Schork NJ, Hamer DH. 2005. A genomewide scan of male sexual orientation. Hum Genet 116:272–278.

63. Bailey JM, Pillard RC, Dawood K, Miller MB, Farrer LA, Trivedi S, Murphy RL. 1999. A family history study of male sexual orientation using three independent samples. Behav Genet 29:79–86.

64. Diamond M. 1993. Some genetic considerations in the development of sexual orientation. In: Haug M, Whalen RE, Aron C, Olsen KL, editors. eds. The development of sex differences and similarities in behavior. Dordrecht, The Netherlands: Kluwer Academic Publishers; 291–309.

65. Hamer DH, Hu S, Magnuson VL, Hu N, Pattatucci AML. 1993. A linkage between DNA markers on the X chromosome and male sexual orientation. Science 261:321–327.

66. Hu S, Pattatucci AM, Patterson C, Li L, Fulker DW, Cherny SS, Kruglyak L, Hamer DH. 1995. Linkage between sexual orientation and chromosome Xq28 in males but not in females. Nat Genet 11:248–256.

67. Sanders AR, Dawood K. 2003. Nature encyclopedia of life sciences. London: Nature Publishing Group.

68. Rice G, Anderson C, Risch N, Ebers G. 1999. Male homosexuality: absence of linkage to microsatellite markers at Xq28. Science 284:665–667.

69. Bocklandt S, Vilain E. 2007. Sex differences in brain and behavior: hormones versus genes. Adv Genet 59:245–266.

70. Ngun TC, Ghahramani N, Sanchez FJ, Bocklandt S, Vilain E. 2011. The genetics of sex differences in brain and behavior. Front Neuroendocrinol 32:227–246.

71. Bogaert AF, Skorska M. 2011. Sexual orientation, fraternal birth order, and the maternal immune hypothesis: a review. Front Neuroendocrinol 32:247–254.

72. Kinsey AC, Pomeroy WR, Martin CE, Gebhard PH. 1953. Sexual behavior in the human female. Philadelphia: Saunders.

73. Bem DJ. 1996. Exotic becomes erotic: a developmental theory of sexual orientation. Psychol Rev 103:320–335.

74. Bem DJ. 2000. Exotic becomes erotic: interpreting the biological correlates of sexual orientation. Arch Sex Behav 29:531–548.

Jacques Balthazart is the associate professor of neuroendocrinology in GIGA Neurosciences at University of Liège in Belgium. He is the former president of the Society for Behavioral Neuroendocrinology and is the co-editor of the Oxford series on Behavioral Neuroendocrinology.

Stanton L. Jones and Alex W. Kwee

Scientific Research, Homosexuality, and the Church's Moral Debate: An Update

Etiological Research

Significant new research on etiology has emerged in six areas: 1) behavioral genetics; 2) genetic scanning, 3) human brain structure studies, 4) studies of "gay sheep" and "gay fruit flies," 5) fraternal birth order research, and 6) familial structure impact.

Behavioral Genetics

Bailey's behavioral genetics studies of sexual orientation in twins and other siblings seemed to provide solid evidence of a substantial degree of genetic influence on formation of homosexual orientation. Jones and Yarhouse criticized these studies severely, most importantly on the grounds that both studies were making population estimates of the degree of genetic influence on sexual orientation on *potentially biased samples,* samples recruited from advertisements in gay publications and hence potentially biased by differential volunteerism by subjects inclined to favor a genetic hypothesis for the causation of their orientation. Later research by Bailey and other associates with a truly representative sample of twins drawn from the Australian Twin Registry in fact refuted the earlier findings by failing to find a significant genetic effect in the causation of homosexual orientation.

Not included in our review was a major behavioral genetics study paralleling the work of Bailey: Kendler, Thornton, Gilman, and Kessler. This study is remarkable in two ways. First, it replicates almost exactly the findings of the earlier Bailey studies in reporting relatively strong probandwise concordances for homosexual monozygotic twins. Kendler et al. report their findings as pairwise concordances, but when the simple conversions to probandwise concordances are done, Kendler et al.'s 48% probandwise concordance for males and females together (reported as a 31.6% pairwise concordance) is remarkably similar to Bailey's reports of probandwise concordances of 52% for men and 48% for women.

Second, the Kendler et al. study is also remarkably similar to the earlier Bailey studies in its methodological weaknesses. Trumpeted as a study correcting the "unrepresentative and potentially biased samples" of the Bailey studies by using a "more representative sample," specifically a "U. S. national probability sample" (p. 1843), this study appears actually to suffer all of the original problems of volunteer sample bias of the 1991 and 1993 Bailey studies. Further, the methodological problems give every sign of compounding one upon the next. The description of the methodology is confusing: Kendler et al. state that their sample comes from a MacArthur Foundation study of 3,032 representatively chosen respondents, but then they note that since this sample produced too few twins and almost no homosexual twins (as would be expected), they turned to a different sample of 50,000 households that searched for twins, and here the clear sampling problems begin: 14.8% of the households reported a twin among the siblings, but only 60% gave permission to contact the twin. There was further erosion of the sample as only 20.6% of the twins agreed to participate if the initial contact was with another family member, compared to 60.4% if the initial contact was a twin him- or herself (and given the lower likelihood of an initial contact being with a twin, this suggests a low response rate for twins overall). Yet further erosion may have occurred at the next step of seeking contact information of all siblings in the family; the write-up is confusing on this point. With all these potential sampling problems, it is then quite striking that the absolute number of identical/monozygotic twin pairs concordant for homosexuality were only 6 (out of a total of 19 pairs where at least one twin was "non-heterosexual"). With such a small absolute number of monozygotic twin pairs concordant for homosexuality, the smallest bias in the assembly of the sample would introduce problems in data interpretation; loss of just two concordant twin pairs would have wiped out the findings. It is remarkable that Kendler et al. give no explicit attention to these problems.

Thus, we must regard this new study, promoted by some as a replication of Bailey's original 1991 and 1993 studies, as having the same fatal flaws as those earlier studies and as rightly superseded by Bailey's report in 2000 that there is no statistically significant indication of genetic influence on sexual orientation.

Genetic Scanning

Mustanski et al. reported on a "full genome scan of sexual orientation in men" (p. 272). This is the third study of genetics and homosexuality to emerge from the laboratory of the associates of Dean Hamer, and this study utilized 146 families; 73 families previously studied by either Hamer, Hu, Magnuson, Hu, and Pattatucci or Hu et al., and 73 new families not previously studied. The same sample limitations are present in these studies as were discussed in Jones and Yarhouse (pp. 79–83). If these studies were attempting to establish population estimates, these would constitute biased samples, but because they explicitly state that they are looking for genetic factors in a subpopulation of homosexual men predetermined to be more likely to manifest genetic factors, these are limitations and not methodological weaknesses. They obtained their sample through "advertisements in local and national homophile publications" and the "sole inclusion criterion was the presence of at least two self-acknowledged gay male siblings" (p. 273), a rare occurrence indeed.

Two findings are worth noting. First, the Mustanski et al. study continued the pattern of failing to replicate the original 1993 Hamer finding of an Xq28 region of the X chromosome being linked to male homosexuality, this despite somewhat heroic statistical focus in this study. This is yet another blow to the credibility of their original findings.

Second, while media outlets headlined the Mustanski et al. study as having found genes linked to homosexuality on chromosomes 7, 8, and 10, this is precisely what they did *not* find, but rather "we found one region of near significance and two regions close to the criteria for suggestive linkage" (p. 273). None of their findings, in other words, achieved statistical significance. It is hard to tell whether these findings represent a cluster of near false positives that will fail future replication, or clues that will lead to more fine-grained and statistically significant findings. If the latter, these genetic segments may be neither necessary nor sufficient to cause homosexual orientation, and may either contribute to the causation of the orientation directly or indirectly. This is an intriguing but ambiguous report.

Human Brain Structure Studies

New brain research allows us to expand the reported findings on the relationship of brain structure to sexual orientation, and to correct one element of our prior presentation of the data in this complex field. We duplicate [here] . . . (Table 1) part of the table summarizing brain findings from pages 68–69 of Jones and Yarhouse.

Our correction is to recategorize in Table 1 the findings of Swaab and Hoffman from our listing, following the

Table 1

Summary of Brain Differences by Biological Sex and Sexual Orientation

| | Brain | | Region | |
Study	INAH1	INAH2	INAH3	INAH4
Swaab & Fliers (1985)	HetM > HetF			
Swaab & Hoffman (1988)	HetM = HomM; (HetM & HomM) > HetF			
Allen et al. (1989)	HetM = HetF	HetM > HetF	HetM > HetF	HetM = HetF
LeVay (1991)	HetM = HetF	HetM = HetF	HetM > (HetF & HomM)	HetM = HetF
Byne et al. (2000)	HetM = HetF	HetM = HetF	HetM > HetF	HetM = HetF
Byne et al. (2001)	HetM = HetF	HetM = HetF	HetM > HetF	HetM = HetF
			HetM = HomM in number of neurons	

HetM = heterosexual males; HetF = heterosexual females; HomM = homosexual males.

original report, as from the SDNH or sexually differentiated nucleus of the hypothalamus to a finding reporting on the INAH1 or interstitial nucleus of the hypothalamus, area 1. The review of Byne et al. pointed out that the SDNH *is* the INAH1; Swaab's 1988 report was an extension of his earlier work and not an exploration of a new area. The new work of Byne et al. continued the pattern of refuting Swaab's reported findings.

The new findings reporting on brain structure and sexual orientation (summarized in Table 1) come from the respected laboratory of William Byne and his colleagues. We cited Byne heavily in our critique of the famous Simon LeVay studies of brain differences in the INAH3 region. Byne et al. replicated the previous findings of sexual dimorphism (male-female differences) in INAH3, and thus it is now safe to say that this is a stable finding. Further, Byne and his team have refined the analysis to be able to say, based on their 2000 study, that the INAH3 size difference by sex "was attributable to a sex difference in neuronal number and not in neuronal size or density." Simply put, the INAH3 area in women is, on average, smaller than it is in men, and this is because women have fewer neurons in this area, and *not* because their neurons are smaller or less dense.

This makes the findings of Byne et al. on sexual orientation yet more curious; they found the size (specifically, volume) of the INAH3s of homosexual males to be intermediate (to a statistically nonsignificant degree) between heterosexual males and heterosexual females. In other words, the volume of the INAH3s was, on average, between the average volumes of heterosexual males and heterosexual females such that the differences did not achieve statistical significance in comparison to either heterosexual males or females. Hence, "Sexual orientation cannot be reliably predicted on the basis of INAH3 volume alone." Further, and to complicate things more, they found that the nonsignificant difference noted between homosexual and heterosexual males was *not* attributable (as it was for the male-female difference) to numbers of neurons, as homosexual and heterosexual males were found to have comparable neuronal counts. So, there may be a difference between homosexual and heterosexual males, but if there is, it is not the same type of difference as that between males and females.

To complicate the analysis even further, Byne et al. point out that these differences, if they exist, are not proof of prenatal, biological determination of sexual orientation. While it is possible that differences in INHA3 may be strongly influenced by prenatal hormones, "In addition, sex related differences may also emerge later in development as the neurons that survive become part of

functional circuits" (p. 91). Specifically, the difference in volume could be attributed to "a reduction in neuropil within the INAH3 in the homosexual group" (p. 91) as a result of "postnatal experience." In other words, if there are brain structure differences between homosexuals and heterosexuals, they could as well be the result rather than the cause of sexual behavior and sexual preference. (The same conclusion about directionality of causation can be drawn about the new study showing activation of sexual brain centers in response to female pheromones by male heterosexuals, and to male pheromones by female heterosexuals *and* male homosexuals. The authors themselves point out that these brain activations could be the result of learning as well as evidence of the "hard-wiring" of the brain.) . . .

Second, and in a rare admission for those advancing biological explanations of sexual orientation, Roselli et al. admit that the direction of causation is at this time completely unclear, in the process echoing the possible causal role of postnatal experience mentioned by Byne et al. above:

> However, the existing data do not reveal which is established first—oSDN size or mate preference. One might assume that the neural structure is determined first and that this, in turn, guides the development of sexual partner preference. However, it is equally possible that some other factor(s), including social influences or learned associations, might shape sexual partner preference first. Then, once a sexual partner preference is established, the continued experiences and/or behaviors associated with a given preference might affect the size of the oSDN. (p. 241)

A new study released in June, 2005 has ignited the latest frenzy about biological causation of sexual orientation. In response to this study, the president of the Human Rights Campaign ("the largest national lesbian, gay, bisexual and transgender political organization") stated that "Science is closing the door on right-wing distortions. . . . The growing body of scientific evidence continues to refute the opponents of equality who maintain that sexual orientation is a 'choice.'" Chairman of the Case Western Reserve University Department of Biochemistry Michael Weiss expressed for the *New York Times* his hope that this study "will take the discussion about sexual preferences out of the realm of morality and put it into the realm of science." Both quotes epitomize the over-interpretation and illogic of those anxious to press findings from science to moral conclusions.

The new study appears to be a strong piece of scientific research that will have important implications for our understanding of the biological bases of sexual behavior. The researchers generated a gene fragment (the *"fruitless (fru)"* allele) that was "constitutively spliced in either the male or the female mode" in the chromosomes of the opposite sex (i.e., male fruit flies had the allele inserted in a female mode and female fruit flies had the allele inserted in a male mode) with dramatic effects: "Forcing female splicing in the male results in a loss of male courtship behavior and orientation, confirming that male-specific splicing of *fru* is indeed essential for male behavior. More dramatically, females in which *fru* is spliced in the male mode behave as if they were males: they court other females" (p. 786). The results reported were indeed powerful; the behavioral distinctions in the modified fruit flies were almost unequivocal.

The authors of this study were reasonably circumspect in their report of the implications of their findings, though others were not as noted before. Three issues deserve attention. First, as in our discussion of "gay sheep," the differences between human and animal (or insect) mating patterns are enormous, and those differences limit application to the human situation. Demir and Dickson noted that male courtship of the female fruit fly is highly scripted, "largely a fixed-action pattern" (p. 785). The finding that the normal, almost robotic mating patterns of this creature are hard-wired is hardly surprising; in contrast, the enormous complexity of human sexual and romantic response indicates that such a finding will be challenging to apply to the human condition. Further, the interpretation that this study establishes a genetic base for "sexual orientation" in fruit flies is careless; the study rather finds genetic determination (to some degree) of an entire pattern of mating/reproductive behavior. The genetic control of mating behavior in this study is of something both more and less than sexual orientation as experienced by humans.

Second, we have plenty of existing data to indicate that no such encompassing genetic determination of sexual behavior exists in humans. The behavior genetics evidence of sexual orientation (see the earlier discussion of the Kendler et al. study) provides strong evidence that genetic factors provide (at most) incomplete determination of sexual orientation, even if genetic factors are part of a multivariant causal array.

Third, we must question the following claim of the authors:

> Thus, male-specific splicing of *fru* is both necessary and *sufficient* [emphasis added] to specify male courtship behavior and sexual orientation. A complex innate behavior is thus specified by the action of a single gene, demonstrating that behavioral switch genes do indeed exist and identifying *fru* as one such gene.

Strictly understood, the authors appear to be claiming that the presence of *fru* elicits, *necessarily and sufficiently*, stereotypical male courtship by males of female fruit flies, but a famous study from a decade before falsifies the sufficiency of *fru* causation. Zhang and Odenwald reported on genetic alterations in male fruit flies which produced "homosexual behavior" in the altered fruit flies. This study too resulted in many tabloid headlines heralding the creation of a "homosexual gene." Media reports failed to cite the other curious finding of the study: when genetically normal or "straight" fruit flies were introduced into the habitat of the "gay" flies without females present, the normal (genetically unaltered) male flies began engaging in the same type of "homosexual" behavior as the genetically altered flies. In other words, genetically normal ("straight") flies began to act like homosexual flies because of their *social environment*. Thus, in a most biological experiment, evidence of environmental ("psychological") influence emerged once again. So if the authors of the 2005 study are claiming that the presence of *fru* elicits (is sufficient to produce) stereotypical male courtship, that claim was falsified a decade before by the finding that normal male fruit flies (presumably with intact *fru* alleles), when exposed to certain social contexts ("gay" flies), engage in behavior that violates the stereotypical male courtship of females; other conditions—specifically, *social* conditions—are also sufficient to elicit homosexual behavior in fruit flies.

Together, these three issues suggest that, as powerful as the recent findings about fruit flies are, interpretive caution in application to humans is indicated.

Fraternal Birth Order Research

The fraternal birth order studies by Ray Blanchard, Anthony Bogaert, and various other researchers purport to show that sexual orientation in men correlates with an individual's number of older brothers. Specifically, it is claimed that male homosexuals tend to be born later in their sibships than male heterosexuals, and that male homosexuality is statistically (and causally) related to the number of older biological brothers (but not sisters) in the family. This purported relationship within the fraternal birth order is such that each additional older brother, it is claimed, increases the odds of homosexuality by 33%, and for gay men with approximately 2.5 older brothers, older brothers equal all the other causes of homosexuality combined.

Blanchard, Bogaert, and others advance the so-called maternal immune hypothesis to explain the fraternal birth order effect. According to this hypothesis, some mothers progressively produce, in response to each succeeding male fetus, antibodies to a substance called the H-Y antigen, which is produced by male fetuses and foreign to female bodies. The maternally produced anti-H-Y antibodies are thought to be passed on to the male fetus, preventing the fetal brain from developing in a male typical pattern, thereby causing the affected sons to develop homosexual orientations in later life. So much hyperbole surrounds the maternal immune causal hypothesis that it appears the assumption is simply being made that the fraternal birth order effect itself is indisputable when, in fact, it is not. We will direct the bulk of our critical attention to the birth order phenomenon. The maternal immune theory underlying the phenomenon can be quite readily dispatched at this point by stating that no direct evidence has ever been found for it, and so it remains purely speculative.

The major flaw of the fraternal birth order research is that the main studies were conducted on nonrepresentative samples. For example, one of the "landmark" studies that demonstrated the birth order effect recruited its sample from the 1994 Toronto Gay Pride Parade and several LGBT community organizations. Nonrepresentative samples are known to be vulnerable to a variety of selection biases. For instance, perhaps later-born gay men were overrepresented in this sample because they were more apt to be "out and proud," participate in Gay Pride events, and affiliate with overtly LGBT groups. If later born siblings tend to be less conventional and more rebellious as some research shows, later-born gay men, accordingly, may be less gender conforming and more likely to flaunt their sexual orientation. This may have resulted in an overrepresentation of later-born gay men and an under-representation of earlier-born gay men at Gay Pride events and within LGBT groups, which naturally exaggerated the fraternal birth order effect in this sample. This is just one of several possible selection biases which may have flawed Blanchard and Bogaert's sample.

To his credit, Bogaert attempted to correct for the methodological flaw of selection bias by examining national probability samples in the United States and Britain respectively. His study yielded a finding of fraternal birth order effects in both samples. While this may appear to replicate initial research results, we must question the size of the effects given the large samples involved—over 1,700 subjects in each of the samples. Bogaert did not clearly report the effect sizes he found. It is well known that using large enough samples, even small differences can be found to be statistically significant. Since statistical significance is a function of both sample size and effect size, and we really care about the effect size (and not merely that it is non-zero), Bogaert's findings are quite unhelpful.

In an even more recent study, Bogaert and Cairney attempted to answer the question of whether there is a fraternal birth order and parental age interaction effect in the prediction of sexual orientation. The researchers examined two samples—a U.S. national probability sample, and the flawed Canadian sample which we discussed above. The study based on the U.S. sample found an interaction, but the data was so flawed—and acknowledged to be so by the authors themselves—that we cannot possibly take its conclusion seriously. Specifically, the preexisting U.S. data allowed for only an examination of absolute (not fraternal) birth order, surmised sexual orientation from behavior alone, and did not separate biological from non-biological siblings. The conclusion was counterintuitive in that while a positive association between (absolute) birth order and the likelihood of homosexuality was found, this association was weakened and in fact *reversed* with increasing maternal age. We believe that this conclusion highlights the problem of bias when researchers attempt to find putative phenomena in data to support a cherished theory. If one is trying to establish a link between maternal age and homosexuality, it seems counterintuitive that the likelihood of homosexuality weakens or is reversed with increasing maternal age. Of course, if there is no relationship between sexual orientation and maternal age (which we suspect), a finding of *any* relationship is probably spurious and a methodological artifact. The researchers acknowledge the counterintuitiveness of their result by stating that they "know of no evidence of a stronger maternal reaction [to the H-Y antigen] in younger (versus older) mothers" (p. 32), betraying their bias towards a theory for which no direct evidence has ever been established, and then calling for new research.

Turning to the Canadian sample, Bogaert and Cairney found a Parental Age x Birth Order interaction. Their weighted analysis (giving larger families a greater impact on the results) revealed that this interaction was carried by a Mother's Age x Older Sisters effect. This finding actually *undermines* the fraternal birth order theory because it provides some evidence that homosexuality is independent of the fraternal birth order effect. The authors acknowledge but downplay this, calling instead for the gathering of new data.

Other studies have falsified the fraternal birth order effect or showed no support for the maternal immune hypothesis. Using an enormous and nationally representative sample of adolescents that we discuss fully below, Bearman and Brückner found "no evidence for a speculative evolutionary model of homosexual preference" (i.e., the older-brother findings; p. 1199).

Despite various methodological problems with the fraternal birth order research, we concede that the evidence as a whole points to some sort of relationship between the number of older brothers and homosexuality. As responsible scientists, we should approach this body of research critically but not ignore the fact that it consistently shows some link between sexual orientation and fraternal but not sororal birth order. Research may well identify some pathway by which some men develop a stable same-sex attraction that is linked to their placement in the birth order. However, those who argue that the maternal immunosensitivity theory explains the fraternal birth order effect run into the problem of having to show that the same hypothesis does not underlie pedophilia, sexual violence, and other forms of sexual deviancy. While Blanchard, Bogaert, and other researchers deny any link between fraternal birth order and pedophilia, or they believe that any such link exists only for pedophiles who are homosexual, other studies have demonstrated a link between fraternal birth order and general (pedophilic and non-pedophilic) sexual offending, raising the possibility that homosexuality shares a common pathway with some forms of sexual deviance.

Research has not clearly established what this pathway is. One of the most natural but politically divisive speculations, which cautiously raises its head in the literature now and then, is that childhood sexualization and abuse has some causative relationship to homosexuality and pedophilia. This speculation is logical in relation to the fraternal birth order effect because younger brothers with higher fraternal birth order indices may have a higher probability of being victimized sexually by older brothers or otherwise experiencing same-sex sexualization. Preadolescent sexualization and abuse underlie the post-natal learning theory of homosexuality and pedophilia, which most recently has been supported by James in his review of several major studies. However plausible this theory appears, it is based on inferences from other studies and the direct empirical evidence for it is extremely weak.

Familial Structure Impact

A particularly powerful study challenging all of the major paradigms asserting biological determination of sexual orientation, and of the claim that there is no meaningful evidence of psychological/experiential causation of orientation, was recently published. Bearman and Brückner reported on analyses of an enormous database of almost 30,000 sexuality interviews with adolescents, with fascinating findings on the determinants of same-sex attraction for males (they found no evidence of significant determinants for females). Their summary of their findings merits citation in full:

> The findings presented here confirm some findings from previous research and stand in marked contrast to most previous research in a number of respects. First, we find no evidence for intrauterine transfer of hormone effects on social behavior. Second, we find no support for genetic influences on same-sex preference net of social structural constraints. Third, we find no evidence for a speculative evolutionary model of homosexual preference. Finally, we find substantial indirect evidence in support of a socialization model at the individual level. (p. 1199)

Their second conclusion is a direct reference to the types of genetic influence posited by Bailey and others; the third conclusion a direct reference to the "older-brother" findings of Blanchard, Bogaert and others. But not only do their findings contradict other research, a new finding of socialization effects on same-sex attraction emerge from their data (see Table 2).

Bearman and Brückner found a single family constellation arrangement that significantly increased the likelihood that an adolescent male would report same-sex attraction, and that was when the adolescent male was a

Table 2

Core Findings of Bearman & Brückner

Relationship (Subject is a . . .)	% Reporting Same-Sex Attraction	N (all males)
Opposite Sex Dizygotic Twin	16.8%	185
Same Sex Dizygotic Twin	9.8%	276
Same Sex Monozygotic Twin	9.9%	262
Opposite Sex Full Sibling	7.3%	427
Same Sex Full Sibling	7.9%	596
Other (adopted non-related; half-sibling)	10.6%	832

dizygotic (fraternal) twin whose co-twin is a sister (what they call "male opposite-sex twins"); in this arrangement, occurrence of same-sex attraction more than doubled over the base-rate of 7% to 8%: "we show that adolescent male opposite-sex twins are *twice as likely* as expected to report same-sex attraction, and that the pattern of concordance (similarity across pairs) of same-sex preference for sibling pairs does not suggest genetic influence independent of the social context" (p. 1181). They advance a socialization hypothesis to explain this finding, specifically proposing that sexual attraction is an outgrowth of gender socialization, and that no arrangement presents as much a challenge to parents to gender socialization than for a boy to be born simultaneous with a girl co-twin. In other words, they suggest that the parental task of accomplishing effective solidification of male sexual identity is challenged by parents having to handle a mixed-sex twin pair. The result of the diminished effectiveness of sexual identity formation in boys on average is the increased probability of same-sex attraction in the group of boys with twin sisters.

Bearman and Brückner go on to explore in their data the possibility that there could be a hormonal explanation for this finding: "Our data falsify the hormonal transfer hypothesis [i.e., the hypothesis posited to explain the fraternal birth order phenomenon], by isolating a single condition that eliminates the OS effect we observe—the presence of an older same-sex sibling" (p. 1181). Put simply, they found their effect disappeared when the boy with the twin sister was born into a family where there was already an older brother, an effect they attributed to the family already having grown accustomed to the process of establishing the sexual identity of a boy child; parents appear to be able to better handle the special challenges of a mixed-sex twin pair when they have already had some practice with an older brother. They firmly suggest that their "results support the hypothesis that less gendered socialization in early childhood and preadolescence shapes subsequent same-sex romantic preferences" (p. 1181). At a moment in time when it is common for many to deny that any firm evidence exists for the influence of non-biological causes on sexual orientation, these are remarkable findings (perhaps especially when the presence of an older brother decreases rather than increases the likelihood of homosexual orientation). . . .

STANTON L. JONES is the provost and professor of psychology at Wheaton College. He is the author of the lead article, "Religion and Psychology," for the *Encyclopedia of Psychology,* jointly published in 2000 by the American Psychological Association and Oxford University Press. His article in the March 1994 *American Psychologist,* titled "A Constructive Relationship for Religion with the Science and Profession of Psychology: Perhaps the Best Model Yet," was a call for greater respect for and cooperation with religion by secular psychologists.

ALEX W. KWEE is an assistant professor at Trinity Western University and a program psychologist at Back in Motion Rehab, where he specializes in pain management. He also maintains a private practice through New Life Christian Counselling in Langley, where he practices psychology in a more spiritually-sensitive context.

EXPLORING THE ISSUE

Is Homosexuality Biologically Based?

Critical Thinking and Reflection

1. Is homosexuality a product of biology or learning? Support your claims with relevant research evidence.
2. Many argue that if it were proven that homosexuality is biologically based, discrimination against homosexuals would decrease. Support this argument with research on discrimination and prejudice. Are there any good reasons to think that discrimination might continue or even increase?
3. Stanton Jones, the first author of the second article, has recently co-authored a book entitled *Ex-Gays?* In this book, he reports a complex research study that he argues is an indicator that homosexuals can change their sexual orientation. If this is true, what would this finding mean for the possibility of biological determination of sexual orientation?

Is There Common Ground?

Understanding the origins and causes of homosexual attraction is a very "hot" topic in society today, often inviting strong opinions and loud confrontations. Whatever position is accepted as constituting the "final word" on homosexuality will undoubtedly have wide-ranging effects in the culture, especially in the political arena. What is often not noted, however, is that in many cases in psychology advocates of both the biological and the environmental views of homosexuality assume a more or less deterministic view of human behavior and sexual desire. That is to say, despite the often contentious nature of the debate, and the passion with which advocates of the two competing sides argue, many seem to share a philosophical commitment to deterministic forms of explanation. On the one hand, homosexuality is thought to be caused by biological forces (e.g., genes and hormones), while, on the other, it is explained as a product of social experiences and environmental forces external to the person.

Of course, there are those who seek to resist deterministic explanations of behaviors like homosexuality. Such folks argue that whatever the case may be regarding biology and environment, human beings are capable of making free and meaningful choices in their lives, even in terms of their sexual desires and attractions. While

many who experience same-sex desires do so in a very compulsory sort of way—that is, as something over which they have no control, but which just is a fundamental part of their very identity—others experience their sexual desires as very much something in which they participate, as an expression of themselves that they have chosen in some way. Deeper exploration of precisely how and why different individuals—all identifying as homosexual—might experience their homosexuality differently, as compelled or as chosen (or, even, as compelled in some ways but not others), is certainly worth further scientific investigation.

Additional Resources

Jones, S. L. (2012). Same-sex science: The social sciences cannot settle the moral status of homosexuality. *First Things: A Monthly Journal of Religion & Public Life, 220,* 27–33.

Rahman, Q. (2005). The neurodevelopment of human sexual orientation. *Neuroscience & Biobehavioral Reviews, 29*(7), 1057–1066.

Wilson, G., & Rahman, Q. (2008). *Born Gay: The Psychology of Sex Orientation.* Peter Owen Publishers, London.

Internet References . . .

Psychology Today

http://www.psychologytoday.com/blog/sexing-the-body/201111/are-we-born-gay

Queer by Choice

http://www.queerbychoice.com/

Scientific American

http://blogs.scientificamerican.com/guest-blog/2012/10/19/is-homosexuality-a-choice/

Same Sex Attraction

http://www.samesexattraction.org/biological-causes-homosexuality.htm

Selected, Edited, and with Issue Framing Material by:
Edwin E. Gantt, *Brigham Young University*

ISSUE

Is Free Will an Illusion?

YES: Arnold Modell, from "The Agency of the Self and the Brain's Illusions," *Psychological Agency: Theory, Practice, and Culture* (2008)

NO: Eddy Nahmias, from "Why We Have Free Will," *Scientific American* (2015)

Learning Outcomes

After reading this issue, you will be able to:

- Determine for yourself whether human freedom is simply an illusion created by the brain, or is rather something fundamental about human beings.
- Understand the strengths and limitations that current neuroscience research has in regard to explaining human behavior.
- Think about whether the debate over free will can be settled by an empirical, scientific psychology, or if it can only be addressed from a more philosophical point of view.

ISSUE SUMMARY

YES: Arnold Modell, a professor of social psychiatry at the Harvard Medical School, argues that free will is simply a necessary illusion in our lives. To support his point, he cites scientific research that seems to provide evidence that the causes of our actions occur before we are conscious of them. He also argues that our feelings arise without our conscious choice or volition.

NO: Eddy Nehmias, a professor of philosophy at Georgia State University, argues an opposing view to those who see free will as an illusion. He argues that we need not accept the conclusion that free will is simply an illusion just because fMRIs show neurons firing a split second before a choice is made. In other words, he argues that brain activity cannot sufficiently account for conscious human actions.

With recent technological advances in the field of cognitive neuroscience, research on the functioning of the brain has become more and more sophisticated and informative. Many brain structures have been identified and their functions correlated with specific human behaviors. As more sophisticated methods of investigation have been developed, researchers have increasingly focused on trying to identify the brain's role in the common experience of agency or free will. Some of this research has suggested that there may be specific neurons responsible for conscious thought and decision-making, and several researchers have begun to argue that this means that our sense of agency and free choice is really an illusion created by our brains.

As a result of such findings, one of the most enduring debates in psychological science and philosophy has found new and interesting life; that is, whether or not human beings really have freedom of choice. Are our conscious choices really just an illusion created by the brain? Do we have any real control over our actual choices, feelings, and decision-making? The outcome of this debate will, of course, have significant implications for how we understand human behavior as well as the reality of the moral precepts that form the basis for so many of our social and cultural institutions. For example, if free will really is just an illusion foisted on us by our brain function, then it may be difficult to see how criminal or civil law—both of which are founded on the notion of human freedom and responsibility—can be valid given that a consequence of the notion that free will is an illusion is that people cannot be held accountable for their behaviors and choices. In other words, if an individual's choices are caused by neurons randomly firing in the brain, then in what sense can they be held to be responsible for those choices? With implications such as that, it is easy to see the importance of settling this important debate, and many researchers and philosophers alike have attempted to explore the issue and come up with workable and intellectually satisfying solutions.

In the YES selection, Modell argues that instead of serving as the cause of our own behavior, human beings merely interpret the feelings and actions that arise in us as a result of unconscious brain activity. There is nothing that we can do about these feelings because they are a direct product of processes outside our awareness and control. The only thing we know for certain, he argues, is that we are the ones experiencing our feelings and engaging in our actions. Thus, we do not experience our free will as causing our actions or feelings, but we do experience control over what interpretations we give to our feelings and actions. Consciousness, Modell argues, is immaterial and, therefore, is unable to be a cause of anything. It is, in reality, only something we observe as a by-product of other, more basic physical causes. Nonetheless, Modell argues that the illusion of agency is important for us in order to

sense the difference between our actions and those of others. In this vein, Modell cites studies that seem to show free will as simply a feeling that is activated by unique parts of the brain, milliseconds before we are conscious of our actions, but which allows us to have a sense of our own effectiveness. He argues that this illusion is ultimately important to our sense of well-being and our ability to fulfill ourselves.

In the NO selection, Nahmias argues that just because recent research may suggest that neurons are activated before we become aware of our decision to act, this does not mean that we are controlled by our brains. In other words, he argues, neuroscience research cannot validly state that free will is an illusion simply based on the physical fact of neurons firing in the brain. He first states that current technology actually lacks the ability to differentiate between conscious decision-making and subconscious thought. Therefore, researchers cannot tell whether any given group of neurons is in reality firing before conscious thought or after. He also confronts the often-advanced point that we as human beings seem to have less conscious control over our actions than we think. He argues that just because we have less control does not mean we have no control at all. Further, he argues that free will cannot be a brain-created illusion by citing recent research that shows that our technology simply is not complex enough to actually validate such a claim.

YES

Arnold Modell

The Agency of the Self and the Brain's Illusions

Our feelings arise from within our bodies without our bidding, and are therefore beyond our control. This fact, that we do not control our feelings, is an aspect of human nature that has been noted since antiquity. This then raises the question, if we do not control our feelings, to what extent we are free, and as a corollary, to what extent are we responsible for our actions?

If we are not free but in bondage to our feelings, our sense of agency is an illusion. Contemporary neuroscience appears to have confirmed this assumption. Although our feeling of agency is an illusion, it is a *necessary* illusion, an illusion that can be enhanced or impaired. . . .

Agency means causality, and strictly speaking, we are never the cause of our feelings but only responsible for their interpretation. If agency implies causality, ownership implies a recognition that I am the one that is having the feeling (Gallagher 2000). But we can never be quite sure whether our feelings originate in our own bodies or have been secondarily placed within us. We do not question that we are the one experiencing the feeling, but we remain uncertain as to how the feeling got there. Feelings have what William James described as an ambiguity of place. Inasmuch as feelings are unconsciously communicated, what we feel may be in response to an unconscious perception of feelings that originate in other minds and are directed toward us by the Other. Our feelings belong to us because they are part of our body, but because our feelings respond to the feelings of the other we can say we are not to blame. . . .

We cannot control what we feel any more than we can control our heartbeat. Our feelings simply happen to us. What we can control, at least potentially, is our *interpretation* of those feelings. . . .

The Feeling of Agency Is an Illusion Created by the Brain

For millennia, philosophers have questioned whether human volition can be considered a causal agent. Kant (1998) famously declared that "freedom of the will" is one

of only three metaphysical problems that lie beyond the powers of the human intellect. Philosophers have long suspected that the belief that our will is a causal agent is an illusion. This ancient problem of free will has recently become a subject of scientific inquiry (Libet, Freeman, and Sutherland 1999; Wegner 2002). Neuroscience appears to have confirmed that our feeling of agency is just that, merely a feeling, an illusion created by the brain. Daniel Wegner has written a book titled *The illusion of Conscious Will*, where he provides evidence that a feeling of agency is no more than an illusion. But he acknowledges that it is a necessary illusion. According to Wegner (2005, 30),

> The creation of our sense of agency is critically important for a variety of personal and social processes, even if this perceived agent is not a cause of action. The experience of conscious will is fundamentally important because it provides a marker of our authorship—what might be called an authorship emotion. Each surge of will we sense in the operation of controlled processes provides a bodily reminder of what we think we have done. In this sense, the function of will is to identify our action with a feeling, allowing us to sense in a very basic way what we're likely to have done, and to distinguish such things from those caused by events in the world or by other people or agents.

Wegner's observation that a sense of agency is simply a feeling that distinguishes our actions from those of the Other was shown experimentally by an investigation using positron-emission tomography (PET) and functional magnetic resonance imagery (fMRJ) (Farrer and Frith 2002; Farrer et al. 2003). These researchers demonstrated that when the subjects used a computer joystick to drive a circle along a given path and did not know whether they or the computer generated the action, different areas of the brain were activated when they believed themselves to be the source of action as compared to action attributed to the Other. When the subjects believed themselves to be the agent, the anterior insula was activated; the right inferior parietal lobe was activated when they attributed the action to another agent. These studies suggest that the feeling of agency is a matter of belief and that it has its own neural circuitry. The feeling of agency is just that, a feeling and nothing more. But it is a feeling that is necessary for our existence in the world. It is hard to imagine living in the world if we had no sense of our own effectiveness.

In a famous set of experiments, Benjamin Libet (1999) has demonstrated that unconscious neural activity precedes conscious intent. Libet's subjects were wired to an EEG and were asked to flex their wrists and indicate on a timing device, which measured fractions of seconds, when they were aware of their intention to act. Neural activity described as a "readiness potential" occurred approximately 500 milliseconds before the subjects were conscious of their intent to move their wrists. Conventional wisdom might have anticipated that conscious thought occurred at the same time as the correlated neural activity. But this was not the case. Unconscious intentionality expressed as a neural event preceded conscious intention, and therefore can be judged as causal. Libet (1999, 51) states that "the initiation of the freely voluntary act appears to begin in the brain unconsciously, well before the person consciously knows he wants to act."

Libet's experiments were confirmed by others and are now established as fact. This would appear to establish the primacy of unconscious thought. Parenthetically, it should be said that Libet himself does not believe that his experiments refute the existence of free will because a willed inhibition was not preceded by neural activity. He believes that conscious will can block or veto an unconscious process. Libet's experiments confirm Freud's assertion that "in psychoanalysis there was no choice first but to assert that mental processes are in themselves unconscious and to liken the perception of them by means of consciousness to the perception of the external world by means of the sense organs" (Freud 1915, 171).

In his book *Wider Than the Sky* (2004), Gerald Edelman insists as does Freud that causality is not a property of consciousness. Causality can only be attributed to physical processes because the physical world is a dosed space and there are no ghosts to activate the machine; there is no causality apart from a neurophysiological process. Consciousness in itself does not cause anything. Consciousness is knowing, not causing. Causality can only be attributed to electrical and chemical forces.

The Self Is Also an Illusion

The current view in neuroscience is that all of what the brain constructs is an illusion. *Illusion* has been defined as a false appearance, a belief that does not have

correlates in the physical world. We see a red rose and inhale its fragrance, but the color red does not exist in the physical world, nor does its fragrance. Colors and odors are the brain's constructions. What exists in the physical world are only packets of energy, photons of varying wavelengths; there are no odors, only chemicals. We constantly attribute and project onto the world that which we construct internally. Our feeling that seeing red is a constant sensation despite alterations in the reflecting light is the consequence of an internal neural process. As the neurophysiologist Semir Zeki (1993, 227) says, "Surfaces are not endowed with codes or labels which allow the brain to analyze them passively with respect to color." Because our perception of the self is a construction of the brain—a construction that does not correspond to anything in the physical world—the self can be justifiably described as an illusion. The illusory nature of the self has been examined in great detail by the German philosopher Thomas Metzinger in his book *Being No One* (2003). According to Metzinger, we essentially imagine ourselves. But we should not depreciate or disparage the belief in illusions as false conceptions; if the self is an illusion, it is an illusion without which we cannot live. We have only to be reminded that the loss of the sense of self—which has been described as annihilation anxiety—is a form of anxiety so horrific that some have been known to commit suicide rather than reexperience this loss.

The self is very difficult to define because it has its origins in our body, in our relation to the Other, and in our culture. There is only one experience of self, but that self can be viewed, as I have just described, as a self-organizing neural construction, and also as a co-construction with the Other—the so-called relational self. This is a view of the self that has been adopted by contemporary psychoanalysis. Finally, the self can be understood as a construction of culture. The idea of the self in Western thought has been constantly evolving from classical antiquity to our own era (Seigel 2005). Western and Eastern cultures have very different views regarding individuality and self-actualization. These different construals of the self have been shown to influence cognition and emotion (Markus and Kitayama 1991). The self is therefore simultaneously a neural construction, a relational construction, and a cultural construction. . . .

Although our sense of agency is an illusion, as I have emphasized, it is an illusion that is necessary for living in the world. As William James (1890, 296–297) said, "The *fons et origo* of all reality . . . is ourselves. Our own reality, that sense of our own life which we at every moment possess is the ultimate of ultimates for our belief." It seems to me that James is saying that *we create what is real in accordance with our needs*. Our sense of agency feels real because we need it to be so.

References

- Edelman, G. 2004. *Wider than the sky*. New Haven, Conn.: Yale University Press.
- Farrer, C., Franck, Georgieff, M., Frith, C., Decety, J., Jeannerod, M. I. 2003. Modulating the experience of agency: A positron emission tomography study. *Neuroimage* 18:324–333.
- Farrer, C., and Frith, C. 2002. Experiencing oneself versus another person as being the cause of action: The neural correlates of the experience of agency. *Neuroimage* 15: 96–603.
- Freud, S. 1915. The unconscious. In *The standard edition of the complete psychological works of Sigmund Freud*, vol. 14. London: Vintage, 2001.
- Gallagher, S. 2000. Philosophical conceptions of the self: Implications for cognitive science. *Trends in cognitive Science* 4:14–21.
- James, W. 1890. *The principles of psychology*. New York: Dover.
- Kant, I. 1998. *Critique of pure reason*. Cambridge: Cambridge University Press. (Original work published 1787.)
- Libet, B. 1999. Do we have free will? *Journal of Consciousness Studies* 6:47–57.
- Libet, B., Freeman, A., and Sutherland K., eds. 1999. The volitional brain. *Journal of Consciousness Studies* 6:1–293.
- Markus, H., and Kitayama, S. 1991. Culture and the self: Implications for cognition, emotion and motivation. *Psychological Review* 98:224–253.
- Metzinger, T. 2003. *Being no one*. Cambridge, Mass.: MIT Press.
- Seigel, J. 2005. *The idea of the self*. Cambridge: Cambridge University Press.
- Wegner, D. 2002. *The illusion of conscious will*. Cambridge, Mass.: MIT Press.
- Wegner, D. 2005. Who is the controller of controlled processes? In R. Hassan, J. Uleman, and J Bargh, eds., *The new unconscious*. New York: Oxford University Press.
- Zeki, S. 1993. *A vision of the brain*. Oxford: Blackwell.

ARNOLD MODELL is a professor of social psychiatry at the Harvard Medical School, and he also serves as a supervising and training analyst at the Boston Psychoanalytic Society and Institute. His research focuses primarily on problems of psychoanalysis and the unconscious self.

Eddy Nahmias  **NO**

Why We Have Free Will

One night last fall I lay awake wondering how I should begin this essay. I imagined a variety of ways I could write the first sentence and the next and the one after that. Then I thought about how I could tie those sentences to the following paragraph and the rest of the article. The pros and cons of each of those options circled back and forth in my head, keeping me from drifting off to sleep. As this was happening, neurons were buzzing away in my brain. Indeed, that neural activity explains *why* I imagined these options, and it explains why I am writing these very words. It also explains why I have free will.

Increasingly, neuroscientists, psychologists and pundits say that I am wrong. Invoking a number of widely cited neuroscientific studies, they claim that unconscious processes drove me to select the words I ultimately wrote. Their arguments suggest our conscious deliberation and decisions happen only after neural gears below the level of our conscious awareness have already determined what we will choose. And they conclude that because "our brains make us do it"—choosing for us one option over another—free will is nothing more than an illusion.

The experiments most often cited to show that our brains take charge behind the scenes were carried out by the late Benjamin Libet in the 1980s at the University of California, San Francisco. There he instructed study participants outfitted with electrodes on their heads to flick their wrists whenever they felt like it. The electrodes detected fluctuations in electrical activity called readiness potentials that occurred about half a second before people made the flicking motion. But participants became aware of their intentions to move only about a quarter of a second before the movement, leading to the conclusion that their brains had decided before they became aware of what had happened. In essence, unconscious brain processes were in the driver's seat.

More recent studies using functional MRI have suggested the unconscious roots of our decisions begin even earlier. In research published in 2013, neuroscientist John-Dylan Haynes of the Bernstein Center for Computational Neuroscience Berlin and his colleagues had volunteers decide whether to add or subtract two numbers while in the fMRI scanner. They found patterns of neural activity that were predictive of whether subjects would choose to add or subtract that occurred four seconds before those subjects were aware of making the choice—a rather long lag time.

Indeed, both these studies—and others like them—have led to sweeping pronouncements that free will is dead. "Our decisions are predetermined unconsciously a long time before our consciousness kicks in," Haynes commented to *New Scientist*, while adding that "it seems that the brain is making the decision before the person." Others share his opinion. Evolutionary biologist Jerry Coyne has written: "So it is with all of our . . . choices: not one of them results from a free and conscious decision on our part. There is no freedom of choice, no free will." Neuroscientist Sam Harris has concluded from these findings that we are "biochemical puppets": "If we were to detect [people's] conscious choices on a brain scanner seconds before they were aware of them . . . this would directly challenge their status as conscious agents in control of their inner lives."

But does the research really show that all our conscious deliberation and planning is just a by-product of unconscious brain activity, having no effect on what we do later on? No, not at all. For many reasons, others, such as philosopher Alfred R. Mele of Florida State University, and I argue that people who insist free will is a mirage are misguided.

Not So Fast

I call those who contend that science shows that free will is an illusion "willusionists." There are many reasons to be wary of the willusionists' arguments. First, neuroscience currently lacks the technical sophistication to determine whether neural activity underlying our imagining and evaluating of future options has any impact on which option we then carry out minutes, hours or days later. Instead the research discussed by willusionists fails to clearly define the border between conscious and unconscious actions.

Consider the Libet experiment. It began with study participants preparing consciously to make a series of repetitive and unplanned actions. When the experiment began, they flexed their wrists when a desire arose spontaneously. The neural activity involved in the conscious planning presumably influenced the later unconscious initiation of movements, revealing an interaction between conscious and unconscious brain activity.

Similarly, the Haynes study, in which people randomly picked whether to add or subtract over the course of many trials, fails to provide convincing evidence against free will. Early brain activity that occurred four seconds before participants were aware of making a choice may be an indication of unconscious biases toward one choice or the other.

But this early brain activity predicted a choice with an accuracy only 10 percent better than could be forecast with a coin flip. Brain activity cannot, in general, *settle* our choices four seconds before we act, because we can react to changes in our situation in less time than that. If we could not, we would all have died in car crashes by now! Unconscious neural activity, however, can prepare us to take an action by cuing us to consciously monitor our actions to let us adjust our behavior as it occurs.

Willusionists also point to psychological research showing that we have less conscious control over our actions than we think. It is true that we are often influenced unknowingly by subtle features of our environment and by emotional or cognitive biases. Until we understand them, we are not free to try to counteract them. This is one reason I think we have less free will than many people tend to believe. But there is a big difference between having less and none at all.

The Libet and Haynes research deals with choices that people make without conscious deliberation at the time of action. Everyone performs repetitive or habitual behaviors, sometimes quite sophisticated ones that do not require much thought because the behaviors have been learned. You put your key in the lock. A shortstop dives for a ground ball. A pianist becomes immersed in playing Beethoven's *Moonlight Sonata*.

The reflexive turning of the key, the lunging for the ball, or the depressing of the white and black keys requires a particular type of mental processing. What I was doing on that sleepless night—conscious consideration of alternative options—is a wholly different activity from engaging in practiced routines. A body of psychological research shows that conscious, purposeful processing of our thoughts really does make a difference to what we do.

This work indicates that intentions we formulate to carry out specific tasks in particular circumstances—what psychologists call "implementation intentions"—increase the likelihood that we will complete the planned behavior. A study performed by psychologist Peter Gollwitzer of New York University and his colleagues revealed that dieters who consciously formed an intention to ignore thoughts about tempting foods whenever they came to mind then ate less of those foods than those dieters who simply set the goal to lose weight.

Psychologist Roy F. Baumeister of Florida State University and his colleagues have demonstrated that conscious reasoning improves performance on logical and linguistic tasks and that it helps in learning from past mistakes and overriding impulsive behaviors. In addition, psychologist Walter Mischel of Columbia University has found that our ability to willfully distract ourselves from a temptation is crucial for self-control.

Every one of us takes actions every day that we have consciously planned for ourselves. It is possible that the neural activity that carries out this planning has no effect on what we do or that it just concocts stories after the fact to explain to ourselves and others what we did. But that would make little evolutionary sense. The brain makes up only 2 percent of the human body's weight but consumes 20 percent of its energy. There would be strong evolutionary pressure against neural processes that enable intricate conscious thought yet are irrelevant to our behavior. The brain circuits responsible for my imagining that this is the best way to write this essay are likely causing it to turn out this way.

Free Will in the Brain

Willusionists, however, suggest this internalized brain processing simply cannot count as free will. They often say that people who believe in free will must be "dualists" who are convinced that the mind somehow exists as a nonphysical entity, separate from the brain. "Free will is the idea that we make choices and have thoughts independent of anything remotely resembling a physical process," wrote neuroscientist Read Montague in 2008. And Coyne has claimed that "true 'free will' . . . would require us to step outside of our brain's structure and modify how it works."

It is true that some people think of free will in this way. But there is no good reason to do so. Most philosophical theories develop a view of free will that is consistent with a scientific understanding of human nature. And despite willusionists' claims, studies suggest that most people accept that we can have free will even if our mental activity is carried out entirely by brain activity. If most people are not dualists about free will, then it is a mistake to tell them that free will is an illusion based on the scientific view that dualism is false.

One way to test people's assumptions about free will is to describe the possibility of brain-imaging technology that would allow perfect prediction of actions based on information about prior brain activity. In fact, Harris has suggested this scenario "would expose this feeling [of free will] for what it is: an *illusion*."

To see whether people's belief in free will would be challenged by the knowledge that the brain is engaged in unconscious information processing that predicts behavior, Jason Shepard of Emory University, Shane Reuter of Washington University in St. Louis and I recently performed a series of experiments in which we presented people with detailed scenarios describing futuristic brain-imaging technology, as posited by Harris.

Hundreds of students at Georgia State University participated in the studies. They read about a woman named Jill who, in the distant future, wore a brain-imaging cap for a month. Using information from the brain scanner, neuroscientists predicted everything she thought and did, even when she tried to fool the system. The scenario concluded that "these experiments confirm that all human mental activity just *is* brain activity such that everything that any human thinks or does could be predicted ahead of time based on their earlier brain activity."

More than 80 percent of the participants reported that they believed that such future technology was possible, yet 87 percent of them responded that Jill still had free will. They were also asked whether the existence of such technology would indicate that individuals lack free will. Roughly 75 percent disagreed. Further results showed that a significant majority felt that as long as the technology did not allow people's brains to be manipulated and controlled by others, they would have free will and be morally responsible for their behavior.

Most participants in the experiments seem to think that the hypothetical brain scanner is just recording the brain activity that is Jill's conscious reasoning and consideration about what to decide. Rather than taking this to mean that Jill's brain is making her do something—and that she has no free will—they may just be thinking that the brain scanner is simply detecting how free will works in the brain.

Why, then, do willusionists believe the opposite? It may have to do with the current state of knowledge. Until neuroscience is able to explain consciousness—which will require a theory to explain how our minds are neither reducible to, nor distinct from, the workings of our brain—it is tempting to think, as the willusionists seem to, that if the brain does it all, there is nothing left for the conscious mind to do.

As neuroscience advances and imaging technology improves, these developments should help reveal more precisely how much conscious control we have and to what extent our actions are governed by processes beyond our control. Finding resolutions for these questions about free will is important. Our legal system—and the moral basis for many of our society's institutions—requires a better understanding of when people are—and are not—responsible for what they do.

EDDY NAHMIAS is a professor in the Department of Philosophy and the Neuroscience Institute at Georgia State University. His research is devoted to the study of human agency: what it is, how it is possible, and how it accords with scientific accounts of human nature. His primary focus is the free will debate.

EXPLORING THE ISSUE

Is Free Will an Illusion?

Critical Thinking and Reflection

1. Compare the arguments from the two articles. In what ways do you agree with the authors? What are your reasons for disagreeing with them?
2. What would be the implications for your own life if free will is simply an illusion? For example, how would it change your ethical/moral ideals?
3. What role does cognitive neuroscience research play in increasing our understanding of human psychology? Does it really have the scientific validity and power to explain agency, and by implication, morality?
4. Imagine that free will is really just an illusion. How might knowing that your thoughts and feelings are not under your control impact your personal identity, or the way you interact with other people?

Is There Common Ground?

The debate over the reality of free will has increasingly moved out of the realm of philosophy and psychology and into areas of neuroscientific research, biology, and anatomy. It is difficult to see where there might be common ground between those who argue that free will and freedom of choice is a fundamental feature of human nature and those who argue that our experience of free will is simply a product of mechanical and deterministic brain functions over which we have no control and are not aware. Indeed, the two camps involved in this debate often proceed from entirely different perspectives as to the viability of scientific experimentation for even addressing such questions. That is, not only do the two approaches disagree about the reality of free will, they also disagree about what methods are best suited to fruitfully addressing the question. Nonetheless, there may be some common ground in so far as a fuller account of free will may need to be one in which the various constraints and context of brain function are taken seriously and not disregarded. That is, perhaps the most fruitful approach will be one in which

the correlations between brain function and meaningful choice are identified, and human choice is seen to be both meaningful and real, even though always occurring in the context of the physical reality of our brains and bodies. Perhaps the best account of human agency is one in which the necessity of brain function for meaningful behavior is admitted, while equally admitted is the fact that brain function is not sufficient to account for meaningful human choice and behavior.

Additional Resources

Baumeister, R. G., Masciampo, E. J., Vohs, K. D. (2011). Do conscious thoughts cause behavior? *Annual Review of Psychology, 62*, 331–361.

Nahmias, E., Shephard, J., Keuter, S. (2014). It's OK if "my brain made me do it": People's intuitions about free will and neuroscientific prediction. *Cognition, 133*(2), 502–516.

Soon, S. C. (2013). Predicting free choices for abstract intentions. *Proceedings of the National Academy of Sciences USA, 110*(15), 6217–6222.

Internet References . . .

Pacific Standard

http://www.psmag.com/health-and-behavior/free-will
-illusion-83861

Human Truth

http://www.humantruth.info/free_will.html

Psychology Today

https://www.psychologytoday.com/blog/psych
-unseen/201411/the-neuroscience-free-will
-and-the-illusion-you

Unit 2

UNIT

Research Issues

*R*esearch methods are the means by which psychologists test their ideas. Yet the way that psychologists conduct their research and interpret their findings is sometimes the subject of controversy. When, for example, are the findings sufficient to support a particular conclusion? Psychological practices, such as psychotherapy, are complicated phenomena, involving not only observable behaviors, the typical province of empirical methods, but also less observable client and therapist meanings. Also, how generalizable are such findings to other cultures? If American researchers dominate the research on a given topic, how applicable are these findings to other cultures, with different customs and social traditions? And what about specific research assumptions, such as scientific determinism, the notion that all things, including humans, are determined by causal forces outside their control? Could these assumptions, when taught to psychology students, affect them in unexpected ways?

Selected, Edited, and with Issue Framing Material by:
Edwin E. Gantt, *Brigham Young University*

ISSUE

Is American Psychological Research Generalizable to Other Cultures?

YES: Gerald J. Haeffel et al., from "Theory, Not Cultural Context, Will Advance American Psychology," *American Psychologist* (2009)

NO: Jeffrey Jensen Arnett, from "The Neglected 95%, a Challenge to Psychology's Philosophy of Science," *American Psychologist* (2009)

Learning Outcomes
After reading this issue, you will be able to: • Describe some of the advantages and disadvantages of basic research compared to cross-culturally sensitive studies.   • Know what determines scientific progress and understanding.

ISSUE SUMMARY

YES: Gerald Haeffel and his colleagues believe that psychological studies of American people often generalize to people of other cultures, especially when basic processes are being studied.

NO: Jeffrey Arnett, psychological research professor, argues that culture is central to the functioning of humans and thus to psychological findings.

We live in a multicultural world, with important and substantial difference among cultures. Unfortunately, however, traditional psychological research has focused almost exclusively on a narrow portion of this multicultural world. Specifically, the majority of academic psychological investigations have been conducted using undergraduate American college students as participants (and generally those enrolled in psychology courses). While there are some variations within this subpopulation, college students are typically more homogenous than the wider population in categories like socioeconomic status, education, ethnicity, age, and values.

The major concern with studying such a narrow segment of the wider multicultural world is the question of *generalizability*—do studies of American college students actually tell us much about other populations in other circumstances? If they do not, then the findings of such research would not count as general knowledge. These findings would be viewed as more local, and thus not necessarily applicable to other populations. The primary issue in the generalizability question is whether contextual and cultural factors are *vital* to understanding humans. Are these factors merely "add-ons," and humans are essentially the same the world over? If so, investigations of *any* humans, including American college students, tell us what is essential about all other humans. Alternatively, if situational and ethnic factors are required to understand the functioning of humans, then humans are not such interchangeable parts.

In the first article, Haeffel and his colleagues believe that concerns about the generalizability of American psychology are overstated. Although they agree that cultural factors are a valid concern for some research topics, such as gender roles and family structure, they consider these factors less relevant to "basic human processes," processes that are universal to all humans, such as perception and cognition. Haeffel and his colleagues also dispute the notion that these basic processes have no real-world implications. They cite several examples, which they believe illustrate the critical role of basic research, including the recent development of cognitive behavioral therapy from basic research on cognition. Science mainly progresses, they argue, on the basis of falsifiable theories that deal with core psychological processes. Cultural factors are important for understanding the particular manifestations of these universals, but these factors do not prevent the generalizability of research on these basic processes.

Psychological researcher Jeffrey Arnett argues that psychological investigations must become dramatically less American to truly make progress in understanding humans. By Arnett's calculations, psychologists conduct research on less than 5 percent of the world's population, and this selective group does *not* automatically represent the other 95 percent. Therefore, as Dr. Arnett maintains, we should be more cautious about assuming the generalizability of psychological findings. Psychologists should do more to train investigators in multicultural issues; rigorous hypothesis testing alone is not sufficient to advance psychological knowledge. Only by broadening psychology's cultural horizons will the research become ecologically valid and truly contribute to an understanding of how people live their lives.

POINT

- Psychology should not focus primarily on culture and diversity issues
- Science progresses by rigorously testing falsifiable theories that include universals.
- Humans around the world have the same basic psychological processes.
- The careful control of variables through the scientific method will answer the basic questions of psychology.

COUNTERPOINT

- Psychology should step up its recognition and promotion of multicultural awareness, especially in research.
- Understanding cultural context is essential to the advancement of psychological science.
- The ways in which humans meaningfully carry out their activities are particular to their context.
- Laboratory control cannot answer many important questions about human nature, development, and experience.

YES ↵

Gerald J. Haeffel et al.

Theory, Not Cultural Context, Will Advance American Psychology

In his recent article, "The Neglected 95%: Why American Psychology Needs to Become Less American," Arnett (October 2008) provided a thought-provoking analysis of the current state of psychology. He made two primary arguments: (a) Psychological research using American samples cannot generalize to the rest of the world, and (b) psychology's emphasis on basic processes should be replaced by an emphasis on context and culture. We agree with the author's call for greater attention to issues of context. However, we[1] fundamentally disagree with his position on issues related to generalizability and basic research. The goal of this comment is to provide a critical evaluation of Arnett's primary arguments as well as to offer alternative strategies for facilitating scientific progress on cultural and diversity issues.

Generalizability

Arnett's (2008) first argument is that American psychology does not represent people everywhere, and thus, its findings are not generalizable. This argument is a variation of the well-known "college sophomore problem." The argument is as follows: Research findings from a select sample such as college sophomores (or Americans, in this case) will not apply to other samples. This is a valid concern, and clearly there are situations in which research on select samples may not generalize. However, the problem of generalizability is often overstated. Studies using one sample of humans (e.g., Americans) often generalize to other samples of humans (e.g., Spaniards), particularly when basic processes[2] are being studied (e.g., Anderson, Lindsay, & Bushman, 1999). The results of studies investigating a wide range of psychological phenomena, including personality, information processing, aggression, and mental illness, tend to hold in a variety of contexts and with a variety of participant samples (see Stanovich, 2007,

for review). The consistency of research findings across contexts and samples should not be surprising given that all humans, whether they live in America or a developing country, share a common genome, brain organization, and capacity for cognition, perception, and emotion.

The college sophomore problem is not new, and it is not clear that Arnett's (2008) discussion advances our understanding of the issue. His case is based largely on "straw man" arguments. He provided numerous examples of when differences between Americans and other samples would be expected, including gender roles, marital relations, family structure, and the nature of formal education. Although subjectively compelling, these examples do not address the issue of the generalizability of research on *basic processes*. The existence of cultural variation does not imply that there are no universals worth studying. The same basic process can generate different products depending on the structure of the environment in which that process operates. It is not enough to show that American culture is different from other cultures. This fact is not disputed. The critical question is what these differences mean for human psychology. That is, what do cultural differences (e.g., gender roles, family structure, formal mathematical skills) say about the basic human processes (e.g., perception, cognition, emotion) that played a role in the development of those differences?

Basic Research

Arnett's (2008) second argument is that psychological research should focus on culture and diversity rather than on basic processes. He went so far as to state, "At a time when there are numerous daunting international problems that psychological science could address, such as religious fundamentalism, terrorism, international ecological crises, war, the HIV pandemic, and growing poverty, the main thrust in American psychology continues to be a research

Haeffel, Gerald J., et al. From *American Psychologist*, vol. 64, no. 6, September 2009, pp. 570–571. Copyright © 2009 by American Psychological Association. Reprinted by permission via Rightslink.

focus on processes and principles that goes forward as if none of these issues existed" (p. 612). This statement demonstrates a fundamental misunderstanding about basic research. His statement is akin to asking why medical research continues to focus on growing stem cells when there are more daunting problems such as Alzheimer's and Parkinson's disease. Basic research in psychology has clear implications for real-world issues. For example, research on information processing and behavioral activation has led to the creation of highly effective treatments (e.g., cognitive behavior therapy) for disorders such as depression and anxiety. Similarly, research on early experience with binocular vision (e.g., Banks, Aslin, & Letson, 1975) demonstrated the critical need for early (as opposed to delayed) detection and treatment of conditions that cause abnormal binocular experience such as esotropia. In addition, research on obedience (e.g., the Milgram studies and Zimbardo's prison experiment) has important implications for understanding the sometimes atrocious behavior of humans (e.g., Abu Ghraib, terrorism, Nazi war crimes). These are just a few of many examples that illustrate the critical role of basic research (both human and animal[3]) in understanding, and creating solutions for, real-world issues.

Cultural Context—Where's the Theory?

Arnett's (2008) argument against basic research raises fundamental questions about how to define science (i.e., the problem of demarcation) and how to evaluate scientific progress. Following Arnett's reasoning, science is defined by its applicability to real-world problems, sample representativeness, and the use of nonexperimental designs. Thus, he concluded that psychological science is "incomplete" because of its focus on basic processes, American samples, and experimental designs. In contrast to Arnett, we subscribe to a philosophy of science described by philosophers such as Popper and Meehl. According to Popper (1959), science is characterized by the falsification of theories. If a theory is falsifiable, it is by definition scientific. Popper's definition of science does not depend on whether the work is basic or applied. It does not depend on the type of research design one uses (longitudinal, cross-sectional, experimental, quasi-experimental, etc). It does not depend on the sample (e.g., American or Nigerian). Science is characterized by testing and falsifying theories (Meehl, 1978).

In light of this philosophy, it is unclear why research on cultural context should be considered more scientifically progressive than research on basic processes. In fact, Arnett's (2008) description of cultural research raises concerns that

it could actually slow progress in psychology. His vision of cultural psychology does not invoke theory or the importance of having testable hypotheses. Rather, cultural psychology appears to be exploratory and descriptive in nature. Will cultural psychology simply be an anecdotal record of cultural differences or a collection of replication studies? Will 100% of the world's population have to be studied before psychology can be considered a "complete science?" Arnett failed to provide any information about how cultural psychology will progress as a science.

From a philosophy of science perspective, Arnett's (2008) distinction between cultural context and basic processes is a false dichotomy. The problem with human psychology is not its focus on basic processes rather than cultural context; it is the lack of strong falsifiable theories (Meehl, 1978). Cultural context cannot exist in a vacuum isolated from basic processes such as cognition, perception, language, and so forth. If cultural research is to take hold in psychology, then it must be theory driven and integrated into work on basic processes. It is not enough to surmise that different cultures may lead to different outcomes. Researchers need to specify the conditions for when they would and would not expect culture to affect basic processes and behaviors.

Cultural context can serve an important purpose in psychological science: It will enable us to test hypotheses about which features of human behavior are acquired through experience and which are basic (or innate). Basic processes are mechanisms via which humans—and other animals—are able to respond adaptively to typical environments; however, these processes can be distinguished from another kind of adaptation, acquired associations or strategies (such as reading), which vary across situations and cultures. Within this framework, cultural adaptations can be thought to arise from the operation of basic processes, such as learning.[4] For example, at one time it was thought that language was acquired solely through imitation of and reinforcement by models within one's sociocultural context (e.g., Skinner's, 1957, *Verbal Behavior*), until Chomsky's synthesis of cross-cultural linguistic variation revealed important similarities across cultures, suggesting that language acquisition also depends on a more basic structure or process that all humans share. Similarly, conventional wisdom suggests that abstract mathematical concepts are learned through years of formal education and training; however, studies of hunter-gatherer cultures (e.g., the Pirahã; Gordon, 2004) and even of nonhuman animals (e.g., monkeys, rats, pigeons; Gallistel & Gelman, 2000) have shown that we all share a common system for representing the abstract concept of number. In clinical psychology, many assume that eating disorders such as anorexia nervosa and bulimia nervosa share a common genetic etiology. However, recent research suggests that the genetic diathesis for bulimia nervosa may exhibit greater pathoplasticity cross-culturally than the diathesis for anorexia nervosa; this finding indicates distinct etiologies for these disorders (Keel & Klump, 2003). These examples highlight the importance of using cultural context to test theories about basic and acquired human behavior.

Conclusion

Focusing on cultural context *rather* than basic processes is not going to advance American psychology, or psychology in general. Neither [is] having students travel abroad or take anthropology classes (as recommended by Arnett), in and of themselves. Rather, science will advance by developing and testing theories. We believe that psychological science can benefit most by using differences in culture and context to develop and test novel hypotheses about basic human processes.

Notes

1. The authors of this commentary represent a broad cross-section of psychological science including clinical, developmental, biological, and cognitive areas.

2. By basic processes, we mean those psychological or biological processes that are shared by all humans at appropriate developmental levels (e.g., cognition, perception, learning, brain organization, genome).

3. In addition to basic research on humans, there is also a large body of animal research to consider. For example, Michael Davis's research delineating the neural basis of fear and anxiety in rats led to the creation of a cognitive enhancer (D-cycloserine), which is currently being used to treat Iraq veterans with posttraumatic stress disorder (Davis, Myers, Ressler, & Rothbaum, 2005). Similarly, Michael Meaney's (2001) research on maternal care and gene expression in rats has tremendous implications for understanding of human attachment, stress reactivity, and even developmental disorders such as autism.

4. Note that this formulation of the purpose of cross-cultural psychology differs markedly from Arnett's (2008), which espouses cultural representativeness as a goal unto itself.

GERALD J. HAEFFEL is an assistant professor of psychology at Notre Dame. His program of research is devoted to understanding the cognitive processes and products that contribute to risk and resilience for depression.

Jeffrey Jensen Arnett  **NO**

The Neglected 95%, a Challenge to Psychology's Philosophy of Science

My goal in writing "The Neglected 95%: Why American Psychology Needs to Become Less American" (Arnett, October 2008) was to fuel a conversation in psychology about whether American psychological research should become more reflective of how human beings in different cultures around the world experience their lives. I am pleased to see that many of my colleagues have taken up this conversation, as represented in the four comments [in] *American Psychologist* . . . [published in September 2009]. The four comments were well chosen in that they represent quite different reactions to my article. Two of the comments were generally in support of my thesis that American psychology is too narrow culturally, and sought to provide additional information on the issues I raised. The other two comments were in opposition to my thesis and presented the grounds for their opposition. In this rejoinder I address the issues raised in [the second of the] opposing comments. Following this, I address the more general problem that cuts across the comments: American psychology's dominant philosophy of science. . . .

What Is Science? What Is Scientific Progress?

The most extensive of the four commentaries is the one offered by Haeffel, Thiessen, Campbell, Kaschak, and McNeil . . . [September 2009, *American Psychologist*], who took the position that "Theory, Not Cultural Context, Will Advance American Psychology" (p. 570). Their main goal was to defend the value of research on basic processes (e.g., cognition, perception, learning) and question the value of culturally diverse research.

Haeffel et al. (2009) are on shaky ground from the beginning. They showed the limits of their perceptions in asserting that "the problem of generalizability is often overstated" (p. 570), offering in support of this statement the

assertion "Studies using one sample of humans (e.g., Americans) often generalize to other samples of humans (e.g., Spaniards)" (p. 570). Even adding Spaniards to Americans (and throwing in Canadians for good measure) still makes for less than 5% of the world's population. Psychologists are far too quick to jump from one study of Americans and one study of Spaniards to a declaration of a universal psychological principle. It is not the problem of generalizability that is overstated but the research findings of psychologists based on a tiny and unusual segment of humanity.

There may be an effective case to be made for the value of psychological research on basic processes, but Haeffel and colleagues (2009) did not make it.[1] They claimed that I suffer from a "fundamental misunderstanding about basic research" and that my position is "akin to asking why medical research continues to focus on growing stem cells when there are more daunting problems such as Alzheimer's and Parkinson's disease" (p. 570). If only the connection between psychological research on basic processes and real-world human problems were as clear as the relation between stem cell research and diseases like Alzheimer's and Parkinson's! The relation between stem cell research and treatments for Alzheimer's and Parkinson's disease is evident even to the nonscientist. The relation between basic research in psychology and real human problems is far less clear even to a research psychologist. There may be value in psychological research on basic processes, especially when the results are linked to cultural contexts, as Haeffel et al. suggested. It is just that research on basic processes alone is not enough for a science of humanity. This approach to research leaves out too much about cultural beliefs, cultural practices, and social relations.

Haeffel et al. (2009) accurately identified the heart of the difference between my perspective and theirs as a divergence in views of "how to define science . . . and how to evaluate scientific progress" (p. 570). They hold to a philosophy of science they attribute to Popper (1959) and Meehl (1978): "If a theory is falsifiable, it is by definition scientific" (Haeffel et al., 2009, p. 570). To some extent, I agree with this view. Certainly testing falsifiable hypotheses is one part of psychological science. However, restricting research to falsifiable theories alone is far too narrow a view of psychology as a human science. A focus on falsifiable theories narrows psychology's intellectual and scientific scope mainly to the laboratory, where experimental situations can be carefully controlled. The problem with this focus is that laboratory studies are often ecologically invalid and have little relation to how people actually live and how they experience their lives. There are many aspects of human development, behavior, and experience that are worth investigating even if they cannot be reduced to falsifiable theories (Rogoff, 2003). Psychology needs to get over its "physics envy" and adapt its methods and theoretical approaches to its uniquely human topic, in all its cultural complexity and diversity, rather than endlessly and fruitlessly aping the natural sciences.

Toward a Broader Philosophy of Our Human Science

The four comments on my article (Arnett, 2008) are diverse, but together they suggest a need for a reexamination of psychology's dominant philosophy of science. Even the two comments that were sympathetic to my thesis did not fully grasp the crux of the problem. Both assumed that a cultural understanding of human psychology could be attained through cross-cultural research, not realizing how transporting American-based theories and methods to other cultures might result in missing the most distinctive and essential features of those cultures. The two opposing comments represented well the traditional approach to psychological research, with its confident assurance that progress in psychology is best served by following the model of the natural sciences, investigating basic processes in search of universal laws, with limited or no attention to that distracting variable, cultural context, that actually means the most to how people behave, how they function psychologically, and how they understand and interpret their lives.

I advocate a broader, more intellectually vibrant and inclusive philosophy of science. The goal of the human sciences should not be simply the pursuit of universal laws and the falsification of theories—no matter how dull or trivial the theory, no matter how little relation the theory has to how people experience life outside the laboratory. The goal of the human sciences should be to use the tools of the scientific method to illuminate our understanding of

human behavior, human functioning, and human development. The tools of the scientific method in psychology should be construed broadly to include not just laboratory tasks but any systematic investigation of human phenomena. In this philosophy of science, the structured interview and the ethnography are no less legitimate as tools of the scientific method than are the laboratory or the questionnaire. Many diverse methods are welcome, and all contribute valuable pieces to the mosaic that makes up a full understanding of humanity.

That mosaic is still missing many large and essential pieces, over a century after psychology was first established as a field. However, many research psychologists are working daily to fill it in, using a wide range of theories and methods (Jensen, 2010). What we need now in American psychology is not a narrowing of theories and methods to those that seem best to mimic the methods of the natural sciences, but a wider range of new, creative theories and methods, synthesizing cultural perspectives from all over the world, that will broaden our understanding of the endlessly fascinating human experience.

Note

1. Haeffel et al. (2009) claimed, "Basic research in psychology has clear implications for real-world issues" (p. 570), but the examples they provided fall flat. Research on information processing and behavioral activation has not "led to the creation of highly effective treatments (e.g., cognitive behavior therapy) for disorders such as depression and anxiety" (p. 570). Cognitive behavior therapy was developed in the 1950s and 1960s by Albert Ellis and Aaron Beck, and its roots are in ancient Greek philosophy, not basic research on information processing and behavioral activation. To find an example of basic research related to any of the problems I suggested that psychology should address (e.g., religious fundamentalism, terrorism, international ecological crises, war), the authors are forced to go back half a century to Milgram's obedience studies and Zimbardo's prison experiment. I agree about the value of the Milgram and Zimbardo studies, and I regard it as a great pity that psychological research today is rarely as creative in its methods as those studies were. As for research on "abnormal binocular experience such as esotropia" (p. 570), this seems more in the realm of optometry than psychology.

Jeffrey Jensen Arnett is a psychological research professor in the Department of Psychology at Clark University. Dr. Arnett is the author of several books on adolescents.

EXPLORING THE ISSUE

Is American Psychological Research Generalizable to Other Cultures?

Critical Thinking and Reflection

1. Arnett accuses psychology of "physics envy" and suggests psychology should develop methods that better reflect the unique nature of humans. Why does he make this accusation, and what sorts of methods might be considered in this development?
2. Haeffel and colleagues make a distinction between "basic research" and the cross-cultural studies suggested by Arnett. What are the advantages and disadvantages of basic research compared to culturally sensitive studies? From your perspective, which is more needed in psychology, and why do you hold this position?
3. Why is generalizability such an important issue for some psychologists? Are there disadvantages to increasing generalizability through greater experimental control?
4. Both articles in this issue are written by scholars at American universities. How might their own cultural perspective inform or limit their view of this issue?
5. A central question debated in these two articles is what counts as scientific progress and understanding. What are the different understandings of these authors on the issue of progress, and how does this understanding impact their respective arguments?

Is There Common Ground?

There can be little doubt that American psychological research in the past has been conducted primarily by Americans and focused almost entirely on Americans. There can also be little doubt that, regardless of any gains in diversity that have been made in American research in recent years, the focus of most research currently continues to be Americans. Despite differences in belief about generalizability of basic human processes across cultures, though, all agree that greater representation of foreign cultures in American psychological research would be beneficial. Whether the purpose of such cross-cultural studies would be to discover legitimate differences in the psychologies of different peoples or to test falsifiable hypothesis about basic human processes in a different context, the field would benefit from research conducted in other cultures.

The similarities, however, usually end there. The author of the NO article, Arnett, could reasonably argue—borrowing from a famous quip by the philosopher Kierkegaard—that most commenters have understood his article so poorly, they do not even understand his complaint about them not understanding it. The problem, according to Arnett, is not merely that American psychologists use too many Americans in their research samples, it is that many in American psychology view their very methods as culturally neutral, failing to realize that the methods themselves carry cultural and philosophical biases that would taint any research done with them in foreign cultures. Thus, while all of the authors in these two pieces may agree that the methods we use in research are important, they find such methods to be important in very different ways. The YES authors believe the methods to be the great equalizer across cultures while the NO author believes them to be the very vehicle of cross-cultural misunderstanding. The only common ground here seems to be the notion that psychology must have a sound philosophical basis, though what exactly that may be is as yet unclear.

Additional Resources

Matsumoto, D., and Hwang, S. H. (2011). Reading facial expressions of emotion. Retrieved from www.apa.org/science/about/psa/2011/05/facial-expressions.aspx

Rubin, B., Gluck, M. E., Knoll, C. M., Lorence, M., and Geliebter, A. (2008). Comparison of eating disorders and body image disturbances between Eastern and Western countries. *Eating and Weight Disorders, 13*(2), 73–80.

Internet References . . .

Psychology Research Issues

http://www.academyprojects.org/est.htm

Selected, Edited, and with Issue Framing Material by:
Edwin E. Gantt, *Brigham Young University*

ISSUE

Are Traditional Empirical Methods Sufficient to Provide Evidence for Psychological Practice?

YES: **APA President Task Force on Evidence-Based Practice**, from "Report of the 2005 Presidential Task Force on Evidence-Based Practice," *American Psychologist* (2006)

NO: **Brent D. Slife** and **Dennis C. Wendt**, from "The Next Step in the Evidence-Based Practice Movement," *Speech or Remarks* (2006)

Learning Outcomes
After reading this issue, you will be able to:
• Understand what has led to traditional empirical methods being considered sufficient evidence for psychological practices.

ISSUE SUMMARY

YES: The APA Presidential Task Force on Evidence-Based Practice assumes that a variety of traditional empirical methods is sufficient to provide evidence for psychological practices.

NO: Psychologist Brent D. Slife and researcher Dennis C. Wendt contend that traditional empirical methods are guided by a single philosophy that limits the diversity of methods.

Imagine that one of your family members needs to see a therapist for a severe depression. Of the two therapists available, the first therapist's practices are supported by evidence obtained through traditional scientific methods. The second therapist's practices are not. The latter's practices could be equally effective or even more effective than the first therapist's practices, but we do not know. Which therapist would you choose for this member of your family?

Most people would readily choose therapists who have scientific evidence for their interventions. They think of psychotherapy much like they think of medicine, with treatments that have stood the test of science. Just as physicians can provide evidence that pain relievers actually relieve pain, so too psychologists hope to provide evidence that their practices deliver their desired results. Because not all psychological treatments come with evidence to support

their use, some psychologists worry that some treatments could actually do more harm than good. It is with this potential harm in mind that many psychologists banded together to establish empirically supported treatments (ESTs). The goal was to establish a list of ESTs for specific psychological disorders. Those involved in this movement (various task forces from different divisions of the American Psychological Association) initially stressed the use of randomized clinical (or controlled) trials (RCTs)—a specific type of research design—to be sure that the scientific examination of these treatments was rigorous and thorough.

In the YES selection, however, the APA Presidential Task Force on Evidence-Based Practice questions whether too much emphasis has been placed on RCT research designs. This Task Force affirms the need for empirically based evidence in psychology but tries to reframe the notion of evidence-based practice so that a diversity of empirical methods, including correlational and even case study methods, are considered important for producing evidence. The Task Force calls for objectivity in gathering all forms of evidence. In fact, it still considers RCTs the most rigorous type of objective method. However, it also acknowledges that other empirical approaches to gathering information and evidence can and do have their place in deciding psychology's evidence-based practices.

In the NO selection, psychologist Brent D. Slife and researcher Dennis Wendt applaud the APA Task Force for taking important steps in the right direction. Nevertheless, they argue that the Task Force's statement is "ultimately and fundamentally inadequate." The Task Force correctly champions the objectivity and diversity of methods and evidence, in their view, but they contend that the Task Force is not objective and diverse enough. They claim that just as the EST movement restricted the gathering of evidence to a single method (RCTs), the Task Force's suggestions assume, but never justify, that evidence-based practice should be restricted to a single *epistemology* of method. They acknowledge that many psychologists view this empirical epistemology as not affecting the outcome of research, but they note that most practices that are considered evidence-based fit the biases of the philosophy of empiricism.

POINT

- Psychological treatments should be supported by evidence.
- Evidence should include RCTs as well as other empirical methods.
- Evidence should be both objective and diverse.
- Evidence should not be limited to a single method (RCT).

COUNTERPOINT

- Not all psychologists agree on what qualifies as evidence.
- Traditional empirical methods are not the only methods by which evidence can be obtained.
- Including only the "empirical" is neither objective nor diverse.
- Evidence should not be limited to a single methodology.

YES ⬅

Report of the 2005 Presidential Task Force on Evidence-Based Practice[1]

From the very first conceptions of applied psychology as articulated by Lightner Witmer, who formed the first psychological clinic in 1896, psychologists have been deeply and uniquely associated with an evidence-based approach to patient care. As Witmer pointed out, "the pure and the applied sciences advance in a single front. What retards the progress of one retards the progress of the other; what fosters one fosters the other." As early as 1947 the idea that doctoral psychologists should be trained as both scientists and practitioners became the American Psychological Association (APA) policy. Early practitioners such as Frederick C. Thorne articulated the methods by which psychological practitioners integrate science into their practice by . . . "increasing the application of the experimental approach to the individual case into the clinician's own experience." Thus, psychologists have been on the forefront of the development of evidence-based practice for decades.

Evidence-based practice in psychology is therefore consistent with the past twenty years of work in evidence-based medicine, which advocated for improved patient outcomes by informing clinical practice with relevant research. Sackett and colleagues describe evidence-based medicine as "the conscientious, explicit, and judicious use of current best evidence in making decisions about the care of individual patients." The use and misuse of evidence-based principles in the practice of health care has affected the dissemination of health care funds, but not always to the benefit of the patient. Therefore, psychologists, whose training is grounded in empirical methods, have an important role to play in the continuing development of evidence-based practice and its focus on improving patient care.

One approach to implementing evidence-based practice in health care systems has been through the development of guidelines for best practice. During the early part of the evidence-based practice movement, APA recognized the importance of a comprehensive approach to the conceptualization of guidelines. APA also recognized the risk that guidelines might be used inappropriately by commercial health care organizations not intimately familiar with the scientific basis of practice to dictate specific forms of treatment and restrict patient access to care. In 1992, APA formed a joint task force of the Board of Scientific Affairs (BSA), the Board of Professional Affairs (BPA), and the Committee for the Advancement of Professional Practice (CAPP). The document developed by this task force—the *Template for Developing Guidelines: Interventions for Mental Disorders and Psychosocial Aspects of Physical Disorders* (Template)—was approved by the APA Council of Representatives in 1995 (APA, 1995). The Template described the variety of evidence that should be considered in developing guidelines, and cautioned that any emerging clinical practice guidelines should be based on careful systematic weighing of research data and clinical expertise. . . .

Although the goal was to identify treatments with evidence for efficacy comparable to the evidence for the efficacy of medications, and hence to highlight the contribution of psychological treatments, the Division 12 Task Force report sparked a decade of both enthusiasm and controversy. The report increased recognition of demonstrably effective psychological treatments among the public, policymakers, and training programs. At the same time, many psychologists raised concerns about the exclusive focus on brief, manualized treatments; the emphasis on specific treatment effects as opposed to common factors that account for much of the variance in outcomes across disorders; and the applicability to a diverse range of patients varying in comorbidity, personality, race, ethnicity, and culture.

In response, several groups of psychologists, including other divisions of APA, offered additional frameworks for integrating the available research evidence. In 1999, APA Division 29 (Psychotherapy) established a task force to identify, operationalize, and disseminate information on empirically supported therapy relationships, given the powerful association between outcome and aspects of the therapeutic relationship such as the therapeutic alliance. Division 17 (Counseling Psychology) also undertook an examination of empirically supported treatments in counseling psychology. The Society of Behavioral Medicine, which is not a part of APA but which has significantly overlapping membership, has recently published criteria for examining the evidence base for behavioral medicine interventions. As of this writing, we are aware that task forces have been appointed to examine related issues by a large number of APA divisions concerned with practice issues. . . .

Definition

Based on its review of the literature and its deliberations, the Task Force agreed on the following definition:

> Evidence-based practice in psychology (EBPP) is the integration of the best available research with clinical expertise in the context of patient characteristics, culture, and preferences.

This definition of EBPP closely parallels the definition of evidence-based practice adopted by the Institute of Medicine as adapted from Sackett and colleagues: "Evidence-based practice is the integration of best research evidence with clinical expertise and patient values." Psychology builds on the IOM definition by deepening the examination of clinical expertise and broadening the consideration of patient characteristics. The purpose of EBPP is to promote effective psychological practice and enhance public health by applying empirically supported principles of psychological assessment, case formulation, therapeutic relationship, and intervention.

Psychological practice entails many types of interventions, in multiple settings, for a wide variety of potential patients. In this document, *intervention* refers to all direct services rendered by health care psychologists, including assessment, diagnosis, prevention, treatment, psychotherapy, and consultation. As is the case with most discussions of evidence-based practice, we focus on treatment. The same general principles apply to psychological assessment, which is essential to effective treatment. The settings include but are not limited to hospitals, clinics, independent practices, schools, military, public health, rehabilitation institutes, primary care, counseling centers, and nursing homes.

To be consistent with discussions of evidence-based practice in other areas of health care, we use the term *patient* in this document to refer to the child, adolescent, adult, older adult, couple, family, group, organization, community, or other populations receiving psychological services. However, we recognize that in many situations there are important and valid reasons for using such terms as *client, consumer,* or *person* in place of patient to describe the recipients of services. Further, psychologists target a variety of problems, including but not restricted to mental health, academic, vocational, relational, health, community, and other problems, in their professional practice.

It is important to clarify the relation between EBPP and ESTs (empirically supported treatments). EBPP is the more comprehensive concept. ESTs start with a treatment and ask whether it works for a certain disorder or problem under specified circumstances. EBPP starts with the patient and asks what research evidence (including relevant results from RCTs) will assist the psychologist to achieve the best outcome. In addition, ESTs are specific psychological treatments that have been shown to be efficacious in controlled clinical trials, whereas EBPP encompasses a broader range of clinical activities (e.g., psychological assessment, case formulation, therapy relationships). As such, EBPP articulates a decision making process for integrating multiple streams of research evidence, including but not limited to RCTs, into the intervention process.

The following sections explore in greater detail the three major components of this definition—best available research, clinical expertise, and patient characteristics—and their integration.

Best Available Research Evidence

A sizeable body of scientific evidence drawn from a variety of research designs and methodologies attests to the effectiveness of psychological practices. The research literature on the effect of psychological interventions indicates that these interventions are safe and effective for a large number of children and youth, adults and older adults across a wide range of psychological, addictive, health, and relational problems. More recent research indicates that compared to alternative approaches, such as medications, psychological treatments are particularly enduring. Further, research demonstrates that psychotherapy can and often does pay for itself in terms of medical costs offset, increased productivity, and life satisfaction.

Psychologists possess distinctive strengths in designing, conducting, and interpreting research studies that can guide evidence-based practice. Moreover, psychology—as a science and as a profession—is distinctive in combining scientific commitment with an emphasis on human relationships and individual differences. As such, psychology can help develop, broaden, and improve the research base for evidence-based practice.

There is broad consensus that psychological practice needs to be based on evidence, and that research needs to balance internal and external validity. Research will not always address all practice needs. Major issues in integrating research in day-to-day practice include: a) the relative weight to place on different research methods; b) the representativeness of research samples; c) whether research results should guide practice at the level of principles of change, intervention strategies, or specific protocols; d) the generalizability and transportability of treatments supported in controlled research to clinical practice settings; e) the extent to which judgments can be made about treatments of choice when the number and duration of treatments tested has been limited; and f) the degree to which the results of efficacy and effectiveness research can be generalized from primarily white samples to minority and marginalized populations. Nevertheless, research on practice has made progress in investigating these issues and is providing research evidence that is more responsive to day-to-day practice. There is sufficient consensus to move forward with the principles of EBPP.

Meta-analytic investigations since the 1970s have shown that most therapeutic practices in widespread clinical use are generally effective for treating a range of problems. In fact, the effect sizes for psychological interventions for children, adults and older adults rival, or exceed, those of widely accepted medical treatments. It is important not to assume that interventions that have not yet been studied in controlled trials are ineffective. Specific interventions that have not been subjected to systematic empirical testing for specific problems cannot be assumed to be either effective or ineffective; they are simply untested to date. Nonetheless, good practice and science call for the timely testing of psychological practices in a way that adequately operationalizes them using appropriate scientific methodology. Widely used psychological practices as well as innovations developed in the field or laboratory should be rigorously evaluated and barriers to conducting this research should be identified and addressed.

Multiple Types of Research Evidence

Best research evidence refers to scientific results related to intervention strategies, assessment, clinical problems, and patient populations in laboratory and field settings as well as to clinically relevant results of basic research in psychology and related fields. APA endorses multiple types of research evidence (e.g., efficacy, effectiveness, cost-effectiveness, cost-benefit, epidemiological, treatment utilization studies) that contribute to effective psychological practice.

Multiple research designs contribute to evidence-based practice, and different research designs are better suited to address different types of questions. These include:

- Clinical observation (including individual case studies) and basic psychological science are valuable sources of innovations and hypotheses (the context of scientific discovery).
- Qualitative research can be used to describe the subjective lived experience of people, including participants in psychotherapy.
- Systematic case studies are particularly useful when aggregated as in the form of practice research networks for comparing individual patients to others with similar characteristics.
- Single case experimental designs are particularly useful for establishing causal relationships in the context of an individual.
- Public health and ethnographic research are especially useful for tracking the availability, utilization, and acceptance of mental health treatments as well as suggesting ways of altering them to maximize their utility in a given social context.
- Process-outcome studies are especially valuable for identifying mechanisms of change.
- Studies of interventions as delivered in naturalistic settings (effectiveness research) are well suited for assessing the ecological validity of treatments.
- Randomized clinical trials and their logical equivalents (efficacy research) are the standard for drawing causal inferences about the effects of interventions (context of scientific verification).
- Meta-analysis is a systematic means to synthesize results from multiple studies, test hypotheses, and quantitatively estimate the size of effects.

With respect to evaluating research on specific interventions, current APA policy identifies two widely accepted dimensions. As stated in the *Criteria for Evaluating Treatment Guidelines,* "The first dimension is *treatment efficacy,* the systematic and scientific evaluation of whether a treatment works. The second dimension is *clinical utility,* the applicability, feasibility, and usefulness of the intervention in the local or specific setting where it is to be offered. This dimension also includes determination of the generalizability of an intervention whose efficacy has been established." Types of research evidence with regard to intervention research in ascending order as to their contribution to conclusions about efficacy include: clinical opinion, observation, and consensus among recognized experts representing the range of use in the field (Criterion 2.1); systematized clinical observation (Criterion 2.2); and sophisticated empirical methodologies, including quasi experiments and randomized controlled experiments or their logical equivalents (Criterion 2.3). Among sophisticated empirical methodologies, "randomized controlled experiments represent a more stringent way to evaluate treatment efficacy because they are the most effective way to rule out threats to internal validity in a single experiment."

Evidence on clinical utility is also crucial. As per established APA policy, at a minimum this includes attention to generality of effects across varying and diverse patients, therapists and settings and the interaction of these factors, the robustness of treatments across various modes of delivery, the feasibility with which treatments can be delivered to patients in real world settings, and the cost associated with treatments.

Evidence-based practice requires that psychologists recognize the strengths and limitations of evidence obtained from different types of research. Research has shown that the treatment method, the individual psychologist, the treatment relationship, and the patient are all vital contributors to the success of psychological practice. Comprehensive evidence-based practice will consider all of these determinants and their optimal combinations. Psychological practice is a complex relational and technical enterprise that requires clinical and research attention to multiple, interacting sources of treatment effectiveness. There remain many disorders, problem constellations, and clinical situations for which empirical data are sparse. In such instances, clinicians use their best clinical judgment and knowledge of the best available research evidence to develop coherent treatment strategies. Researchers and practitioners should join together to ensure that the research available on psychological practice is both clinically relevant and internally valid. . . .

Clinical Expertise[2]

Clinical expertise is essential for identifying and integrating the best research evidence with clinical data (e.g., information about the patient obtained over the course of treatment) in the context of the patient's characteristics and preferences to deliver services that have the highest probability of achieving the goals of therapy. Psychologists are trained as scientists as well as practitioners. An advantage of psychological training is that it fosters a clinical expertise informed by scientific expertise, allowing the psychologist to understand and integrate scientific literature as well as to frame and test hypotheses and interventions in practice as a "local clinical scientist."

Cognitive scientists have found consistent evidence of enduring and significant differences between experts and novices undertaking complex tasks in several domains. Experts recognize meaningful patterns and disregard irrelevant information, acquire extensive knowledge and organize it in ways that reflect a deep understanding of their domain, organize their knowledge using functional rather than descriptive features, retrieve knowledge relevant to the task at hand fluidly and automatically, adapt to new situations, self-monitor their knowledge and performance, know when their knowledge is inadequate, continue to learn, and generally attain outcomes commensurate with their expertise.

However, experts are not infallible. All humans are prone to errors and biases. Some of these stem from cognitive strategies and heuristics that are generally adaptive and efficient. Others stem from emotional reactions, which generally guide adaptive behavior as well but can also lead to biased or motivated reasoning. Whenever psychologists involved in research or practice move from observations to inferences and generalizations, there is inherent risk for idiosyncratic interpretations, overgeneralizations, confirmatory biases, and similar errors in judgment. Integral to clinical expertise is an awareness of the limits of one's knowledge and skills and attention to the heuristics and biases—both cognitive and affective—that can affect clinical judgment. Mechanisms such as consultation and systematic feedback from the patient can mitigate some of these biases.

The individual therapist has a substantial impact on outcomes, both in clinical trials and in practice settings. The fact that treatment outcomes are systematically related to the provider of the treatment (above and beyond the type of treatment) provides strong evidence for the importance of understanding expertise in clinical practice as a way of enhancing patient outcomes. . . .

Patient Characteristics, Culture, and Preferences

Normative data on "what works for whom" provide essential guides to effective practice. Nevertheless, psychological services are most likely to be effective when responsive to the patient's specific problems, strengths, personality, sociocultural context, and preferences. Psychology's long history of studying individual differences and developmental change, and its growing empirical literature related to human diversity (including culture[3] and psychotherapy), place it in a strong position to identify effective ways of integrating research and clinical expertise with an understanding of patient characteristics essential to EBPP. EBPP involves consideration of patients' values, religious beliefs, worldviews, goals, and preferences for treatment with the psychologist's experience and understanding of the available research.

Several questions frame current debates about the role of patient characteristics in EBPP. The first regards the extent to which cross-diagnostic patient characteristics, such as personality traits or constellations, moderate the impact of empirically tested interventions. A second, related question concerns the extent to which social factors and cultural differences necessitate different forms of treatment or whether interventions widely tested in majority populations can be readily adapted for patients with different ethnic or sociocultural backgrounds. A third question concerns maximizing the extent to which widely used interventions adequately attend to developmental considerations, both for children and adolescents and for older adults. A fourth question is the extent to which variable clinical presentations, such as comorbidity and polysymptomatic presentations, moderate the impact of interventions. Underlying all of these questions is the issue of how best to approach the treatment of patients whose characteristics (e.g., gender, gender identity, ethnicity, race, social class, disability status, sexual orientation) and problems (e.g., comorbidity) may differ from those of samples studied in research. This is a matter of active discussion in the field and there is increasing research attention to the generalizability and transportability of psychological interventions.

Available data indicate that a variety of patient-related variables influence outcomes, many of which are cross-diagnostic characteristics such as functional status, readiness to change, and level of social support. Other patient characteristics are essential to consider in forming and maintaining a treatment relationship and in implementing specific interventions. These include but are not limited to a) variations in presenting problems or disorders, etiology, concurrent symptoms or syndromes, and behavior; b) chronological age, developmental status, developmental history, and life stage; c) sociocultural and familial factors (e.g., gender, gender identity, ethnicity, race, social class, religion, disability status, family structure, and sexual orientation); d) current environmental context, stressors (e.g., unemployment or recent life event), and social factors (e.g., institutional racism and health care disparities); and e) personal preferences, values, and preferences related to treatment (e.g., goals, beliefs, worldviews, and treatment expectations). Available research on both patient matching and treatment failures in clinical trials of even highly efficacious interventions suggests that different strategies and relationships may prove better suited for different populations.

Many presenting symptoms—for example, depression, anxiety, school failure, bingeing and purging—are similar across patients. However, symptoms or disorders that are phenotypically similar are often heterogeneous with respect to etiology, prognosis, and the psychological processes that create or maintain them. Moreover, most patients present with multiple symptoms or syndromes rather than a single, discrete disorder. The presence of concurrent conditions may moderate treatment response, and interventions intended to treat one symptom often affect others. An emerging body of research also suggests that personality variables underlie many psychiatric syndromes and account for a substantial part of the comorbidity among syndromes widely documented in research. Psychologists must attend to the individual person to make the complex choices necessary to conceptualize, prioritize, and treat multiple symptoms. It is important to know the person who has the disorder in addition to knowing the disorder the person has.

EBPP also requires attention to factors related to the patient's development and life-stage. An enormous body of research exists on developmental processes (e.g., attachment, socialization, and cognitive, social-cognitive, gender, moral, and emotional development) that are essential in understanding adult psychopathology and particularly in treating children, adolescents, families, and older adults.

Evidence-based practice in psychology requires attention to many other patient characteristics, such as gender, gender identity, culture, ethnicity, race, age, family context, religious beliefs, and sexual orientation. These variables shape personality, values, worldviews, relationships, psychopathology, and attitudes toward treatment. A wide range of relevant research literature can inform psychological practice, including ethnography, cross-cultural psychology, psychological anthropology, and cultural psychotherapy. Culture influences not only the nature and expression of psychopathology but also the patient's understanding of psychological and physical health and illness. Cultural values and beliefs and social factors such as implicit racial biases also influence patterns of seeking, using, and receiving help; presentation and reporting of symptoms, fears and expectations about treatment; and desired outcomes. Psychologists also understand and reflect upon the ways their own characteristics, values, and context interact with those of the patient.

Race as a social construct is a way of grouping people into categories on the basis of perceived physical attributes, ancestry, and other factors. Race is also more broadly associated with power, status, and opportunity. In Western cultures, European or white "race" confers advantage and opportunity, even as improved social attitudes and public policies have reinforced social equality. Race is thus an interpersonal and political process with significant implications for clinical practice and health care quality. Patients and clinicians may "belong" to racial groups, as they choose to self-identify, but the importance of race in clinical practice is relational, rather than solely a patient or clinician attribute. Considerable evidence from many fields suggests that racial power differentials between clinicians and their patients, as well as systemic biases and implicit stereotypes based on race or ethnicity, contribute to the inequitable care that patients of color receive across health care services. Clinicians must carefully consider the impact of race, ethnicity, and culture on the treatment process, relationship, and outcome.

The patient's social and environmental context, including recent and chronic stressors, is also important in case formulation and treatment planning. Sociocultural and familial factors, social class, and broader social, economic, and situational factors (e.g., unemployment, family disruption, lack of insurance, recent losses, prejudice, or immigration status) can have an enormous influence on mental health, adaptive functioning, treatment seeking, and patient resources (psychological, social, and financial).

Psychotherapy is a collaborative enterprise, in which patients and clinicians negotiate ways of working together that are mutually agreeable and likely to lead to positive outcomes. Thus, patient values and preferences (e.g., goals, beliefs, and preferred modes of treatment) are a central component of EBPP. Patients can have strong preferences for types of treatment and desired outcomes, and these preferences are influenced by both their cultural context and individual factors. One role of the psychologist is to ensure that patients understand the costs and benefits of different practices and choices. Evidence-based practice in psychology seeks to maximize patient choice among effective alternative interventions. Effective practice requires balancing patient preferences and the psychologist's judgment, based on available evidence and clinical expertise, to determine the most appropriate treatment. . . .

Conclusions

Evidence-based practice in psychology is the integration of the best available research with clinical expertise in the context of patient characteristics, culture, and preferences. The purpose of EBPP is to promote effective psychological practice and enhance public health by applying empirically supported principles of psychological assessment, case formulation, therapeutic relationship, and intervention. Much has been learned over the past century from basic and applied psychological research as well as from observations and hypotheses developed in clinical practice. Many strategies for working with patients have emerged and been refined through the kind of trial and error and clinical hypothesis generation and testing that constitute the most scientific aspect of clinical practice. Yet clinical hypothesis testing has its limits, hence the need to integrate clinical expertise with best available research.

Perhaps the central message of this task force report, and one of the most heartening aspects of the process that led to it, is the consensus achieved among a diverse group of scientists, clinicians, and scientist-clinicians from multiple perspectives that EBPP requires an appreciation of the value of multiple sources of scientific evidence. In a given clinical circumstance, psychologists of good faith and good judgment may disagree about how best to weight different forms of evidence; over time, we presume that systematic and broad empirical inquiry—in the laboratory and in the clinic—will point the way toward best practice in integrating best evidence. What this document reflects, however, is a reassertion of what psychologists have known for a century: that the scientific method is a way of thinking and observing systematically and is the best tool we have for learning about what works for whom.

Clinical decisions should be made in collaboration with the patient, based on the best clinically relevant evidence, and with consideration for the probable costs, benefits, and available resources and options. It is the treating psychologist who makes the ultimate judgment regarding a particular intervention or treatment plan. The involvement of an active, informed patient is generally crucial to the success of psychological services. Treatment decisions should never be made by untrained persons unfamiliar with the specifics of the case.

The treating psychologist determines the applicability of research conclusions to a particular patient. Individual patients may require decisions and interventions not directly addressed by the available research. The application of research evidence to a given patient always involves probabilistic inferences. Therefore, ongoing monitoring of patient progress and adjustment of treatment as needed are essential to EBPP.

Moreover, psychologists must attend to a range of outcomes that may sometimes suggest one strategy and sometimes another and to the strengths and limitations of available research vis-à-vis these different ways of measuring success. Psychological outcomes may include not only symptom relief and prevention of future symptomatic episodes but also quality of life, adaptive functioning in work and relationships, ability to make satisfying life choices, personality change, and other goals arrived at in collaboration between patient and clinician.

EBPP is a means to enhance the delivery of services to patients within an atmosphere of mutual respect, open communication, and collaboration among all stakeholders, including practitioners, researchers, patients, health care managers, and policy-makers. Our goal in this document, and in the deliberations of the Task Force that led to it, was to set both an agenda and a tone for the next steps in the evolution of EBPP.

Notes

1. This document was received by the American Psychological Association (APA) Council of Representatives during its meeting of August, 2005. The report represents the conclusions of the Task Force and does not represent the official policy of the American Psychological Association. The Task Force wishes to thank John R. Weisz, PhD, ABPP for his assistance in drafting portions of this report related to children and youth. The Task Force also thanks James Mitchell and Omar Rehman, APA Professional Development interns, for their assistance throughout the work of the Task Force.

2. As it is used in this report, clinical expertise refers to competence attained by psychologists through education, training, and experience resulting in effective practice; clinical expertise is not meant to refer to extraordinary performance that might characterize an elite group (e.g., the top two percent) of clinicians.

3. Culture, in this context, is understood to encompass a broad array of phenomena (such as shared values, history, knowledge, rituals, and customs) that often result in a shared sense of identity. Racial and ethnic groups may have a shared culture, but those personal characteristics are not the only characteristics that define cultural groups (e.g., deaf culture, inner-city culture). Culture is a multifaceted construct, and cultural factors cannot be understood in isolation from social, class and personal characteristics that make each patient unique.

THE APA 2005 PRESIDENTIAL TASK FORCE ON EVIDENCE-BASED PRACTICE defines and discusses evidence-based practice in psychology (EBPP).

Brent D. Slife and Dennis C. Wendt

 **NO**

The Next Step in the Evidence-Based Practice Movement

Nearly everyone agrees that psychological practice should be informed by evidence (Westen & Bradley, 2005, p. 266; Norcross, Beutler, & Levant, 2006, p. 7). However, there is considerable disagreement about what qualifies as evidence (e.g., Reed, 2006; Kihlstrom, 2006; Messer, 2006; Westen, 2006; Stirman & DeRubeis, 2006). This disagreement is not a simple scientific dispute to be resolved in the laboratory, but rather a "culture war" between different worldviews (Messer, 2004, p. 580). As Carol Tavris (2003) put it, this "war" involves "deeply held beliefs, political passions, views of human nature and the nature of knowledge, and—as all wars ultimately involve—money, territory, and livelihoods" (as qtd. in Norcross et al., p. 8).

How does one address a cultural battle of deeply held worldviews and political passions? We believe the approaches that have tried to address it so far in psychology have been well-intended and even headed in the right direction, but are ultimately and fundamentally inadequate. We will first describe what we consider the two major steps in this regard, beginning with the empirically supported treatment (EST) movement, which still has considerable energy in the discipline, and then moving to the "common factors" approach, which recently culminated in a policy regarding evidence-based practice (EBP) in psychology from the American Psychological Association (APA, 2006). We specifically focus on the latter, extolling its goals, but noting their distinct lack of fulfillment. We then offer what seems to us the logical extension of these first two steps—what could be called "objective methodological pluralism" in the spirit of one of our discipline's founding parents, William James (1902/1985; 1907/1975).

The First Step: The EST Movement

Psychology's first step in addressing this evidence controversy involved a succession of APA Division 12 (Clinical) task forces. Beginning in 1993, these task forces have "constructed and elaborated a list of empirically supported, manualized psychological interventions for specific disorders" (Norcross et al., 2006, p. 5). In other words, this first step assumed that the battle of worldviews would be resolved through rigorous scientific evidence. "Rigorous evidence," in this case, was idealized as the randomized clinical (or controlled) trial (RCT), widely esteemed as the gold standard of evidence in medicine. The advantages of this step were obvious. Third-party payers were familiar with this gold standard from medicine, and many psychologists believed that an EST list would provide a clear-cut index of "proven" treatments, not to mention greater respect from medicine.

Unfortunately, this seemingly rigorous, clear-cut approach has manifested more than a few problems (Westen & Bradley, 2005; Messer, 2004). Much like the testing movement in education, where teachers found themselves "teaching to the test," psychologists found their practices being shaped by the RCT "test." The critics of the RCT showed how professional practices were conforming, consciously or unconsciously, to the RCT worldview in order to make the EST list. In other words, the practices being studied tended to accommodate the particular RCT perspective on treatments, therapists, and patients.

With regard to treatments, this medical-model worldview of the RCT is biased toward "packaged" treatments for well-defined, compartmentalized disorders (e.g., Bohart, O'Hara, & Leitner, 1998). This model of treatment took its cues from the pharmaceutical industry, where "one must specify the treatment and make sure it is being applied correctly" (p. 143). According to this model, every patient would receive the same thing, and it is this thing, not the therapist or patient, that is considered the agent of change. Critics have argued that this view of treatment undermined many types of therapy, such as humanistic or psychodynamic therapies, in which "treatment" does not entail a manualized set of principles (e.g., Bohart et al.; Safran, 2001).

A related argument against this packaged view of treatment concerned the role of therapists. The assumptions or worldview of the RCT, these critics contended, turned the therapist into an interchangeable part, discounting the importance of the therapist's distinctive personality, practical wisdom, and unique relationship with the patient. Many researchers have worried, to use the words of Allen Bergin (1997), that the RCT manualization of treatments turned therapists into "cookie cutters" and researchers into "mechanotropes" (pp. 85–86). This worry has been validated by research suggesting that manualization often hinders important therapeutic factors, such as the therapeutic alliance and the therapist's genuineness, creativity, motivation, and emotional involvement (Duncan & Miller, 2006; Piper & Ogrodniczuk, 1999).

Third, critics have noted that the biases of RCTs shaped one's view of the patient, assuming that researchers and clinicians work with pure patient pathologies only. According to this argument, RCTs are limited to patients with textbook symptoms of a single DSM disorder; thus, their results "may apply only to a narrow and homogeneous group of patients" (Butcher, Mineka, & Hooley, 2004, p. 563). This limitation is no small problem, critics have warned, because the vast majority of U.S. patients are not pathologically "pure" in this narrow RCT sense. Rather, they are co- or "multi"-morbid in the sense that they are an amalgam of disorders (Morrison, Bradley, & Westen, 2003; Westen & Bradley, 2005). The prevalence of these "messy" patients is corroborated by the 35%–70% exclusion rates of RCTs for major disorders (Morrison et al., p. 110).

The common theme behind the above criticisms is that the biases of the EST movement stem from its narrow framework for validating evidence. Thus, it is not mere coincidence, critics have argued, that therapies that exemplify this type of treatment (e.g., behavioral or cognitive-behavioral treatments) are the most frequently listed as ESTs (Messer, 2004). The exclusion of other types of therapy (e.g., humanistic and psychodynamic therapies) has prompted critics to contend that the EST movement constitutes a methodological bias toward behavioral and cognitive-behavioral therapies (e.g., Slife, Wiggins, & Graham; Messer, 2004). If this first step has taught psychologists anything, it has taught that what the evidence seems to say has a great deal to do with what one considers evidence.

The Second Step: The Common Factors Movement

The second step—the common factors movement—was, in part, an attempt to learn from the shortcomings of the EST movement. Common factors advocates have argued that a focus on specific, "packaged" treatments for specific disorders is a narrow way of conceptualizing psychological research and practice (e.g., Westen & Bradley, 2005; Bohart et al., 1998). An alternative approach is to discover and validate factors of therapeutic change that are common across treatments. In this way, responsibility for change is not just attributed to the treatment, as in ESTs. Change is considered the result of a dynamic relationship among the "common factors" of therapy, which include the therapist, patient, and technique (APA, 2006, p. 275).

A common factors approach is especially appealing to the majority of practitioners, who consider themselves eclectics or integrationists. Its popularity has helped it to play a significant role in shaping APA's (2006) new policy statement on evidence-based practice. For this policy statement, evidence was liberalized not only to include studies of therapist and patient variables but also to include other methods than RCTs for conducting these studies (pp. 274–75). The main guideposts for selecting these methods, according to the underlying rationale of the APA policy, were their objectivity and their diversity. Methods should be *objective* to prevent the intrusion of human error and bias that would distort the findings (p. 276), and they should be *diverse* to prevent the shaping of practice that a focus on only one method might produce, such as the problems created by RCTs (pp. 272–74).

The problem, from our perspective, is that the APA culmination of this common factors approach is not objective and diverse enough. In other words, we applaud the goals but criticize the implementation. The APA policy is a clear step forward, in our view, but its conceptions of objectivity and diversity are inadequate. As we will attempt to show, this inadequacy means that the lessons of the EST movement have not been sufficiently learned. Recall that this first step restricted itself to a single ideal of evidence, the RCT, and thus disallowed any true diversity of methods. Recall also that several biases resulted from this restriction, obviating objectivity and shaping practice even before investigation. As we will argue, this same lack of diversity and objectivity has continued into the second approach to the evidence controversy.

Our basic criticism is this: Just as an EST framework uncritically restricts acceptable evidence to a *single method* ideal (the RCT), so does the APA policy uncritically restrict acceptable evidence to a *single epistemology*. By "epistemology" we mean the philosophy of knowing that provides the logic and guides the conduct of a group of methods (Slife & Williams, 1995). Although the EST framework is biased toward a certain *method,* the common factors framework is biased toward a certain *methodology*—a narrow brand of *empiricism*.

According to this empiricist epistemology, "we can only know, or know best, those aspects of our experience that are sensory" (Slife, Wiggins, & Graham, 2005, p. 84). This narrow conception of empiricism is fairly traditional in psychology. More liberal usages of empiricism differ substantially, such as William James' radical empiricism. James' empiricism encompasses "the whole of experience," including *non*-sensory experiences such as thoughts, emotions, and even spiritual experiences (James, 1902/1985; 1907/1975). Still, psychologists have interpreted the natural sciences to be grounded in the narrow empiricism. Historically, psychologists have wanted to be both rigorously scientific and comparable to medicine, leading them to embrace the narrower empiricism. As we will attempt to show, however, this restriction to a single epistemology is not based on evidence. Analogous to the EST restriction to a single method, the APA policy merely assumes and never justifies empiricism as the only appropriate epistemology for evidence-based practice, in spite of other promising epistemologies.

The reason for this lack of justification seems clear. Throughout much of the history of psychology, empiricism has been mistakenly understood not as a *particular* philosophy of science, but as a *non*-philosophy that makes reality transparent. Analogous to the way in which many EST proponents view RCTs, empiricism is not *a* way to understand evidence, but *the* way. Consequently, nowhere in the APA policy or its underlying report is a rationale provided for a commitment to empirical research, and nowhere is a consideration given for even the possibility of a "non-empirical" contribution to evidence-based practice.

This equation of evidence with empiricism is directly parallel to the EST movement's equation of evidence with RCT findings. Just as Westen and Bradley (2005) noted that "EBP > EST" (p. 271), we note that EBP > empirical. After all, there is no empirical evidence for empiricism, or for RCTs, for that matter. Both sets of methods spring from the human invention of philosophers and other humanists. Moses did not descend Mt. Sinai with the Ten Commandments in one hand and the principles of science in the other. Moreover, these principles could not have been scientifically derived, because one would need the principles (before their derivation) to conduct the scientific investigations to derive them.

Indeed, the irony of this epistemology's popularity is that many observers of psychology have long considered empiricism to be deeply problematic for psychological research. Again, the parallel to the dominance of RCTs is striking. Just as the majority of real-world patients, therapists,

and treatments were perceived to defy RCT categories, so too the majority of real-world phenomena can be perceived to defy empirical categories. Indeed, many of the common factors for evidence-based practice are not, strictly speaking, empirical at all. Rather, they are experiences and meanings that are not sensory, and thus not observable, in nature (Slife et al., 2005, p. 88).

Consider, for example, the efforts of APA Division 29 (Psychotherapy) to provide empirical support for therapy relationships, such as therapeutic alliance and group cohesion (Norcross, 2001; APA, 2006, p. 272). Although patients and therapists probably experience this alliance and cohesion, these relationships literally never fall on their retinas. The people involved in these relationships are observable in this sense, to be sure, but the "betweenness" of these relations—the actual alliance or cohesion themselves—never are. Their unobservability means, according to the method requirements of empiricism, that they must be operationalized, or made observable. Thus, it is not surprising, given its commitment to a narrow empiricism, that the APA policy report presumes that operationalization is a requirement of method (p. 274).

The problem with this requirement, however, is that any specified operationalization, such as a patient's feelings about the relationship (e.g., Norcross, 2002), can occur without the therapeutic alliance, and any such alliance can occur without the specified operationalization. The upshot is that the construct (e.g., alliance) and the operationalization are two different things, yet the operationalization is the only thing studied in traditional research. Moreover, one can never know empirically the relation between the construct and its operationalization because pivotal aspects of this relation—the construct and relation itself—are never observable. Thus, APA's policy runs the risk of making psychotherapy research a compendium of operationalizations without any knowledge of how they relate to what psychologists want to study.

Problems such as these are the reason that alternative philosophies of science, such as qualitative methods, were formulated. Many qualitative methods were specifically formulated to investigate unobservable, but experienced, meanings of the world (Denzin & Lincoln, 2000; Patton, 1990; Slife & Gantt, 1999). The existence of this alternative philosophy of science implies another problem with the unjustified empiricist framework of the APA policy report—it runs roughshod over alternative frameworks, such as qualitative methods. Although the policy includes qualitative research on its list of acceptable methods (APA, p. 274), it fails to understand and value qualitative research as a different philosophy of science.

A clear indication of this failure is the use of the word "subjective" when the report describes the purpose of qualitative research (p. 274). In the midst of a report that extols "objective" inquiry, relegating only qualitative methods to the "subjective" is second-class citizenship, at best. More importantly, this relegation only makes sense within an empiricist framework. In non-empiricist philosophies, such as those underlying many qualitative methods, the notions of "objective" and "subjective" are largely irrelevant because most non-empiricist conceptions of science do not assume the dualism of a subjective and objective realm (Slife, 2005).

The bottom line is that a common factors approach to the evidence controversy is a clear advancement of the EBP project, but it is not an unqualified advance. Indeed, it recapitulates some of the same problems that it is attempting to correct. In both the EST and the common factors approaches, criteria for what is evidence shape not only the studies conducted but also the practices considered supported. Indeed, we would contend there is no method or methodology that is not ultimately biased in this regard. As philosophers of science have long taught, all methods of investigation must make assumptions about the world *before* it is investigated (Curd & Cover, 1998). The question remains, however, whether there can be a framework for understanding evidence that does not *automatically* shape practice before it is investigated.

Presaging the Next Step: The Ideas of William James

The answer, we believe, is "yes," and we do not have to reinvent the wheel to formulate this alternative. One of the intellectual parents of our discipline, William James, has already pointed the way. Consequently, we will first briefly describe three of James' pivotal ideas: his radical empiricism, his pluralism, and his pragmatism. Then, we will apply these ideas to the evidence-based practice issue, deriving our alternative to the current monopoly of empiricism—objective methodological pluralism.

James was actually quite critical of what psychologists consider empirical today. As mentioned above, his radical empiricism embraces the whole of experience, including non-sensory experiences such as thoughts, emotions, and spiritual experiences (James, 1902/1985; 1907/1975). His position implies, as he explicitly recognizes, that there are several epistemologies of investigation ("ways of knowing") rather than just one. As James (1909/1977) put it, "nothing includes everything" (p. 145). In other words,

no philosophy of science is sufficient to understand everything.

Psychology needs, instead, a *pluralism* of such philosophies, which is the second of James's ideas and an intriguing way to actualize APA's desire for diversity. In other words, we not only need a diversity of methods, which the APA report (2006) clearly concedes (p. 274), we also need a diversity of *methodologies* or philosophies underlying these methods. It is not coincidental, in this regard, that James (1902/1985) used qualitative methods to investigate spiritual meanings in his famous work, *Varieties of Religious Experiences.* His pluralism of methods dictated that he should not change or operationalize his phenomena of study to fit the method, but that he should change his method to best illuminate the phenomena—spiritual phenomena, in this case.

This approach to method implies the third of James's ideas—his pragmatism. According to James:

> Rationalism sticks to logic and . . . empiricism sticks to the external senses. Pragmatism is willing to take anything, to follow either logic or the senses and to count the humblest and most personal of experiences. [Pragmatism] will count mystical experiences if they have practical consequences. (James, 1907/1975, p. 61)

As James implies, the heart of pragmatism is the notion that one should never approach the study or understanding of anything with fixed schemes and methods. There is too much danger that the method will distort understanding of the phenomena being studied. This is not to say that one can or should approach such phenomena without some method or interpretive framework. Yet this framework does not have to be cast in stone; psychologists should allow the phenomenon itself to guide the methods we choose to study it.

This pragmatism may sound complicated, but it is not significantly different from what good carpenters do at every job—they let the task dictate the tools they use. They have a pluralism of tools or methods, rather than just one, because many tasks cannot be done with just one tool, such as a hammer. Moreover, not every carpentry job can be "operationalized" into a set of "nails." As Dupré (1993) and others (e.g., Feyerabend, 1975; Viney, 2004) have noted, this pragmatism is the informal meta-method of physics, where the object of study is the primary consideration, and the method of studying it is a secondary consideration.

By contrast, APA's version of evidence-based practice is method-driven rather than object-driven. That is to say, psychologists have decided the logic of their investigation before they even consider what they are studying. If the object of study does not fit this logic, they have no choice but to modify it to fit this logic through operationalization. For example, an unobservable feeling, such as sadness, becomes operationalized as an observable behavior, such as crying.

The irony of this familiar research practice is that psychologists are driven more by an unrecognized and unexamined philosophy of science, as manifested through their methods, than by the objects they are studying. Indeed, they are changing their object of study—from sadness to crying—to accommodate this philosophy. We believe that this accommodation is contrary to good science, where everything including the philosophies that ground one's methods, should be subject to examination and comparison.

The Next Step: Objective Methodological Pluralism

This description of James' three pivotal ideas—his radical empiricism, pluralism, and pragmatism—sets the stage for our proposal on evidence-based practice: "objective methodological pluralism." First, this pluralism assumes a broader empiricism, in the spirit of James. To value only sensory experiences, as does the conventional empiricist, is to affirm a value that is itself unproven and non-empirical. There simply is no conceptual or empirical necessity to value only the sensory. We recognize that many would claim the success of this value in science, but we also recognize that no scientific comparison between such philosophical values has occurred. These claims of success, then, are merely opinion, uninformed by scientific findings.

In practical terms, this move from conventional empiricism to radical empiricism means that alternative methods, such as qualitative methods, are no longer second class citizens. They are no longer "subjective" and experimental methods considered "objective," because all methods ultimately depend on experiences of one sort or another. This creates more of a level playing field for methods—a pluralism—and allows for an even-handed assessment of each method's advantages and disadvantages.

Unlike the APA policy's conception, the criteria of this assessment are not already controlled by one, unexamined philosophy of science. They are guided, instead, by the object of one's study. This is the reason for the term "objective" in our alternative, *objective* methodological pluralism. Methods, we believe, should be driven not by some philosophy of method that is deemed to be correct *before* the object of study has even been considered. Methods should be driven by consideration of the objects themselves.

This consideration is itself evaluated pragmatically, in terms of the practical differences it makes in the lives of patients. As James realized, any evaluation of practical significance begs the question of "significant to what?" In other words, any methodological pluralism requires thoughtful disciplinary discussion of the moral issues of psychology, a discussion that has begun in a limited way in positive psychology (Seligman, 2002): What is the good life for a patient? When is a life truly flourishing? Such questions cannot be derived from the "is" of research; they must be discussed as the "ought" that guides this research and determines what practical significance really means.

Obviously, much remains to be worked out with a Jamesian pluralism. Still, we believe that this particular "working out" is not only possible but also necessary. The monopoly and problems of empiricism—the lessons of our first two steps in the evidence controversy—do not go away with a rejection of this pluralism. This is the reason we titled this article "the next step"—the difficulties with empiricism and APA's desire for diversity lead us logically, we believe, to this next general step. Admittedly, this kind of pluralism is a challenging prospect. Still, if carpenters can do it in a less complex enterprise, surely psychologists can. In any case, it is high time that psychologists face up to the challenge, because ignoring it will not make it go away.

Brent D. Slife is currently a professor of psychology at Brigham Young University, where he chairs the doctoral program in theoretical and philosophical psychology and serves as a member of the doctoral program in clinical psychology.

Dennis C. Wendt is a predoctoral fellow for the University of Michigan Substance Abuse Research Center (UMSARC), funded through a NIDA training grant.

EXPLORING THE ISSUE

Are Traditional Empirical Methods Sufficient to Provide Evidence for Psychological Practice?

Critical Thinking and Reflection

1. The label "objective" is typically used only in reference to empirical evidence. Why is this typical, and what would Slife and Wendt say about this practice?
2. The APA Task Force bases its definition of evidence-based practice on a conception formulated by the Institute of Medicine. Find out what this definition is and form your own informed opinion about its relevance or irrelevance to psychotherapy. Support your answer.
3. Many people think they would feel safer if their therapist used practices that have been validated by science. Explain what it is about science that leads people to feel this way.
4. William James is known as the father of American psychology. Why do you think the APA has largely neglected to take his pluralism into consideration?
5. Slife and Wendt believe that the methods of psychology (and any other science, for that matter) are based on and guided by philosophies, yet few psychology texts discuss these philosophies. Why do you feel that this is the case, and is the absence of this discussion justified?

Is There Common Ground?

One of the primary goals of psychotherapy is to relieve the suffering of those afflicted with an emotional and psychological disorders. The authors of each of these articles agree that in attempting to relieve the suffering of clients, therapists and psychologists need to utilize counseling methods and techniques that can be shown to be genuinely effective. Additionally they would agree that techniques that are ineffective, or which further harm psychotherapy clients, must be identified and their use proscribed. Establishing which particular forms of therapy work best, and for whom and in which instances, is most certainly a worthy project for psychological researchers to undertake. Without the information that this sort of research would provide, there would be no way to adequately assess how useful particular psychotherapies are. Not only would treatment advances in the field likely grind to a halt, but actually harmful practices might well be approved.

Although the authors of these two articles differ as to which type of method should be employed to establish evidenced-based psychological practice, each would certainly agree that empirical observational methods are needed. Furthermore, although they clearly differ in regards to which methods are best suited for determining effective treatment practices, each of the authors of these articles would no doubt agree that multiple methods and a variety of investigatory perspectives are necessary in order to provide as broad and deep an understanding of the therapeutic process as possible. In the end, treatment outcome research is essential for researchers and practitioners alike if this field is expect to flourish and help those who stand in need.

Additional Resource

James, W. (2006, November 15). A pluralistic universe. *BiblioBazaar.* Retrieved from http://www.gutenberg.org/ebooks/11984

Internet Reference . . .

Journal of Mind and Behavior

www.**umaine.edu/jmb/archives/volume29/v30n3.ht**m

Selected, Edited, and with Issue Framing Material by:
Edwin E. Gantt, *Brigham Young University*

ISSUE

Is Psychology a Science?

YES: Robert E. Silverman, from "Is Psychology a Science?" *Skeptic Magazine* (2011)

NO: Peter Rickman, from "Is Psychology Science?" *Philosophy Now* (2009)

Learning Outcomes

After reading this issue, you will be able to:

- Understand what basic assumptions underlie science and the scientific method.
- Decide for yourself if the discipline of psychology meets the qualifications to be considered a science like the physical sciences.
- Understand alternative possible visions of science that may be beneficial in informing psychology as a discipline.

ISSUE SUMMARY

YES: Robert E. Silverman, an academic psychologist writing in *Skeptic Magazine*, presents a brief history of psychology and a few of its main figures while addressing the role of science in psychology. He argues that over time psychology has become more scientific (i.e., more objective in observations and measurement). He concludes that as the current partnership of psychology and neuroscience grows stronger there will be no question that psychology is indeed a science.

NO: Peter Rickman, formerly professor of philosophy at City University in London, argues that psychology is not a science like physics and other natural sciences because although it shares certain aspects of the scientific method, it must and does rely on the methods of hermeneutics. He argues that because observable facts are not the data being studied in psychology, but rather meaningful communication, psychology must always consider context and background in its research. The scientific method is not sufficient for psychology to accomplish this task.

Psychologists, philosophers, and scientists have long debated the legitimacy of psychology as a natural science. In fact, even before psychology became a recognized academic discipline philosophers such as Immanuel Kant argued for the impossibility of a science of the mind. There are several issues imbedded in this debate that must be addressed. The first and most obvious is whether psychology as it is known today actually meets the conceptual requirements necessary to be counted as science, in the same way that the more established natural or "hard" sciences do. If it does, should it be held to the same methodological and quantitative standards as the physical sciences? Another issue in this debate has to do with the implications of being considered a natural science. Is it still possible for psychology to be recognized as having intellectual merit without it being considered as one of the hard sciences? Can the information produced by psychologists be beneficial to society even if psychology does not employ the same methods or achieve the same predictive results as the physical sciences?

A third issue within this debate has to do with the assumptions underlying the view of the primary subject matter of psychology: human beings. Throughout the history of psychology different aspects of human being have been the focus of research (e.g., the mind, the brain, behavior, etc.), but there has been little argument that human beings are the primary interest of psychology. Each side of the debate at hand has fundamentally different views of what human beings are. Because of these differing views of human nature, the methods used in studying human beings also tend to differ. The camp which argues for psychology as a science typically sees human beings as fundamentally no different than any other natural objects to be found in the world, and, thus, argue that the same basic laws that govern in physics also govern the human world. In contrast, those who argue that psychology is not akin to the natural sciences see human beings as fundamentally different from nonliving, non-choosing objects. The existence of consciousness, purposiveness, and free will (among other things) dictate that the same methods used to study physical phenomena are not adequate to the study of human behavior.

In the YES selection, Robert Silverman presents a brief history of psychology. While doing so he admits that historically psychology has not met the criteria for being truly scientific. He gives various examples of the poor science or nonscience that was conducted by Wundt, the Gestalt psychologists, and Freud. However, he then shows that with the progression of the discipline, psychology has steadily grown closer to being genuinely scientific. He highlights the quantifiable, measurable, and systematic nature of behaviorism and shows that other approaches lost steam because their lack of objective verifiability. He concludes with a clear statement that with the current neuroimaging technology and the strongly biological focus of psychology, there will soon be solid empirical and scientific backing for a scientific study of mental activity. With such solid evidence, he argues, there will be no question as to psychology's status as a natural science.

It is clear that Silverman's focus in the debate is on demonstrating that psychology does indeed meet the criteria for being a science. His article does not deal so much with the issue of whether psychology must be considered a science in order to be beneficial to society, but because of the manner in which he presents the pioneers of psychology who did not live up to scientific standards it is clear that for him a genuinely scientific psychology is of greater worth to us than a nonscientific one. Silverman also does not take up the ontological question of human nature in his analysis. That is, he does not spend much time discussing what he presumes to be fundamentally true about the nature of human beings, though some of the assumptions he makes are clear. Silverman's focus on psychology's goal of being a science is restricted primarily to the

methodology that psychologists must employ. Thus, it is not so much the nature of human nature that is at stake in this debate for Silverman, as it is the use of proper investigatory method. He concludes his analysis by commenting on the benefits of a partnership between neuroscientists and psychologists, a perspective that would seem to presuppose that human behavior and thought are best understood as the product of material/biological conditions and the mechanical laws of nature that govern them. If one assumes this to be true about human nature, then it makes sense that the proper use of the scientific method is all that stands in the way of psychology being considered a legitimate natural science.

In the NO selection, Peter Rickman points out that psychology cannot be a science because unlike physics and chemistry it is not primarily concerned with observable or measurable facts. He argues that even attempts such as can be found in behaviorism are failed attempts at making human beings measurable objects. He states that instead of dealing with observable or measurable facts, psychology is always addressing meaningful and interpretive communication and relationships. He argues that because this is the case other alternative and nonscientific methodologies are better suited for fruitful investigation in psychology. He highlights one such methodological approach: hermeneutics. He argues that the focus on the individual (as opposed to the group) and the careful consideration of context and meaning present in the hermeneutic perspective will greatly benefit psychology as a discipline by helping psychologists to focus on human behavior as meaningful and creative. He then finishes by saying that both the physical sciences and the human sciences can benefit from borrowing the methods of the other.

For Rickman, psychology does not meet the criteria to be considered a natural science, nor should it. He argues that psychology (because of the nature of its subject matter) must rely on alternative methods and conceptual starting points. Indeed, he argues that by attending to a more hermeneutic approach, psychology's ability to shed light on the meaning of human action will be much improved. He believes that psychology does not need to be recognized as a science to be an influential discipline in the academic and practical world. His argument is directly related to the issue on human nature. He clearly illustrates his beliefs that humans cannot be adequately studied in the same way that the physical subject matter of the "hard" sciences is studied.

YES ←

Robert E. Silverman

Is Psychology a Science?

The American Psychological Association's spokespersons have a number of favorite phrases when they discuss psychology. They often refer to the "the basic science of psychology," or to the "scientific research" that helps to provide the foundations of the discipline. Somehow the term science has become linked to descriptions of what psychology's researchers and practitioners do. However, there are skeptics who wonder about the accuracy of these descriptions. Are they reasonable representations stemming from the time in 1879 when Wilhelm Wundt ushered psychology into the family of sciences in Leipzig? Or are they ways of paying lip service to the discipline's desire to appear scientific when in fact the field has a long way to go to achieve scientific status?

When Wundt, a physiologist by training, took the position that the centuries-long philosophical disputes about the nature of mind needed to be set aside and replaced by the approaches favored by the natural sciences, he asked: Why can't the study of mind be based on observation? Just as physics observes the events of the physical world, why shouldn't psychology observe the events of the mental world?[1]

These were good questions and the emphasis on observation was a positive step, but Wundt and his followers were handicapped by the methodology they chose to use and by their lack of appreciation of the whole of science. They were right about the importance of observation and could have moved mental science forward if they had not been stymied by their reliance on the technique of introspection, a form of disciplined, self-observation aimed at looking at mental activity. Such self-reports, even under the most stringently controlled conditions, did not have the kind of repeatability and reliability on which science depends. Moreover, while it is true that the scientific method relies on observation, more is involved. Knowledge is not advanced by the mere collection of facts. The facts have to be systematized and ordered in a way that helps to generate hypotheses (or questions) that can lead to more research. Although Wundt and his student E. B. Titchener (at Cornell University) were interested in analyzing mental experiences into their elemental components as well as in finding out how these elements combine, they did not have a well-ordered, systematic position in which their observations tended to produce hypotheses or call up new questions. Even if introspection provided data, they needed something more to give their findings the kind of structure that had the potential to lead to more knowledge.

While a number of researchers were turning their attention to the new mental science emerging from Wundt's laboratory and were acknowledging the view that objective observation had much to offer, there were scholars who preferred to work from a theoretical base. For them, mind was not merely a concept or a shorthand term for mental processes; it was the controller, the process that managed to organize the input from the outside. Just as Immanuel Kant argued in 1781 that the human mind imposes order on the sensations it receives, so did the triumvirate of Gestalt psychology, Max Wertheimer, Kurt Koffka, and Wolfgang Kohler take the position that the brain organizes incoming stimuli into wholes, or "gestalts."[2] With this preconception as their guide, they set out to find ways to demonstrate how the principle of organization affects perception. While they did perform something like experiments, the observations they sought to make were primarily designed to demonstrate the worth of their ideas. It was not science, but it did keep alive a viewpoint about what the mind does that would provide a basis for the development a few decades later of cognitive psychology.

During the first two decades of the 20th century, when the gestaltists were working around the edges of science and Wundtian laboratory work still had its adherents, William James was emerging as a major influence in American psychology. Here was another point of view about mental science, a position that underscored the mental aspect and downplayed the science features of this new discipline. Although his title at Harvard University was professor of psychology, James was a philosopher at heart and unwilling to give science a central or commanding role in the search for knowledge, especially knowledge of the mind. Moreover, James was unwilling to confine psychology to the laboratory, referring with distaste to the "brass-instrument" psychology that grew out of Wundt's approach. He was skeptical that science—any science—could deal with something as complex and in "constant flux" as consciousness.[3]

While James's influence was spreading in American academic circles, the quest to understand the mysteries of the mind continued in Europe and it extended beyond the research laboratories. It found its way into the clinical setting where, in 1895, Sigmund Freud set out to develop the elaborate theory of psychoanalysis.[4] Although Freud was a clinician, he had been well trained in the principles of scientific research and knew the value of observation. However, he also felt that standard observation would not suffice; he could not limit his inquiries to the kind of evidence appropriate for physics or chemistry, or for that matter to laboratory psychology. And, unlike Wundt, he did not focus on objectivity. Instead, he sought to find ways to analyze subjective material. To accomplish this goal, Freud made the therapy setting his laboratory by seeing to it that the situation was unstructured as possible. He encouraged his patients to say any and all things that came to mind without attempting to restrain or censor their thoughts. The reliance on this "free-association" technique, combined with his idea that dreams could also be very revealing, gave Freud the special tools he felt he needed.

The fact that the information provided by free association and dream interpretation was not constrained by the standards of observation used in natural science did not bother Freud. As he saw it, he was delving into the mysteries of the unconscious and he felt free to interpret this material rather than taking it at face value. If others would not accept this approach, that was their problem, not his.

Despite the voluminous outpouring of work from Freud, many scholars became convinced that psychoanalytic theory was not defensible science. Some simply called it bad science and others insisted it had no place within scientific inquiry, likening it to a kind of counterfeit science. These negative judgments also included psychoanalytic therapy, the form of treatment derived from the theory. The therapy still continues to be the focus of disputes and has failed to garner much objective support, but a recent report does offer some findings that seem to defend the "efficacy of psychodynamic therapy." However, studies designed to test or evaluate therapy are difficult to judge because of the problems inherent in measuring—or even estimating—the many possible outcomes of a treatment procedure. In the absence of hard data, statements that tell us, "For many people, psychodynamic therapy may foster inner resources and capabilities that allow richer, freer, and more fulfilling lives" do little to add to the body of knowledge relating to questions about psychology-based treatment techniques.[5] Phrases such as "inner resources," and "richer, freeing, and more fulfilling lives," indicate little about how such poetically-endowed events are to be assessed and possibly measured.

During the period from the late 1880s to the early 1920s, when the study of mind dominated psychology, questions continued to lurk about the role of science. Wundt's position about the need for observational methods had some influence, but the use of the scientific method and the investigation of mental processes still did not quite fit together. There were too many gaps between what to observe and how to do it. Moreover, concepts, especially those heavily laden with preconceptions about mind and mental processes, tended to put forward conclusions without factual support. However, around 1910 something new began to surface in the United States when questions started to be raised about whether psychology should focus exclusively on mental processes as such. Ironically, the possibility of some change in outlook arose from the writings of William James who, despite his interest in consciousness and mental activities, called attention to the fact that these processes ultimately affect how we behave. In other words, they have functional consequences, many of which are observable.

In 1913, emboldened by the awakening interest in behavior and helped by the research in conditioning by Ivan Pavlov[6] and the studies of learning conducted by E. L. Thorndike,[7] John B. Watson set out to overthrow mind-centered psychology. Watson insisted that the goal of the discipline should be the "prediction and control of behavior."[8] He wanted psychology to be a behavioral science, not the so-called science of mind. After all, both Pavlov and Thorndike had shown that the manipulation of stimuli and responses—even if the research had been done with animals—can be carried out in ways that show how behavior can be controlled and predicted.

Watson's bold pronouncements were not a function of his devotion to science. He was a promoter not a scientist, and although he set a movement in motion, he was more interested in shaking up the establishment than in conducting systematic inquiry himself. It remained for others to give life to this revolutionary approach to psychology. Such scientists as B. F. Skinner, Clark Hull, and E. C. Tolman entered the picture but it was Skinner's work which brought behaviorism to center stage in 1938 with the publication of *The Behavior of Organisms*.[9] This book, as well as the bulk of the research that followed, showed

Skinner to be a no-frills, hands-on researcher who believed that the gathering and organizing of data is fundamental to a science of psychology. Moreover, he emphasized Watson's central tenet that the science of psychology should focus on the prediction and control of behavior.

By the 1950s, however, mind-centered inquiry was still the defining feature of psychology and was gaining strength helped by the developments in information-processing technology. Behaviorism was still finding adherents. As might be expected, a rift developed between the scholars who sought to study mental processes and those who preferred to devote their attention to behavior. The differences in outlook also led to questions about the role science played for each group. Unsurprisingly, the behaviorists felt they had science on their side. Their research, much of which involved the study of learning, was objective and their findings verifiable. Furthermore, the data they gathered were quantifiable, amenable to display in graphic form, and could often stand on their own. However, those who focused on mental processes were not willing to concede the emphasis on science to the behav-iorists. They were sure that they could make effective use of the scientific method, insisting that theorizing was an integral part of science.

Both factions were, in some sense, correct. Neither group had a better grasp of science than the other but they used science in different ways. As behaviorism developed and morphed into what Skinner referred to as "the experimental analysis of behavior," it emphasized observation and with it the accumulation of data.[10] With this approach the facts were made to speak for themselves. Most behaviorally-oriented researchers were more concerned with finding out what is happening than in figuring out what could happen. By contrast, the psychologists who focused on mental activity had to make use of some form of speculation as they went about their searches. At the same time, they needed to be on guard about endowing the concepts that arose from their speculation with extra explanatory powers that were not amenable to objective verification.

Despite differences in outlook, the majority of scholars in each group were aware (without always openly expressing this awareness) that the process of observation defined their connection to science. What Albert Einstein and others referred to as "external validation" had to be the crucial ingredient, whether the emphasis was on gathering data or creating theories.[11] A body of data that leads to a set of generalizations or theoretical formulations must be challenged by subjecting it to tests in which the generalizations or the formulations can be disconfirmed. It is this testing and possible falsification that defines science,

and both behaviorism and mental science could—under some conditions—meet this criterion.

The growth of information-processing technology and a renewed interest in the study of memory combined to provide frameworks for systematizing the study of mental processes. Questions about mental function could now be approached from the vantage point of positing central processing systems that deal with the flow of information from outside the person to inside and to outside again. Models were available (or could be constructed) that might help to analyze how information gets in, how it is stored, and then how it is retrieved. In 1985, Howard Gardner, a prominent psychologist, went as far as to assert that "the computer also serves as the most viable model of how the human mind functions."[12] It is easy at this point to say he was wrong, but during the 1970s and 1980s computer modeling of mental function was useful, even if the models were only elaborate metaphors aimed at creating hypotheses and not really intended to represent actual events. And to some extent they served a purpose as was shown by the research they helped to stimulate when they raised questions about how mental operations might process, store and retrieve information. Although none of this research had the air of finality, some of it pointed the way toward issues that could later prove productive.

As stimulating as the information-processing models seemed to be, the research they helped to encourage was limited. The models were, in effect, too simple. The processing of information by the central nervous system is enormously more complex than any serial or even parallel-processing models is able to represent. Perhaps that was the reason that research dealing with mental processes (now beginning to be referred to as "cognitive science") began to make more extensive use of theoretical concepts. Ideas about the organizing properties of the brain and how language operates according to rules built into our mental systems made their way into the theories being developed within cognitive science.[13] It also became obvious—at least to some—that it was time to regard these ideas in terms of the data being brought to light by neuroscience. What were guesses or suppositions about mental functions might now be looked at in terms of the known features of the central nervous system. A good example of this approach, whereby cognitive science and neuroscience join forces, may be seen in Michael Gazzaniga's work in which he found that the left hemisphere of the brain seems to be involved in making sense of unclear or incomplete information and may be the locus of the kinds of organizing involved in categorizing and explaining (in other words, interpreting) the inputs we receive.[14]

Research such as Gazzinaga's and the many studies now emerging from the laboratories and clinics of neuroscientists are having a profound effect on cognitive science. The brain-imaging methods and the technology of electrode implanting have become increasingly precise to the point that questions about central processes—their locations, extent, interactions, and changes—are becoming answerable. For the first time it is also becoming feasible to turn speculations about neural events into direct observation of such events. As this happens, ideas about the nature of cognitions can be translated into actual targets of study that lend themselves to examination. However, it is still necessary to avoid endowing these conceptual depictions of cognitive activity with surplus meaning that can lead research astray. It should be obvious by now that one of the most vexing problems that intrudes so often into psychology is the discipline's continuing attempts to deal with the idea of mind and the many meanings and misconceptions that concept brings along with it.

Even as the dangers of mind's many meanings are still present and the temptations to invent ad hoc explanatory concepts lie in waiting, we can acknowledge that Wundt's original goal is becoming more reachable. It now appears that the increasing cooperation between neuroscience and psychology is leading toward the moment when psychologists and neuroscientists (as partners) should be able to observe mental events. As this begins to happen, there will be no further need to worry about the role of science in psychology.

References

1. Wundt, W. 1897. *Outlines of Psychology*. Leipzig: Engelmann.

2. Wertheimer, 1950. Gestalt Theory. In W. D. Ellis (Ed.) *A Source Book of Gestalt Psychology*. New York: Humanities Press.

3. James, William. 1890. *Principles of Psychology*. New York: Henry Holt.

4. Breuer, J. and S. Freud. 1895. *Studies in Hysteria*. Leipzig: Franz Deuticke.

5. Shedler, J. 2010. "The Efficacy of Psychoanalytic Therapy." *American Psychologist*. 65, 98–109.

6. Pavlov, I. P. 1927. *Conditioned Reflexes* (G. V. Anrep, trans.). London: Oxford University Press.

7. Thorndike, E. L. 1911. *Animal Intelligence*. New York: Macmillan.

8. Watson, John B. 1913. "Psychology As the Behaviorist Views It." *Psychological Review*. 20, 158-177.

9. Skinner, B. F. 1938. *The Behavior of Organisms: An Experimental Analysis*. New York: Appleton-Century-Crofts.

10. Skinner, B. F. 1953. *Science and Human Behavior*. New York: The Macmillan Company.

11. Holton, G. 1979. "Einstein's Model." *The American Scholar*. Summer, 309–338.

12. Gardner, H. 1985. *The Mind's New Science*. New York: Basic Books.

13. Chomsky. N. 1957. *Syntactic Structures*. The Hague: Mouton.

14. Gazzaniga, M. S. and J. E. LeDoux. 1978. *The Integrated Mind*. New York: Plenum. See also Gazzaniga, M. S. 2008. *Human: The Science behind What Makes Us Unique*. New York: Harper Collins.

ROBERT E. SILVERMAN is an academic psychologist, frequent contributor to *Skeptic Magazine*, and author of several widely used introductory textbooks in psychology.

Peter Rickman  **NO**

Is Psychology Science?

I was slightly taken aback when I heard a speaker at a psychology lecture meeting claiming confidently that psychology was a science. Of course, if we define science broadly, as the systematic search for knowledge, psychology would qualify for that label. But it is not terminology that is at issue here, but a matter of substantial importance.

When we talk of science, we primarily think of physical science. If a mother said that her son was studying science at Cambridge, would psychology come first to the listener's mind? The paradigm of the physical sciences is physics, because its elegant theories based on ample observation and experimentation provide clear explanations and reliable predictions. It also provides the foundations for the technologies which have transformed our lives. The man on the Clapham bus may not understand the laws of physics, but he happily relies on the means of transport based on those laws.

In consequence, the methods of physics become the model of scientific methodology. The different disciplines concerned with the study of humanity, such as psychology, sociology and anthropology, seem to fall woefully short of this. The concepts and theories of these disciplines are not consistently coordinated; and their application does not compare with that of physical sciences. While aeroplanes are pretty reliable, and millions of people enjoy television programmes, there are still too many divorces and mental breakdowns. Groups of violent youths still roam the city streets.

Unobservable Truths

Many students of the mind sought the remedy for their failures and their lack of public esteem in modelling the methods of psychology on the physical sciences. An extreme example of this is *behaviourism*. Why not focus on studying observable human behaviour, as you can study the movements of falling bodies and theorise on that evidence? After all, humans are behaving bodies. There are various flaws in this approach, and one of them is illustrated by a well-targeted joke. Two behaviourists spend a

night passionately making love. In the morning, one says to the other, "It was good for you. How was it for me?"

A proper starting point is to recognise the disciplines which study human nature as a distinct group which require, if not a complete alternative to the scientific method, at least some essential supplementary methodology.

The fact is that the bulk of the evidence given to the student of humanity on which to theorise, are not *observable facts*, but *communications*. These do not correspond to anything observable. In other words, what is in front of the psychologist are statements from interviews or completed questionnaires (eg, I am afraid of dying, I was abused in childhood, etc), responses to tests such as the Rorschach pictures, diaries, and the like. Similarly, sociologists use interviews, questionnaires and legal documents, while historians use biographies, letters, inscriptions on gravestones, eyewitness accounts of battles and revolutions and similar material. The same is true of other human studies such as social anthropology or politics.

All this is pretty obvious and non-controversial. It needs mentioning because of widespread error of taking what is communicated in this material as simple data whose meaning is transparent. What is thus ignored is the immense complexity of the process of communication. For instance, the question, as well as the answers, may be misunderstood, or respondents may be lying to please the questioner, motivated by pride or shame or simply by wanting to get rid of the questioner. A lady confessed to me that when canvassers of different parties come to the door at election time, she says to all of them, "Yes I shall vote for you," and closes the door. Or, if a stranger rings your doorbell and asks you how often you have sex, will you necessarily tell him the truth? Certainly, commercial companies have been the loser when trying to sell goods because of so many people trying to be liked when answering their questionnaires.

An anecdote I quoted in one of my books illustrates one type of miscommunication. An investigator was puzzled when a man in prison answered 'no' to the questionnaire query 'Were you ever in trouble with the police?' He went to see the man and asked: "How come you gave that answer? After all, you are serving a prison sentence." The man answered: "Oh, I thought you meant *trouble*."

A case of partial failure in understanding is the famous study of the Authoritarian Personality, which successfully demonstrated some personality traits of fascists. It was later shown that the characteristics pinpointed were not confined to fascists, but also shared by members of left-wing parties. Here the interpretation of the data was flawed by political naïvety.

It follows that the human studies cannot naïvely ape physical science. If they don't want to resign themselves to being woolly and merely anecdotal, they must therefore address themselves systematically to the complex problems of communication.

Hermes and Hermeneutics

There is an ancient discipline concerned with the interpretation of communications. In Ancient Greece, education focused on the study of literary texts. The theory and methodological approach for the understanding of such texts was called *hermeneutics*, after Hermes, the messenger of the gods. With the advent of Christianity, quarrels and schisms arose over the exact meaning of Biblical texts. To help settle these differences of opinion hermeneutics then became a branch of theology. This systematic textual interpretation continued throughout Antiquity and the Middle Ages up to modern times. Schleiermacher, philosopher, theologian and translator of Plato, was a professor of hermeneutics who widened the concept of this discipline. Not only texts but all other kinds of communication needed interpretation and could be subjected to this type of examination. Wilhelm Dilthey, a pupil of some of Schleiermacher's followers, systematically developed Schleiermacher's approach, demonstrating the vital contribution hermeneutics had to make to the human studies.

This is not the place for a full, systematic account of hermeneutics, but it is the place for drawing attention to some distinctive features of its methodology which are highly relevant. First, one needs to emphasise that unlike physical science, the focus of understanding in hermeneutics is not *classes* but *individuals*. Primarily, we aim to understand a poem, not poetry in general; a particular person, not the group to which he belongs. By contrast, in physics or chemistry, the example investigated is not of intrinsic interest. Once the experiment is finished, the contents of the test tube may be poured down the sink: they're only useful inasmuch as they help form general laws. Yet in the human studies, the individual thing studied—it may be a person, a family or a whole community—remains of

interest. The classic sociological study of 'Middletown' or the analyses of Sigmund Freud are examples.

Physical objects are substantially explained in terms of the class to which they belong. This is a diamond, this is a table, etc, and *they* behave in such-and-such ways. But such explanations of human beings—eg, she is a woman, he is a teenager, etc—are inadequate, and often rightly condemned as stereotyping. Instead, we tend to better understand individuals by placing them their context. A simple example concerns the way in which the correct meaning of a word is only specified by the sentence and general context in which it occurs. Terms such as "club" or "file" have several distinct definitions, and the meaning is determined only in the particular statement in which they occur. Similarly, a gesture like raising your hand might be understood as a greeting, a threat, or otherwise, according to other aspects of the circumstances which accompany the act.

Each meaningful expression is a crossing point of contexts. Take, for example, the John Donne poem 'The Sun Rising':

> Busy old fool, unruly Sun,
> Why dost thou thus,
> Through windows, and through curtains, call on us?
> Must to thy motions lovers' seasons run?
> Saucy pedantic wretch, go chide
> Late school-boys and sour prentices,
> Go tell court-huntsmen that the king will ride,
> Call country ants to harvest offices;
> Love, all alike, no season knows nor clime,
> Nor hours, days, months, which are the rags of time.

Its grammar and vocabulary is obviously one of its contexts; but the context is also the history of the sonnets, Donne's personality, and the conditions and conventions of his age. To understand the poem with insight—though on one level it appears to be immediately accessible—we have to trace the different contexts as far as is fruitful and practicable.

Different Types of Disciplines

Because of the distinct methodologies involved, the distinction between the two groups of disciplines, the physical sciences and the human studies, is both necessary and justified. Of course, there are features common to both groups. Such processes as checking data, forming and testing hypotheses and the like, are required for all systematic research. Some of the methods of the physical sciences are also required in the social studies. The authenticity of manuscripts may need to be chemically tested, vital statistics analysed, and the like. Typical methods of the human studies are also not wholly absent from the physical sciences. For example, in astronomy, the movements of planets may be explained with reference to their contexts, such as their relation to other planets or against the background of the stars.

It remains true, however, that a human study such as psychology is not a science in the same sense as physics, because whatever it shares with the scientific method, it also receives essential support from the methods of hermeneutics. Faced with communications, we need to establish the background, likely knowledge and personal motives of the communicator.

PETER RICKMAN, deceased, was professor of philosophy at City University in London, England, and the author of numerous books on the nature of philosophy, literature, and critical reasoning.

EXPLORING THE ISSUE

Is Psychology a Science?

Critical Thinking and Reflection

1. What are possible implications for the discipline of psychology if it is considered a science like physics or chemistry? What if it is not considered to be a natural science?
2. In the No selection, Peter Rickman offers hermeneutics as a perspective that may benefit psychology. What are other possible disciplines or approaches to intellectual inquiry that may provide beneficial methods for psychology?
3. In the Yes selection, Robert Silverman briefly outlines the history of psychology as a discipline. In his description, it is evident that in its history many different schools of thought formed in psychology. Can psychology even be considered a single discipline? Are certain forms or approaches to psychology more scientific than others? Should those that are less scientific still be considered psychology?
4. What are the implications for human beings if psychology is considered a physical science? Does considering psychology from a humanities or other perspective change these implications?

Is There Common Ground?

The debate over the role of science in psychology is perhaps more philosophical and theoretical than most psychologists care to admit. It brings into question not only the assumptions of methodology but also basic (ontological) assumptions about subject matter (i.e., the nature of human nature). The breadth of the debate raises the question as to whether there is in fact one answer to the question. Must all of psychology be committed to the scientific method, and its focus on measurement, prediction, and control, or is there enough intellectual flexibility to allow science to be integral while still drawing on the insights and methods of other disciplines and traditions?

Any common ground that may exist between the two sides will likely be found in the flexibility of methodology. This is because if psychology were to be considered fully scientific, only scientific methods would be considered viable. Conversely, the "psychology cannot be a science" camp rests their argument on the assumption that human beings are fundamentally different than the purely physical objects, and, therefore, cannot be studied in the same way or by the same methods. Both camps, however, could come together and allow that human behavior could

be profitably studied from a variety of methodologies, some scientific and others coming from other disciplines. Clearly, advocates in both camps are equally committed to better understanding of human beings, as well as to using knowledge for the betterment of human life.

Additional Resources

Dooley, P. K. (1977). The structure of a science of psychology: William James and B. F. Skinner. *Philosophy in Context, 6,* 54–69. Retrieved from http://search.proquest.com/docview/42620100?accountid=4488

Skrupskelis, I. K. (1995). James's conception of psychology as a natural science. *History of the Human Sciences, 8*(1), 73–90. Retrieved from http://search.proquest.com/docview/42814933?accountid=4488

Williams, A. (2010). The importance of distinguishing between the theoretical attitude and the natural scientific attitude in the discipline of psychology. *Studia Phaenomenologica: Romanian Journal of Phenomenology, 10,* 235–250. Retrieved from http://search.proquest.com/docview/878587381?accountid=4488

Internet References . . .

Is Psychology a Science?

www.arachnoid.com/psychology/

Scientific American

http://blogs.scientificamerican.com/the-curious
-wavefunction/2013/08/13/is-psychology-a-real
-science-does-it-really-matter/

Simply Psychology

http://www.simplypsychology.org/science
-psychology.html

Psych Your Mind

http://psych-your-mind.blogspot.com/2013/08/the
-psychology-of-psychology-isnt.html#more

Science 2.0

http://www.science20.com/science_20/biologist
_and_psychologist_square_over_definition
_science-92172

Unit 3

UNIT

Development Issues

*T*he objective of most developmental psychologists is to document the course of physical, social, and cognitive changes over the entire span of our lives. But what has the greatest influence on human development? Some have said that today's youth have been raised with such material affluence and parental indulgence that they have learned to become self-centered rather than other-centered. Is that true? Moreover, the amount of time spent online has led some psychological researchers to be curious about the effect of digital social connections, such as online friendships, on development. How are these online friendships affecting today's youth? Are they different from the youth of a generation ago?

Selected, Edited, and with Issue Framing Material by:
Edwin E. Gantt, *Brigham Young University*

ISSUE

Are Violent Video Games Harmful to Children and Adolescents?

YES: Steven F. Gruel, from "Brief of *Amicus Curiae* in Case of *Brown v. Entertainment Merchants Association*," *U.S. Supreme Court* (2010)

NO: Patricia A. Millett, from "Brief of *Amici Curiae* in Case of *Brown v. Entertainment Merchants Association*," *U.S. Supreme Court* (2010)

Learning Outcomes

After reading this issue, you will be able to:

- Discuss and critically evaluate the arguments about the strength of scientific evidence that either supports or discredits the relationship between playing violent video games and engaging in aggressive behavior among youth.
- Understand the ways in which playing video games can influence neurological structure and functioning.
- Evaluate the extent to which playing violent video games by young people can lead to academic problems.
- Compare the rationale used by the government to regulate other media such as television and radio and the arguments made for and against the regulation of violent video game sales to children.
- Consider the similarities and differences between passively watching a violent movie and actively participating in a violent video game.

ISSUE SUMMARY

YES: Prosecutor Steven F. Gruel, in arguing before the Supreme Court, cites what he says is an overwhelming amount of research support to conclude that viewing violence causes children to act more violently.

NO: Defense attorney Patricia A. Millett argues before the Supreme Court that psychological research about the effects of media violence on children is inconclusive, with these researchers making claims about causation that cannot be substantiated.

With the introduction of any new media—film, television, Internet—its dangers and benefits are inevitably debated. Video games, the newest such technology, are no exception. Advances in video game graphics, as well as an increasing mass-market appeal, have resulted in larger numbers of gamers and more lifelike depictions of simulated violence. These large numbers and lifelike depictions have led, in turn, to some parents and policymakers raising concerns about the potential for real-life violence, what some have called "murder simulators." These concerns seemed to come to a head, at least legally, when a California law that would ban the sale of violent video games to minors was recently proposed.

The possibility of legal restrictions mobilized video game enthusiasts and free-speech supporters. They bristled at not only the restrictions but also the implication that video games controlled their actions. When the California law came before the U.S. Supreme Court, psychological research was called upon to help decide the issue. Both sides seemed to focus on neuroscience research, which some consider a specialty of psychology, as ammunition for their arguments. Eventually the Court ruled the law unconstitutional on the grounds that it limited free speech. However, the battle over the ultimate effects of media violence continues.

In the YES selection Steven F. Gruel probably represents those who consider video games a danger. A former federal prosecutor and lead legal counsel for the case before the Supreme Court, Gruel claims that neuroscience research indicates that playing video games increases violent behavior, and thus presents a clear risk to the nation's youth. He believes that a general conclusion from the scientific literature "can be drawn without any reasonable doubt": video game use is a "causal risk factor" resulting in several negative outcomes, including physically aggressive behavior, lowered school performance, loss of "proactive

control" to inhibit impulsive actions, damaged higher level thinking, and decreased emotional control. From Gruel's perspective, "the scientific debate about whether exposure to media violence causes increases in aggressive behavior is over."

In the NO selection, however, Patricia A. Millett, counsel of record for opponents to the California law, argues that this debate is *not* over. She says that the conclusion of the opposition "is based on profoundly flawed research." Millett rejects this research on the basis of its methodological limitations, noting that it not only fails to show causation but also is suspect even as a correlation. She criticizes the research for relying on "proxies for aggression that do not correlate with aggressive behavior in the real world." Millett argues that whatever correlations may or may not be in play between video game use and violent behavior, there are other, more relevant variables that confound the research, such as family violence at home, antisocial personality tendencies, and the influence of peers.

POINT

- The scientific community has come to an overwhelming consensus about the effects of violent video games on children.

- Studies show that exposure to simulated violence increases aggression in children.

- Numerous studies show a significant correlation between viewing and then performing aggressive acts.

- Neuroscience research shows that playing violent video games rewires the brain for later physical violence.

COUNTERPOINT

- No such consensus exists, and there is much research arguing that there is no negative effect of violent video games on children's behavior.

- Previous studies have used poor definitions of aggression, which do not correlate with real-world behavior.

- Correlation can never be causation, which means that other factors can account for violent behavior, such as violence at home.

- Neuroscience studies describe changes in the brain, but cannot adequately address the causes of those changes.

YES

Steven F. Gruel

Brief of *Amicus Curiae* in Case of *Brown v. Entertainment Merchants Association*

I. Science Confirms That Violent Video Games Are Harmful to Minors Allowing the State Clear Justification in Regulating Children's Access to These Materials

. . .

1. A Minor's Exposure to Violent Video Games—More Time Spent Playing Games With Increasing Graphic Violence

A minor's exposure to the avalance of violent video games is staggering. Video games first emerged in the 1970s, but it was during the 1990s that violent games truly came of age. In 1992, *Wolfenstein 3D*, the first major "first-person shooter" game was released. In a first-person shooter, one "sees" the video game world through the eyes of the player, rather than seeing it as if looking on from afar. The player is the one fighting, killing, and being killed. Video game historian Steven Kent noted that "part of *Wolfenstein 3D* popularity sprang from its shock value. In *Wolfenstein 3D*, enemies fell and bled on the floor."

With ever changing advancements in technology, the dramatic increases in speed and graphic capability have resulted in more realistic violence. As an example, in the video game *Soldier of Fortune*, the player/shooter can wound an enemy causing exposed bone and sinew.

As the video games became more graphically violent, the average time children played these games continued to climb. In the book, *Violent Video Game Effects on Children and Adolescents*, the authors note that in the early 1990s, boys averaged 4 hours a week and girls 2 hours a week playing video games. In a few years these averages jumped to 7.1 and 4.5, respectively. In a recent survey of over 600 eighth and ninth-grade students, children averaged 9 hours per week with boys averaging 13 hours per week and girls averaging 5 hours per week.

In 1993, United States Senators Joseph Lieberman and Herbert Kohl noticed the increasing violence in video games and held hearings to examine the issue. Although there was much less research on the effects of violent video games, the senators put pressure on the video game industry to create a rating system. The goal of the rating system was to provide information to parents about the content of games so that they could make informed decisions about which games their children could play. However, these industry "voluntary" labels rating video games are inherently flawed and have failed due to "invalid assumptions about what is safe versus harmful."

In 2003, more than 239 million computer and video games were sold in the United States; that is almost two games for every household in the United States. More than 90% of all U.S. children and adolescents play video games. The National Youth Violence Prevention Resource Center has stated that a 2001 review of the 70 top-selling video games found 49% contained serious violence. In 41% of the games, violence was necessary for the protagonists to achieve their goals. There is no doubt, violent video games are among the most popular entertainment products for teens and adolescents, especially for boys.

New generation violent video games contain substantial amounts of increasingly realistic portrayals of violence. Elaborate content analyses revealed that the favored narrative is a "human perpetrator engaging in repeated acts of justified violence involving weapons that results in some bloodshed to the victim."

2. Scientific Studies Confirm that Violent Video Games Have Harmful Effects Minors

In a nutshell, teens and adolescents play video games frequently, and a significant portion of the games contain increasingly realistic portrayals of violence. Viewing violence increases aggression and greater exposure to media violence is strongly linked to increases in aggression.

Playing a lot of violent games is unlikely to turn a normal youth with zero, one or even two other risk factors into a killer. But regardless of how many other risk factors are present in a youth's life, playing a lot of violent games is likely to increase the frequency and the seriousness of his or her physical aggression, both in the short term and over time as the youth grows up. These long-term effects are a consequence of powerful observational learning and desensitization processes that neuroscientists and psychologists now understand to occur automatically in the human child. Simply stated, "adolescents who expose themselves to greater amounts of video game violence were more hostile, reported getting into arguments with teachers more frequently, were more likely to be involved in physical fights, and performed more poorly in school.

In a recent book, researchers once again concluded that the "active participation" in all aspects of violence: decision-making and carrying out the violent act, result in a greater effect from violent video games than a violent movie. Unlike a passive observer in movie watching, in first-person shooter and third-person shooter games, you're the one who decides whether to pull the trigger or not and whether to kill or not. After conducting three very different kinds of studies (experimental, a cross-sectional correlational study, and a longitudinal study) the results confirmed that violent games contribute to violent behavior.

The relationship between media violence and real-life aggression is nearly as strong as the impact of cigarette smoking and lung cancer: not everyone who smokes will get lung cancer, and not everyone who views media violence will become aggressive themselves. However, the connection is significant.

In an upcoming publication concerning children and violent video games, three complementary theoretical perspectives are discussed when contemplating the effects of playing video games. The *General Aggression Model* and its offshoot the *General Learning Model* describe the basic learning processes and effects involved in both short-term and long-term effects of playing various types of games. The *Five Dimensions of Video Game Effects* perspective describes different aspects of video games and video game play that influence the specific effects likely to occur. The *Risk and Resilience* perspective describes the effects of video game play—prosocial, antisocial, and other—take place within a complex set of social and biological factors, each of which contribute[s] to development of the individual's thoughts, feelings, and behaviors.

The main findings can be succinctly summarized: playing violent video games causes an increase in the likelihood of physically aggressive behavior, aggressive thinking, aggressive affect, physiological arousal, and desensitization/low empathy. It also decreases helpful or prosocial behavior. With the exception of physiological arousal (for which there are no cross-sectional or longitudinal studies), all of the outcome variables showed the same effects in experimental, cross-sectional, and longitudinal studies. The main effects occurred for both males and females, for participants from low-violence collectivistic type Eastern countries (*e.g.*, Japan), and from high-violence individualistic type Western countries (*e.g.*, USA, Europe).

Research also indicates that the aggression carried out by video game characters is usually portrayed as justified, retributional, necessary to complete the game, rewarded and followed by unrealistic consequences. The overall level and realism of violent depictions, use of guns and likelihood of being killed by a gun has risen substantially over time; additionally, female victims and police officer victims rose significantly across time.

Many researchers have begun studying the concept of video game "addiction" and most researchers studying the pathological use of computer or video games have defined it similarly to how pathological gambling is defined—based on damage to family, social, school, occupational, and psychological functioning. The pace of studies has increased greatly in the past decade. In 2007, the American Medical Association released a report on the "addictive potential" of video games. The report concluded with a recommendation that the "AMA strongly encourage the consideration and inclusion of 'Internet/video game addiction' as a formal diagnostic disorder in the upcoming revision of the *Diagnostic and Statistical Manual of Mental Disorders*-IV."

The most comprehensive study to date in the US used a national sample of over 1,100 youth aged 8 to 18, in which 8.5% of video game players were classified as pathological demonstrates that it is not a trivial number of people who are suffering damage to their lives because of their game play.

School Performance

Several studies have documented a negative relation between amount of time playing video games and school performance among children, adolescents, and college students. The displacement hypothesis, that games displace time on other activities, is the most typical explanation for this relation. It could be argued, however, that the relation might be due to the children themselves, rather than to game time. It is highly likely that children who perform more poorly at school are likely to spend more time playing games, where they may feel a sense of mastery that eludes them at school. Nevertheless, each hour a child spends playing entertainment games (in contrast to educational games, which have been demonstrated to have educational benefits) is an hour not spent on homework, reading, exploring, creating, or other things that might have more educational benefit. Some evidence has been found to support the displacement hypothesis. In one nationally representative US sample of 1,491 youth between 10 and 19, gamers spent 30% less time reading and 34% less time doing homework. Therefore, even if poor school performance tends to cause increases in time playing video games, large amounts of video game play are likely to further hurt their school performance.

In short, the recent explosion in research on video game effects has greatly improved our understanding of how this medium affects its consumers. Several conclusions can be drawn without any reasonable doubt. First, there are many different effects of playing video games on the player. Some of these are short term, whereas others are long term. Second, the specific effects depend on a host of factors, including the content, structure, and context of the game. Third, the same game can have multiple effects on the same person, some of which may be generally beneficial whereas others may be detrimental. Fourth, playing violent video games is a causal risk factor for a host of detrimental effects in both the short and the long term[s], including increasing the likelihood of physically aggressive behavior.

Negative Effects on the Brain

Studies have shown evidence that exposure to violent video games reduces the player's use of some brain areas involved in higher order thought and impulse control.

In addition to behavioral–psychological theories explaining the relationship between media violence exposure and aggressive behavior, recently attention has turned to neuro-psychological theories. These theories attempt to identify areas of brain functioning that may be affected by media violence exposure and that may underlie aggressive behavior.

As recently as June 2010, another study of violent video game effects on frontal lobe activity was published wherein it was concluded that playing a violent video game for only 30 minutes immediately produced lower activity levels (compared to a nonviolent video game) in prefrontal regions thought to be involved in cognitive inhibition. This study shows that playing a violent video game for 30 minutes causes a decrease in brain activity in a region of the frontal lobe that is known to be important in the ability to inhibit impulsive behavior. The study also suggested that . . . violent games may also impair emotional functioning when it noted that "an impaired role of DLPFC (dorsolateral prefrontal cortex) in inhibition, therefore, may yield impaired emotional functioning following violent video game play."

Other studies of the neurological underpinnings of aggressive behavior, for example, indicate that a neural circuit that includes parts of the frontal cortex, amygdale, and temporal lobes is important in emotional regulation and violence. Research strongly suggests an underactivity of brain inhibitory mechanisms in the frontal cortex and striatum, coupled with hyperarousal of the amygdala and temporal lobe regions, is responsible for chronic, explosive, and/or severe aggressive behavior.

Research clearly indicates that areas in the frontal lobe and amygdale may be activated by viewing violent television and playing violent video games.

With the use of functional magnetic resonance imaging (fMRI), research has shown a direct alteration in brain functioning from exposure to media violence. Researchers found that teenagers who played a violent videogame exhibited increased activity in a part of the brain that governs emotional arousal and the same teenagers showed decreased activity in the parts of the brain involved in focus, inhibition, and concentration.

Youth who play a lot of violent video games (but who have not been diagnosed with a behavioral disorder) show a similar pattern of brain activity when doing complex executive control tasks as youth who have been diagnosed with some type of aggression-related behavior disorder. This pattern is very different from control-group youth who do not play a lot of violent games (and who have not been diagnosed with a behavioral disorder).

Youth who play a lot of violent video games show a deficit in a specific type of executive control known as proactive control. Proactive control is seen as necessary to inhibit impulsive reactions. This difference shows up in the brain wave patterns as well as in behavioral reactions.

Additionally, video game violence exposure and aggressive behavior to brain processes have been linked reflecting a desensitization in the aversive motivational system. Repeated exposure to media violence reduces its psychological impact and eventually produced aggressive approach-related motivational states theoretically leading to a stable increase in aggression.

Finally, in a functional magnetic resonance imaging study on players of the first-shooter game *Tactical Ops: Assault on Terror*, the violent portions of a video game activated the regions in the brain known to be active in fight-or-flight situations. In other words, the brain reacted to the fictional violence of a video game in much the same way as it reacts to real violence.

In short, neuroscience research supports a critical link between perpetration of virtual violence with reduced activation of a neural mechanism known to be important for self-control and for evaluation of affect. These findings strongly suggest that focusing on the activity of prefrontal cortical structures important for executive control could provide important mediational links in the relationship between exposure to violent media and increased aggression.

3. Recent Studies and Researchers Continue to Find Harmful Effects To Minors From Playing Violent Video Games

In March 2010, leading researchers in the area of media violence from the United States and Japan worked together to conduct a meta-analytic procedure testing the effects of violent games on aggressive behavior, aggressive cognition, aggressive affect, physiological arousal, empathy/desensitization, and prosocial behavior. In conducting their meta-analysis on the effects of video game violence, these researchers retrieved over 130 research reports which entailed scientific tests on over 130,000 participants. This study has been described as "probably about as exhaustive a sampling of the pre-2009 research literature as one could obtain and far more than that used in any other review of violent video game effects."

This extensive meta-analysis of the effects of violent video games confirms what many theories predicted and what prior research about other violent mass media found: that violent video games stimulate aggression in the players in the short run and increase the risk for aggression behaviors by the players later in life. The effects occur for males and females and for children growing up in Eastern and Western cultures. Also, the effects were stronger for more violent than less violent outcomes.

From their overarching analysis, these researchers concluded that the scientific debate should move beyond the simple question whether violent video game play is a causal risk factor for behavior because: "scientific literature has effectively and clearly shown the answer to be 'yes.'"

Regardless of research method (experimental, correlational, or longitudinal) and regardless of cultures tested (East and West) the same effects are proven: exposure to violent video games is a causal risk factor for aggressive thoughts and behavior, and decreased empathy and prosocial behavior in youths. In fact, Dr. Anderson, one of three 2010 American Psychological Association Distinguished Scientist Lecturers, has stated that this recent meta-analysis on violent video games may be his last because of its "definitive findings."

4. The Shortcomings of Purported "Research" Contesting the Scientific Studies Showing the Harmful Effects to Minors Playing Violent Video Games

The Video Software Dealers Association and the Entertainment Software Association will likely contest the science showing the harmful effects of violent video games on minors. Apart from the self-serving motive for such opposition, one need only consider a professional organization that clearly does not doubt the serious aggression-teaching abilities of violent video games—the United States Department of Defense. Both the U.S. Army and U.S. Marines have their own video games used to train soldiers as tactical "first-person shooters" leading teams in "close-quarters urban combat." Many of these military combat training videos, such as *Full Spectrum Warrior* and *First To Fight* have been adapted and placed on the commercial market for minors to play.

Also, alleged "scientific" studies may be suggested by Respondents to argue that there are no harmful effects from violent video game playing. These "findings" can be explained by small sample size, poor test conditions, and chance. The simple response to these studies is the recent and clear findings of the meta-analysis comprising 130 studies of the effects of violent video games showing the like between violent video games and aggression.

II. Conclusion

The scientific debate about whether exposure to media violence causes increases in aggressive behavior is over. All major types of research methodologies have been used, including experiments, cross-sectional correlational studies, longitudinal studies, intervention studies, and meta-analyses. For each category exposure to media violence was significantly associated with increased aggressions or violence. Likewise, the harmful effects on minors from playing violent video games are documented and not seriously contested.

Much research over several decades documents how witnessing violence and aggression leads to a range of negative outcomes for children. Negative outcomes result both from witnessing real violence [and] from viewing media violence. The most recent comprehensive review of the media violence literature documents the "... unequivocal evidence that media violence increases the likelihood of aggressive and violent behavior in both immediate and long-term contexts."

In the end, we need only to circle back from this rising ocean of research and return to simple commonsense.

Society has a direct, rational, and compelling reason in marginally restricting a minor's access to violent video games. . . .

STEVEN F. GRUEL is a practicing criminal defense attorney and former federal prosecutor with over 25 years of experience. Voted California's top "SuperLawyer" for three consecutive years, he was previously the chief of the Major Crimes Section in the U.S. Attorney's office. He has received a law degree from the University of Wisconsin Law School.

Patricia A. Millett

Brief of *Amici Curiae* in Case of *Brown v. Entertainment Merchants Association*

Introduction and Summary of Argument

As respondents explain, California's ban on the sale and rental of certain video games to minors is subject to strict scrutiny because it directly regulates video games based on the content of a game, i.e., whether the game is deemed "violent." California asserts that its law is necessary to "prevent[] psychological or neurological harm to minors who play violent video games." Under strict scrutiny, California must both provide "substantial evidence" that the video games it regulates cause psychological or neurological harm to minors who play them, and demonstrate that the restriction will "alleviate these harms in a direct and material way."

California has done neither. Indeed, California does not offer any reliable evidence, let alone substantial evidence, that playing violent video games causes psychological or neurological harm to minors. California confesses it cannot prove causation, but points to studies that it says show a "correlation" between the two. But the evidence does not even do that.

California and Senator Yee also cite studies that purport to show a link between the playing of violent video games and violent, aggressive, and antisocial behavior by minors. But in the court of appeals, California expressly disclaimed any interest in regulating video games sales and rentals to minors to prevent such conduct, and therefore these studies are waived because the argument was waived. The studies are of no help to California in any event because they document neither a causal connection nor a correlation between the playing of violent video games and violent, aggressive, or antisocial behavior.

Indeed, whether attempting to link violent video games with psychological and neurological harm or with violent, aggressive, and antisocial behavior, all of the studies that California and Senator Yee cite suffer from inherent and fundamental methodological flaws.

- The survey of aggressive behavior. The courts below carefully considered this survey and correctly discredited it because the questions it posed are simply not valid indicators for actual violent or aggressive behavior and because it fails to account or control for other variables that have been proven to affect the behavior of minors.

- The laboratory experimental study of aggression. This study, too, was rightly discounted by the courts below because it relies on proxies for aggression that do not correlate with aggressive behavior in the real world.

- The "meta-analysis" of video game violence research. A meta-analysis combines the results of many other studies on a particular subject. But the accuracy and utility of any meta-analysis depends on the quality of the underlying studies themselves. Put another way a meta-analysis of scientifically unreliable studies cannot cure the studies' flaws. Here, the meta-analysis on which Senator Yee relies was compromised because it was based on studies that used invalid measures of aggression.

- "Longitudinal" studies of aggression. A longitudinal study analyzes participants on many occasions over an extended period. The studies that Senator Yee cites are not longitudinal because they observed participants on only a few occasions and over just a short period of time. Additionally, those studies both failed to account for other variables that may explain aggressive behavior and used invalid measures of aggression.

- Neuroscience studies. These studies supposedly show a connection between playing violent video games and altered brain activity. The courts below properly concluded that they do not. Further, the neuroscience studies are rooted in fundamentally flawed statistical methodologies and do not address the cause of brain activation and deactivation in children.

Methodological flaws are only the beginning of the studies' problems. Both California and Senator Yee repeatedly exaggerate the statistical significance of the studies' findings, failing to inform the Court of express disclaimers and cautionary statements in the studies about the nature of their findings.

Finally, California and Senator Yee ignore a weighty body of scholarship, undertaken with established and reliable scientific methodologies, debunking the claim that the video games California seeks to regulate have harmful effects on minors.

Argument

I. California's Asserted Interest in Preventing Psychological and Neurological Harm to Minors Is Not Supported by Any Reliable, Let Alone, Substantial Evidence

A. California's Studies Do Not Show a Causal Link, or Even a Correlation, Between Playing Violent Video Games and Psychological or Neurological Harm to Minors

California's ban on the sale and rental of violent video games to minors rests on the same flawed studies that court after court has rejected.

The courts were right to reject these studies because they do not even establish the "correlation" between violent video games and psychological harm to minors that California says exists, let alone the causation of harm that, as respondent explains, the First Amendment requires. Nor do the studies show a connection between playing violent video games and violent or aggressive behavior of minors, which explains why California disclaimed that interest below.

First, California points to a 2004 study by Douglas Gentile of approximately 600 eighth and ninth-grade students. These students completed surveys that asked questions about the types of video games they preferred and how "violent" they were. (The survey did not provide any definition of "violent.") The survey also recorded how often the students played the games; the students' hostility level; how often they had argued with teachers during the past year; their average grades; and whether they had been in a physical fight in the past year. From the survey answers, Gentile concluded that "[a]dolescents who expose themselves to greater amounts of video game violence" were more hostile and reported getting into more arguments with teachers and physical fights and performing poorly in school.

Although California relies heavily on the Gentile survey, it has absolutely no relevance here. The survey examines only the purported connection between video game violence and "aggressive behavior" or "physical aggression" towards third parties. It does not study, and says nothing about, the psychological or neurological

harm allegedly caused to those who play violent video games, which is the only interest that California defended below and thus is the only interest that is properly before this Court.

Even if the Gentile survey were relevant, it simply does not say what California says it does. California states that the survey "suggest[s] a causal connection between playing violent video games and aggressive behavior." It does no such thing. The survey makes absolutely no finding that exposure to violent video games leads to physical aggression. To the contrary, it explicitly cautions against making that inference: "It is important to note . . . that this study is limited by its correlational nature. Inferences about causal direction should be viewed with caution." ("Are young adolescents more hostile and aggressive because they expose themselves to media violence, or do previously hostile adolescents prefer violent media? Due to the correlational nature of this study, we cannot answer this question directly.").

Beyond that, the Gentile survey is rife with methodological flaws that undermine even the suggested correlation. For example, the measures of "aggressive behavior" that Gentile employed are highly suspect. Having an argument with a teacher—without any further exploration into the nature of the event—does not even suggest violent or aggressive behavior. And simply asking students whether they had been in a fight—again, without any further analysis of the event—is not a valid indicator for violent or aggressive behavior.

Additionally, there are many factors that may influence youth violence or aggressive behavior, including: family violence, antisocial personality traits, and association with delinquent peers. . . . Because Gentile's survey failed to control for, or even consider, those other variables, its conclusion that there is a correlation between video games and hostility to third parties lacks scientific grounding. In fact, controlling for gender alone removes most of the variance from which Gentile finds a correlation. In other words, the correlation Gentile claims to find is equally explainable by the effect of gender: boys tend to play more violent video games and tend to be more aggressive.

Second, California points to a 2004 study of 130 college students by Craig Anderson. That study measured the blood pressure of students before, during, and after playing selected video games and had students take a "word completion" test after playing selected video games. Based on the resulting measurements, Anderson concluded that the students' blood pressure increased while playing certain video games he labeled "violent" and that game play "increase[d] . . . the accessibility of aggressive thoughts."

The Anderson study is no help to California, because it does not show that a rise in students' blood pressure has any relationship to whether violent video games cause psychological or neurological harm. Nor does California show how "aggressive thoughts" leads to psychological harm.

Laboratory experiments, like Anderson's, that measure aggression immediately following the playing of a video game are common in the field of media effects research. And like Anderson's, these experiments rely on proxies for real aggressive or violent behavior, such as the participants' willingness to administer blasts of white noise against an unseen (and non-existent opponent). The problem is that the proxies bear no relationship to whether someone is going to act aggressively or violently in the real world. Similarly giving participants words with blank spaces and evaluating whether they make "aggressive" or "non-aggressive" words with the letters they fill in (i.e., "explo_e" could be completed as "explore" or "explode"), as Anderson did in his experiment, has no known validity for measuring aggressive behavior (or even aggressive thinking).

Third, California points to a 2004 study of fourth and fifth grade students by Jeanne Funk, and claims it "found that playing violent video games was correlated with lower empathy as well as stronger pro-violence attitudes." But the Funk study specifically disclaimed any proof of causality. As Funk admitted, the children in her study whose scores indicated lower empathy or stronger pro-violence attitudes may simply have been drawn to violent video games. Moreover, the small sample size—just 150 children—and the failure to control for or consider any other variables undermine even the study's tentative conclusion of a correlation between violent video games and pro-violence attitudes. . . .

B. California and Senator Yee Ignore the Large Body of Empirical Evidence That Shows No Causal Connection, or Even a Correlation, Between Violent Video Games and Harm to Minors

California and Senator Yee ignore a wealth of recent empirical evidence disabusing the notion that violent video games are harmful to minors. Here is just a snapshot of that body of scholarship:

- A study of 603 Hispanic youths (ages ten to fourteen), recently published in The Journal of Pediatrics, examined various risk factors for youth violence, including video game violence, delinquent peer association, family conflict, depression, and others. The children listed television shows and video games and rated how often they viewed or played the media—a reliable and valid method of evaluating violent media exposure. The children were then evaluated using the Child Behavior Checklist, a well-researched and well-validated tool for measuring behavioral problems in children and adolescents. A statistical analysis of the results revealed that exposure to video games had a negligible effect size and was not predictive of youth violence and aggression.

- A study of 1,254 seventh and eighth-grade students examined the influence of exposure to violent video games on delinquency and bullying behavior. The Entertainment Software Ratings Board ratings were employed as a standardized measure of participants' exposure to violence in video games. The study applied a multivariate statistical method that considered other factors that might be predictive of aggressive behavior (such as level of parental involvement, support from others, and stress). This study did not use abstract measures of aggression, but instead focused on specific negative behaviors such as delinquency and bullying. A statistical analysis revealed insignificant effect sizes between exposure to violent video games and delinquency or bullying. The authors accordingly concluded that exposure to such games was not predictive of delinquency or bullying.

- A study of 213 participants examined the influence of violent video game play on aggressive behavior. The 213 participants were divided into a 75-person treatment group that played a single game, Asheron's Call 2, a type of "massively multi-player online role-playing game" that is "highly violent" and has "a sustained pattern of violence," for at least five hours over a one-month period, and a 138-person control group that did not play the game. Participants then completed self-reported questionnaires that included a range of demographic, behavioral, and personality variables. Aggression-related beliefs were measured according to the Normative Beliefs in Aggression general scale, a well-validated scale for measuring beliefs about the acceptability of aggression, and aggressive social interactions were measured using specific behavioral questions. Both measurement techniques had been successfully used in previous studies of violent television and video game effects. The results of this study found no effects associated with aggression caused by playing violent video games.

These studies are just the tip of the iceberg. They rate barely a mention in Senator Yee's brief, which disparages them as "alleged 'scientific studies'" that involved "small sample size, poor test conditions and chance." That is wrong. The studies employed large sample sizes, long-standing and validated measures of aggression, and superior statistical controls. Ironically, the studies also include the work of researchers whom California and Senator Yee cite favorably. For example, as noted above, California relies on the research of Jeanne Funk. But, in a separate study that California does not mention, Funk "fail[ed] to find" even a correlation between violent video games and aggressive emotions and behavior. Notably, this second Funk study employed the Child Behavior Checklist, which is a better validated measure of aggression than measures utilized in the studies on which California and Senator Yee rely.

At minimum, the scholarship that California and Senator Yee ignore belies the notion that the "substantial evidence of causation" standard imposes an "insurmountable hurdle" on science or legislatures. These studies show unequivocally that the causation research can be done, and, indeed, has been done. The problem confronting California and Senator Yee thus is not the constitutional standard; it is simply their inability to meet that standard in this case because validated scientific studies prove the opposite, leaving no empirical foundation for the assertion that playing violent video games causes harm to minors.

PATRICIA A. MILLETT has argued more than 30 cases before the Supreme Court, and was named one of the 100 most influential lawyers by the *National Law Journal*. She graduated summa cum laude from Harvard Law School.

EXPLORING THE ISSUE

Are Violent Video Games Harmful to Children and Adolescents?

Critical Thinking and Reflection

1. Imagine that you have to argue this case before the Supreme Court, based on the evidence cited. What in your view is the most convincing piece of research evidence for or against violent video games as a danger to children? Why is this study so convincing to you?
2. What is the difference between correlation and causation in psychological research? Could a study determine causation conclusively? If so, describe what would be required for such a study. If not, explain why.
3. Gruel argues his point based on the methodological strengths of longitudinal research and meta-analyses, while Millett attempts to undermine that argument by exposing flaws in the methodologies of those studies. How important is methodology in rating the worth of a study? Why?
4. Both sides of the debate cited neuroscience research as an important part of their arguments. What can descriptions of the physical brain tell you about psychological concepts such as aggression? What can they not tell you?
5. Based on the arguments given by both sides, how much agreement is there in the psychological community about this topic? What would be needed to reach a consensus?

Is There Common Ground?

The stunning improvement of computer technology has brought about a significant increase in the number of people using it as a means of personal and group entertainment. Video games have become one of the most common forms of entertainment for children and adolescents. From strategy games to role-playing games, and from "first-person shooters" to educational, age-appropriate games, the video gaming industry seeks to provide a wide-range of entertainment options for children and teens. However, many scientists, worried parents, and public policy makers have sought to know if violent video games can have just many negative effects on children's behavior as educational games can have beneficial ones. The debate has long gone on back and forth.

The articles presented here address four main points: (1) whether or not scientific research has indeed reached a consensus as to the effects of video games regarding aggressive behaviors in children and adolescents; (2) if the instances of increased aggression that are studied in the laboratory actually correspond to real-world behaviors; (3) if any correlations that are found can actually be used to support drawing causal inferences; and (4) if recent neuroscientific findings that suggest that changes in brain activity and function that occur in the presence of violent video games suggest a causal link or are simply descriptive of brain activity and nothing more. Is it really possible to prove a causal relationship between violent video games and aggression in the presence of so many confounding variables? Clearly, this question is one that animates each side of this important debate and one that psychologists of varying opinions seek to answer by means of more careful scientific analysis.

Additional Resources

Kutner, L., and Olson, C. K. (2011). *Grand Theft Childhood: The Surprising Truth About Violent Video Games and What Parents Can Do*. New York, NY: Simon & Schuster.

Nije Bijvank, M., Konijn, E. A., and Bushman, B. J. (2012). "We don't need no education": Video game preferences, video game motivations, and aggressiveness among adolescent boys of different educational ability levels. *Journal of Adolescence, 35*(1), 153–162. doi:10.1016/j.adolescence.2011.04.001

Polman, H., de Castro, B., and van Aken, M. G. (2008). Experimental study of the differential effects of playing versus watching violent video games on children's aggressive behavior. *Aggressive Behavior, 34*(3), 256–264. Retrieved from web.ebscohost.com.silk.library.umass.edu/ehost/ detail?vid=7&hid=7&sid=0e2bl9af-8751-4d92-826d-7fc8403f873%40sessionmgrl5&bdata=JnN

pdGU9ZWhvc3OtbG12ZSZzY29wZTlzaXRl#db= a ph&AN=31875598

Sacks, D. P., Bushman, B. J., and Anderson, C. A. (2011). Do violent video games harm children? Comparing the scientific amicus curiae "experts" in *Brown v. Entertainment Merchants Association, Northwestern Law Review, 106,* 1–12.

Internet References . . .

Quarterly Newsletter of the Entertainment Merchants Association

http://www.entmerch.org/government-relations/ema-v -schwarzenegger-faqs.html

Research Findings Suggesting That Video Games Encourage Moral Disengagement

http://www.ncbi.nlm.nih.gov/pubmed/22766175

A Satirical View of Various Societal Problems for Which Video Games Are Blamed

http://www.wired.com/geekdad/2013/01/video-games -violence/

Selected, Edited, and with Issue Framing Material by:
Edwin E. Gantt, *Brigham Young University*

ISSUE

Does Parent Sexual Orientation Affect Child Development?

YES: Peter Sprigg, from "New Study on Homosexual Parents Tops All Previous Research: Children of Homosexuals Fare Worse on Most Outcomes," *Family Research Council* (2012)

NO: Carmine D. Boccuzzi, Jr. et al., from "Brief of Amicus Curiae of the American Sociological Association on Behalf of Appellants," *American Sociological Association* (2013)

Learning Outcomes

- Understand and discuss some ways in which children of homosexual parents differ from those with heterosexual parents.
- Discuss some of the strengths and weaknesses of Mark Regnerus' recent research on the effects of homosexual parenting on psychological development in children.
- Identify numerous research findings that provide support for both the idea that having homosexual or heterosexual parents produces no significant difference in the psychological development of children and the idea that they do produce significant differences.

ISSUE SUMMARY

YES: Peter Sprigg of the Family Research Council recapitulates the arguments and findings of Mark Regnerus, concluding that the idea that children of homosexual parents are no different than children of heterosexual parents and, thus, are unharmed by the gender of their parents is a myth.

NO: Attorney Carmine Boccuzzi and colleagues, critiquing that the methods and findings of the Regnerus study and other similar studies, argue that children of homosexual parents are just as well off as children of heterosexual parents in most aspects of life.

In 2011 Zach Whals, the 19-year-old son of two lesbian women, testified before the Iowa House of Representatives stating, "The sexual orientation of my parents has had no effect on the content of my character" (Whals, 2011). Whals' testimony reflects one side of a major issue confronting psychologists—the question that titles this issue. As sincere as Whal's testimony apparently was, testimony is not the same as scientific evidence. Part of the job of psychologists is to systematically and scientifically investigate such issues, especially given the significance of this one. In fact, the political and public discourse surrounding same-sex marriage has recently intensified with the passing of California's Proposition 8. This proposition could be viewed as one aspect of the "other" side of the issue, since it proposed that only a man and woman can legitimately practice marriage. Underlying each of these "sides" is the well-being of the children reared by such couples, so a lot is at stake. Can psychologists help to resolve this important issue?

The research addressing this question so far has focused almost exclusively on determining the effects of parents' sexual orientation on child development. These investigations have assessed a variety of vital aspects of the controversy, including depression, gender identity, and education attainment, to name but a few. To date, psychologists are divided on the issue, with some echoing Whals' (2011) claims—children reared by same-sex couples are "no different" from those reared by heterosexual couples on developmental outcomes. Yet other investigators assert that their results indicate the opposite of these claims, suggesting that there are notable "differences" with significant negative consequences. This controversy also involves mutual critiques, with each side repeatedly describing flaws in their opponents' research methodology.

The articles included here are representative of the controversy. In the second article, Carmine Boccuzzi and his colleagues argue that parent sexual orientation does not negatively affect a child's well-being or development. They approach the issue through a comprehensive citation and analysis of existing research. The analysis focuses on several specific child outcomes: academic performance, cognitive development, early sexual activity, mental health, and substance abuse and behavioral problems. Boccuzzi et al. also strongly critique Mark Regnerus' landmark study on the issue in an attempt to show how Regnerus'

claims are unmerited. Boccuzzi and his colleagues believe that their analysis shows that "children of same-sex parents fare just as well as children of different sex parents."

On the other hand, in the first article, Peter Sprigg argues that there are indeed developmental negative differences in children raised by same-sex couples compared to heterosexual couples. He cites data and recapitulates the arguments made by Mark Regnerus and Loren Marks in their research. Sprigg's analysis restates the eight different family structures studied by Regnerus including intact biological families, mother with a same-sex romantic relationship, father with a same-sex romantic relationship, and several others on 40 different outcome measures. Sprigg comes to the same conclusion as Regnerus; that is, despite previous research "the myths that children of homosexual parents are 'no different' from other children and suffer 'no harm' from being raised by homosexual parents have been shattered forever."

YES ↵

Peter Sprigg

New Study On Homosexual Parents Tops All Previous Research: Children of Homosexuals Fare Worse on Most Outcomes

In a historic study of children raised by homosexual parents, sociologist Mark Regnerus of the University of Texas at Austin has overturned the conventional academic wisdom that such children suffer no disadvantages when compared to children raised by their married mother and father. Just published in the journal *Social Science Research*,[1] the most careful, rigorous, and methodologically sound study ever conducted on this issue found numerous and significant differences between these groups—with the outcomes for children of homosexuals rated "suboptimal" (Regnerus' word) in almost every category.

The Debate Over Homosexual Parents

In the larger cultural, political, and legal debates over homosexuality, one significant smaller debate has been over homosexual parents. Do children who are raised by homosexual parents or caregivers suffer disadvantages in comparison to children raised in other family structures—particularly children raised by a married mother and father? This question is essential to political and ethical debates over adoption, foster care, and artificial reproductive technology, and it is highly relevant to the raging debate over same-sex "marriage." The argument that "children need a mom and a dad" is central to the defense of marriage as the union of one man and one woman.

Here is how the debate over the optimal family structure for children and the impact of homosexual parents has usually gone:

- Pro-family organizations (like Family Research Council) assert, "Social science research shows that children do best when raised by their own biological mother and father who are committed to one another in a life-long marriage." This

statement is true, and rests on a large and robust collection of studies.
- Pro-homosexual activists respond, "Ah, but most of those studies compared children raised by a married couple with those raised by divorced or single parents—not with homosexual parents." (This is also true—in large part because the homosexual population, and especially the population of homosexuals raising children, is so small that it is difficult to obtain a representative sample.)
- The advocates of homosexual parenting then continue, "Research done specifically on children raised by homosexual parents shows that there are no differences (or no differences that suggest any disadvantage) between them and children raised by heterosexual parents."
- Pro-family groups respond with a number of critiques of such studies on homosexual parents. For example, such studies usually have relied on samples that are small and not representative of the population, and they frequently have been conducted by openly homosexual researchers who have an ideological bias on the question being studied. In addition, these studies *also* usually make comparisons with children raised by divorced or single parents—rather than with children raised by their married, biological mother and father.

In fact, an important article published in tandem with the Regnerus study (by Loren Marks, Louisiana State University) analyzes the 59 previous studies cited in a 2005 policy brief on homosexual parents by the American Psychological Association (APA).[2] Marks debunks the APA's claim that "[n]ot a single study has found children of lesbian or gay parents to be disadvantaged in any significant respect relative to children of heterosexual parents." Marks also points out that only four of the 59 studies cited by the APA even met *the APA's own standards* by "provid[ing] evidence of statistical power." As Marks so carefully documents, "[N]ot one of the 59 studies referenced in the 2005 APA Brief compares a large, random, representative sample of lesbian or gay parents and their children with a large, random, representative sample of married parents and their children."

To summarize, we have been left with large, scientifically strong studies showing children do best with their married mother and father—but which do not make comparisons with homosexual parents or couples; and studies which purportedly show that children of homosexuals do just as well as other children—but which are methodologically weak and thus scientifically inconclusive.

The New Family Structures Study— Restoring the "Gold Standard"

This logjam of dueling studies has been broken by the work that Regnerus has undertaken. Unlike the many large studies previously undertaken on family structure, Regnerus has included specific comparisons with children raised by homosexual parents. Unlike the previous studies on children of homosexual parents, he has put together a representative, population-based sample that is large enough to draw scientifically and statistically valid conclusions. For these reasons, his "New Family Structures Study" (NFSS) deserves to be considered the "gold standard" in this field.

Another improvement Regnerus has made is in his method of collecting data and measuring outcomes for children in various family structures. Some previous studies collected data while the subjects were still children living at home with their parent or parents—making it impossible to know what the effects of the home environment might be once they reach adulthood. Some such studies even relied, in some cases exclusively, on the self-report of the *parent*. This raised a serious question of "self-presentation bias"—the tendency of the parent to give answers that will make herself and her child look good.

Regnerus, on the other hand, has surveyed young adults, ages 18 to 39, and asked them about their experiences growing up (and their life circumstances in the present). While these reports are not entirely objective, they are likely to be more reliable than parental self-reports, and allow evaluation of long-term impacts.

The study collected information from its subjects on forty different outcomes. They fall into three groups:

- Some are essentially yes-or-no questions: are you currently married, are you currently unemployed, have you thought recently about suicide?

- Other questions asked respondents to place themselves on a scale—for example, of educational attainment, happiness or depression, and household income.
- Finally, "event-count" outcomes involve reporting the frequency of certain experiences—e.g., smoking marijuana or being arrested—and the number of sex partners.

Nearly 15,000 people were "screened" for potential participation in the study; in the end almost 3,000, a representative sample, actually completed the survey questionnaire. Of these, 175 reported that their mother had a same-sex romantic relationship while they were growing up, and 73 said the same about their father. These are numbers just large enough to make some statistically robust conclusions in comparing different family structures.

What the Study Found

The study looked at 40 different outcomes, but reported data for children with "lesbian mothers" and those with "gay fathers" separately. Therefore, there actually were 80 outcome measures that could be said to compare children with "homosexual parents" to those from other family structures. When compared with outcomes for children raised by an "intact biological family" (with a married, biological mother and father), *the children of homosexuals did worse (or, in the case of their own sexual orientation, were more likely to deviate from the societal norm) on 77 out of 80 outcome measures.* (The only exceptions: children of "gay fathers" were more likely to vote; children of lesbians used alcohol less frequently; and children of "gay fathers" used alcohol at the same rate as those in intact biological families).

Of course, anyone who has had a college course in statistics knows that when a survey shows there are differences between two groups, it is important to test whether that finding is "statistically significant." This is because it is always possible, by chance, that a sample may not accurately reflect the overall population on a particular point. However, through statistical analysis researchers can calculate the likelihood of this, and when they have a high level of confidence that a difference identified in the survey represents an actual difference in the national population, we say that finding is "statistically significant." (This does not mean the other findings are *unimportant*—just that we cannot have as high a level of confidence in them.)

Regnerus has analyzed his findings, and their statistical significance, in two ways—first by a simple and direct comparison between what is reported by the children of homosexual parents and the children of "intact biological families" ("IBFs"), and second by "controlling" for a variety of other characteristics. "Controlling for income," for example, would mean showing that "IBF" children do not do better just because their married parents have higher incomes, but that they do better even when the incomes of their households and the households of homosexual parents are the same. Again, Regnerus has done these comparisons for "LMs" (children of "lesbian mothers") and "GFs" (children of gay fathers) separately.

There are eight outcome variables where differences between the children of homosexual parents and married parents were not only present, and favorable to the married parents, but where these findings were statistically significant for *both* children of lesbian mothers and "gay" fathers and *both* with and without controls. While all the findings in the study are important, these are the strongest possible ones—virtually irrefutable. Compared with children raised by their married biological parents (IBF), children of homosexual parents (LM and GF):

- Are *much* more likely to have received welfare (IBF 17%; LM 69%; GF 57%)
- Have lower educational attainment
- Report less safety and security in their family of origin
- Report more ongoing "negative impact" from their family of origin
- Are more likely to suffer from depression
- Have been arrested more often
- If they are female, have had more sexual partners—both male *and* female

The high mathematical standard of "statistical significance" was more difficult to reach for the children of "gay fathers" in this study because there were fewer of them. The following, however, are some additional areas in which the children of *lesbian mothers* (who represented 71% of all the children with homosexual parents in this study) differed from the IBF children, in ways that were statistically significant in both a direct comparison and with controls. Children of lesbian mothers:

- Are more likely to be currently cohabiting
- Are almost 4 times more likely to be currently on public assistance
- Are less likely to be currently employed full-time
- Are more than 3 times more likely to be unemployed
- Are nearly 4 times more likely to identify as something *other than* entirely heterosexual
- Are 3 times as likely to have had an affair while married or cohabiting

- Are an astonishing *10 times more likely to have been "touched sexually by a parent or other adult caregiver."*
- Are nearly 4 times as likely to have been "physically forced" to have sex against their will
- Are more likely to have "attachment" problems related to the ability to depend on others
- Use marijuana more frequently
- Smoke more frequently
- Watch TV for long periods more frequently
- Have more often pled guilty to a non-minor offense

Differences in Sexuality

When comparing children of homosexuals with children of married biological parents, the differences in sexuality—experiences of sexual abuse, number of sexual partners, and homosexual feelings and experiences among the children themselves—were among the most striking. While not all of the findings mentioned below have the same level of "statistical significance" as those mentioned above, they remain important.

At one time, defenders of homosexual parents not only argued that their children do fine on psychological and developmental measures, but they also said that children of homosexuals "are no more likely to be gay" than children of heterosexuals. That claim will be impossible to maintain in light of this study. It found that children of homosexual fathers are nearly 3 times as likely, and children of lesbian mothers are nearly 4 times as likely, to identify as something other than entirely heterosexual. Children of lesbian mothers are 75% more likely, and children of homosexual fathers are 3 times more likely, to be currently in a same-sex romantic relationship.

The same holds true with the number of sexual partners. Both males and females who were raised by both lesbian mothers and homosexual fathers have more *opposite-sex (heterosexual)* partners than children of married biological parents (daughters of homosexual fathers had twice as many). But the differences in *homosexual* conduct are even greater. The daughters of lesbians have *4 times as many female (that is, same-sex) sexual partners* than the daughters of married biological parents, and the daughters of homosexual fathers have *6 times as many*. Meanwhile, the sons of both lesbian mothers and homosexual fathers have *7 times as many* male (same-sex) sexual partners as sons of married biological parents.

The most shocking and troubling outcomes, however, are those related to sexual abuse. Children raised by a lesbian mother were *10 times more likely* to have been "touched sexually by a parent or other adult caregiver"

(23% reported this, vs. only 2% for children of married biological parents), while those raised by a homosexual father were 3 times more likely (reported by 6%). In his text, but not in his charts, Regnerus breaks out these figures for only female victims, and the ratios remain similar (3% IBF; 31% LM; 10% GF). As to the question of whether you have "ever been physically forced" to have sex against your will (not necessarily in childhood), affirmative answers came from 8% of children of married biological parents, 31% of children of lesbian mothers (nearly 4 times as many), and 25% of the children of homosexual fathers (3 times as many). Again, when Regnerus breaks these figures out for females (who are more likely to be victims of sexual abuse in general), such abuse was reported by 14% of IBFs, but 3 times as many of the LMs (46%) and GFs (52%).

These data require more detailed exploration and explanation. A number of researchers have pointed out that self-identified homosexual adults (both men and women) are more likely to report having been victims of child sexual abuse. However, Family Research Council and other pro-family organizations have been criticized for also pointing to evidence suggesting that homosexual *men* are more likely to *commit* acts of child sexual abuse than are heterosexual men. And experts in child sexual abuse in general say that men are most often the perpetrators, regardless of the sex of the victim. Therefore, the finding that children of *lesbian mothers* are significantly more likely to have been victims of sexual touching by "a parent or adult caregiver" than even the children of homosexual fathers is counter-intuitive.

However, it is important to note what we do *not* know about such experiences from the data that have been published. The fact that a child of a lesbian mother was touched by "a parent or adult caregiver" *does not mean that the lesbian mother was herself the parent or caregiver who did the "touching."* An alternative scenario mentioned by Regnerus, for example—hypothetical, but plausible—is one in which a child is molested by her biological father; her mother divorces her father; and the mother *later* enters into a lesbian relationship.

Limitations of the Study

While the Regnerus study is a vast improvement over virtually all the prior research in the field, it still leaves much to study and learn about homosexual parents and their effect on children. Author Mark Regnerus emphasizes the traditional caveat in social science, warning against leaping to conclusions regarding "causality." In other words, just because there are statistical correlations between having a

homosexual parent and experiencing negative outcomes does not automatically prove that having a homosexual parent is what *caused* the negative outcomes—other factors could be at work.

This is true in a strict scientific sense—but because Regnerus carefully *controlled* for so many other factors in the social environment, the study gives a clear indication that it is this parental characteristic which best defines the household environment that produces these troubling outcomes. The *large number* of *significant* negative outcomes in this study gives legitimate reason for concern about the consequences of "homosexual parenting."

The definition of what it means to have a homosexual parent is also a loose one in this study—by necessity, in order to maximize the sample size of homosexual parents. Not all of those who reported that a parent was in a same-sex relationship even lived with that parent during the relationship; many who did, did not live with the partner as well. Only 23% of those with a lesbian mother, and only 2% of those with a homosexual father, had spent as long as three years living in a household with the homosexual parent and the parent's partner at the same time. Details like this involving the actual timeline of these children's lives can reportedly be found in Regnerus' dataset, which is to be made available to other researchers later this year.

Figures like these suggest a need for more research, to distinguish, for example, the effects of living with a homosexual parent from having a non-custodial one, or the effects of living with a homosexual single parent vs. a homosexual couple. But they also point out something of note for public policy debates on "gay families"—the stereotype put forward by pro-homosexual activists, of a same-sex couple jointly parenting a child from birth (following either adoption or the use of artificial reproductive technology), represents a scenario that is extraordinarily rare in real life. Most "homosexual parents" have their own biological children who were conceived in the context of a previous *heterosexual* relationship or marriage, which then ended before the person entered into homosexual relationships.

Conclusion

The articles by Marks and Regnerus have completely changed the playing field for debates about homosexual parents, "gay families," and same-sex "marriage." The myths that children of homosexual parents are "no different" from other children and suffer "no harm" from being raised by homosexual parents have been shattered forever.

References and Notes

1. Mark Regnerus, "How different are the adult children of parents who have same-sex relationships? Findings from the New Family Structures Study," *Social Science Research* Vol 41, Issue 4 (July 2012), pp. 752–770; online at: http://www.sciencedirect.com/science/article/pii/S0049089X12000610

2. Loren Marks, "Same-sex parenting and children's outcomes: A closer examination of the American Psychological Association's brief on lesbian and gay parenting," *Social Science Research* Vol 41, Issue 4 (July 2012), pp. 735–751; online at: http://www.sciencedirect.com/science/article/pii/S0049089X12000580

PETER SPRIGG is a senior fellow for policy studies at the Family Research Council in Washington, D.C. His research and writing have addressed issues of marriage and family, human sexuality, the arts and entertainment, and religion in public life.

Carmine D. Boccuzzi, Jr. et al.

 **NO**

Brief of Amicus Curiae of the American Sociological Association on Behalf of Appellants

I. Scholarly Consensus Is Clear: Children of Same-Sex Parents Fare Just as well as Children of Differentsex Parents

The social science consensus is clear: children raised by same-sex parents fare just as well as children raised by different-sex parents. Numerous nationally representative, credible, and methodologically sound social science studies form the basis of this consensus. These studies reveal that children raised by same-sex parents fare just as well as children raised by different-sex parents across a wide spectrum of child-well-being measures: academic performance, cognitive development, social development, psychological health, early sexual activity, and substance abuse.

. . .

A) Academic Performance and Cognitive Development

Social science research confirms that the academic performance of children raised by same-sex parents is indistinguishable from that of children raised by different-sex parents. A leading study by Daniel Potter based on nationally representative, longitudinal data found no significant difference in academic achievement between children of same-sex parents and children of different-sex parents. Similarly, another leading 2009 study by sociologists Alicia Fedewa and Teresa Clark employing nationally representative data that examined the academic achievement of first-grade children reported no significant differences in academic achievement between children raised by same-sex and different-sex parents. The same pattern holds true among older children. For example, in another nationally representative study, social scientists found similar GPA levels among adolescents living with same-sex and different-sex parents.

Research also reveals similar cognitive development between children raised by same-sex parents and different-sex parents. In fact, a report of children with same-sex parents reveals that they score at least as well as—and sometimes better than—children of different-sex parents on numerous indicators of educational achievement and involvement.

B) Social Development

The social development of children raised by same-sex parents is equivalent to that of children raised by different-sex parents. Analysis of nationally representative data reveals no differences in social adjustment depending on whether children were raised by same-sex or different-sex parents. Nationally representative studies of adolescents find that the number, support, and quality of peer relationships and friendships are similar for teens raised by female same-sex parents and those raised by different-sex parents.

C) Mental Health

Social science studies also confirm that children of same-sex parents are just as psychologically healthy as children of different-sex parents. According to a nationally representative study, adolescents raised by same-sex and different-sex parents report similar levels of self-esteem and depression.

. . .

Recent research focusing on young children reports that the ability of adopted children to externalize and internalize behaviors does not depend on whether they are raised in male same-sex, female same-sex, or different-sex parented families. As Dr. Lamb outlined in his comprehensive literature review of the social science evidence, "numerous studies of children and adolescents raised by same-sex parents" conducted over now approximately 30 years "by respected researchers and published in peer-reviewed academic journals conclude that they are as successful psychologically, emotionally, and socially as children and adolescents raised by heterosexual parents." Similarly, surveys reveal no greater levels of anxiety or Attention Deficit Disorder among teenagers raised by same-sex parents than among those raised by different-sex parents.

This social science evidence confirms the evidence presented by Dr. Lamb in both cases below. For example, as Dr. Lamb affirmed in *Jackson*, social science "overwhelmingly rejects the notion that . . . adolescents with same-sex parents suffer any developmental disadvantages compared with those with two [different]-sex parents." Dr. Lamb went on to state in *Sevcik* that:

> The body of research that has examined children's and adolescents' adjustment in the specific context of parenting by same-sex couples represents approximately 30 years of scholarship and includes more than 50 peer-reviewed empirical reports. . . . The results of these studies further demonstrate that adjustment is not affected by the gender or sexual orientation of the parent(s).

D) Early Sexual Activity

The social science studies also demonstrate that teenagers raised by same-sex parents and those raised by different-sex parents engage in similar levels of teenage sexual activity. For instance, nationally representative studies show that similar proportions of teenagers raised by same-sex parents and by different-sex parents have had sexual intercourse or a romantic relationship. In fact, reports by 17-year-olds raised by same-sex mothers of their sexual behavior indicate that the age at which they first engage in sexual intercourse was slightly older than those in a gender- and age-matched national sample of children raised by different-sex parents. Moreover, the odds of having a sexually transmitted disease, becoming pregnant, or impregnating someone were statistically similar. And none of the children raised by same-sex parents examined in the National Longitudinal Lesbian Family Study reported any physical or sexual abuse by a parent or caregiver.

E) Substance Abuse and Behavioral Problems

Finally, social science studies confirm that children of same-sex parents are no more likely to abuse substances than children of different-sex parents. A nationally representative sample of adolescents living with female, same-sex parents reveals that the adolescents are similar to their counterparts raised by different-sex parents in terms of frequency of substance use (*i.e.*, tobacco, alcohol, and marijuana), problems with substance use, and delinquent behavior. Furthermore, children of different-sex and same-sex parents report similar levels of problematic, rule-breaking, and inappropriately aggressive behaviors.

In sum, as the overwhelming body of social science research confirms, whether a child is raised by same-sex or different-sex parents has no bearing on a child's well-being. Instead, the consensus is that the key factors affecting child well-being are stable family environments and greater parental socioeconomic resources, neither of which is related to the sex or sexual orientation of a child's parents. As the testimony of Dr. Lamb concluded, "[the studies] demonstrate that the adjustment of children and adolescents of same-sex parents is determined by the quality of the youths' relationships with the parents, the quality of the relationship between the parents, and the resources available to the families." These factors indicate that in order to further enhance child outcomes and well-being, we should encourage stable and financially secure family units—including same-sex parented families—rather than exclude the hundreds of thousands of children living with same-sex couples from the stability and economic security that marriage provides.

II. The Research Claimed to Undermine the Consensus Either Does Not Address Same-Sex Parents and Their Children or Is Mischaracterized

Studies relied on by . . . opponents of marriage for same-sex couples fail to support the claim that children fare better with different-sex parents than same-sex parents because nearly all of the studies do not examine same-sex parents or their children. Specifically, in an effort to undermine the social science consensus, . . . opponents of marriage for same-sex couples often rely on two papers by Mark Regnerus, which are referred to herein as "Regnerus 2012a" and "Regnerus 2012b." But for the reasons articulated below, and as Regnerus himself acknowledges, these papers do not examine, and provide no conclusions regarding, the well-being of children who lived with and were raised by same-sex parents.

Beyond Regnerus, other reports cited by opponents of marriage for same-sex couples also fail to support their arguments. For example, Appellees in both *Sevcik* and *Jackson* cite to a study published by Child Trends to support their propositions, but the authors of that study have explicitly disclaimed the use of their work for this purpose. Similarly, HFF cites to studies by David Popenoe as authoritative in spite of the fact that his work does not analyze samesex parented families.

In short, the reports put forth by Appellees have no bearing on the issue of same-sex parents because they seek to draw inappropriate apples-to-oranges comparisons and often do not address same-sex parents at all. Moreover, some of the findings in the studies are mischaracterized by the Appellees and, in fact, affirm that family stability and greater parental socioeconomic resources are the principal factors affecting child well-being.

A) The Regnerus Papers Do Not Support Conclusions about Children Raised by Same-Sex Parents

The Regnerus 2012a paper—a principal assertion relied on by the Appellees to support the proposition that children of different-sex parents fare better than those of same-sex parents—did not specifically examine children raised by same-sex parents, and provides no support for the conclusions that same-sex parents are inferior parents or that the children of same-sex parents experience worse outcomes. This critique of Regnerus 2012a was made in an internal audit in the very journal in which Regnerus's article was published, and this audit went so far as to state that the Regnerus 2012a paper should not have been published. Dr. Lamb confirmed these assertions when he stated that "[the Regnerus 2012a paper] did not actually assess individuals raised by same-sex partners."

1. The Regnerus 2012a Study Offers No Basis for Conclusions about Same-Sex Parents

First, the Regnerus 2012a paper does not specifically examine children born or adopted into same-sex parent families, but instead examines children who, from the time they were born until they were 18 or moved out, had a parent who at any time had "a same-sex romantic relationship." As Regnerus noted, the majority of the individuals characterized by him as children of 'lesbian mothers' and 'gay fathers' were the offspring of failed different-sex unions whose parent subsequently had a same-sex relationship. In other words, Regnerus did not study or analyze the children of two same-sex parents.

Second, when the Regnerus 2012a paper compared the children of parents who at one point had a "same-sex romantic relationship," most of whom had experienced a family dissolution or single motherhood, to children raised by two biological, married different-sex parents, the study stripped away all divorced, single, and stepparent families from the different-sex group, leaving only stable, married, different-sex parented families as the comparison. Thus, it was hardly surprising that the different-sex parented group had better outcomes given that stability, as noted above, is a key predictor of positive child well-being. By so doing, the Regnerus 2012a paper makes inappropriate apples-to-oranges comparisons.

Third, the Regnerus 2012a data analysis failed to consider whether the children lived with, or were raised by, the parent who was, at some point, apparently involved in "a romantic relationship with someone of the same sex" and that same-sex partner. Instead, Regnerus categorized children as raised by a parent in a same-sex relationship regardless of whether they were in fact raised by the parent and the parent's same-sex romantic partner and regardless of the amount of time that they spent under the parent's care. As a result, so long as an adult child believed that he or she had *had* a parent who at some point had a relationship with someone of the same sex, then he or she was counted by Regnerus as having been "raised by" a parent in a same-sex relationship.

Fourth, in contrast to every other study on same-sex parents, Regnerus 2012a identified parents who had purportedly engaged in a same-sex relationship based solely on the child's own retrospective report of the parent's romantic relationships, made once the child was an adult. This unusual measurement strategy ignored the fact that the child may have limited and inaccurate recollections of the parents' distant romantic past.

Finally, Regnerus failed to account for the fact that the negative outcomes may have been caused by other childhood events or events later in the individual's adult life, particularly given that the vast majority (thirty-seven of forty) of the outcomes measured were adult and not childhood outcomes. Regnerus himself recognizes that the survey data he relied upon—the New Family Structures Study (NFSS)—"is poised to address [questions] about the lives of young adults between the ages of 18 and 39, but not about children or adolescents." Regnerus 2012a at 755. Factors other than having same-sex parents are likely to explain these outcomes in the Regnerus 2012a study. Regnerus himself concludes that "I am thus not suggesting that growing up with a lesbian mother or gay father causes suboptimal outcomes *because of* the sexual orientation or sexual behavior of the parent."

In sum, by conflating (1) children raised by same-sex parents with (2) individuals who reportedly had a parent who had "a romantic relationship with someone of the same sex," and referring to such individuals as children of "lesbian mothers" or "gay fathers," the Regnerus 2012a study obscures the fact that it did not specifically examine children raised by two same-sex parents. Accordingly, it cannot speak to the well-being of children raised by same-sex parents.

2. The "Re-Stated" Regnerus 2012b Study Offers No Basis for Conclusions about Same-Sex Parents

A group of over one hundred social scientists signed an article faulting the Regnerus 2012a paper for failing to take account of family structure and family instability. The article specifically criticized Regnerus 2012a's failure to "distinguish between the impact of having a parent who has a continuous same-sex relationship from the impact of having same-sex parents who broke-up from the impact of living in a same sex stepfamily from the impact of living with a single parent who may have dated a same-sex partner." Regnerus acknowledged the merit of these scholarly critiques regarding the underlying aspects of his research and subsequently published a second analysis of the data, which is referred to as Regnerus 2012b. Through Regnerus 2012b, Regnerus attempted to remedy the fact that Regnerus 2012a did not analyze whether the children had actually lived with the parent who, according to the adult child, had at some point, been "romantically involved" with someone of the same sex.

Nevertheless, the Regnerus 2012b analysis does *not* resolve the problems inherent in the initial analysis and contains many of the same shortcomings. First, a recently published review of Regnerus 2012a elaborated on these shortcomings. Second, Regnerus 2012b maintained the same flawed and extremely broad definition of what constitutes "lesbian mothers" and "gay fathers"—that is, a mother or father who ever had a romantic relationship with someone of the same-sex during the period from the birth of the child until the child turned eighteen (or left home to be on their own). Accordingly, Regnerus 2012b continues to ignore stability as the primary factor in child outcomes. Third, Regnerus 2012b still fails to account for the duration of time spent with a mother who was "romantically involved" with a same-sex partner and that partner. Only *two* of the eighty-five children who at some point lived with a mother who was "romantically involved" with another woman reported that they did so for the entire duration of their childhood. Finally, the Regnerus 2012b paper is still not informative of same-sex parents because Regnerus did not determine whether the recorded childhood experiences occurred while the mother lived with a same-sex partner *or* during another family living arrangement.

If any conclusion can be reached from Regnerus 2012a and 2012b, it is that family stability is predictive of child well-being. As Regnerus himself notes, family structure (for instance whether the family has a single parent or two parents) matters significantly to child outcomes. As the social science consensus described above demonstrates, the evidence regarding children raised by same-sex parents overwhelmingly indicates that they fare just as well as children raised by different-sex parents, and that children raised by same-sex parents are likely to benefit from the enhanced stability the institution of marriage provides to their families. All told, the Regnerus studies, even as revised, simply do not undermine the consensus that children raised by same-sex parents fare just as well as those raised by different-sex parents.

B) Other Studies Cited by Opponents of Marriage for Same-Sex Couples Do Not Address Same-Sex Parents and Therefore Do Not Undermine the Consensus

Various other studies often cited by opponents of marriage for same-sex couples, including Appellees here, do not undermine the consensus of social science research that children of same-sex couples fare just as well as those of different-sex couples. In continued apples-to-oranges fashion, opponents rely on studies analyzing *inter alia* stepparents, single parents, and adoptive parents—none of which address same-sex parents or their children—in order to make speculative statements about the well-being of children of same-sex parents. Instead, the studies confirm that parental stability and higher parental socio-economic resources are the key drivers of positive child outcomes.

1. Studies Regarding the Impact of Stepparents, Divorced Parents, or Single Parents

Those opposing marriage for same-sex couples often rely on studies examining the impact of stepparents, divorced parents, and single parents on child well-being outcomes, and use these studies to argue that two biological parents are necessary to positive child outcomes. Contrary to these assertions, these studies in no way examine same-sex parents or their impact on child well-being. As Dr. Lamb described below, social science evidence that does not explicitly consider same-sex parents cannot be used to argue that same-sex parented families impede child well-being. Accordingly, they cannot be relied upon as scientific evidence regarding the effects of same-sex parents.

Aside from not specifically addressing same-sex parents, the studies regarding stepparents and divorce indicate that child outcomes are, on average, not as positive because of the disruption caused by divorce or the introduction of a new parent into the family, but do not indicate that the source of the negative outcomes is related to the fact that the stepparent is not biologically related to the child.

. . .

Therefore, the argument that research regarding stepparents is relevant to same-sex parents because at least one of the same-sex parents is not the biological parent, and is therefore "step," is misplaced. In a planned, same-sex parented family, both parents have brought the child into the family and raised the child from infancy. Moreover, in many states, including Nevada and Hawaii, both parents in same-sex parented families may be legal parents to the children. Accordingly, any studies cited by Appellees analyzing the effects of single parents and stepparents are mischaracterized. The research on children in divorced, single parent, and stepparented families simply says nothing about the well-being of children raised by same-sex parents.

Finally, the authors of one of the principal studies relied on by all Appellees—the Child Trends study—have publicly responded that their study focused on children being raised in families headed by single parents, stepparents, and married, different-sex parents—not same-sex parents. In fact, before the Supreme Court considered *Windsor* and *Perry*, the authors of the Child Trends study expressly disclaimed the misuse of their study by the Bipartisan Legal Advisory Group, which defended DOMA, explaining that "no conclusions can be drawn from this research about the well-being of children raised by same-sex parents or adoptive parents." The study concluded that "when researchers have compared marriage to cohabitation, they have found that marriage is associated with better outcomes for children." Extending this logic to the context of samesex couples and their children, recognition of marriage rights of such couples would improve, not impair, the well-being of children being raised by currently unmarried same-sex parents.

2. Studies Purporting to Examine the Effect of Two Biological Parents

Opponents of marriage for same-sex couples often cite studies purporting to show the superiority of biological parents over adoptive parents and problems faced by children conceived by donor sperm. It is hard to see the relevance of reports about the significance of biological parenting on the issue of marriage rights for same-sex couples given that both adoption and assisted reproduction are widely used by heterosexual couples, as reflected in the very sources cited in support of the Nevada and Hawaii Marriage Bans.

But in any case, there is no basis for the assertion that adoption or assisted reproduction leads to negative child outcomes. In fact, studies indicate that children raised in adoptive families since infancy or in families utilizing assisted reproduction techniques fare just as well as other children.

3. Studies Regarding Gender Roles in Families with Different-Sex Parents

Opponents of marriage for same-sex couples also rely on a number of studies that examine the parental roles of mothers and fathers within the context of different-sex parented families and claim that these studies demonstrate that child well-being depends on having both a male and female parent. But these studies do not support this suggestion, and reliance on them is misplaced for multiple reasons.

First, like the other studies cited by opponents of marriage for same-sex couples, these studies do not examine the parenting and disciplinary dynamics of same-sex parents. Without any social science evidence to support their conclusion, it is asking a court to deduce that a child raised by two gay husbands would not receive the necessary neural development or improvement in emotional and communicative skills. No such conclusion is proper based on any study published to date. Second, these opponents ignore the fact that the research regarding different parenting roles and styles indicates that those roles are relative, and nothing in the research indicates that same-sex couples are not able to provide such relative parenting dynamics. Third, the research also indicates that there is a range of parenting styles, that no couple parents identically, and that children do not need their parents to adopt particular parenting styles to be well adjusted.

. . .

Fourth, arguments based on rigid gender roles should be rejected as courts routinely decline to rely upon "outdated misconceptions" and "loose-fitting characterizations" regarding gender. Again, as the District Court in *Perry* concluded after examining testimony from Dr. Lamb, "[c]hildren do not need to be raised by a male parent and a female parent to be well-adjusted, and having both a male and a female parent does not increase the likelihood that a child will be well-adjusted."

Finally, the studies relied on by the Appellees that examine the role of absentee fathers do not establish that, within the context of same-sex parents, fathers are necessary to the child's well-being. In fact, the research regarding the negative impact of absentee fathers, such as David Popenoe's, has nothing to do with the unique contributions of fathers, but rather with the loss of a parental relationship.

. . .

In sum, the studies relied upon by Appellees here (as well as opponents of marriage for same-sex couples at large) examine child outcomes within the context of different-sex relationships, and do not address the impact of same-sex parents on child well-being. These studies do not undermine the social science consensus, supported by the most reliable studies available, that children raised by same-sex parents fare just as well as children raised by different-sex parents across a broad spectrum of indicators.

Conclusion

The social science consensus is both conclusive and clear: children fare just as well when they are raised by same-sex parents as when they are raised by different-sex parents. This consensus holds true across a wide range of child outcome indicators and is supported by numerous nationally representative studies. Accordingly, assuming that any of the Nevada and Hawaii Marriage Bans has any effect on whether children are raised by different-sex or same-sex parents, there is no basis to prefer different-sex parents over same-sex parents. The research supports the conclusion that extension of marriage rights to same-sex couples has the potential to improve child well-being insofar as the institution of marriage may provide social and legal support to families and enhances family stability, which are key drivers of positive child outcomes. The Regnerus papers and other sources relied on by opponents of marriage for same-sex couples provide no basis for their arguments because they do not directly examine the well-being of children raised by same-sex parents. These studies therefore do not undermine the consensus from the social science research and do not establish a legitimate basis for the Nevada and Hawaii Marriage Bans.

CARMINE D. BOCCUZZI is a partner with Cleary and Gottlieb. His litigation and arbitration practice covers a broad range of complex civil litigation matters, with an emphasis on international disputes, including those involving foreign states and state-owned entities, and domestic disputes involving the capital markets and antitrust issues. He received a JD from the Yale Law School in 1994 and a BA, *magna cum laude,* from Yale College in 1990.

EXPLORING THE ISSUE

Does Parent Sexual Orientation Affect Child Development?

Critical Thinking and Reflection

1. Sprigg's argument is based on and recapitulates the work of psychological researcher Mark Regnerus in the attempt to show that children of homosexual parents fair worse than the children of heterosexual parents. In your opinion, what are some of the weaknesses of using the work of another author to prove the validity of your own research? On the other hand, why might it be a good strategy?
2. Boccuzzi and his colleagues spend the majority of their time critiquing the methodology of Regnerus' research findings, but do not spend much time offering new evidence in support of their own position. In your opinion, what are some factors other than parent sexual orientation that might play a role in a child's gender role behavior? Explain.
3. Choose a current public policy issue being highlighted in the media that has relevance to this issue and discuss how either of these articles might be used to support or oppose the policy.
4. Boccuzzi and colleagues attempt to discredit arguments like those made by Sprigg by appealing to a majority scientific consensus, claiming that "the social science consensus is both conclusive and clear: children fare just as well when they are raised by same-sex parents as when they are raised by different-sex parents." Why might there be a problem with simply appealing to a majority opinion, without providing much citation, as opposed to appealing directly to scientific inquiry?
5. The study by Regnerus that Sprigg employs as a basis for his argument contained data collected at one particular point in time. Does such a technique provide enough insight about the lives of those being studied and the subsequent effects of their family experience? Provide three reasons explaining your view.

Is There Common Ground?

It is arguable that there is no current social issue more complex, more hotly debated and more intensely researched in our society today than homosexuality. The political discussions and the scientific literature are rife with debates concerning the origins, consequences, and ethical impact of homosexuality across a wide swath of human behavior and experience. One issue that is particularly salient in the current debate is the effect that homosexual partnerships may or may not have on child-rearing outcomes for those raised by homosexual parents, as opposed to children raised by heterosexual parents.

Though clearly controversial, Mark Regnerus' recent research is widely considered one of the most groundbreaking attempts to study this particular issue. The Regnerus study is central to the analyses of both articles presented here. The YES article attempts to recapitulate Regnerus' findings to support the claim that the research method employed is superior to all previous investigations of homosexual parenting, and, thus, the findings generated are more informative and insightful. The NO article, on the other hand, argues against the Regnerus study, citing an array of competing research that purports to show that, at least in regards to many important developmental outcomes, all children fair the same regardless of the sexual orientations of their parents. A central concern running through both articles centers on the definitions of homosexual orientation and the various outcomes that have been identified as important. In short, it has proved very difficult so far for psychologists to agree on how exactly to define what homosexual orientation means and how to most clearly define successful parenting outcomes in order to study them best.

Additional Resources

Biblarz, T. J., & Stacey, J. (2010). How does the gender of parent matter? *Journal of Marriage and Family, 72(1)*, 3–22.

Crowl, A., Ahn, S., & Baker, J. (2008). A meta-analysis of development outcomes for children of same-sex and heterosexual parents. *Journal of GLBT Family Studies, 4*, 385–407.

Regnerus, M. (2012). How different are the adult children of parents who have same-sex relationships? Findings from the new family structures study. *Social Science Research, 41*, 752–770

Spitzer, R. L. (2003). Can some gay men and lesbians change their sexual orientation? 200 participants reporting a change from homosexual to heterosexual orientation. *Archives of Sexual Behavior, 32(5)*, 403–417

Tasker, F. (2010). Same-sex parenting and child development: Reviewing the contribution of parental gender. *Journal of Marriage and Family, 72*, 35–40

Internet References . . .

The APA's Official Stance on Sexual Orientation

http://www.apa.org/helpcenter/sexual-orientation
.aspx

The APA's Report on "Appropriate Therapeutic Responses to Sexual Orientation"

http://www.apa.org/pi/lgbt/resources/therapeutic-
response.pdf

The Official Sight of the Family Research Council

http://www.frc.org

Unit 4

UNIT

Cognitive–Emotional Issues

*A*long with behavior, our cognitive and emotional abilities are of vital interest to psychologists. Many people, for example, are concerned with a particular emotion—how to become and remain happy. Could psychological research on the factors that facilitate and maintain well-being help us to be happier? What about emotions in general? Is there a skill or sensitivity regarding emotions that is akin to intelligence? Are some people better than others at empathizing, reading emotions, or knowing how to manipulate them?

Selected, Edited, and with Issue Framing Material by:
Edwin E. Gantt, *Brigham Young University*

ISSUE

Can Positive Psychology Make Us Happier?

YES: Stephen M. Schueller and Acacia C. Parks, from "The Science of Self-Help: Translating Positive Psychology Research into Increased Individual Happiness" *European Psychologist* (2014)

NO: Laurel C. Newman and Randy J. Larsen, from "How Much of Our Happiness Is Within Our Control?" *Original Essay* (2009)

Learning Outcomes
After reading this issue, you will be able to: • Determine if it is possible to adapt strategies to improve one's happiness.   • Discuss how the manipulation of environmental variables could impact happiness.   • Discuss what it means to be "happy" and determine if it is the sort of thing that can actually be manipulated.

ISSUE SUMMARY

YES: Positive psychologists Stephen M. Schueller and Acacia C. Parks present a summary of the current state of positive psychological interventions as they pertain to self-help, interventions that have been shown to lead to increases in individual happiness.

NO: Psychologists Laurel Newman and Randy Larsen challenge the external validity and sustainability of the effects of these strategies, arguing that most of what influences our long-term happiness is outside our control.

Who wants to be happy? Or perhaps the more empirical question is, how *can* we be happy? The U.S. Declaration of Independence lists the pursuit of happiness as an unalienable right, but no psychological researcher was around in 1776 to teach U.S. citizens how best to pursue it. Nor is the quest for happiness an exclusively U.S. business; the country Bhutan, for instance, has a Gross National Happiness (GNH) index to help guide government policy. Still, in the Western world of psychological research, Maslow's hierarchy of needs seems to be at play. In Maslow's hierarchy, we must satisfy our most basic needs (e.g., hunger) before we can concern ourselves with higher level needs, such as happiness and flourishing. If this is true, then only the more affluent countries, those that have satisfied their citizens' more basic needs, can even afford to ask the happiness question.

With this affluence, the positive psychology movement has risen during the last decade with the study of human flourishing as its major aim. Its focus on examining and nurturing what is best in humans is grounded in ancient Greek philosophies and more recent humanistic psychological theories, such as that of Carl Rogers. Recently, happiness has become a popular emphasis of the movement, with a host of psychological researchers attempting to answer many important questions. Is happiness biologically based? Is it environmental? How much is under our personal control? Sonja Lyubomirsky's early book described research that she contended would achieve lasting happiness, but many critics examined her results with skepticism. Is the research now substantial enough for psychologists to finally tell people how they can become happy?

Stephen M. Schueller and Acacia C. Parks seem to think so. In the YES article, they argue that previous research has provided substantial evidence that individual happiness can increase. Schueller and Parks believe that this increase in individual happiness can be achieved by imitating the behaviors of those who are "naturally" happy. They hold that current research shows small-to-moderate increases in well-being and decreasing depressive symptoms result from the teaching and encouraging of unhappy people to learn and apply these "happy" behaviors. They contend that less happy people can not only learn strategies (e.g., savoring, gratitude, kindness, and creating meaning), but also apply these strategies to increase their levels of happiness. Indeed, psychological studies seem to show that careful interventions can be effective in facilitating happiness.

Laurel Newman and Randy Larsen, in contrast, believe that psychologists should be cautious before making public announcements about how people can make ourselves happier. According to Newman and Larsen, psychologists are misleading when they say that 40 percent of happiness is within our control. Although they do agree that roughly half of the difference in happiness scores (within a group) may be attributed to genetics, they also believe that most life-changing events (those that affect happiness) are out of a person's control. This means, perhaps most important, that strategies and techniques for increasing happiness are not likely to endure, because people have a surprising tendency to return to preexisting levels of happiness after good and bad events have produced temporary changes in happiness levels. Moreover, Newman and Larsen contend that the experimental effects of the most oft-cited happiness interventions are at best weak and require very specific circumstances to produce any effect.

POINT

- According to some models, 40 percent of happiness may be within our control.
- Circumstantial factors do not adequately explain different levels of happiness.
- Studies with happiness-inducing strategies show people can increase their levels of happiness.
- Individual differences in adaptation show that people can use strategies to help themselves stay happy, even after a less-than-happy event.

COUNTERPOINT

- Heritability estimates describe variations in groups and do not apply to individuals.
- A variety of environmental variables predict happiness, and many of them are uncontrollable.
- These strategies have weak statistical effects that show up only under very specific circumstances.
- People adapt quickly to negative and positive changes, returning to previous levels of happiness.

YES

Stephen M. Schueller and Acacia C. Parks

The Science of Self-Help: Translating Positive Psychology Research into Increased Individual Happiness

A recent initiative by Martin Seligman, the founder of positive psychology, aims to increase global well-being, with the goal being 51% of the world population "flourishing" by 2051. Considerable evidence supports that effective interventions exist to help achieve this goal. Many of these interventions, however, use resources (such as therapists' and coaches' time) that can only benefit one person at a time. Promoting the flourishing of 51% of the world population by 2051, however, requires developing resources that can aid multiple people without additional investment of professional time. Indeed, psychological researchers have long acknowledged that psychosocial interventions can be disseminated via various less traditional approaches and this notion has been echoed in recent calls for the translation of in-person psychosocial interventions into new, more innovative, and cost-effective modes of delivery.

One mode is to provide resources directly to those who are interested without professional assistance, known simply as self-help. Although evidence supports that self-help can be efficacious, a majority of the current self-help resources are not based on scientifically supported principles or have not been evaluated. Thus, happiness-seekers have to sort through an array of resources to try to find evidence-based techniques. With regard to increasing happiness, many people use a "do-it-yourself" approach, drawing on ancient wisdom, scientific evidence, and lessons from popular approaches without professional guidance. Although this may work for some people, others might need more guidance, and it is thus important to help those interested in pursuing happiness to identify what is most likely to work based on the current scientific evidence.

This paper aims to provide the current state of research in increasing happiness especially as it pertains to self-help in order to help scientists and therapists interested in contributing to the study and application of positive psychology for self-help purposes.

We begin by briefly defining happiness and discussing its mutability, and then turn to defining a positive psychological intervention (hereafter: PPI) and to describing the current evidence base for a selection of evidence-based PPIs. We . . . highlight specific concerns related to developing self-help interventions based on positive psychology principles. We close with future directions and conclusions for the field.

What Is Happiness and Can It Change?

The predominant conception of happiness in Western cultures is that happiness is characterized by positive subjective appraisals and feelings. This conception, deemed the hedonic approach, preferences emotions and subjective evaluations rather than character, achievements, or objective life circumstances (which is deemed a eudaimonic approach). Thus, one is happy if he or she says so. These subjective states include two key components: (1) a cognitive appraisal that one's life is good, and (2) reports of frequently experiencing positive emotions and infrequently experiencing negative emotions. Accordingly, increasing happiness is a combination of helping people to view the circumstances of their lives more positively, as well as to experience more positive emotions and fewer negative emotions.

Although whether individual happiness could increase used to be a major debate, research throughout the past decade has provided substantial evidence that it can. Furthermore, research findings overwhelmingly support that the best way to do so is to change what one does to be more aligned with the behaviors of happy people. Self-help should therefore teach these scientifically supported behaviors to help people increase their own happiness.

. . . Some theories have . . . emerged to help explain the underlying mechanisms that drive the efficacy of PPIs. For example, Fredrickson's Broaden and Build Model posits that deliberately increasing positive emotions leads to greater resources (e.g., creativity, resilience, and openness to new experiences), which in turn can spur individuals to engage in behaviors that further promote well-being (Fredrickson, 2001). This cycle results in a positive feedback loop that might improve cognitive appraisals, positive emotions, and possibly even life circumstances. While not specific to any particular PPI, the model provides a solid empirical justification for the goal of increasing happiness and describes a cascade of benefits that is empirically testable. It has only been in very recent years, however, that questions of mechanisms and potential moderators of particular PPIs' effectiveness have started to receive empirical attention. . . .

Defining Positive Psychological Interventions

Behaviors related to happiness have been translated into several PPIs. . . . The most comprehensive and exclusive definition of a PPI . . . posits that an intervention can only be deemed a PPI if evidence exists that it successfully increases positive feelings, behaviors, and/or cognitions. Therefore, while many interventions could be potentially considered PPIs, they may not qualify as a PPI due to the lack of an empirical basis. . . .

Based upon our review of the literature, the resulting interventions can be classified into five categories: (1) savoring experiences and sensations, (2) cultivating (and sometimes expressing) gratitude, (3) engaging in kind acts, (4) promoting positive relationship processes, and (5) pursuing hope and meaning. Thus, these categories are a description of the evidence-base rather than a theoretical proposal of what could exist. We do not include strengths, a prominent research area within positive psychology, as a category itself because each of the identified categories corresponds to specific strengths and research suggests that mere strength-identification is an insufficient strategy to promote well-being. From this research, it appears as though strength-identification may not be valuable above and beyond the specific strategies it inspires. In the context of self-help, thus, we focus on these specific strategies as included in the categories above.

It is also important to note that whether or not a specific activity will actually lead to increased happiness is related to additional factors of the activity (e.g., dosage and variety) or the person (e.g., personality, strengths, and motivation); we will return to some of these issues at the end of the paper, as they provide additional layers of complexity to the somewhat simple story that disseminating an effective intervention leads to increased happiness.

Evidence for Positive Psychological Interventions

A considerable evidence base for PPIs exists. Two recently published meta-analyses suggest that on average PPIs lead to small-to-moderate increases in well-being and decreases in depressive symptoms. We review specific studies and PPIs below, but rather than present effect sizes for each study, we believe the effect sizes found in these meta-analyses provide a more useful summary of the field and the degree to which well-being might change over time in response to PPIs. Sin and Lyubomirsky (2009) found average increases in well-being of $r = .29$ and decreases in depressive symptoms of $r = .3 1$. Bolier and colleagues (2013), with their more restricted definition and fewer studies, however, found smaller effects of $d = 0.34$ for measures of subjective well-being, $d = 0.20$ for psychological well-being, and $d = 0.23$ for depressive symptoms. One reason we believe that it is useful to view these summary effect sizes rather than the effect sizes from individual studies is that characteristics of the application of the interventions were more predictive of differences in the effect sizes obtained than the specific techniques used. Longer intervention duration, greater degree of participant self-selection, and high level of initial participant distress (i.e., depression or other psychosocial problems) all corresponded to larger effect sizes. Most relevant to this review, however, is that supported interventions were more efficacious than self-help. We return to issues related to the widespread implementation of self-help after our review of specific PPI strategies. Overall, however, it appears that one can reasonably expect small but significant and lasting changes in well-being resulting from engaging in PPIs and even smaller effects when doing so on one's own. We now turn to a review and description of the specific PPIs that align with the definition of PPIs we offered.

Positive Psychology Interventions

Savoring

Savoring aims to intensify (through focused awareness) and prolong (through elaboration skills) momentary pleasurable experiences. The concept of savoring is derived from one of the most basic activities in mindfulness meditation wherein one deliberately and systematically attends to every aspect of an experience. While easiest to apply to a sensory experience, such as eating, savoring can be used with any type of experience, including memories. Individuals who engage in savoring more often have higher levels of happiness, life satisfaction, optimism, and perceived control, and lower levels of depression. Several factors have been proposed to increase the savoring of experiences including savoring in the presence of others, writing about the experience, considering counterfactuals, incorporating humor, focusing on the meaning of the activity, and maintaining an awareness of the fleeting nature of the experience. Savoring interventions fall into two categories: (1) those that teach and encourage the practice of the general principles of savoring and (2) those that teach a specific savoring skill and encourage the use of that skill.

Teaching a wide range of savoring strategies and encouraging the application of these strategies in one's life is an effective way to promote well-being. For example, Schueller (2010) instructed participants to reflect daily for at least 2–3 min on two pleasurable experiences and to make the pleasure last as long as possible. For example, when drinking hot chocolate, one might prolong that experience by focusing first on the various features of the whipped cream (i.e., the taste, texture, and temperature), then on the drink itself, and lastly, on the interplay of those flavors, textures, and temperatures together. Participants who engaged in this simple exercise reported higher levels of happiness one week later. More structured instruction in savoring also appears to contribute to well-being. An intervention taught participants savoring strategies through a 20-min audio recording and then instructed them to brainstorm ways they could have savored three positive activities they experienced within the past week. Participants were instructed to use these skills throughout the week and track the number of times they savored events in a savoring log. Participants who completed this savoring intervention experienced significant reductions in negative emotions but no significant boosts in positive emotions. Thus it might be that savoring serves to buffer against negative life events.

Another way to promote savoring is to teach specific strategies to enhance a person's focus and recall of pleasant aspects in one's environment and life. In "mindful photography," people spend at least 15 min daily taking photographs that are creative, beautiful, and hold personal meaning. Participants who took mindful photographs for a two-week period reported significantly more positive mood compared to participants who took photographs but received no specific instruction to the types of photographs to take. Similar strategies have been used for savoring positive memories, referred to as reminiscence. Reminiscence has been used particularly for older populations with positive benefits on life satisfaction.

Gratitude

Gratitude refers to the emotional response accompanying the acknowledgment that some outside force is responsible for something good that has happened to oneself. Gratitude interventions include both grateful reflection and gratitude-motivated activities. Both have demonstrated efficacy at increasing well-being including increasing positive emotions, reducing depressive symptoms, and improving physical health. Grateful reflection, exemplified by gratitude journaling, refers to listing things for which one is grateful. In gratitude journaling, people write down what they are thankful for, most often completing this in private. Some instructions emphasize the importance of writing both the thing that one is grateful for as well as the reason why that thing happened, however, benefits have been found with only noting the events. Gratitude-motivated activities encourage public expressions of gratitude. In a direct comparison of expressing gratitude versus merely promoting positive thoughts toward a relationship partner, it was found that grateful expressions were considerably more effective at enhancing the strength of the relationship. The PPI known as the "gratitude letter" instructs an individual to express gratitude to another person that he or she has never had a proper chance to thank. The instructions emphasize the importance of conducting a gratitude visit (i.e., a face-to-face meeting) after writing the letter; however, studies suggest that this is not the essential component and that simply writing a letter may also boost well-being, albeit perhaps to a slightly lesser degree.

Kindness

Common wisdom states that one of the most reliable ways to feel better is to do good for someone else. Indeed, happier people tend to act more kindly, and performing kind acts, in turn, boosts happiness. Furthermore, happiness and kindness appear to exist in some kind of "positive feedback loop" such that one encourages the other. In this way, acts of kindness interact with gratitude to create reciprocity between givers and recipients. Even more interesting, reflecting on one's acts of kindness, even without deliberately increasing the frequency of kind acts, also increases happiness.

Kindness research has examined a variety of kind acts, ranging from brief, cost-free behaviors, such as holding the door or complimenting a stranger to behaviors that come at a personal cost, such as buying a gift or helping a colleague with a project at work. One type of kind act that has received particular research attention is prosocial spending – that is, spending money on other people. Compared to spending money on oneself, spending money on others leads to increases in happiness. This line of research suggests that while, on average, money does not "buy" happiness, using money to promote kindness provides an important exception. Even interventions, however, that promote kindness more generally appear to lead to significant boosts in well-being. In a study by Lyubomirsky, Tkach, and Sheldon (2004) undergraduate students who performed five kind acts weekly for 6 weeks experienced significant increases in well-being compared to a no-treatment control group, but only if these kind acts were performed all in one day rather than spread throughout the week.

Promoting Positive Relationship Processes

In his three-word summary of positive psychology, "Other people matter," Chris Peterson (2006) emphasizes the centrality of positive relationships for happiness. Indeed, robust findings support this claim. In fact, relationships are so central to happiness that one analysis of the happiest people led to the conclusion that "good social relationships might be a necessary condition for high happiness" (Diener & Seligman, 2002, p. 82). Thus, increasing the amount of social contact a person has and improving the quality of one's interpersonal relationships are both strong pathways to promoting happiness.

One intervention designed to improve a positive process in one's social interactions is active-constructive responding. This intervention draws on research that noted that individuals respond to good news in either an active versus passive and constructive versus destructive manner and that couples that use more active-constructive responding have more satisfying and stable relationships. Active-constructive responding means reacting to the good news with authentic displays of excitement and expanding the discussion of the event through active questioning. For example, if one's spouse received a job promotion, an active-constructive response would be "That is great news! I am so happy for you! We should go out to dinner to celebrate. Tell me exactly what happened when you found out." In many ways, this is similar to savoring as

it serves to intensify and elongate a positive experience through encouraging, retelling, and re-experiencing, but is circumscribed to the interpersonal domain and the sharing of positive news. Instruction in active-constructive responding has been provided as a standalone exercise and incorporated into programs such as Group Positive Psychotherapy and the Masters of Resilience Training (MRT) Program. Although, active-constructive responding is well liked, it has limited support for its efficacy as a standalone exercise. More research needs to assess whether it can increase its impact on happiness when delivered experimentally.

Creating Meaning

Various conceptualizations of meaning in life exist, encompassing an understanding of relationships among people, things, and events to a general sense that one's life is significant. Despite these various definitions, empirical findings have consistently indicated that meaning in life predicts well-being, happiness, and life satisfaction. Thus, interventions aimed at facilitating the construction of meaning and purpose can contribute to individual happiness.

One way that PPIs seek to promote meaning is through expressive writing paradigms. Life narratives have a powerful influence over people's construction of meaning and their individual happiness. The cognitive change theory of expressive writing posits that writing can enhance well-being and emotional adjustment through facilitating the construction of a coherent and meaningful narrative of the event. In the basic paradigm underlying this research, people write about a past trauma on consecutive days with instructions to facilitate specific styles of expression; participants instructed to include both the facts of the trauma and their emotions experienced fewer illness-related doctor's visits in the weeks to follow compared to other styles of writing. While the expressive writing paradigm is not itself a PPI, research examining the effects of writing expressively about positive events is, and has found similar benefits. Expressive writing is a useful tool for self-help because it can be done independently with minimal instruction and has demonstrated benefits even when the writing is repeated over several days. An important caveat is the same style of writing might not be useful for both positive and negative events. In a series of studies, Lyubomirsky, Sousa, and Dickerhoof (2006) found that analyzing events, facilitated through writing, improved well-being and health with negative but not positive events. For positive events, on the other hand, participants benefited more from talking through the event aloud or adopting an approach where they replayed but did not analyze the event.

Another way in which meaning can be promoted is through increasing hope for the future – and more specifically, the belief that one's goals are within one's reach. The more abstract idea of pursuing hope has typically been operationalized as the formulation and pursuit of personally meaningful goals, which according to Self-Determination Theory contributes substantially to one's happiness. Writing about life goals, for instance, can bring about greater clarity and awareness to those goals. [T]he "Best Possible Self" intervention increases focus on one's life goals by requiring people to visualize and write about their "ideal future life," in as much detail as possible. Participants who completed this writing assignment over a 4-week period experienced increases in positive emotions and displayed more interest and higher degrees of motivation compared with a control group who merely wrote about life details. It is worth noting that although this exercise is useful at bringing clarity and awareness of goals, it does not provide support at putting those goals into action.

Other research has demonstrated that teaching people goal setting and planning skills is an effective way to increase happiness. Goal setting and planning relate to the other major component of Snyder's (2002) conceptualization of hope, "pathways thinking." "Pathways thinking" involves brain-storming and planning the specific routes one can use to achieve a given goal. The first portion of MacLeod and colleagues' (2008) intervention is similar to the "Best Possible Self" intervention; participants receive instructions to envision their goals. However, participants are also instructed on how to select and refine goals, to plan to achieve those goals, to address obstacles and potential solutions to achieving those goals, and lastly to review the implementation of the plan. This program was effective in both group and individual self-directed formats.

. . .

Concerns and Caveats Regarding the Widespread Implementation of Self-Administered PPIs

Thus far, we have told a simple story: effective PPIs exist, and if individuals can access them – and we believe that self-help is the best vehicle by which this access will occur in a scalable and sustainable way – they will become happier. However, in reality, this story is much more complex; compared to professionally-delivered or supported interventions,

self-help has several unique challenges, which must be addressed.

Motivation and Engagement

When people seek out self-help resources, their motivation is often quite high, however this motivation often drops over time resulting in a reduced use of the techniques. Indeed, with regard to the *Live Happy* iPhone app, only a small portion of the people who downloaded the app used it and left enough data to allow analysis of the changes in their mood scores. This is quite consistent with other work that finds that an overwhelming number of people who begin an Internet intervention drop out, with very few even progressing past a first lesson. Thus self-help interventions need to be designed to help hook people in early and facilitate long-term behavior change.

The Fogg Behavior Model (FBM) offers several insights into design considerations to do so. In the FBM, three factors influence one's performance of a target behavior: motivation, ability, and triggers. When motivation is high, people are able to complete more difficult behaviors (i.e., finding a self-help resource). When motivation is low, however, people's ability to complete difficult behaviors drops. In order to be successful, self-help programs should provide structure such that when motivation drops people will continue to practice a target behavior. . . . Having a scheduled, weekly activity will promote follow through in the future, even when motivation drops, because of the commitment made and the social reinforcement of getting together with a friend. Another insight from the FBM is that behavior change should begin with small behaviors that through repeated practice will increase one's ability to complete larger behaviors. Thus, a person might begin by gratitude journaling a single thing each day and begin to challenge himself by noting more and more things he is grateful for as time goes on.

Motivation is a critical element of intervention efficacy as well. Indeed, some research suggests that only those motivated to increase their happiness benefit from PPIs. In a study by Lyubomirsky and colleagues (2011), they compared participants recruited either through advertisements for a happiness intervention or cognitive exercises. Recruitment source was deemed to be a proxy for motivation. All participants, regardless of the recruitment ad that attracted them, were randomly assigned to one of three conditions: two included previously supported active PPIs (gratitude or optimism) and one a control condition (listing experiences of the week). Both the gratitude and optimism conditions led to increases in well-being compared to the control condition but only for the "motivated" participants who were recruited into the study with the "happiness intervention" ad. The results of this study provide both reservations and promise for PPIs. First, the lack of efficacy within the "unmotivated" group expecting to receive "cognitive exercises" demonstrates the PPIs may not be effective for all people. One could interpret these findings to be suggestive of possible placebo effects for PPIs; however, it seems unlikely given that well-being did not improve among the "motivated" group who received the control condition. Lyubomirsky and colleagues (2011) took these findings to illustrate the critical importance of motivation. They concluded the PPIs require both a proper "way" and the "will" to follow through and do the suggested technique. Fortunately, PPIs are well-liked and compared to other strategies with the same goal (i.e., promoting a better mood) are viewed as more useful and used more often. So although motivation is an important concern for self-help, PPIs might be particularly effective at overcoming this concern.

Variety and Flexibility

Variety appears to be a critical factor in supporting both initial and sustained benefits of any life changes related to increased happiness. Professionals often adapt interventions to consider a person's current needs and capacities, as well as offering suggestions to continue to challenge a person to apply their skills in new ways to promote growth. Self-help interventions can, *and should*, be designed to support long-term practice. For example, to add variety to the "Best Possible Self" intervention, Lyubomirsky and colleagues (2011) modified the instructions to include writing about different topics each week (i.e., romantic life, educational attainment, hobbies or personal interests, family life, career situation, social life, community involvement, and physical/mental health). Variations such as these should be developed drawing on the current theories of happiness and tested to ensure they contribute to sustainable benefits in happiness.

Person-Activity Fit

Perhaps the most important caveat to the proposal that widespread dissemination of PPIs would be beneficial to the general population is the need for a more nuanced approach that considers person-activity fit. Initial work in the PPI literature looking at individual differences suggests substantial variation exists among happiness-seekers – Parks and colleagues (2012) identified two distinct "clusters" that differ substantially in their baseline levels of life satisfaction, positive emotion, and depressive symptom

levels. One of these subgroups was consistent with population norms reported in other research: reasonably happy, experiencing few or no depressive symptoms. The other, however, reported well-being scores low enough to suggest clinical depression. While self-help approaches can be effective even for people suffering from mental disorders, presumably, these two subgroups might require different self-help techniques. For instance, individual differences in depression levels have practical significance when it comes to gratitude. In one study, a gratitude intervention was ineffective, and in some cases led to reduced well-being, among depressed individuals who were also interpersonally "needy." Given the existence of cases where the efficacy of PPIs varies by individual differences, we recommend that the widespread dissemination of PPIs to the general population be balanced with further attention to questions of person-activity fit.

Rigorous Designs

Rigorous scientific research studies on self-help are limited. Indeed, as previously mentioned, many self-help resources do not draw on empirically-based principles and lack validation on their own. This issue is mirrored in positive psychology research, where PPIs are often not tested against rigorous control conditions. Furthermore, results suggest that although PPIs are efficacious when compared to no-treatment controls, the effects are considerably lower when compared to "treatment as usual" or placebo controls. Positive findings for PPIs may be circumscribed within specific groups (e.g., motivated individuals) and differences among samples may result in an inability to replicate key findings. Thus, although we have presented considerable evidence that PPIs do work, we provide the caveat – not always. Although we believe further exploration of factors such as motivation, variety, and person-activity fit will help explain some of these inconsistences, it is nevertheless critical that investigations use high-quality methods to examine the limits of the effectiveness of these techniques.

Future Directions and Conclusions

Positive psychology has helped develop a variety of intervention strategies that can reliably boost individual happiness. An important next step is to research important questions of what interventions work for whom, under what circumstances, and in what contexts to ensure that when interventions are provided as self-help, people will receive the most effective and relevant techniques. Some research has begun to address these questions but much additional work is needed to fully disentangle these issues.

In order to do so, however, studies should evaluate the effectiveness of these methods when provided in real-world settings and the complications and nuances that arise when doing so. Indeed, promoting the flourishing of the world population requires bringing resources directly to people as opposed to assuming they will find these resources themselves.

In conclusion, PPIs can lead to reliable boosts in well-being, yet these benefits are smaller when provided as self-help resources. In this paper, we have outlined specific positive psychological strategies including savoring, gratitude, kindness, promoting positive relationship processes, and pursuing hope and meaning. Beyond their efficacy, PPIs are useful for self-help not merely because they increase well-being but because they are also well liked. Effectively using PPIs for self-help, however, requires a consideration of the role that motivation and engagement, variety and flexibility, and person-activity fit play in supporting long-term behavior change.

Moreover, in order to begin to achieve Seligman's goal of promoting flourishing worldwide, PPI researchers must think beyond questions of efficacy and begin to tackle the problem of dissemination. What are the best modalities for distributing PPIs to the general population? How can PPIs be made available in a way that is affordable and accessible for all? How will we accurately assess whether PPIs "work" in the more inherently messy real-world environments through which they will ultimately be offered to users? . . . We hope . . . that readers will be inspired to do that work, as we believe it will ultimately benefit a substantial portion of the world population.

References

Bolier, L., Haverman, M., Westerhof, G. J., Riper, H., Smit, F., & Bohlmeijer, E. (2013). Positive psychology interventions: A meta-analysis of randomized controlled studies. *BMC Public Health, 13*, 119. Retrieved from http://www.biomedcentral.com/1471-2458/13/119.doi:10.1186/1471-2458-13-119

Diener, E., & Seligman, M. E. (2002). Very happy people. *Psychological Science, 13*, 81–84.

Fredrickson, B. L. (2001). The role of positive emotions in positive psychology: The broaden-and-built theory of positive emotions. *American Psychologist, 56*, 218–226.

Lyubomirsky, S., Dickerhoof, R., Boehm, J. K., & Sheldon, K. M. (2011). Becoming happier takes both a will and a proper way: An experimental longitudinal intervention to boost well-being. *Emotion, 11*, 391–402.

Lyubomirsky, S., Sousa, L., & Dickerhoof, R. (2006). The costs and benefits of writing, talking, and thinking about life's triumphs and defeats. *Journal of Personality and Social Psychology, 90*, 692–708.

Lyubomirsky, S., Tkach, C., & Sheldon, K. M. (2004). *Pursuing sustained happiness through random act of kindness and counting one's blessings: Tests of two six-week interventions*. Unpublished manuscript, University of California, Riverside.

MacLeod, A. K., Coates, E., & Hetherton, J. (2008). Increasing well-being through teaching goal-setting and planning skills: Results of a brief intervention. *Journal of Happiness Studies, 9*, 185–196.

Parks, A. C., Della Porta, M. D., Pierce, R. S., Zilca, R., & Lyubomirsky, S. (2012). Pursuing happiness in everyday life: The characteristics and behaviors of online happiness seekers. *Emotion, 12*, 1222–1234.

Peterson, C. (2006). *A primer in positive psychology*. New York, NY: Oxford University Press.

Schueller, S. M. (2010). Preferences for positive psychology exercises. *Journal of Positive Psychology, 5*, 192–203.

Sin, N. L., & Lyubomirsky, S. (2009). Enhancing well-being and alleviating depressive symptoms with positive psychological interventions: A practice-friendly metaanalysis. *Journal of Clinical Psychology, 65*, 467–487.

Snyder, C. R. (2002). Hope theory: Rainbows in the mind. *Psychological Inquiry, 13*, 249–275.

STEPHEN M. SCHUELLER, PhD, is a research assistant professor in the Department of Preventive Medicine at Northwestern University's Feinberg School of Medicine and a faculty member of the Center for Behavioral Intervention Technologies (CBITs). His research focuses on the use of Internet and mobile interventions for the treatment and prevention of depression and the promotion of happiness and well-being.

ACACIA C. PARKS, PhD, is an assistant professor of psychology at Hiram College. Her research focuses on the efficacy of positive psychological interventions and the psychological and behavioral characteristics of individuals who use them.

Laurel C. Newman and Randy J. Larsen    **NO**

How Much of Our Happiness Is Within Our Control?

In reviewing articles for the "no" side of this issue, there were several individual perspectives on why we psychologists should take caution before announcing to the public that we know how to make people happier. However, there was no culminating piece containing the variety of lines of logic and research that inspire this warning. Thus, the purpose of this piece is not to insist that we have absolutely zero control over our own happiness. Rather, it is to summarize the evidence suggesting that we have much less control over it than positive psychologists typically espouse.

1. **The heritability of happiness:** In 1989, a group of researchers began a wildly ambitious and comprehensive study of twins called the Minnesota Twin Family study. They used comparisons of identical twins, fraternal twins, and other family members to determine the proportion of the variation in the public's happiness scores that is caused by genetic factors, which is called the *heritability* of happiness. In 1996, two of the researchers (David Lykken and Auke Tellegen) published a paper reporting that the heritability is around .50, which means about half of the variability we see in the population's happiness scores is caused by people's genes, and about half by other things. Most psychologists would concede that a person cannot change his or her genes, so it follows that at least one major cause of happiness lies outside of our control.

2. **The hedonic treadmill:** In 1978, Brickman, Coates, and Janoff-Bulman published a well-cited study showing that people who had befallen great fortune (lottery winners) or great tragedy (recent paraplegics) returned to their preexisting levels of happiness within a year following the event. A re-analysis of the data from the study showed that the paraplegics' level of happiness really never fully returned to baseline.

Nevertheless, follow-up research has been done on the topic, and most psychologists agree that people do adapt emotionally to most of the good and bad events in life and have a surprising tendency to remain very near their preexisting level of happiness despite life's slings and arrows. This has been called the "hedonic treadmill theory" because no matter how fast or slow people "run," they stay in the same place (emotionally, of course). This is good news because it means we have the capacity to adapt to the inevitable tragedies and problems of life, but it is also bad news because, for most people, it precludes ever attaining everlasting bliss.

The two points made thus far comprise the portion of this "no we cannot make ourselves happier" argument that is generally accepted, and even pointed out, by most positive psychologists. The points that follow may be viewed as more controversial.

3. **The famous 40 percent:** Sonja Lyubomirsky is most often cited by positive psychologists and the media as the person who has cracked the happiness code and made the fruits available to all. In her book, *The How of Happiness: A New Approach to Getting the Life You Want,* she summarizes the research showing that happiness is 50 percent heritable and 10 percent due to well-studied demographic variables. She claims *that means* the remaining 40 percent of happiness is within our control. To illustrate this concept, the cover of her book contains a pie with 40 percent removed and the claim, "this much happiness—up to 40 percent—is within your power to change." Her book has been touted by many as scientific evidence of great news: We have a surprisingly high level of control over our own happiness. There are a few problems with this conclusion, though.

a. She misuses heritability estimates. Heritability estimates estimate the proportion of individual differences, or variation, in scores *among a group of people* that can be attributed to their genes. They describe variation in a group, and cannot be applied to any individual person.[1] There are undoubtedly people whose happiness lies largely within their control, and others who suffer from life circumstances that will likely cause lasting and inescapable misery. It is the job of positive psychologists to study these sorts of distinctions rather than making the misleading claim that everyone has an equal capacity for increasing his or her happiness.

b. Even if the 40 percent estimate were valid (which, as I just explained, it isn't), it is not accurate to claim that whatever portion of our happiness is not due to genetics and not due to as-of-yet carefully studied demographic variables is by default within our control. That 40 percent estimate would simply include *everything else*—everything besides genes and the demographic variables that have been carefully studied. That leaves room for many situational and personality variables that likely have a strong impact on our emotional state. Home foreclosures, lost jobs, unfaithful spouses, chronic illness, unplanned pregnancies, miscarriages, broken down cars and other daily hassles, work/life conflict, marital discord—the list is practically endless of things that would be included in that "everything else" portion, and the very important question remains as to which of those variables matter most, and to what extent those variables are actually within our control.

c. The evidence for the effectiveness of existing happiness interventions is shaky and unclear. Several positive psychologists have their own prescriptions for how to increase one's own happiness. These prescriptions are generally based on scientific research,[2] and most involve happiness exercises you can do easily at home to boost your happiness. There are currently two lines of research that have received the most attention that claim to increase happiness. In her book, Sonja Lyubomirsky describes exercises such as a *gratitude exercise* (wherein you contemplate 5 things you are grateful for at the end of each week), committing regular acts of kindness toward others, and distracting yourself when things are going badly rather than ruminating. Seligman and colleagues

have tested 5 similar strategies and found scattered effects with 3 of them (though they also found temporary effects with an unconvincing placebo exercise). Although these interventions are often referred to by positive psychologists as promising evidence that we can boost our own happiness, the actual effects of these interventions are unimpressive. Though Lyubomirsky's book does not include actual data from her studies, a careful reading of the original journal articles reporting her results shows that many of the strategies have weak, improperly derived, or even unreported statistical effects that only show up at all under a very specific set of circumstances. Her 2005 paper is most commonly cited as scientific evidence that happiness-boosting interventions can work. However, in the actual paper, the *gratitude exercise* only mattered for people who did it once per week (not three times per week) and the *acts of kindness* exercise only mattered for people who did 5 acts of kindness all in one day for 6 weeks straight (not people who spread the acts out). Additionally, I use the term "mattered" rather than "worked" because the data were not reported in the article, nor were the results of any statistical tests.[3] Indeed, Boehm and Lyubomirsky's chapter in the *Handbook of Positive Psychology* reviews 8 studies, each testing several of what they call successful activities for increasing happiness. But the whole of the chapter contains mention of only one statistically significant result. The situation is surprisingly bleak considering the methodological features of her studies that should stack the results in her favor.[6] Nevertheless, her book has been translated into 11 languages and she is cited by positive psychologists and the media alike as having uncovered lasting keys to happiness. Several crucial questions remain: Do these exercises really increase happiness at all? If so, what boundary conditions are necessary for them to work? Are they ineffective for some people, and can they even have drawbacks?[4] Will any boost to happiness resulting from these exercises be long-lasting?[5] Given what we know about the hedonic treadmill, and given that emotional adaptation is even faster for good events than for bad ones, it seems likely that any benefits that people might gain from these interventions would dissipate quickly over time.

4. **The trouble with the denominator:** It might be surprising to most people to learn that personality

psychologists have found that positive and negative affect (PA and NA) are independent of each other. This means the people who experience the most positive emotions are not necessarily the people who experience the least negative emotions. Furthermore, most psychologists accept the proposition that our subjective well-being is defined, in emotional terms, as our ratio of positive to negative affect. So to make a person happier, you could increase the numerator (PA) *or* decrease the denominator (NA). Unfortunately, there is also a well-documented pattern of findings across various subfields of psychology that "bad is stronger than good." Bad events have a deeper and longer lasting impact on us emotionally than good events. This is called the *negativity bias*, and it is interpreted by most as having an evolutionary purpose: avoiding threats helps us survive; relishing accomplishments does not. What all this suggests is that people would get more bang for their buck by trying to eliminate the causes of negative emotion in their lives than by trying to increase the positive. This has been pointed out in the positive psychology literature,[7] but it remains largely ignored or even dismissed by most positive psychologists, as their "declaration of independence" depends on their determination to focus on increasing the positive and not dwelling on the negative. To make matters worse, while bad is stronger than good, it also seems evident that many key sources of negative affect (such as those listed in paragraph 3b) are largely if not fully outside of people's control. Indeed, Diener and colleagues recently stressed the need for a *revised adaptation (hedonic treadmill) theory* based on results from a large longitudinal study investigating whether or not people's life satisfaction levels are stable across time. They concluded that most people's were largely stable (which fits with hedonic treadmill theory), but that a portion of people (about 25 percent) have more fluctuating levels of life satisfaction. What variables did they find have a significant and lasting impact on life satisfaction? Unemployment and widowhood (both negative and outside of our control) had the strongest effects, with divorce having significant but smaller effects (an event most people view as negative and often outside of their control). It was in this article that they pointed out that paraplegics and other disabled people (again, negative and outside of their control) actually do not return fully to baseline. The lottery winners did not gain any lasting happiness from their wins (a positive event outside of their control). In fact, almost all the data cited in their review shows that, though life satisfaction may fluctuate, it seems to be lastingly influenced primarily by events that are negative and outside of our control. Another comprehensive study by Diener and colleagues compared well-being data from large samples of people from 55 nations and found that subjective well-being was higher among people who lived in nations that were wealthier, individualistic, and that protected their citizens' human rights. Few people in countries that lack these characteristics are there by choice.

There is some debate as well among psychologists as to whether we *should* be trying to increase happiness in the American public, most of whom report being pretty happy already. That is an issue for another day. The question here is, *if* we concede that boosting happiness is a worthwhile goal to pursue for psychologists, to what extent is doing so *possible*? Careful research has shown that happiness is by no means predetermined or "fixed" by genetics. Psychologists have uncovered a variety of environmental variables that predict (correlate with or cause) happiness. However, we must not confuse prediction with control. Nobody chooses to become a widow, be confined to a wheelchair, live in an impoverished nation, or lose their job. Many of the most influential environmental variables in our lives are every bit as uncontrollable as our genes.

In the field of psychology, unbridled enthusiasm often gives way to skepticism, and this is a good thing for the field. Psychology has a long history of demonstrating that people like to be in control of their surroundings, and they like to be happy. It comes as no surprise that they would embrace the finding that they are in control of making themselves happy. But the job of psychologists is to make claims based on objective interpretation of scientific evidence. Objective interpretation seems to point more to the idea that most of what influences our happiness in large and lasting ways lies outside the realm of the controllable.

Notes

1. See Diener, 2008, for a lengthier explanation of this concept.
2. Psychologists agree that any finding in the field of psychology as well as any claims for treatment or intervention must be based on scientific research, so this is a good thing. However, claiming that one's opinions are based on scientific research has become somewhat of a free pass to say whatever you want as long as there is at least some trend

in your data that is consistent with your theory. Most psychologists are not going to take the time to sift through the details of others' (often unpublished) data and publish purposeful criticisms of others' work, and most laypersons do not have the skills to judge the quality of research. Therefore, whether or not the quality and results of the research actually warrant the claims being made is a question that often goes unchecked.

3. The results were described by bar graphs, which showed increases in well-being of .4 points for the acts of kindness exercise and .15 points (identical to the magnitude of change for the control group, incidentally) for the gratitude exercise. However, because there was no information on the scale or its end points and no statistical analyses were presented, it is impossible to judge what these values mean. One can only assume the results were not statistically significant, in which case it is misleading to refer to this article as evidence that these two activities increase happiness.

4. For example, the advice to stop ruminating probably has a lot of cash value for a chronic ruminator, but for most normal, well-adjusted people, ruminating can signal to us that we need to do something about a problem in our environment. Indeed, evolutionary and personality psychologists agree that negative emotions exist because they serve a purpose. Stifling the emotion, though more affectively pleasant, may not always be in our best interest.

5. Occasionally, researchers do conduct follow-up studies several months down the road. When they do, they often find mixed success, meaning that people are still a little happier who engaged in some of the exercises, but people who completed other exercises have returned to baseline (if they ever budged at all).

6. For example, lack of a convincing placebo control group (even though there is evidence that placebos have an effect in these types of studies), multiple measures of happiness and subjective well-being as dependent variables (which increases the overall probability of finding a significant result due to chance), and instructions telling participants that the researchers *expect* the exercises to boost people's moods (which can influence participants' responses).

7. Larsen and Prizmic estimate that bad events impact us about 3.14 times as strongly as good events.

LAUREL NEWMAN is an associate professor of psychology, and department of behavioral sciences chair at Fontbonne University in St. Louis, MO. Dr. Newman's research interests include studying the ways personality traits and situational and contextual factors combine to influence people's thoughts, feelings, and behavior. Her recent work has focused on identifying the predictors of adjustment and success in college among undergraduate students, as well as providing a critical analysis of the conclusions contained in the positive psychology literature.

RANDY J. LARSEN is a personality psychologist interested in emotion. He does research on such topics as emotion/cognition interactions, emotional aging, emotion regulation, and subjective well-being. He currently serves as a member of the Publication Committee of the Society for Personality and Social Psychology. Additionally, he is a fellow of both APA and APS, serves on several journal editorial boards, and is currently serving as Chair of the Psychology Department at Washington University.

EXPLORING THE ISSUE

Can Positive Psychology Make Us Happier?

Critical Thinking and Reflection

1. Imagine you are an unhappy person who wishes to become happier. How would each of the viewpoints presented in these articles influence your decision whether or not to seek therapy? What might you expect to gain from therapy in each case?
2. Which of these viewpoints do you agree with most? How does your choice make a difference in how you, as a hypothetical therapist, might address an unhappy client's needs?
3. What does it mean to be "happy" in each of the views expressed in these two articles? Does defining happiness have an impact on whether or not positive psychology techniques? If yes, how so? If no, then why not?
4. Psychologists debate whether or not we should try to increase happiness in the American public. What arguments might either side make?
5. Larsen and Newman argue that psychologists should take caution before making public announcements about how we can make ourselves happier. What problems might result from a lack of caution?

Is There Common Ground?

Being able to determine how to increase happiness and relieve suffering is one of the main goals of psychology, especially psychotherapy. Additionally, happiness is widely held to be an essential component of individual well-being. Most people can agree that if an individual is able to increase their happiness, his or her quality of life will also improve as a result. Indeed, the authors of both articles agree that those who are happier tend to have particular behavioral characteristics (gratitude, kindness, promoting positive relationships, etc.) related to their perceived happiness. However, whether or not an increase in happiness is within our personal control is still very much up for debate.

Both articles agree that there are limitations to using positive psychology interventions to increase happiness, although they may not agree on the severity of these limitations. Some of the less severe limitations include flexibility and variability of interventions, person-activity fit, and motivation to be happy. Some of the more severe limitations indicate that happiness is really outside of our control,

including the heritability of happiness and the "hedonic treadmill theory" of happiness. If happiness is truly outside of our control, could it be possible that positive changes in the environment can promote happiness, just as negative changes in the environment (e.g., loss of job and death of loved one) decrease happiness?

Additional Resource

Boehm, J. K., and Lyubomirsky, S. (2009). The promise of sustainable happiness. In *The Oxford Handbook of Positive Psychology*, 2nd ed. Oxford University Press.

Held, B.S. (2004). The negative side of positive psychology. *Journal of Humanistic Psychology*, 44(1), 9–41.

McMahon, D. M. (2006). *Happiness: A History*. Boston, MA: Atlantic Monthly Press.

Niemiec, R., and Wedding, D. (2008). *Positive Psychology at the Movies: Using Films to Build Virtues and Character Strengths*. Cambridge, MA: Hogrefe.

Internet References . . .

ABC News

http://abcnews.go.com/Health/story?id=4115033&page=1&singlePage=true

New York Times

http://www.nytimes.com/2010/06/01/health/research/01happy.html?_r=1

U.S. News

http://health.usnews.com/health-news/family-health/brain-and-behavior/articles/2009/06/24/positive-emotional-psychology-have-a-daily-diet-of-positive-emotions

Selected, Edited, and with Issue Framing Material by:
Edwin E. Gantt, *Brigham Young University*

ISSUE

Is Emotional Intelligence Valid?

YES: John D. Mayer, Peter Salovey, and David R. Caruso, from "Emotional Intelligence: New Ability or Eclectic Traits?" *American Psychologist* (2008)

NO: Gerald Matthews, Moshe Zeidner, and Richard Roberts, from "The Science, the Myth, and the Future of Emotional Intelligence," *Emotional Intelligence: Science and Myth* (2002)

Learning Outcomes

After reading this issue, you will be able to:

- Discuss whether the narrowing of the definition of Emotional Intelligence (EI) has reduced its misinterpretation.
- Understand whether discriminating between emotions is a learned skill.
- Discuss whether there is any connection between EI and either brain or cognitive structures.
- Take and successfully defend a position on whether EI is uniquely capable of predicting specific behaviors.

ISSUE SUMMARY

YES: Psychologists John Mayer, Peter Salovey, and David Caruso maintain that some individuals have a greater emotional intelligence (EI), a greater capacity than others to carry out sophisticated information processing about emotions.

NO: Psychologists Gerald Matthew, Moshe Zeidner, and Richard Roberts contend that the concept of emotional intelligence, as currently understood, is fundamentally flawed, having no reliable foundation in biological, cognitive, coping, or personality models of human behavior.

Do you have a friend who seems to understand everyone, who just seems to "know" how others are feeling or what they are thinking? Is it simply a phenomenon of personality, or do some individuals possess a type of intelligence that facilitates this social skill? Could there be a social or emotional intelligence apart from that measured by standard intelligence tests? From as early as the 1920s, psychologists such as Thorndike, Wechsler, and Gardner have sought to explain performance outcomes that could not be explained by traditional intelligence models. The term emotional intelligence (EI) was coined as early as 1966 to account for some of that unexplained portion, but it was not until the 1990s that psychologists developed models and tests for measuring EI. After *Time* magazine ran a 1996 cover story on EI, the

term became a buzzword in the popular media and among professionals, some of whom assert that EI may be more important to business success than standard intelligence.

The concept of EI has taken on a life of its own since Harvard psychologist Daniel Goleman's 1995 book on EI promised to redefine what it means to be smart. Seminars and books appeared advising leaders about the importance of EI in the workplace, and some psychologists attempted to incorporate EI into their models of intelligence. However, many other psychologists disagreed. Apart from the confusion of what exactly EI means, some researchers insist that the original definition of EI is not a true form of intelligence but rather a matter of awareness and introspection. They argued that intelligence factors have to be part of a single, general mental ability.

In the YES article, John Mayer, Peter Salovey, and David Caruso concede that the popularization of EI has led to considerable confusion as to what EI is or should be. They argue, however, that their own scientific conception of EI qualifies as a valid intelligence because it refers to a mental ability that may exist apart from general intelligence or personality. Further, EI reliably and uniquely predicts behaviors, such as the ability to maintain positive personal commitments. They note that individuals high in EI have a differentiated ability to comprehend and use emotions to benefit themselves and others. Even when personality traits are controlled, EI measurements can predict deviancy and problem behaviors.

In the NO article, Gerald Matthews, Moshe Zeidner, and Richard Roberts contend that many of the promises and claims of EI scholars are myths. They argue that no compelling explanation of a mechanism for emotional intelligence exists. Neither neurobiological nor cognitive approaches to EI have presented any link between EI and known or supposed neural or cognitive architectural structures. Beyond that, the contextual nature of emotional situations and the changing criterion for what counts as an effective response make the creation of a generalized, rank-ordered EI impossible. Any and all differences between people that may be attributed to EI are already explicable under extant personality and intelligence theories—EI adds nothing to our current understanding of humans.

POINT

- The earliest model of EI was in some respects overly broad and therefore interpreted incorrectly.
- Emotions are signals that convey information, so one can use them to facilitate thinking.
- Measures of EI significantly increase the prediction of standard intelligence tests.
- Whereas emotional knowledge (the *information* that EI operates on) can be learned easily, EI is a stable aptitude not easily learned.

COUNTERPOINT

- Most definitions are so all-inclusive that they make the concept unintelligible.
- One cannot reason with emotion. Reason and emotion are two distinct processes.
- What is termed emotional intelligence is simply intelligence applied to emotions.
- Discriminating between emotions is a learned skill, just as is detecting a given emotion.

YES ↵

John D. Mayer, Peter Salovey, and David R. Caruso

Emotional Intelligence: New Ability or Eclectic Traits?

The notion that there is an emotional intelligence (EI) began as a tentative proposal (Mayer, DiPaolo, & Salovey, 1990; Salovey & Mayer, 1990). The original idea was that some individuals possess the ability to reason about and use emotions to enhance thought more effectively than others. Since 1990, EI has grown into a small industry of publication, testing, education, and consulting (Matthews, Roberts, & Zeidner, 2004; Matthews, Zeidner, & Roberts, 2002). Matthews et al. (2002) have outlined the dramatic growth of the psychological literature concerning an EI. Yet the apparent size of the field dwarfs what we regard as relevant scientific research in the area. In fact, one commentator recently argued that EI is an invalid concept in part because it is defined in too many ways (Locke, 2005, p. 425).

The original definition of EI conceptualized it as a set of interrelated abilities (Mayer & Salovey, 1997; Salovey & Mayer, 1990). Yet other investigators have described EI as an eclectic mix of traits, many dispositional, such as happiness, self-esteem, optimism, and self-management, rather than as ability based (Bar-On, 2004; Boyatzis & Sala, 2004; Petrides & Furnham, 2001; Tett, Fox, & Wang, 2005). This alternative approach to the concept—the use of the term to designate eclectic mixes of traits—has led to considerable confusion and misunderstandings as to what an EI is or should be (Daus & Ashkanasy, 2003; Gohm, 2004; Mayer, 2006). Many features, such as self-esteem, included in these models do not directly concern emotion or intelligence or their intersection (Matthews et al., 2004, p. 185). We agree with many of our colleagues who have noted that the term *emotional intelligence* is now employed to cover too many things—too many different traits, too many different concepts (Landy, 2005; Murphy & Sideman, 2006; Zeidner, Roberts, & Matthews, 2004). "These models," wrote Daus and Ashkanasy (2003, pp. 69–70), "have done more harm than good regarding establishing emotional intelligence as a legitimate, empirical construct with incremental validity potential." In this article, we explore these key criticisms of

the field, contrasting what we believe to be a meaningful theory of EI with models describing it as a mix of traits.

Our principal claim is that a valid EI concept can be distinguished from other approaches. This valid conception of EI includes the ability to engage in sophisticated information processing about one's own and others' emotions and the ability to use this information as a guide to thinking and behavior. That is, individuals high in EI pay attention to, use, understand, and manage emotions, and these skills serve adaptive functions that potentially benefit themselves and others (Mayer, Salovey, & Caruso, 2004; Salovey & Grewal, 2005). As we use the term, *emotional intelligence* is an instance of a standard intelligence that can enrich the discussion of human capacities (Mayer, Salovey, Caruso, & Sitarenios, 2001).

The deeper question raised by Locke's (2005) and others' assertions that EI has become overgeneral is "How does one decide something ought or ought not to be called emotional intelligence?" To address this question, in the first section of this article, The Schism in the Field, we examine the central conception of EI and the current confusion in the field. In the second section, The Four-Branch Model of EI, we further describe our approach to EI. In the third section, The Significance of EI, we examine the various reasons why EI is important as a discrete variable. Finally, in the Discussion and Recommendations section, we consider how the term *emotional intelligence* has come to be so misused and the steps that can be taken to improve terminology and research in the area.

The Schism in the Field

Initial Ideas

Our initial view of EI was that it consists of a group of related mental abilities. For example, we first defined EI as "the ability to monitor one's own and others' feelings and emotions, to discriminate among them and to use this information to guide one's thinking and actions" (Salovey & Mayer, 1990, p. 189). An empirical companion piece operationalized aspects of EI as an ability: Participants examined a set of colors, faces, and designs and had to identify each one's emotional content (Mayer et al., 1990). In a subsequent editorial in the journal *Intelligence*, we discussed the difference between traits such as extraversion, self-confidence, and EI, noting,

> Although a trait such as extraversion may depend on social skill, or result in it, [it] is a . . . preference rather than an ability. Knowing what another person feels, in contrast, is a mental ability. Such knowledge may stem from *g*, or be somewhat independent of it. The way in which we have defined emotional intelligence—as involving a series of mental abilities—qualifies it as a form of intelligence. (Mayer & Salovey, 1993, p. 435) . . .

External Factors

A journalistic rendering of EI created and also complicated the popular understanding of it. Goleman's (1995) best-selling book *Emotional Intelligence* began with the early version of our EI model but mixed in many other personality traits including persistence, zeal, self-control, character as a whole, and other positive attributes. The book received extensive coverage in the press, including a cover story in *Time* magazine (Gibbs, 1995). Because the book included, in part, the theory we developed, some investigators wrongly believed that we endorsed this complex and, at times, haphazard composite of attributes as an interpretation of EI.

The journalistic version became the public face of EI and attracted further attention, in part, perhaps, owing to its extraordinary claims. Goleman (1995, p. 34) wrote of EI's importance that "what data exist, suggest it can be as powerful, and at times more powerful, than IQ." A few years later, Goleman (1998a, p. 94) remarked that "nearly 90% of the difference" between star performers at work and average ones was due to EI. Although these ideas appeared in trade books and magazine and newspaper articles, they influenced scientific articles as well. For example, one refereed journal article noted that "EI accounts for over 85% of outstanding performance in top leaders" and "EI—not IQ—predicts top performance" (Watkin, 2000, p. 89). Our own work never made such claims, and we actively critiqued them (Mayer, 1999; Mayer & Cobb, 2000; Mayer & Salovey, 1997; Mayer, Salovey, & Caruso, 2000). More

recently, Goleman (2005, p. xiii) wrote that others who believed that EI predicts huge proportions of success had misunderstood his 1995 book.

The Advent of Mixed Models

With EI defined in the public mind as a variety of positive attributes, subsequent approaches continued to expand the concept. One defined EI quite broadly as, "an array of noncognitive capabilities, competencies, and skills that influence one's ability to succeed in coping with environmental demands and pressures" (Bar-On, 1997, p. 14). Although the model included emotion-related qualities such as emotional self-awareness and empathy, into the mix were added many additional qualities, including reality testing, assertiveness, self-regard, and self-actualization. It was this mixing in of related and unrelated attributes that led us to call these *mixed models* of EI (Mayer et al., 2000). A second mixed model of EI included such qualities as trustworthiness, adaptability, innovation, communication, and team capabilities as emotional competencies (Goleman, 1998b). The additions of this model led to the characterization of such an approach as "preposterously all-encompassing" (Locke, 2005, p. 428).

Still another research team defined a trait EI as referring to "a constellation of *behavioral dispositions* and *self-perceptions* concerning one's ability to recognize, process, and utilize emotion-laden information. It encompasses . . . empathy, impulsivity, and assertiveness as well as elements of social intelligence . . . and personal intelligence" (Petrides & Furnham, 2003, p. 278). At this point, the pattern is clear: A large number of personality traits are amassed, mixed in with a few socioemotional abilities, and the model is called one of EI or trait EI. (The "trait" designation is particularly confusing, as *trait* is typically defined as a distinguishing quality, or an inherited characteristic, and could apply to any EI model.) Generally speaking, these models include little or no justification for why certain traits are included and others are not, or why, for that matter, certain emotional abilities are included and others are not, except for an occasional mention that the attributes have been chosen because they are most likely to predict success (e.g., Bar-On, 1997).

Such approaches are disappointing from a theoretical and construct validity standpoint, and they are scientifically challenging in that, with so many independent qualities, it is hard to identify a global theme to these lists of attributes. There is, however, an alternative to such a state of (what we see as) disorganization. We believe that our four-branch model of emotional intelligence, for example, provides one conceptually coherent approach (Mayer & Salovey, 1997). It is to this model that we turn next.

The Four-Branch Model of EI

General Introduction to EI

Intelligence Considered

It is possible to develop a coherent approach to the concept of EI. In order to describe an EI, we need first to define intelligence. From the beginning of intelligence theorizing and testing, debates have raged regarding not only the nature of intelligence but also how many intelligences exist (Neisser et al., 1996). However, even the fiercest of *g* theorists, those proposing that intelligence is best described as consisting of a single, general mental ability factor, allow for the existence of more specific ability factors (e.g., Carroll, 1993).

Intelligences can be divided up in different ways, for example, according to whether they address crystallized (memory-dependent) or fluid (process-dependent) abilities or, alternatively, according to the type of information that is their focus. The approach that divides intelligences into information areas, for example, yields a verbal/propositional intelligence that deals with words and logic and a spatial intelligence that deals with arranging and rotating objects in space, among others. Analogously, an EI would address (a) the capacity to reason with and about emotions and/or (b) the contribution of the emotions system to enhancing intelligence.

One longstanding grouping of intelligences divides them into verbal/propositional and perceptual/organizational areas (e.g., Kaufman, 2000). For decades, researchers have searched for an elusive third intelligence, believing that these two core intelligences by themselves were insufficient to describe individual differences in mental abilities (Walker & Foley, 1973; Wechsler, 1943). In 1920, Thorndike (p. 228) suggested the existence of a social intelligence, which involved "the ability to understand and manage men and women, boys and girls—to act wisely in human relations" (see also Bureau of Personnel Administration, 1930; Thorndike & Stein, 1937). Social intelligence began to be investigated, although it had vocal critics—whose criticisms may have impeded the field's growth (Cronbach, 1960).

None of the proposed earlier intelligences, however, explicitly concerned an EI—reasoning validly about emotions and then using emotions in the reasoning process. By the early 1980s, there was a greater openness to the idea of specific (or multiple) intelligences (Gardner, 1983; Guilford, 1959; Sternberg, 1985), and at the same time, research in emotions was blossoming. Ekman (1973) and others had resurrected Darwin's ideas that some types of emotional information—for example, human facial expressions of certain emotions—are universal; others examined how events lead to cognitive appraisals that in turn generate emotions (Dyer, 1983; Roseman, 1984; Scherer, 1993; Sloman & Croucher, 1981; Smith & Ellsworth, 1985).

Perhaps the elusive intelligence that could complement the traditional dichotomy of verbal/propositional and perceptual/organizational might be one of EI. An EI, after all, when compared with social intelligence, arguably could have a more distinct brain locus in the limbic system and its cortical projections (Damasio, 1994; LeDoux, 2000; MacLean, 1973; TenHouten, Hoppe, Bogen, & Walter, 1985). An initial theory of EI developed these ideas along with a first demonstration study to indicate how aspects of it might be measured (Mayer et al., 1990; Salovey & Mayer, 1990).

Emotions as Signals

To describe convincingly what it means to reason with emotions, however, one must understand their informational content. Initially, some people express surprise that emotions convey information at all. Emotions often are viewed as irrational, will-o'-the-wisp states—even pathological in their arbitrariness (Young, 1943). Although this does describe the operation of emotion at times, it is far from a complete picture of a normal, functioning emotion system.

. . . [T]here is compelling evidence that many emotion meanings are in large part universal—and play a key role in helping people to understand their own and others' actions (e.g., Dyer, 1983; Ekman, 1973).

By the 1990s, the significance of emotions and their meanings were better appreciated and were increasingly studied empirically. The functional role of emotions as communication signals became widely accepted, although further issues remain to be explored, such as the meanings of affective dimensions and how social influences may modify emotional expression (Averill, 1992; Barrett & Russell, 1999). . . .

EI and the Four-Branch Model

Emotional abilities can be thought of as falling along a continuum from those that are relatively lower level, in the sense of carrying out fundamental, discrete psychological functions, to those that are more developmentally complex and operate in the service of personal self-management and goals. Crucial among lower level, fundamental skills is the capacity to perceive emotions accurately. Higher level skills include, for example, the capacity to manage emotions properly. These skills can be arranged in a rough hierarchy of four branches (these branches refer to a treelike diagram; Mayer & Salovey, 1997). These include the abilities to (a) perceive emotions in oneself and others accurately,

(b) use emotions to facilitate thinking, (c) understand emotions, emotional language, and the signals conveyed by emotions, and (d) manage emotions so as to attain specific goals (Mayer & Salovey, 1997). . . .

Measuring EI

Ability Measures of EI

Individual differences exist in each of these four processes. For example, some people are more accurate in initially perceiving how each individual . . . might be feeling, recognizing their feelings from faces and postures. Such individual differences can be measured. Each ability area of our four-branch model of EI can be operationalized formally as a set of to-be-solved problems, and test takers' responses can be checked against a criterion of correctness. There are a number of ability-based scales of emotional perception (Archer, Costanzo, & Akert, 2001; Matsumoto, LeRoux, & Wilson-Cohn, 2000), emotional identification and understanding (Geher, Warner, & Brown, 2001), and emotional integrative complexity (Lane, Quinlan, Schwartz, Walker, & Zeitlin, 1990).

One measure that spans these areas is the Mayer-Salovey-Caruso Emotional Intelligence Test (MSCEIT). It consists of eight tasks, two for each of the four branches of our EI model (Mayer, Caruso, & Salovey, 1999; Mayer, Salovey, & Caruso, 2002; Mayer, Salovey, Caruso, & Sitarenios, 2003). For example, Perceiving Emotions is assessed by asking participants to identify emotions in pictures of faces, in one task, and in photographs and artwork, in another. . . .

Theory of the Measurement of EI

There are two powerful theoretical reasons why only such a clearly focused, ability-based approach can best measure EI. First, intelligences most generally are defined as mental abilities, and measuring mental abilities involves asking test takers relevant questions and then evaluating their answers against a criterion of correctness (e.g., Carroll, 1993). The MSCEIT expert scoring system identified correct answers by using the pooled responses of 21 emotions researchers (Mayer et al., 2003). . . .

Key Findings Concerning EI and Other Psychological Traits

If, as we claim, EI involves a unique source of variation that reflects a new intelligence, then it should exhibit some overlap with other intelligence scales. Studies indicate that EI, as measured by the MSCEIT and its precursor test the Multifactor Emotional Intelligence Scale (MEIS), correlates about .35 or so with verbal intelligence, and lower with perceptual/organizational IQ (Ciarrochi, Chan, & Caputi,

2000; Mayer et al., 1999). Most of the overlap with verbal intelligence is accounted for by the third branch of the MSCEIT, Understanding Emotions.

EI also should be relatively independent of more traditional personality scales. To test this, one can correlate scales of EI with the Big Five personality traits. The Big Five traits are Extraversion–Introversion, Neuroticism–Stability, Openness–Closedness, Agreeableness–Disagreeableness, and Conscientiousness–Carelessness. Each of the Big Five traits can be divided into more specific traits. For example, one approach to the Big Five divides Extraversion–Introversion into such facets as gregariousness, assertiveness, and warmth (Costa & McCrae, 1992). The Big Five represents a good starting point for frequently studied personality dimensions, although some traits arguably are not measured by the Big Five (e.g., educated–uneducated, diplomatic–humorous, religious–unreligious; Saucier & Goldberg, 1998).

EI, defined here as an ability, should have minimal correlations with Big Five traits such as Extraversion or Neuroticism: Whether or not people are sociable or emotional, they can be smart about emotions. We did predict that EI would have a modest relation to Openness, as Openness often correlates with intelligences (Mayer & Salovey, 1993). The scale correlated .25 with Openness and .28 with Agreeableness, a trait that includes empathic and interpersonally sensitive content, and had lower correlations with the rest (Brackett & Mayer, 2003). . . .

A number of observers and commentators on the field have expressed reservations about whether such tests are adequate measures of EI and whether they predict important outcomes (e.g., Brody, 2004; Oatley, 2004; Zeidner, Matthews, & Roberts, 2001). The recent *Annual Review of Psychology* examination of EI and its measurement covers such concerns in greater detail and summarizes many of the central, continuing issues (Mayer et al., 2008). To date, however, we believe that ability scales provide the best benchmark for this new construct, although existing scales still have room for substantial improvement.

The Significance of EI

General Considerations of the Validity of an EI Measure

We recognize that the MSCEIT has important limitations (see, e.g., our Recommendation 5 below), and yet we consider it among the better and most widely used of the valid measures available. As such, we focus on it in this section. The measurement issues surrounding EI are elements of broader questions: Is a measure such as the MSCEIT a valid assessment of EI? And can a test such as the MSCEIT account for new variance in important outcomes? In the mid-20th century, psychologists believed that such questions about validity could be answered on the basis of findings from key correlational and experimental studies of the test itself (e.g., Barley, 1962). . . .

Thus far, the measurement evidence tends to favor the ability-based EI approach described here over other research alternatives (such as dismissing EI or using mixed models). Valid approaches to EI can be divided into two central areas: specific-ability approaches, such as the study of accurate emotional perception, and integrative models of EI, one example of which is the four-branch model and the MSCEIT (see Mayer et al., 2008, for other measures). Drawing on revised criteria for test validity (AERA, APA, & NCME, 1999), a research team (including one of the present authors) surveyed such EI measures and concluded that tests based either on specific or integrative ability approaches to measurement exhibited generally good evidence for their validity. Tests based on mixed models, by contrast, did not adequately measure EI (Mayer et al., 2008). . . .

EI and Understanding Feelings

Higher EI does appear to promote better attention to physical and mental processes relevant to clinical outcomes. For example, people higher in some EI skills are more accurate in detecting variations in their own heartbeat—an emotion-related physiological response (Schneider, Lyons, & Williams, 2005). Higher EI individuals also are better able to recognize and reason about the emotional consequences of events. For example, higher EI individuals are more accurate in affective forecasting—that is, in predicting how they will feel at some point in the future in response to an event, such as the outcome of a U.S. presidential election (Dunn et al., 2007).

EI and Subjective Symptoms

Abilities such as affective forecasting are important, for example, because psychotherapy patients from a wide diversity of backgrounds seek help with the hope of gaining insight into their feelings and motives (Evans, Acosta, & Yamamoto, 1986; Noble, Douglas, & Newman, 1999). If EI increases an individual's attention to and accuracy about his or her feelings under various conditions, this could, in turn, minimize the individual's psychiatric symptoms. David (2005) examined EI and psychiatric distress on the Symptom Checklist–90–Revised (SCL-90-R). The higher a person's EI, the lower their reports of symptoms on the Positive Symptom Total ($r = 2.38$), including, for example, fewer headaches and less trouble concentrating. Scores on the Symptom Distress Index, which measures symptom intensity, also declined

as EI rose ($r = -.22$). After she controlled for the Big Five personality dimensions, EI still accounted for between 1% and 6% of the variance in SCL-90-R scales—supporting the incremental validity of EI. Other reports have indicated that, for example, those diagnosed with dysthymia have lower EI scores than other psychiatric groups (Lizeretti, Oberst, Chamarro, & Farriols, 2006).

EI and Understanding Social Relationships

Many psychotherapy clients hope to improve what have become problematic social behaviors and relationships (Evans et al., 1986; Noble et al., 1999). Research on EI indicates that people with high EI tend to be more socially competent, to have better quality relationships, and to be viewed as more interpersonally sensitive than those lower in EI (Brackett et al., 2006; Brackett, Warner, & Bosco, 2005; Lopes et al., 2004; Lopes, Salovey, Côté, & Beers, 2005; Lopes, Salovey, & Straus, 2003). Many associations between EI and these kinds of variables remain significant even after one controls for the influence of traditional personality variables and general intelligence on the measured outcome.

In one study of friendships, the relationship between EI and participants' engagement in destructive responses to life events experienced by their friends was often significant, even after the researchers controlled for the Big Five, psychological well-being, empathy, life satisfaction, and Verbal SAT scores, but for men only (Brackett et al., 2006); MSCEIT correlations ranged from $-.02$ to $-.33$.

Although the findings described above were based on self-evaluated outcome criteria, similar findings have come from observer reports of the same individuals. For example, judges' positive ratings of a videotaped "getting acquainted" social interaction were predicted by the MSCEIT, although again, only for men and not for women. Ratings of the ability to work well with others as well as overall judged social competence correlated .53 and .51, respectively, with EI. The authors noted that significant correlations remained after they partialed out the Big Five (Brackett et al., 2006).

Just as higher EI predicts better social outcomes, lower EI predicts interpersonal conflict and maladjustment. Teenagers lower in EI were rated as more aggressive than others and tended to engage in more conflictual behavior than their higher EI peers in two small-sample studies (Mayer, Perkins, Caruso, & Salovey, 2001; Rubin, 1999). Lower EI also predicted greater drug and alcohol abuse. For example, levels of drug and alcohol use are related to lower EI among males (Brackett, Mayer, & Warner, 2004). Inner-city adolescents' smoking is also related to their EI (Trinidad & Johnson, 2002).

EI and Understanding Work Relationships

High EI correlates with better relationships in business settings as well. Managers higher in EI are better able to cultivate productive working relationships with others and to demonstrate greater personal integrity according to multirater feedback (Rosete & Ciarrochi, 2005). EI also predicts the extent to which managers engage in behaviors that are supportive of the goals of the organization, according to the ratings of their supervisors (Côté & Miners, 2006). In one study, 38 manufacturing supervisors' managerial performance was evaluated by their 1,258 employees. Total EI correlated .39 with these managerial performance ratings, with the strongest relations for the ability to perceive emotions and to use emotions (Kerr, Garvin, & Heaton, 2006). . . .

Discussion and Recommendations

EI as a Valid and Significant New Concept

In this article, we have argued that there exists a valid and conceptually important new variable for investigators and practitioners. EI can be defined as an intelligence that explains important variance in an individual's problem solving and social relationships. Yet the acceptance of the construct is threatened less by its critics, perhaps, than by those who are so enthusiastic about it as to apply the term indiscriminately to a variety of traditional personality variables (as pointed out by Daus & Ashkanasy, 2003, and Murphy & Sideman, 2006).

Why Do Some Investigators and Practitioners Use the Term Emotional Intelligence Overly Broadly?

Expansion of the Emotional and Cognitive Areas of Thinking
Why are traits such as the need for achievement, self-control, and social effectiveness (let alone character and leveraging diversity) sometimes referred to as EI? Perhaps one contributing cause is a lack of perspective on personality as a whole. Psychology needs good overviews of the central areas of mental function—models that define personality's major areas. Yet few such overviews reached any level of currency or consensus in the psychology of the 1980s and 1990s. Hilgard (1980) indicated that psychology is thrown out of balance by the absence of such models. Indeed, the cognitive revolution of the 1960s and 1970s (Miller, 2003), followed by the intense interest in affective (emotional) sciences in the 1980s and 1990s (e.g.,

Barsade, Brief, & Spataro, 2003), contributed to a sense that cognitive and emotional systems were dominant aspects of the whole of personality. Many psychologists and other investigators began to refer to cognition, affect, and behavior, as though they provided complete coverage of the study of mental life (e.g., Thompson & Fine, 1999). In that impoverished context, the term emotional intelligence could be mistaken as a label for much of mental processing. In fact, however, the three-legged stool of cognition, affect, and behavior underemphasizes such areas of personality as representations of the self, motivation, and self-control processes; more comprehensive models have since been proposed (Mayer, 2003, 2005; McAdams & Pals, 2006). . . .

Our Viewpoint
We agree with a number of observers of this area of study that the term emotional intelligence is used in too all-inclusive a fashion and in too many different ways (Landy, 2005; Locke, 2005; Matthews et al., 2004; Murphy, 2006). Referring in particular to the broadened definitions of EI, Locke (2005) remarked, "What does EI . . . not include?" (p. 428). We believe that there is a valid EI concept. However, we certainly agree that there is widespread misuse of the term to apply to concepts that simply are not concerned with emotion or intelligence or their intersection. The misuses of the term are, to us, invalid in that they attempt to overthrow or subvert the standard scientific language in psychology, with no apparent rationale for doing so. Other investigators similarly have pointed out that it is important to distinguish between valid and invalid uses of the concept (Daus & Ashkanasy, 2005; Gohm, 2004); to date, however, this message has not been heeded as we believe it should be.

Recommendations

. . . Those investigators interested in EI increasingly are asking for clarification of what is and is not legitimate work in the field. Murphy and Sideman (2006, p. 296) put it as a need to "succeed in separating the valid work from the hype." One central concern of ours (and of others), here and elsewhere, has been to distinguish better from poorer approaches to EI.

From our perspective, renaming the Big Five and other classic personality traits as "emotional intelligence" reflects a lack of understanding of personality theory and undermines good scientific practice. It obscures the meaning of EI, and EI is an important enough new construct as to make that unfortunate and problematic. Only when researchers revert to using the term to refer to its legitimate meaning within the conceptual, scientific network can it be taken seriously (AERA, APA, & NCME, 1999; Cronbach & Meehl, 1955). There are a good number of researchers who understand this and who have used the term consistently in a meaningful fashion. As for the others, one of our reasons for writing this article is to convince them of the common sense of using the current personality terminology. On a very practical level, it is often impossible to evaluate a journal article purporting to study EI on the basis of keywords or the abstract: The study may examine well-being, assertiveness, self-perceptions of emotional abilities, or actual abilities.

We have provided an overview of EI in particular with an eye to helping distinguish EI from other more traditional personality variables. We have attempted to make it clearer than before where EI begins and ends and where other personality approaches pick up. Much of the mixed-model research on EI (sometimes called EQ), can be described by what Lakatos (1968, cited in G. T. Smith, 2005, p. 401) referred to as a "degenerating research program," which consists of a series of defensive shifts in terminology and hypotheses "unlikely to yield new knowledge or understanding."

We realize that the recommendations below may be obvious to many, even to those who have not read our article. To be as clear as we can be, however, we propose a set of simple recommendations that we believe will help to safeguard the field and foster its progress.

Recommendation 1

In our opinion, the journalistic popularizations of EI frequently employ inadequate and overly broad definitions of EI, implausible claims, and misunderstandings of the concepts and research more generally. We urge researchers and practitioners alike to refer to the scientific literature on emotions, intelligence, and emotional intelligence to guide their thinking. Simply put, researchers need to cite the research literature rather than journalistic renderings of scientific concepts, which serve a different purpose.

Recommendation 2

Referring to the diverse approaches to EI, one research group observed, "It is precisely because of this heterogeneity that we need clear conceptualization and definition" (Zeidner et al., 2004, p. 247). To restore clarity to the study of EI, we recommend that the term *emotional intelligence* be limited to abilities at the intersection between emotions and intelligence—specifically limited to the set of abilities involved in reasoning about emotions and using emotions to enhance reasoning.

Recommendation 3

We recommend that those interested in EI refocus on research relevant to the ability conception of EI. This includes studies using emotional knowledge measures, emotional facial recognition ability, levels of emotional awareness, emerging research on emotional self-regulation, and related areas (e.g., Elfen-bein & Ambady, 2002b; Izard et al., 2001; Lane et al., 1990; Mayer et al., 2003; Nowicki & Mitchell, 1998).

Recommendation 4

We recommend that groups of widely studied personality traits, including motives such as the need for achievement, self-related concepts such as self-control, emotional traits such as happiness, and social styles such as assertiveness should be called what they are, rather than being mixed together in haphazard-seeming assortments and named emotional intelligence.

Recommendation 5

Much remains unknown about EI (Matthews, Zeidner, & Roberts, 2007). Our final recommendation is that, following the clearer terminology and conceptions above, good theorizing and research on EI continue until more is known about the concept and about human mental abilities more generally. Enough has been learned to indicate that EI is a promising area for study but also that significant gaps in knowledge remain. For example, there needs to be greater attention to issues of culture and gender and their impact on theories of EI and the measurement of EI. Further progress in the measurement of EI generally also is required. Applications of EI must be conducted with much greater attention to the research literature, be grounded in good theory, and reject outlandish claims. . . .

In this article, we hope to have separated this EI from other constructs that may be important in their own right but are ill-labeled as *emotional intelligence*. By clarifying our model and discussing some of the confusion in the area, we hope to encourage researchers and practitioners to distinguish EI from other domains of study. Such distinctions will help pave the way for a healthier, more convincing, and better understood EI, one that best can serve the discipline of psychology and other fields.

JOHN D. MAYER is professor of psychology at the University of New Hampshire. He received his PhD and MA in psychology at Case Western Reserve University and his BA from the University of Michigan. Dr. Mayer has served on the editorial boards of *Psychological Bulletin*, the *Journal of*

Personality and Social Psychology, and the *Journal of Personality,* among others, and has been an Individual National Institute of Mental Health postdoctoral scholar at Stanford University. He has published extensively in emotional intelligence, integrative models of personality, and the effects of personality on an individual's life.

PETER SALOVEY, provost at Yale University, is the Chris Argyris Professor of Psychology and a professor of management and of epidemiology and public health at Yale University. He directs the Health, Emotion and Behavior Laboratory. He also has affiliations with the Yale Cancer Center and the Institution for Social and Policy Studies. Dr. Salovey received a BA in psychology and a coterminal MA in sociology from Stanford University in 1980. He holds three Yale degrees in psychology: an MS (1983), an MPhil (1984), and a PhD (1986). He was president of the Graduate and Professional Student Senate at Yale in 1983–1984. He joined the Yale faculty as an assistant professor in 1986 and has been a full professor since 1995.

DAVID R. CARUSO is a research affiliate in the Department of Psychology at Yale University and the coauthor of the Mayer, Salovey, Caruso Emotional Intelligence Test (MSCEIT). He was a National Institute of Child Health and Human Development predoctoral fellow and received a PhD in psychology from Case Western Reserve University. He was then awarded a National Institute of Mental Health fellowship and spent two years as a postdoctoral fellow in Developmental Psychology at Yale University.

Gerald Matthews, Moshe Zeidner, and Richard D. Roberts

The Science, the Myth, and the Future of Emotional Intelligence

Emotional intelligence has caught the imagination of the general public, the commercial world, and the scientific community. It matches the current zeitgeist of self-awareness and understanding, redressing a perceived imbalance between intellect and emotion in the life of the collective Western mind. Emotional intelligence also connects with several cutting-edge areas of psychological science, including the neuroscience of emotion, self-regulation theory, studies of metacognition, and the search for human cognitive abilities beyond traditional academic intelligence.

The supposed malleability of emotional intelligence has considerable appeal to practitioners tackling personal and social problems. It is perceived as a panacea for clinical patients locked into private misery; obstructive, unproductive employees; and violent, antisocial children. Beyond the more dramatic manifestations of emotional illiteracy, many essentially adjusted people feel their lives would benefit from greater skills in understanding their own emotions and those of other people.

. . .

Biological Bases of Emotional Intelligence

Biological approaches to emotional intelligence claim that specific brain systems, notably the amygdala and areas of frontal cortex, directly control emotion recognition, emotional conditioning, encoding and retrieval of emotional memories, and real-world decision making. EI may be seen as some overall quality of these several brain systems. There is little doubt that lesions to these brain areas disrupt emotional functioning (although the role of the amygdala in humans seems often to be overstated). Biological models have a significant contribution to make to understanding abnormalities of emotional functioning, but we identified various difficulties in linking normal variation in EI directly to brain systems. There are methodological difficulties associated with generalizing animal models to humans, with the distributed and modular nature of brain systems for emotion, with using brain-lesion studies to infer sources of normal variation in emotional functioning, and with the use of emotion as a construct whose existence is inferred (rather than directly measured).

There are also three serious constraints on how successful biological models are ever likely to be, even with improved methods. First, biological models tend to neglect the distinction between hardware and software levels of explanation, although there are some promising developments in using connectionist, neural-net models to interrelate the levels. If some internal program based on abstract representations controls emotional behavior, then localization of emotion provides, at most, only some indirect clues to the nature of the programming. Second, although in animals specific emotions may be tightly coupled to stereotyped responses, such as flight in the case of fear, the link between emotion and behavior in humans is much looser. There is no simple isomorphism between emotion and response: studies of emotion and information processing demonstrate finely tuned cognitive control of behavior. Third, biological accounts tend to neglect cognitive control of outputs from the brain systems identified with emotion. No doubt, lower-level brain systems such as the amygdala provide signals that are coded symbolically and processed by higher-level, language-based cognition, but equally, the outputs of cognition feed downward to influence lower-level emotional functioning.

It follows that purely neurological accounts of emotional intelligence are unlikely to take us very far in understanding individual differences in emotion-regulation. Contrary to claims made in the literature, there is little evidence that neural processes directly control either irrational emotional outbursts or self-control. For example, panic attacks in part reflect a biologically based oversensitivity to stress. However, research shows that much of the panic-disorder patient's vulnerability derives from cognitive factors: beliefs about the harmfulness of somatic reactions, low perceived control, and a tendency toward catastrophic cognitions.

. . .

Cognitive Bases of Emotional Intelligence

The more sophisticated theoretical accounts of emotional intelligence are rooted in cognitive psychology. It seems plausible that people may differ in the processing routines that evaluate the emotional connotations of events, and select coping responses.

Two of the main attractions of the cognitive-psychological approach are its high degree of engagement with empirical data on emotion and behavior, and its scope for deriving testable predictions about individual differences in behavior. Furthermore, the cognitive psychology of self-regulation, by distinguishing self-referent metacognitive processing from immediate and possibly unconscious stimulus appraisal processes, may serve to differentiate emotional intelligence from emotion itself. Indeed, some evidence links EI to mood regulation. Perhaps EI relates to some overall self-regulative efficiency that underpins accurate and detailed evaluation of emotions, and selection and control of responses. Concepts related to self-regulation and meta-cognition are at the cutting edge of the cognitive psychology of emotion, and these are important issues to explore. However, there are various barriers for such a cognitive psychology of EI to overcome.

Some of these barriers reflect misunderstandings of cognitive psychology. Goleman, for example, appears to identify cognition with slow, deliberate reasoning processes. This view is ill informed: cognition refers to the complete array of computational processes performed on abstract data representations, processes that include free-wheeling parallel processing and unconscious, implicit processing, as well as step-by-step reasoning.

At a somewhat more sophisticated level, it is similarly erroneous to distinguish an emotional from a rational mind. As Clore and Ortony discuss in their important commentary, both implicit and explicit thinking are equally cognitive. It may well be productive to differentiate cognitive systems, such as implicit and explicit cognition. To suppose, however, that there is some mysterious intuitive emotional system that does not operate cognitively is to abandon contact with both the empirical evidence and the conceptual clarity offered by cognitive science.

Cognition is better conceptualized as a complex of many separate but interacting components, regulated in part by a supervisory executive that can itself be split into component parts. The conscious experience of emotion may be identified with specific key components, such as control signals for self-regulation. Although we can loosely speak of interaction between cognition and emotion, it is more accurate to refer to interaction between different subsystems of the cognitive architecture, a subset of which control conscious emotional experience. This perspectives support detailed accounts of changes in information-processing during emotional states, referring to cognitive functions such as selective attention, working memory, and decision making.

Although we might suppose that some individuals are generally superior in maintaining efficient function while emotional, the distributed, modular nature of cognition raises serious difficulties. Processing emotional stimuli depends on many independent subroutines at different levels of the cognitive architecture, some of which are stimulus-driven and automatic, and others of which are strategy-driven and controlled. Even appraisal itself is probably controlled by multiple mechanisms. Cognitive theories of EI do not differentiate clearly between these different mechanisms, or link EI to an explicit cognitive architecture. There is little in the available empirical evidence to suggest any general factor for individual differences in the multiple processes that support self-regulation (e.g., conscious and unconscious appraisal processes), although further evidence is undoubtedly required. Furthermore, a description of how more and less emotionally intelligent individuals process information still fails to tackle the key issue of the adaptive value of those processing differences.

Coping and Adaptation

Individual differences in neural and cognitive architectures may bias individuals towards more or less efficient emotional functioning. However, understanding how people may be generally more or less adapted to emotional circumstances requires a knowledge-level analysis of EI. The transactional theory of emotion provides an account of emotion and its behavioral consequences in terms of the personal meaning of events and of high-level appraisal and coping processes (i.e., without formal computational specification). This level of analysis may well be the most appropriate one for understanding EI as an index of individual differences in adaptation (or adaptability) to emotional demands. In particular, the emotionally intelligent person should cope more adaptively than the low-EI person, perhaps in part due to superior abilities to appraise emotions of self and others. There is indeed some research that links EI to individual differences in coping.

Unfortunately, the existing research literature does not support the notion of a continuum of adaptive competence. It is central to the transactional approach that emotions must be understood within the specific context in which they occur. Nevertheless, there is no necessary connection between how well different events are handled (although there are empirical links established by personality research). It is entirely consistent with the transactional approach that a former president of the United States should appear emotionally intelligent in connecting with the concerns of ordinary people on the campaign trail and emotionally unintelligent in handling romantic encounters. As discussed in Chapter 8, there are fundamental difficulties in rating the outcomes of events in terms of adaptive success or failure, due to the many and sometimes conflicting criteria for adaptation that can be applied. Furthermore, the empirical literature on individual differences in coping suggests that particular strategies are only weakly related to coping outcomes. Although the concept is superficially appealing, we cannot identify EI with emotional adaptivity.

Personality Revisited

It is safe to say that nothing resembling EI emerges from the voluminous literature on stress and coping. Perhaps, though, coping researchers have focused too much on specific contexts, and neglected stable individual differences that may only become evident when data are aggregated across studies. There is a large personality literature that links traits to general styles of coping, although the extent to which these styles control coping within specific situations is moot. The psychometric evidence suggests that personalitylike questionnaires for EI are fatally compromised by their redundancy with existing personality scales, but perhaps we can reconceptualize these existing traits in terms of EI. Perhaps too there may be major adaptive processes for EI that generalize across psychometrically distinct traits.

. . . However, the concept of EI adds nothing to existent personality theory. Indeed, to describe those individuals who are emotionally unstable or introverted or disagreeable or unconscientious as "emotionally unintelligent" is confusing on two counts. First, normal personality traits are neither adaptive nor maladaptive in any overall sense. Emotionally instability (neuroticism) confers benefits associated with threat sensitivity, introverts are superior to extroverts at handling monotony and sustaining performance, disagreeable persons may be more resilient

in social conflict situations, and lack of conscientiousness relates to creativity and spontaneity. Instead, traits appear to specialize individuals for thriving in certain environments, at the expense of others. To describe traits as markers for emotional intelligence obscures the subtle balance between dispositional costs and benefits.

. . .

Theory: Conclusions

. . .

- To equate EI with neurological properties of brain systems is conceptually naive and of little use in explaining empirical data on human emotional function. The executive role of the orbitofrontal cortex and other frontal systems, such as the cingulate cortex, is a potentially important component of the theory of EI. However, current research does not provide either an adequate account of the emotional information processing that these brain systems support or of biological bases for individual differences in processing.

- EI may potentially be linked to individual differences in the information-processing routines of self-regulation and executive control. However, EI does not appear to map onto the component processes of self-regulation in any coherent way, and the construct offers a highly impoverished view of higher-order emotion regulation, that represents a step backward from existing cognitive models. Much EI work rests on a false separation of conscious reason and unconscious passion, and neglects the key issue of the cognitive architecture supporting different aspects of information-processing related to emotion.

- It appears attractive to link EI to knowledge-level emotional constructs such as the personal meaning of events, appraisal, and coping. However, research in this area provides little conceptual basis or empirical evidence for rank-ordering people in terms of degree of adaptedness or adaptivity. Whether people cope effectively or ineffectively is often dependent on both the context, and on the criteria chosen to define effectiveness.

- The personality traits that overlap with EI as defined by self-report are richly correlated with various subjective and objective indices of emotional functioning, and with neural and cognitive processes supporting adaptation. However, traits such as those of the FFM appear to relate to various adaptive specializations rather than to overall emotional adaptedness. Work on narrow traits sometimes linked to EI, such as empathy and alexithymia has been valuable in understanding personality and emotion, but there is no psycometric or theory-based rationale for grouping these traits together under the umbrella of EI.

Overall, our conclusions concerning the prospect for a coherent theory of EI supported by empirical evidence are pessimistic for both ability and mixed (i.e., personality-like) approaches to the construct. We do not find any clear continuum of emotional competence in brain function, in basic information-processing, in high-level cognitions of person-environment interaction, or by reconceptualizing existing personality traits. Within the normal range of function, it is difficult to link neural and cognitive architectures to adaptive constructs. From the ability perspective, it is certainly worth probing further into individual differences in emotion processes. Perhaps abilities such as emotion perception can be linked to specific brain systems or information-processing routines. Such research is of course at an early stage of development, and no definitive conclusion is possible. So far, there appears little evidence that would suggest that abilities defined in terms of objectively assessed processing efficiencies would prove to be linked either to each other (and hence to some general intelligence) or to real-world adaptive outcomes.

Research on stress and personality deals with adaptive constructs but fails to support the idea that some people are geniuses of adaptation, handling all challenges with equal facility, whereas others struggle to cope regardless of circumstances. Instead, personality traits define multiple and independent patterns of context-dependent strength and weakness, with emotional outcomes primarily representing the person's capabilities for handling the specific demands of the context concerned. For example, neurotic individuals tend to be anxious in stressful social situations because they are cognitively (and, arguably, neurologically) ill equipped to handle specific demands such as handling criticism from others, not because of any generalized deficit in EI. The personalitylike side of EI research appears to be based on fundamental misconceptions about the nature of individual differences in managing emotional encounters.

. . .

Myths of Emotional Intelligence

We hold that myth is, in its most general and comprehensive nature, the spontaneous and imaginative form in which the human intelligence and human emotions conceive and represent themselves and things in general.

Tito Vignoli, 1882

Despite some promising research developments, we have identified various 'mythical' beliefs about EI that are not scientifically supported. There appear to be four central, defining myths around which the multiple shortcomings we have identified cohere:

Emotional intelligence is a generalized, far-reaching personal quality covering almost all aspects of emotional functioning   Goleman and, to some extent, Bar-On appear to claim that all desirable aspects of emotional function reflect a general factor of EI. Such a factor would be on a par with IQ in bringing together many apparently distinct personal qualities. [We've] seen that tests of EI fail, thus far, to meet psychometric criteria, or even to correlate highly with one another. In addition, the extensive literature on personality shows that qualities such as resilience under stress, self-control, sensitivity to others and social assertiveness are distinct constructs that relate to differing fundamental personality dimensions, and to differing psychological processes. Ability-based approaches to EI generally make more modest claims, though it remains an open question whether there is some general factor for emotional information-processing. Thus far, the search for EI has discovered not some new continent, but what may be a rather minor province of terrain already charted.

Emotional intelligence is directly based on brain systems for emotion   Goleman seeks to give EI scientific credibility by linking the construct to brain structures such as amygdala and orbitofrontal cortex. The link is not entirely mythical, in that brain lesions to these structures produce deficits in behaviors related to emotion. Nevertheless, there is no evidence that individual differences, in the normal range, map in any direct way to variation in brain function. The evidence from personality studies is critical here. Certainly, the personality traits that correlate with EI are substantially heritable, indicating a biological basis for personality. However, psychophysiological studies of personality implicate a wide variety of brain structures, going beyond the traditional emotion centers. In addition, biological models have fared poorly in attempting to explain objective behavioral correlates of personality, and, in general, cognitive-psychological models have greater explanatory power and more predictive success empirically.

Emotional intelligence is critical for real-world success   It is claimed that EI may be the single most important factor predicting job success, especially within a given job category or profession. There is no evidence in peer-reviewed journals to support this claim. The personality literature suggests that the validity of EI measures as predictors of job performance is likely to be modest, and often less than IQ. Similarly, the patterning of adaptive costs and benefits associated with the personality traits linked to EI, suggests that measures of EI cannot be used to index some overall "aptitude for life." The overlap of EI-as-personality with emotional stability (low neuroticism) ensures that tests such as the EQ-i and SSRI will robustly predict happiness and life satisfaction, but this subjective outcome dissociates from objective behavioral indices.

Raising emotional intelligence is essential for countering social disintegration The preface to Goleman's book highlights what he perceives as a social crisis, described in flowery phrases such as "the disintegration of civility and safety," "surging rage and despair," and "the rotting of the goodness of our communal lives." The remedy is the teaching of emotion intelligence in schools and, a theme developed in a later book, promoting EI in the workplace. It is questionable whether civilization is falling apart quite so catastrophically. In any case, while it is plausible that school-based programs for EI are beneficial, there is no convincing evidence showing dramatic changes in adaptation, in part because of methodological deficiencies in studies conducted so far. In the occupational and clinical domains, interventions based on EI appear to add little to existing techniques.

GERALD MATTHEWS is currently an associate research professor at the Applied Cognition and Training in Immersive Virtual Environments (ACTIVE) Lab of the University of Central Florida. His research focuses on human factors, cognitive models of personality and individual differences, and task-induced states of stress and fatigue. He has published over 300 journal articles and book chapters, and co-authored several books including *Human Performance: Cognition, Stress and Individual Differences, Emotional Intelligence: Science and Myth*, and *Personality Traits*.

MOSHE ZEIDNER is a professor of educational psychology in the Faculty of Education at the University of Haifa. He is the co-founder and director of the Center for the Interdisciplinary Research on Emotions and the director of the Laboratory for Personality and Individual Differences. Among his main areas of research interest are emotions, personality, intelligence, emotional intelligence, brain and education, giftedness, and psycho-educational assessment. Zeidner has co-authored or co-edited 10 books and has authored or co-authored over 200 articles and book chapters published in the scientific literature. He received the Lifelong Achievement Award in July 2003 from the "Society of Stress and Anxiety Research."

RICHARD D. ROBERTS is the managing principal research scientist in the Educational Testing Service's Center for New Constructs and is the associate editor of *International Journal of Psychology*. His main areas of specialization are assessment and human individual differences, and he has conducted research on cognitive abilities, emotional intelligence, personality, health and well-being, motivation, self-confidence, sensory processes, aging, processing speed, situational judgment tests, and human chronotype.

EXPLORING THE ISSUE

Is Emotional Intelligence Valid?

Critical Thinking and Reflection

1. In what ways does the definition of EI put forth by the authors of the YES article differ from the earlier definitions/perceptions that they critique?
2. What is the difference between emotional knowledge and EI as conceptualized by the authors of the YES article?
3. Does the concept of EI actually add to our understanding of persons beyond general intelligence and personality? If so, how so? If not, then is EI already captured by general intelligence, personality, or both? In what way?
4. The authors of the NO article contend that the contextual nature of emotional situations makes it impossible to create a rank-ordered EI, where higher is always better. Do you think that having a higher IQ (the traditional, general intelligence) is always better, regardless of context? Would the same apply to EI?
5. Can emotions actually inform rational thinking, or do emotions get in the way of rational thinking?

Is There Common Ground?

A well-developed theory of emotional intelligence (EI) has the potential to help people understand and improve their relationships with one another. It is a noble goal. In the pursuit of this improvement, EI has already swept the worlds of business and psychology by storm. A simple Google search will reveal hundreds of articles and companies proclaiming the necessity of hiring emotionally intelligent employees, the health and social benefits of emotional intelligence, and offering the tools to measure one's emotional intelligence. It is a popular concept with a wide following.

It may or may not, however, even exist. If we are to allow EI to have such a large influence, then we must ensure that we are building on a strong foundation, not casting in our lots with a passing fad of psychological thought. It is imperative that more research be conducted in order to firmly establish whether EI even exists.

At the very least, no one is denying that we need to be smart with our emotions. We are emotional beings, and to ignore that fact is to ignore a large part of what makes up our relationships with others and what gives us meaning in our lives. The difficult question is whether there is an independent category of intelligence that deals strictly with our own and other's emotions. Whether you believe this to be so—or whether you believe that one's ability to recognize, process, and react to emotional stimuli is a part of one's general intelligence or personality—it is possible to accept that it is a good thing to be aware of one's own and other's emotions and to be able successfully to respond to them (and that some, for whatever reason, are better at this than others). Even if it turns out not to be real, perhaps the pursuit of emotional intelligence will make us more aware of ourselves and others.

Additional Resource

Austin, E. J., & Saklofske, D. H. (2014). Introduction to the special issue on emotional intelligence. *Personality and Individual Differences, 65*, 1–2.

Baker, A., Ten Brinke, L., & Porter, S. (2013). Will get fooled again: Emotionally intelligent people are easily duped by high-stakes deceivers. *Legal and Criminological Psychology, 18*(2), 300–313.

Goleman, D. (2011). *The Brain and Emotional Intelligence: New Insights*. More Than Sound LLC.

Locke, E. A. (2005). Why emotional intelligence is an invalid concept. *Journal of Organizational Behavior, 26*(4), 425–431.

Mayer, J. D., Roberts, R. D., & Barsade, S. G. (2008). Human abilities: Emotional intelligence. *Annual Review of Psychology, 59*, 507–536.

Internet Reference . . .

Consortium for Research on Emotional Intelligence in Organizations

http://www.eiconsortium.org/index.html

Daniel Goleman: Emotional Intelligence, Social Intelligence, Ecological Intelligence

http://www.danielgoleman.info/

London Psychometric Laboratory at UCL

http://www.psychometriclab.com

Unit 5

UNIT

Mental Health Issues

A *mental disorder is often defined as a pattern of thinking or behavior that is either disruptive to others or harmful to the person with the disorder. This definition seems straightforward, yet there is considerable debate about whether some disorders truly exist. For example, does a child's disruptive behavior and short attention span unquestionably warrant that he or she be diagnosed with attention-deficit hyperactive disorder (ADHD)? When does "curiosity" and "fidgetiness" become pathological and warrant medication? When, also, are life events, such as elective abortions, considered sufficiently traumatic that they can cause mental health issues, such as posttraumatic stress disorder?*

Selected, Edited, and with Issue Framing Material by:
Edwin E. Gantt, *Brigham Young University*

ISSUE

Is Attention-Deficit Hyperactivity Disorder (ADHD) a Real Disorder?

YES: National Institute of Mental Health, from "Attention Deficit Hyperactivity Disorder," *National Institute of Mental Health* (2006)

NO: Sami Timimi and Nick Radcliffe, from "The Rise and Rise of ADHD," *Clinical Psychology, Leicester* (2005)

Learning Outcomes

After reading this issue, you will be able to:

- Understand whether ADHD is a legitimate psychiatric disorder.
- Discuss what sorts of situations might lead to the over-diagnosis of ADHD.
- Discuss the possible ramifications of over-diagnosing or misdiagnosing ADHD.
- Explain the arguments for and against ADHD being classified as a medical disorder.
- Understand both medical and social construct-explanations of behaviors associated with ADHD.

ISSUE SUMMARY

YES: The National Institute of Mental Health asserts that ADHD is a real disorder that merits special consideration and treatment.

NO: Timimi and Radcliffe insist that ADHD is not a medical disorder as it has no demonstrable biological cause; rather, it is not a disorder at all, but an agenda-driven, socially constructed entity invented by Western society.

Diagnosis presents considerable challenges for mental health professionals. *The Diagnostic and Statistical Manual (DSM)*, now in its fifth edition, defines widely recognized disorders in terms of clusters of symptoms that typically characterize these disorders. Because mental disorders are usually defined in terms of symptoms, there has been significant room for debate as to which groupings of symptoms constitute legitimate disorders that merit professional attention. Indeed, through its multiple revisions the DSM has added some disorders, redefined others, and set aside yet others as these diagnostic debates have shifted the ways we understand mental disorders.

Attention-deficit hyperactivity disorder, or ADHD, has been a particularly controversial diagnosis from the time it first appeared in the DSM-III nearly 30 years ago. Parents, teachers, psychologists, legislators, and even celebrities have debated not only whether ADHD is a real disorder but also whether the pharmacological treatments that are frequently prescribed are appropriate. Some people worry that we are pathologizing behaviors that are normal and typical of young children (e.g., curiosity, exploration, and fidgetiness). Others worry that dismissing the diagnosis and leaving affected children untreated will place these children at a social, academic, and emotional disadvantage.

In the first selection, the National Institute of Mental Health (NIMH) argues that ADHD is a neurologically based disorder that affects 3–5 percent of school-age children. According to the NIMH, we can all be occasionally distracted, impulsive, and hyperactive. However, the scientists at the NIMH assert that children with ADHD struggle not only with these sorts of behaviors in greater frequency and intensity but also in a manner that is inappropriate for their age group. Moreover, the NIMH argues that there are treatments—which typically should include medicine—that will prevent greater problems in a child's later life.

In the second article, Timimi and Radcliffe claim that ADHD is not, in fact, a medical disorder at all. They argue that the lack of any demonstrable biological deficiency in children diagnosed with ADHD, the lack of any medical test for its diagnosis, and the lackluster long-term performance of chemical treatments (medicine) in reducing symptoms or causing permanent change show that the medical model of ADHD is a fallacy. A confluence of many factors nonetheless makes the medical model, however, incorrect, appealing to Westerners. For example,

(1) it is insisted upon by the doctors we trust (i.e., doctors who ignore and dismiss non-medical explanations), (2) it generates non-conclusive research hinting at possible biological explanations, which implicitly make ADHD a part of the broader medical field, and (3) powerful social groups ranging from the pharmaceutical industry to the educational system stand to benefit from a view of ADHD that takes responsibility for a child's actions away from caretakers and places it squarely inside of the child, subject only to and requiring medication to change. Rejecting the medical model understanding of ADHD, Timimi and Radcliffe insist that ADHD is a socially constructed entity unique to the West, one whose prevalence and diagnosis are highly subjective and whose very existence is a symptom of a deeper illness—Western society's contempt for children.

POINT

- There is mounting research evidence that ADHD is a diagnosable disorder that is neurologically based and strongly linked to genetics.

- Hyperactivity and distractibility are common among all children, but these symptoms are more pervasive and inappropriate in children with ADHD.

- ADHD can be diagnosed by assessing whether a person's behavior matches the criteria indicated by the DSM-IV-TR for ADHD.

- Research suggests that the best treatments for ADHD should include medication as part of their regimen.

COUNTERPOINT

- ADHD is a "fad diagnosis" that does not exist, like other similar diagnoses that have come and gone.

- Even when symptoms are more pervasive and inappropriate, these are more often signs of excessive fatigue or stress.

- The cluster of symptoms attributed to ADHD leads mental health professionals to treat a diverse group of people as having a single problem that requires a single solution.

- Pharmaceutical treatments for ADHD can create problems and are often unnecessary when the true cause of symptoms is understood.

YES ↵

National Institute of Mental Health

Attention Deficit Hyperactivity Disorder

Attention Deficit Hyperactivity Disorder (ADHD) is a condition that becomes apparent in some children in the preschool and early school years. It is hard for these children to control their behavior and/or pay attention. It is estimated that between 3 and 5 percent of children have attention deficit hyperactivity disorder (ADHD), or approximately 2 million children in the United States. This means that in a classroom of 25 to 30 children, it is likely that at least one will have ADHD.

A child with ADHD faces a difficult but not insurmountable task ahead. In order to achieve his or her full potential, he or she should receive help, guidance, and understanding from parents, guidance counselors, and the public education system.

Symptoms

The principal characteristics of ADHD are inattention, hyperactivity, and impulsivity. These symptoms appear early in a child's life. Because many normal children may have these symptoms, but at a low level, or the symptoms may be caused by another disorder, it is important that the child receive a thorough examination and appropriate diagnosis by a well qualified professional. Symptoms of ADHD will appear over the course of many months, often with the symptoms of impulsiveness and hyperactivity preceding those of inattention that may not emerge for a year or more. Different symptoms may appear in different settings, depending on the demands the situation may pose for the child's self-control. A child who "can't sit still" or is otherwise disruptive will be noticeable in school, but the inattentive daydreamer may be overlooked. The impulsive child who acts before thinking may be considered just a "discipline problem," while the child who is passive or sluggish may be viewed as merely unmotivated. Yet both may have different types of ADHD. All children are sometimes restless, sometimes act without thinking, sometimes daydream the time away. When the child's hyperactivity, distractibility, poor concentration, or impulsivity begin to affect performance in school, social relationships with other children, or behavior at home, ADHD may be suspected. But because the symptoms vary so much across settings, ADHD is not easy to diagnose. This is especially true when inattentiveness is the primary symptom.

According to the most recent version of the Diagnostic and Statistical Manual of Mental Disorder (DSM-IV-TR), there are three patterns of behavior that indicate ADHD. People with ADHD may show several signs of being consistently inattentive. They may have a pattern of being hyperactive and impulsive far more than others of their age. Or they may show all three types of behavior. This means that there are three subtypes of ADHD recognized by professionals. These are the predominantly hyperactive-impulsive type (that does not show significant inattention); the predominantly inattentive type (that does not show significant hyperactive-impulsive behavior) sometimes called ADD—an outdated term for this entire disorder; and the combined type (that displays both inattentive and hyperactive-impulsive symptoms).

Hyperactivity-Impulsivity

Some signs of hyperactivity-impulsivity are:

- Feeling restless, often fidgeting with hands or feet, or squirming while seated
- Running, climbing, or leaving a seat in situations where sitting or quiet behavior is expected
- Blurting out answers before hearing the whole question
- Having difficulty waiting in line or taking turns.

Inattention

The DSM-IV-TR gives these signs of inattention.

- Often becoming easily distracted by irrelevant sights and sounds

National Institute of Mental Health. From *Attention Deficit Hyperactivity Disorder*, NIH Publication No. 3572, 2006. Published by The National Institutes of Mental Health. www.nimh.nih.go.

- Often failing to pay attention to details and making careless mistakes
- Rarely following instructions carefully and completely losing or forgetting things like toys, or pencils, books, and tools needed for a task
- Often skipping from one uncompleted activity to another.

Is It Really ADHD?

Not everyone who is overly hyperactive, inattentive, or impulsive has ADHD. Since most people sometimes blurt out things they didn't mean to say, or jump from one task to another, or become disorganized and forgetful, how can specialists tell if the problem is ADHD?

Because everyone shows some of these behaviors at times, the diagnosis requires that such behavior be demonstrated to a degree that is inappropriate for the person's age. The diagnostic guidelines also contain specific requirements for determining when the symptoms indicate ADHD. The behaviors must appear early in life, before age 7, and continue for at least 6 months. Above all, the behaviors must create a real handicap in at least two areas of a person's life such as in the schoolroom, on the playground, at home, in the community, or in social settings. So someone who shows some symptoms but whose schoolwork or friendships are not impaired by these behaviors would not be diagnosed with ADHD. Nor would a child who seems overly active on the playground but functions well elsewhere receive an ADHD diagnosis.

To assess whether a child has ADHD, specialists consider several critical questions: Are these behaviors excessive, long-term, and pervasive? That is, do they occur more often than in other children the same age? Are they a continuous problem, not just a response to a temporary situation? Do the behaviors occur in several settings or only in one specific place like the playground or in the schoolroom? The person's pattern of behavior is compared against a set of criteria and characteristics of the disorder as listed in the DSM-IV-TR.

Diagnosis

Professionals Who Make the Diagnosis

If ADHD is suspected, to whom can the family turn? What kinds of specialists do they need?

Ideally, the diagnosis should be made by a professional in your area with training in ADHD or in the diagnosis of mental disorders. Child psychiatrists and psychologists, developmental/behavioral pediatricians, or behavioral neurologists are those most often trained in differential diagnosis. Clinical social workers may also have such training. The family can start by talking with the child's pediatrician or their family doctor. Some pediatricians may do the assessment themselves, but often they refer the family to an appropriate mental health specialist they know and trust. In addition, state and local agencies that serve families and children . . . can help identify appropriate specialists.

Within each specialty, individual doctors and mental health professionals differ in their experiences with ADHD. So in selecting a specialist, it's important to find someone with specific training and experience in diagnosing and treating the disorder.

Whatever the specialist's expertise, his or her first task is to gather information that will rule out other possible reasons for the child's behavior. Among possible causes of ADHD-like behavior are the following:

- A sudden change in the child's life—the death of a parent or grandparent; parents' divorce; a parent's job loss.
- Undetected seizures, such as in petit mal or temporal lobe seizures
- A middle ear infection that causes intermittent hearing problems
- Medical disorders that may affect brain functioning
- Underachievement caused by learning disability
- Anxiety or depression

Next the specialist gathers information on the child's ongoing behavior in order to compare these behaviors to the symptoms and diagnostic criteria listed in the DSM-IV-TR. This also involves talking with the child and, if possible, observing the child in class and other settings.

The child's teachers, past and present, are asked to rate their observations of the child's behavior on standardized evaluation forms, known as behavior rating scales, to compare the child's behavior to that of other children the same age.

The specialist interviews the child's teachers and parents, and may contact other people who know the child well, such as coaches or baby-sitters. Parents are asked to describe their child's behavior in a variety of situations. They may also fill out a rating scale to indicate how severe and frequent the behaviors seem to be.

In most cases, the child will be evaluated for social adjustment and mental health. Tests of intelligence and learning achievement may be given to see if the child has a learning disability and whether the disability is in one or more subjects.

The specialist then pieces together a profile of the child's behavior.

A correct diagnosis often resolves confusion about the reasons for the child's problems that lets parents and child move forward in their lives with more accurate information on what is wrong and what can be done to help. Once the disorder is diagnosed, the child and family can begin to receive whatever combination of educational, medical, and emotional help they need. This may include providing recommendations to school staff, seeking out a more appropriate classroom setting, selecting the right medication, and helping parents to manage their child's behavior.

What Causes ADHD?

One of the first questions a parent will have is "Why? What went wrong?" "Did I do something to cause this?" There is little compelling evidence at this time that ADHD can arise purely from social factors or child-rearing methods. Most substantiated causes appear to fall in the realm of neurobiology and genetics. This is not to say that environmental factors may not influence the severity of the disorder, and especially the degree of impairment and suffering the child may experience, but that such factors do not seem to give rise to the condition by themselves.

The parents' focus should be on looking forward and finding the best possible way to help their child. Scientists are studying causes in an effort to identify better ways to treat, and perhaps someday, to prevent ADHD. They are finding more and more evidence that ADHD does not stem from home environment, but from biological causes. Knowing this can remove a huge burden of guilt from parents who might blame themselves for their child's behavior.

Genetics. Attention disorders often run in families, so there are likely to be genetic influences. Studies indicate that 25 percent of the close relatives in the families of ADHD children also have ADHD, whereas the rate is about 5 percent in the general population. Many studies of twins now show that a strong genetic influence exists in the disorder.

Researchers continue to study the genetic contribution to ADHD and to identify the genes that cause a person to be susceptible to ADHD. Since its inception in 1999, the Attention-Deficit Hyperactivity Disorder Molecular Genetics Network has served as a way for researchers to share findings regarding possible genetic influences on ADHD.

Recent Studies on Causes of ADHD. Some knowledge of the structure of the brain is helpful in understanding the research scientists are doing in searching for a physical basis for attention deficit hyperactivity disorder. One part of the brain that scientists have focused on in their search is the frontal lobes of the cerebrum. The frontal lobes allow us to solve problems, plan ahead, understand the behavior of others, and restrain our impulses. The two frontal lobes, the right and the left, communicate with each other through the corpus callosum (nerve fibers that connect the right and left frontal lobes).

The basal ganglia are the interconnected gray masses deep in the cerebral hemisphere that serve as the connection between the cerebrum and the cerebellum and, with the cerebellum are responsible for motor coordination. The cerebellum is divided into three parts. The middle part is called the vermis.

All of these parts of the brain have been studied through the use of various methods for seeing into or imaging the brain. These methods include functional magnetic resonance imaging (fMRI), positron emission tomography (PET), and single photon emission computed tomography (SPECT). The main or central psychological deficits in those with ADHD have been linked through these studies. By 2002 the researchers in the NIMH Child Psychiatry Branch had studied 152 boys and girls with ADHD, matched with 139 age- and gender-matched controls without ADHD. The children were scanned at least twice, some as many as four times over a decade. As a group, the ADHD children showed 3–4 percent smaller brain volumes in all regions—the frontal lobes, temporal gray matter, caudate nucleus, and cerebellum.

This study also showed that the ADHD children who were on medication had a white matter volume that did not differ from that of controls. Those never-medicated patients had an abnormally small volume of white matter. The white matter consists of fibers that establish long-distance connections between brain regions. It normally thickens as a child grows older and the brain matures.

The Treatment of ADHD

Every family wants to determine what treatment will be most effective for their child. This question needs to be answered by each family in consultation with their health care professional. To help families make this important decision, the National Institute of Mental Health (NIMH) has funded many studies of treatments for ADHD and has conducted the most intensive study ever undertaken for evaluating the treatment of this disorder. This study is known as the Multimodal Treatment Study of Children with Attention Deficit Hyperactivity Disorder (MTA).

The MTA study included 579 (95–98 at each of 6 treatment sites) elementary school boys and girls with ADHD, randomly assigning them to one of four treatment programs: (1) medication management alone; (2) behavioral treatment alone; (3) a combination of both; or (4) routine community care.

In each of the study sites, three groups were treated for the first 14 months in a specified protocol and the fourth group was referred for community treatment of the parents' choosing. All of the children were reassessed regularly throughout the study period. An essential part of the program was the cooperation of the schools, including principals and teachers. Both teachers and parents rated the children on hyperactivity, impulsivity, and inattention, and symptoms of anxiety and depression, as well as social skills.

The children in two groups (medication management alone and the combination treatment) were seen monthly for one-half hour at each medication visit. During the treatment visits, the prescribing physician spoke with the parent, met with the child, and sought to determine any concerns that the family might have regarding the medication or the child's ADHD-related difficulties. The physicians, in addition, sought input from the teachers on a monthly basis. The physicians in the medication-only group did not provide behavioral therapy but did advise the parents when necessary concerning any problems the child might have.

In the behavior treatment-only group, families met up to 35 times with a behavior therapist, mostly in group sessions. These therapists also made repeated visits to schools to consult with children's teachers and to supervise a special aide assigned to each child in the group. In addition, children attended a special 8-week summer treatment program where they worked on academic, social, and sports skills, and where intensive behavioral therapy was delivered to assist children in improving their behavior.

Children in the combined therapy group received both treatments, that is, all the same assistance that the medication-only received, as well as all of the behavior therapy treatments.

In routine community care, the children saw the community-treatment doctor of their parents' choice one to two times per year for short periods of time. Also, the community-treatment doctor did not have any interaction with the teachers.

The results of the study indicated that long-term combination treatments and the medication-management alone were superior to intensive behavioral treatment and routine community treatment. And in some areas—anxiety, academic performance, oppositionality, parent-child relations, and social skills—the combined treatment was usually superior. Another advantage of combined treatment was that children could be successfully treated with lower doses of medicine, compared with the medication-only group.

Medications

For decades, medications have been used to treat the symptoms of ADHD.

The medications that seem to be the most effective are a class of drugs known as stimulants.

Some people get better results from one medication, some from another. It is important to work with the prescribing physician to find the right medication and the right dosage. For many people, the stimulants dramatically reduce their hyperactivity and impulsivity and improve their ability to focus, work, and learn. The medications may also improve physical coordination, such as that needed in handwriting and in sports.

The stimulant drugs, when used with medical supervision, are usually considered quite safe. . . . [T]o date there is no convincing evidence that stimulant medications, when used for treatment of ADHD, cause drug abuse or dependence. A review of all long-term studies on stimulant medication and substance abuse, conducted by researchers at Massachusetts General Hospital and Harvard Medical School, found that teenagers with ADHD who remained on their medication during the teen years had a lower likelihood of substance use or abuse than did ADHD adolescents who were not taking medications.

The stimulant drugs come in long- and short-term forms. The newer sustained-release stimulants can be taken before school and are long-lasting so that the child does not need to go to the school nurse every day for a pill. The doctor can discuss with the parents the child's needs and decide which preparation to use and whether the child needs to take the medicine during school hours only or in the evening and weekends too.

About one out of ten children is not helped by a stimulant medication. Other types of medication may be used if stimulants don't work or if the ADHD occurs with another disorder. Antidepressants and other medications can help control accompanying depression or anxiety.

Side Effects of the Medications

Most side effects of the stimulant medications are minor and are usually related to the dosage of the medication being taken. Higher doses produce more side effects. The most common side effects are decreased appetite, insomnia, increased anxiety and/or irritability. Some children report mild stomach aches or headaches.

When a child's schoolwork and behavior improve soon after starting medication, the child, parents, and teachers tend to applaud the drug for causing the sudden changes. Unfortunately, when people see such immediate improvement, they often think medication is all that's needed. But medications don't cure ADHD; they only control the symptoms on the day they are taken. Although the medications help the child pay better attention and complete school work, they can't increase knowledge or improve academic skills. The medications help the child to use those skills he or she already possesses.

Behavioral therapy, emotional counseling, and practical support will help ADHD children cope with everyday problems and feel better about themselves.

Facts to Remember about Medication for ADHD

- Medications for ADHD help many children focus and be more successful at school, home, and play. Avoiding negative experiences now may actually help prevent addictions and other emotional problems later.
- About 80 percent of children who need medication for ADHD still need it as teenagers. Over 50 percent need medication as adults.

The Family and the ADHD Child

Medication can help the ADHD child in everyday life. He or she may be better able to control some of the behavior problems that have led to trouble with parents and siblings. But it takes time to undo the frustration, blame, and anger that may have gone on for so long. Both parents and children may need special help to develop techniques for managing the patterns of behavior. In such cases, mental health professionals can counsel the child and the family, helping them to develop new skills, attitudes, and ways of relating to each other. In individual counseling, the therapist helps children with ADHD learn to feel better about themselves. The therapist can also help them to identify and build on their strengths, cope with daily problems, and control their attention and aggression. Sometimes only the child with ADHD needs counseling support. But in many cases, because the problem affects the family as a whole, the entire family may need help. The therapist assists the family in finding better ways to handle the disruptive behaviors and promote change. If the child is young, most of the therapist's work is with the parents,

teaching them techniques for coping with and improving their child's behavior.

Several intervention approaches are available. Knowing something about the various types of interventions makes it easier for families to choose a therapist that is right for their needs.

Psychotherapy works to help people with ADHD to like and accept themselves despite their disorder. It does not address the symptoms or underlying causes of the disorder. In psychotherapy, patients talk with the therapist about upsetting thoughts and feelings, explore self-defeating patterns of behavior, and learn alternative ways to handle their emotions. As they talk, the therapist tries to help them understand how they can change or better cope with their disorder.

Behavioral therapy (BT) helps people develop more effective ways to work on immediate issues. Rather than helping the child understand his or her feelings and actions, it helps directly in changing their thinking and coping and thus may lead to changes in behavior. The support might be practical assistance, like help in organizing tasks or schoolwork or dealing with emotionally charged events. Or the support might be in self-monitoring one's own behavior and giving self-praise or rewards for acting in a desired way such as controlling anger or thinking before acting.

Social skills training can also help children learn new behaviors. In social skills training, the therapist discusses and models appropriate behaviors important in developing and maintaining social relationships, like waiting for a turn, sharing toys, asking for help, or responding to teasing, then gives children a chance to practice. For example, a child might learn to "read" other people's facial expression and tone of voice in order to respond appropriately. Social skills training helps the child to develop better ways to play and work with other children.

Attention Deficit Hyperactivity Disorder in Adults

Attention Deficit Hyperactivity Disorder is a highly publicized childhood disorder that affects approximately 3 to 5 percent of all children. What is much less well known is the probability that, of children who have ADHD, many will still have it as adults. Several studies done in recent years estimate that between 30 percent and 70 percent of children with ADHD continue to exhibit symptoms in the adult years.

Typically, adults with ADHD are unaware that they have this disorder—they often just feel that it's impossible to get organized, to stick to a job, to keep an appointment. The everyday tasks of getting up, getting dressed and ready for the day's work, getting to work on time, and being productive on the job can be major challenges for the ADHD adult.

Diagnosing ADHD in an Adult

Diagnosing an adult with ADHD is not easy. Many times, when a child is diagnosed with the disorder, a parent will recognize that he or she has many of the same symptoms the child has and, for the first time, will begin to understand some of the traits that have given him or her trouble for years—distractability, impulsivity, restlessness. Other adults will seek professional help for depression or anxiety and will find out that the root cause of some of their emotional problems is ADHD. They may have a history of school failures or problems at work. Often they have been involved in frequent automobile accidents.

To be diagnosed with ADHD, an adult must have childhood-onset, persistent, and current symptoms. The accuracy of the diagnosis of adult ADHD is of utmost importance and should be made by a clinician with expertise in the area of attention dysfunction. For an accurate diagnosis, a history of the patient's childhood behavior, together with an interview with his life partner, a parent, close friend or other close associate, will be needed. A physical examination and psychological tests should also be given. Comorbidity with other conditions may exist such as specific learning disabilities, anxiety, or affective disorders.

A correct diagnosis of ADHD can bring a sense of relief. The individual has brought into adulthood many negative perceptions of himself that may have led to low esteem. Now he can begin to understand why he has some of his problems and can begin to face them.

THE NATIONAL INSTITUTE OF MENTAL HEALTH has the mission to transform the understanding and treatment of mental illnesses through basic and clinical research, paving the way for prevention, recovery, and cure.

Sami Timimi and Nick Radcliffe    **NO**

The Rise and Rise of ADHD

Something's Happening Here

Something strange has been happening to children in Western society in the past couple of decades. The diagnosis of Attention Deficit Hyperactivity Disorder (ADHD) has reached epidemic proportions, particularly amongst boys in North America. The diagnosis is usually made by a child psychiatrist or paediatrician with advocates of the diagnosis claiming that children who present with what they consider to be over-activity, poor concentration and impulsivity are suffering from a medical condition which needs treatment with medication. The main medications used for children with a diagnosis of ADHD are stimulants such as Ritalin, whose chemical properties are virtually indistinguishable from the street drugs, speed and cocaine. Boys are four to ten times more likely to receive the diagnosis and stimulants than girls, with children as young as two being diagnosed and prescribed stimulants in increasing numbers.

By 1996 over 6 percent of school-aged boys in America were taking stimulant medication with more recent surveys showing that in some schools in the United States over 17 percent of boys have the diagnosis and are taking stimulant medication. In the UK prescriptions for stimulants have increased from about 6,000 in 1994 to about 345,000 in the latter half of 2003, suggesting that we in the UK are rapidly catching up with the US. Concerned professionals and parents are increasingly vocal in their criticism of the excessive use of stimulants and there are debates among clinicians proposing that ADHD is better regarded as a 'cultural construct' than a bona-fide medical disorder.

Despite the assertion from ADHD industry insiders that 'ADHD' is a medical disorder, even they have to concede that despite years and millions of dollars spent on research (it is the most thoroughly researched child psychiatric label—from a biological perspective that is) no medical test for it exists, nor has any proof been forthcoming of what the supposed physical deficit is, and so diagnosis is based on the subjective opinion of the diagnoser. Indeed its validity as a distinct diagnostic entity is

widely questioned as it cannot reliably be distinguished from other disorders in terms of aetiology, course, cultural variation, response to treatment, co-morbidity and gender distribution. Furthermore there is no evidence that treatment with stimulants leads to any lasting improvement. Indeed a recent meta-analysis of randomised controlled trials showed the trials were of poor quality, there was strong evidence of publication bias, short-term effects were inconsistent across different rating scales, side effects were frequent and problematic and long-term effects beyond four weeks of treatment were not demonstrated.

In the absence of objective methods for verifying the physical basis of ADHD, we also conceptualise ADHD as primarily a culturally constructed entity. The cultural dynamics of this label cannot be understood without first understanding the cultural discourses and power hierarchies that exist in contemporary Western society. It is a very compelling and dominating story invented and perpetuated by those whose interests are served by its telling and retelling (ADHD was literally voted into existence in the 1980s by the American Psychiatric Association when drawing up the third edition and third edition-revised versions of the Diagnostic and Statistical Manual). By focusing on within-child explanations for presenting behaviours, ADHD divorces a child from their context, and real life experiences, including traumatic ones, become clinically less important. In this article we explore how ADHD manages to occupy and hold onto such a dominant position despite the growing criticism and lack of evidence supporting its alleged medical origins.

The Claim That ADHD Is a Medical Disorder

To believers, ADHD is a diagnosable neuro-developmental disorder. Its identification is based on the observation of a constellation of behaviours that must be found across different settings and that are said to reveal abnormalities in children's activity levels, impulsiveness and concentration.

Commonly, when a child is diagnosed the first-line treatment of choice is a stimulant such as Methylphenidate. Stimulants are portrayed as safe and effective and children that are diagnosed and treated in this way are said to show vast improvements in their behaviour, activity levels, concentration and achievements. In the real world the picture is not so straightforward.

ADHD in Practice

In practice, the diagnosis of ADHD relies on adults in varying caring relationships with the child, reporting the above behaviours to a medical diagnostician. As diagnosis is based on the observation of behaviours alone, this has led to a kind of 'open season' where anyone can 'have a go': teachers, parents, school doctors, welfare officers, and so on. As the construct becomes more widely known within any community, confidence in making provisional diagnoses grows too. What is alarming is the apparent lack of awareness of the self-fulfilling nature of this process.

This self-fulfilling process occurs at many levels. For example, when a parent and child meet a specialist medical practitioner, the meeting is likely to be organised to elicit the type of information needed to fulfill predetermined diagnostic criteria. The relationship between the people's beliefs, expectations and subjective reporting will shape and inform the questions asked, responses given, and of course the child's behaviour in the room. Basically, some observable behaviours in children (such as inattention and hyperactivity) change in status from behaviours containing no more or less information (in isolation) than the inattention or hyperactivity as described by an observer, to becoming the basis of a primary diagnosis. The biomedical template is applied and the behaviours are interpreted as a sign of a physical disorder. This leaves out several layers of experience and context that could contribute to any observed behaviour as well as alternative meanings that could be given to that behaviour. This also denies the participant observers an opportunity to witness the child demonstrating exceptional behaviours.

This medical explanatory model has enormous cultural power. Naturally, most of the population will assume that once doctors have named these behaviours as a disorder, such a categorisation must have a natural and scientific basis. This leads to the huge differences in the experiences of children with the label being interpreted as of lesser importance when compared to the assumed similarities children with a disorder are felt to possess.

Behaviour rating scales have become a key part of the diagnostic process and are presented as an objective tool. Critics point out that agreeing a cut-off point for the behaviours in question is a culturally and subjectively driven process which is reflected in the fact that epidemiological studies (using rating scales) have produced very different prevalence rates for ADHD (in its various forms), ranging from about 0.5 percent of school age children to 26 percent of school age children. The criteria used for rating behaviours are based on Likert-type frequency descriptors (for example, often, seldom, never, and so on), thus reliable diagnoses depend on how consistently raters share a common understanding of the behaviours to be rated. Despite attempts at standardising criteria and assessment tools in cross-cultural studies, major and significant differences between raters from different countries, as well as between raters from different ethnic minority backgrounds, continue to be apparent.

If trained professionals cannot agree on how to rate behaviours relative to some sort of agreed (all be it arbitrary) 'norm', it is not surprising that non-professional observers and informants have different thresholds. For example, Reid et al. cite several studies reporting that specialist teachers tend to be more tolerant of misbehaviour and judge students' behaviours as less deviant than general class teachers.

ADHD is thus ideally placed as a convenient diagnostic 'dumping ground' allowing all of us (parents, teachers, doctors, politicians) to avoid the messy business of understanding human relationships and institutions and their difficulties, and our common responsibility for nurturing and raising well-behaved children. Loose, subjective diagnostic criteria with no established medical basis lend themselves to the 'elastic band' effect of ever stretching boundaries as the drug companies help themselves and the medical professions develop new markets. This has resulted in stimulants being prescribed for their perceived performance enhancing properties and with more children in classrooms taking stimulants many parents end up feeling their child is at a disadvantage if they do not. Stimulants are also being prescribed to children without them even fulfilling broad diagnostic criteria. This trend has now become so established that in some areas of the United States, less than half the children prescribed stimulants reach even the broad formal criteria for making a diagnosis of ADHD. In the UK you can now get a diagnosis via a 25-minute telephone consultation, without the child concerned being seen.

So Why Such a Strong Belief in ADHD?

ADHD exists as a concept because it has been positioned within the empiricist tradition of medical and psychological research. Writing on schizophrenia, Boyle draws attention to some of the devices that psychiatry uses to create the impression of a brain disorder despite the absence of supporting evidence. Firstly, she points out that by using their powerful status doctors can simply assert that it is a medical disorder, in such a way as to minimise opposition. In the case of ADHD, the Barkley et al. consensus statement would be a good example of such rhetoric. Here a group of eminent psychiatrists and psychologists produced a consensus statement to forestall debate on the merits of the widespread diagnosis and drug treatment of ADHD. Secondly, to support the assertion of a medical disorder, apparently meaningful associations with biological processes are created. For example, funding research that supports claims of biological or genetic causes (whether this delivers results or not), leads to the construct implicitly being regarded as if it is part of a larger field (in the case of ADHD, neuro-developmental psychiatry). Thirdly, the medical discourse prevails by ignoring or rejecting other non-biological accounts of (in this case, children's) behaviour, or by co-opting them as peripheral or consequential rather than antecedent.

Privileged social groups, who hold important and influential positions, have a powerful effect on our common cultural beliefs, attitudes and practices. Child Psychiatry in the UK does appear to have re-invented itself in the last ten years. Having struggled with a crisis of identity about being doctors, influential child psychiatrists successfully influenced the UK's professional discourse convincing it that there were more personal rewards for the profession by it adopting a more medicalised American style approach. ADHD has, along with a string of other so-called disorders, helped construct the field of neuro-developmental psychiatry, which the public, trusting such high status opinions, has come to view as real.

The development of diagnostic categories such as ADHD is of course of huge interest to the pharmaceutical industry. Indeed some argue that ADHD has been conceived and promoted by the pharmaceutical industry in order for there to be an entity for which stimulants could be prescribed. It is after all a multi-million dollar industry, with the US National Institute of Mental Health and the US Department of Education and the Food and Drug Administration all having been involved in funding and promoting treatment which calls for medicating

children with behavioural problems. The situation with drug companies controlling the agenda of scientific debate has become so prevalent that it is virtually impossible to climb up the career ladder without promotional support from drug companies. Most senior academics have long-standing financial links with drug companies inevitably compromising the impartiality of their opinions.

Similarly the impartiality of patient support organisations has to be questioned. In recent years it has become apparent that drug companies are using such consumer lobbying groups to their advantage not only by (often secretly) generous donations, but also on occasion by setting up patient groups themselves. The main pro-medication pro-ADHD consumer support group in North America is CHADD, which receives substantial amounts from drug companies, receiving an estimated $500,000 in 2002. There are other support groups: for example, in the United Kingdom the parent support group 'Overload' have been campaigning for prescribing doctors to provide more information to parents about the cardiovascular and neurological side effects of stimulants, believing that many more parents would be likely to reject such medication if they were being properly informed about it by the medical profession. However, without the financial support of the multinational giants, their message rarely gets heard.

ADHD is now also firmly entrenched in the cultural expectations of our education system. The defining of a disability requiring special needs help at school is now shaped by the disciplines of medicine and psychology. The adherence of these two fields to measuring physical and mental competence in order to determine normality inevitably conveys assumptions about deviance and failure and these labels then become attached to both individuals and groups who have failed to measure up or conform. Special needs practice in schools rests on within-child explanations. Psychiatric diagnoses have thus become an acceptable device for raising funds to meet children's perceived special needs. Increasing experience of children rendered less troublesome (to a school) by taking a stimulant, when coupled with a belief that these children's non-compliant behaviours were caused by a medical condition has also increased demand from teachers for children to be diagnosed and medicated.

Effects of This New Category of Childhood

What are the effects of embracing practices that impose descriptions such as ADHD onto children's behaviour? Children quickly become objects of such descriptions.

Their creativity, capacity for 'exceptional behaviours' and diversity go unnoticed. ADHD pushes teachers, parents and medical practitioners into self-doubt about their capacity to teach and care for children. The opportunities for developing reflexive, appreciative child management practices and skills are lost.

In mental health settings, the chance to build a repertoire of therapeutic skills and practices that might facilitate people to talk about their experience in ways that can create more empowering meanings that build on their own knowledge is also lost. Instead children are persuaded to take highly addictive and potentially brain disabling drugs for many years and may well be cultured into the attitude of 'a pill for life's problems'. Children and their carers risk developing 'tunnel vision' about their problems rendering them unnecessarily 'disabled' and dependent on 'experts'. The effect this has not only on the physical health of our children in the West, but also on our ways of viewing childhood is incalculable. Behind the rise in diagnoses and the liberal prescription of such dangerous medicines lurks a deep malaise that is infecting Western culture—hostility to children—for in our modernist, hyperactive, individualistic lifestyles children 'get in the way'.

SAMI TIMIMI is a consultant child and adolescent psychiatrist and director of postgraduate education in the National Health Service in Lincolnshire and a visiting professor of child and adolescent psychiatry at the University of Lincoln, UK. He writes from a critical psychiatry perspective on topics relating to child and adolescent mental health and has published many articles on many subjects including eating disorders, psychotherapy, behavioral disorders, and cross-cultural psychiatry.

NICK RADCLIFFE is a veteran clinical psychologist, having worked as a family psychotherapist for the NHS in Great Britain for 25 years before resigning to begin practice at the Shrewsbury Psychology Centre and lead the Connecting Minds group—an association of psychologists dedicated to delivering relationship-based therapy to the community.

EXPLORING THE ISSUE

Is Attention-Deficit Hyperactivity Disorder (ADHD) a Real Disorder?

Critical Thinking and Reflection

1. According to these authors, how does normal distractibility differ from disordered distractibility? What motivations might some people have to label ordinary distractibility as a mental disorder?
2. According to Timimi and Radcliffe, the subjectivity involved in the diagnosis of ADHD is an argument against its existence as a medical disorder. Should there be any degree of subjectivity in medical diagnoses? Is it tolerable in the diagnosis of non-medical mental illness?
3. Based on your readings, do you believe that ADHD is a real disorder? Why or why not? What does it mean if ADHD is or is not a real disorder? If it is a disorder, is it a medical disorder?
4. There are many people involved in the question of ADHD's legitimacy as a disorder, including children themselves, parents, doctors, psychologists, politicians, and the media. Who should decide whether ADHD is a real disorder? Might any of these groups have motives that could bias them toward one conclusion or the other?

Is There Common Ground?

The authors in this section disagree quite firmly on the issue of whether ADHD is, in fact, a medical disorder. No one is denying the existence of the behaviors that are being diagnosed as ADHD, but the question still remains of whether these behaviors are negative at all or whether they are the sign of anything pathological in nature. It is possible that ADHD is a medical issue whose underlying biological premises are yet to be discovered. It is also possible that ADHD is a social construct. A firm answer is still to be had.

Of course, these are not the only positions that could be taken on this controversial issue. For example, a number of scholars argue that ADHD is really the result of bad parenting, while yet others claim that ADHD really just reflects boredom. Those who claim that ADHD is a reflection of bad or lax parenting argue that parents of ADHD children do not seem to teach their children to focus or organize their time and materials well.

Those claiming boredom as the cause of ADHD note that students who tend not to focus well in some classes are often very attentive and successful when placed in a more advanced, exciting, or demanding courses. These critics also often lay the blame for ADHD at the feet of our educational systems, stating that public schools are not designed to be conducive to multiple styles of learning and, thus, often leave many students disengaged and bored. They cite examples of struggling students who, after being removed from public schools and placed in schools with atypical styles of assignments and assessments, no longer exhibit symptoms of ADHD.

For many of those who are unconvinced that ADHD is a diagnosable illness, there is also much concern about the frequency with which medications are prescribed to youngsters as a way of treating behavior problems. They fear, for example, the long-term effects of such medications on the developing brain (as Timimi and Radcliffe note, the drugs used to treat ADHD are similar to amphetamines and cocaine), as well as question whether the widespread use of medications might not be a form of social control that does not adequately address the underlying problems that are causing inattention and disruptive behavior in children. It is worth considering how the debate regarding the nature of ADHD might change if medications were no longer promoted as a primary means of treating the behavioral problems of children? Also, how might the debate be altered if studies were able to clearly show that ADHD always occurs with depression or other mental illnesses?

Additional Resources

Kessler, R. C., Adler, L., Ames, M., et al. (2005). The World Health Organization Adult ADHD Self-Report Scale (ASRS): A short screening scale for use in the general population. *Psychological Medicine, 35*(2), 245–256.

Polanczyk, G., de Lima, M. S., Horta, B. L., et al. (2007). The worldwide prevalence of ADHD: A systematic review and metaregression analysis. *American Journal of Psychiatry, 164*(6), 942–948.

Southall, A. (2007). *The Other Side of ADHD: Attention Deficit Hyperactivity Disorder Exposed and Explained.* Abingdon, UK: Radcliffe.

Internet References . . .

Attention Deficit Hyperactivity Disorder Controversies

http://en.wikipedia.org/wiki/Attention_deficit_
hyperactivity_disorder_controversies

Centers for Disease Control and Prevention

http://www.cdc.gov/ncbddd/adhd/

WebMD

http://www.webmd.com/add-adhd/default.htm

ISSUE

Selected, Edited, and with Issue Framing Material by:
Edwin E. Gantt, *Brigham Young University*

Is Addiction a Disease?

YES: **National Institute on Drug Abuse**, from *The Science of Addiction* (2007)

NO: **Peter Hitchens**, from "The Fantasy of Addiction," *First Things* (2017)

Learning Outcomes

After reading this issue, you will be able to:

- Determine whether addiction is a disease.

- Discuss whether the evidence for the brain disease model of addiction is sufficient to rule out all other models.

- Understand the debate of free will versus determinism and its role in the disease model of addiction.

- Articulate the argument against the disease model that spontaneous recoveries give.

ISSUE SUMMARY

YES: The National Institute on Drug Abuse describes drug abuse and addiction as a disease of the brain. Although initial drug use may be voluntary, the resulting physical changes to brain circuits explain the compulsive and self-destructive behaviors of addiction. Environmental and genetic factors explain why some become addicted more readily than others.

NO: Journalist and author Peter Hitchens argues that because the disease model of addiction is deterministic, it fundamentally misunderstands human nature and the ability people have to make meaningful choices regarding how they are going to live their lives.

For many decades, the public and psychological researchers alike viewed drug addiction as a symptom of flawed character or moral failure. It was assumed that those who were addicted to drugs or alcohol had the ability to avoid or overcome these problems simply by developing a greater sense of moral character and choosing to quit their addictions by force of will. However, with the rise of cognitive neuroscience research in recent decades, investigators have increasingly begun to view drug addiction as a chronic brain illness, and, as such, something that is outside the control of those suffering from it. In this view, drug and alcohol addictions are similar—at least conceptually—to other well-known diseases, such as cancer, Alzheimer's

disease, or Parkinson's disease. This new model views addiction as a relapsing ailment of the brain that compels those suffering from it to engage in continued drug and alcohol use. In 1987, with the infamous "This Is Your Brain on Drugs" public service announcement sponsored by the Partnership for a Drug-Free America, the notion of drug addiction as a brain problem entered the mainstream of public thinking. Since that time, the brain disease model of drug addiction has become a dominant theory of addiction in both the public and academic realms.

In contrast, much recent research on drug and alcohol addiction indicates that the brain disease model may not be capturing the subtle nuances of the actual experiences of those who are addicted to drugs. The reality is that some drug addicts are able to successfully quit drug use instantaneously (sometimes referred to as "quitting cold turkey"), contradicting the chronic and relapsing characteristics presumed in the brain disease model. If addiction is a disease, then it should not be possible for anyone to simply choose not to have the disease anymore. After all, someone who has cancer or diabetes cannot simply choose not to have cancer or diabetes anymore. There is no "going cold turkey" with such diseases. Similarly, another anomaly of the brain disease model is that drug addicts report that they use drugs for a variety of reasons and frequently choose for themselves how to administer these substances to their body. Understanding these incongruities, is the brain disease model of addiction still a suitable conceptual framework for addiction research and treatment?

The YES article, published by the National Institute on Drug Abuse, reviews the basic functions and structures of the brain. The article claims that drug use can permanently alter how these structures function, and thus change and reinforce an addict's behavior. These changes constitute a disease of the brain because, once effected, they are outside of the control of the individual. Whether or not someone who uses drugs will end up with an addiction can be explained by environmental and genetic factors in the same way that one might have risk factors for (or protective factors from) any other disease.

The NO article, written by English journalist Peter Hitchens, claims that the disease model of addiction is inherently contradictory to human experience. Hitchens believes that defining addiction as an uncontrollable force that is stronger than the will makes the philosophical claim that all human behavior is determined and that there is no such thing as free will; a claim that has yet to adequately demonstrate in either science or philosophy. The debate of free will versus determinism is still inconclusive today. In particular, Hitchens believes that the presence of even one person that has recovered from an addiction spontaneously completely undermines the idea that addiction is a disease. He describes the disease model of addiction as a fundamental misunderstanding of human nature that discounts the ability of people to make meaningful choices.

YES

National Institute on Drug Abuse

The Science of Addiction

Drug Abuse and Addiction

What Is Drug Addiction?

Addiction is defined as a chronic, relapsing brain disease that is characterized by compulsive drug seeking and use, despite harmful consequences. It is considered a brain disease because drugs change the brain—they change its structure and how it works. These brain changes can be long lasting, and can lead to the harmful behaviors seen in people who abuse drugs.

Is Continued Drug Abuse a Voluntary Behavior?

The initial decision to take drugs is mostly voluntary. However, when drug abuse takes over, a person's ability to exert self control can become seriously impaired. Brain imaging studies from drug-addicted individuals show physical changes in areas of the brain that are critical to judgment, decisionmaking, learning and memory, and behavior control. Scientists believe that these changes alter the way the brain works, and may help explain the compulsive and destructive behaviors of addiction.

Why Do Some People Become Addicted to Drugs, While Others Do Not?

As with any other disease, vulnerability to addiction differs from person to person. In general, the more risk factors an individual has, the greater the chance that taking drugs will lead to abuse and addiction. "Protective" factors reduce a person's risk of developing addiction.

What Factors Determine If a Person Will Become Addicted?

No single factor determines whether a person will become addicted to drugs. The overall risk for addiction is impacted by the biological makeup of the individual—it can even be influenced by gender or ethnicity, his or her developmental stage, and the surrounding social environment (e.g., conditions at home, at school, and in the neighborhood).

Which Biological Factors Increase Risk of Addiction?

Scientists estimate that genetic factors account for between 40 and 60 percent of a person's vulnerability to addiction, including the effects of environment on gene expression and function. Adolescents and individuals with mental disorders are at greater risk of drug abuse and addiction than the general population.

The Brain Continues to Develop into Adulthood and Undergoes Dramatic Changes During Adolescence

One of the brain areas still maturing during adolescence is the prefrontal cortex—the part of the brain that enables us to assess situations, make sound decisions, and keep our emotions and desires under control. The fact that this critical part of an adolescent's brain is still a work-in-progress puts them at increased risk for poor decisions (such as trying drugs or continued abuse). Thus, introducing drugs while the brain is still developing may have profound and long-lasting consequences.

Drugs and the Brain

Introducing the Human Brain

The human brain is the most complex organ in the body. This three-pound mass of gray and white matter sits at the center of all human activity—you need it to drive a car, to enjoy a meal, to breathe, to create an artistic masterpiece, and to enjoy everyday activities. In brief, the brain regulates your basic body functions; enables you to interpret and respond to everything you experience, and shapes your thoughts, emotions, and behavior.

The brain is made up of many parts that all work together as a team. Different parts of the brain are responsible for coordinating and performing specific functions. Drugs can alter important brain areas that are necessary for life-sustaining functions and can drive the compulsive

Published by National Institutes of Health, NIH Pub. no. 07-5605, April 2007, pp. 5, 7–8, 10, 15–20.

drug abuse that marks addiction. Brain areas affected by drug abuse—

- *The brain stem* controls basic functions critical to life, such as heart rate, breathing, and sleeping.
- *The limbic system* contains the brain's reward circuit—it links together a number of brain structures that control and regulate our ability to feel pleasure. Feeling pleasure motivates us to repeat behaviors such as eating—actions that are critical to our existence. The limbic system is activated when we perform these activities—and also by drugs of abuse. In addition, the limbic system is responsible for our perception of other emotions, both positive and negative, which explains the mood-altering properties of many drugs.
- *The cerebral cortex* is divided into areas that control specific functions. Different areas process information from our senses, enabling us to see, feel, hear, and taste. The front part of the cortex, the frontal cortex or forebrain, is the thinking center of the brain; it powers our ability to think, plan, solve problems, and make decisions.

How Does the Brain Communicate?

The brain is a communications center consisting of billions of neurons, or nerve cells. Networks of neurons pass messages back and forth to different structures within the brain, the spinal column, and the peripheral nervous system. These nerve networks coordinate and regulate everything we feel, think, and do.

- *Neuron to Neuron*
  Each nerve cell in the brain sends and receives messages in the form of electrical impulses. Once a cell receives and processes a message, it sends it on to other neurons.
- *Neurotransmitters—The Brain's Chemical Messengers*
  The messages are carried between neurons by chemicals called neurotransmitters. (They transmit messages between neurons.)
- *Receptors—The Brain's Chemical Receivers*
  The neurotransmitter attaches to a specialized site on the receiving cell called a receptor. A neurotransmitter and its receptor operate like a "key and lock," an exquisitely specific mechanism that ensures that each receptor will forward the appropriate message only after interacting with the right kind of neurotransmitter.
- *Transporters—The Brain's Chemical Recyclers*
  Located on the cell that releases the neurotransmitter, transporters recycle these neurotransmitters

(i.e., bring them back into the cell that released them), thereby shutting off the signal between neurons.

How Do Drugs Work in the Brain?

Drugs are chemicals. They work in the brain by tapping into the brain's communication system and interfering with the way nerve cells normally send, receive, and process information. Some drugs, such as marijuana and heroin, can activate neurons because their chemical structure mimics that of a natural neurotransmitter. This similarity in structure "fools" receptors and allows the drugs to lock onto and activate the nerve cells. Although these drugs mimic brain chemicals, they don't activate nerve cells in the same way as a natural neurotransmitter, and they lead to abnormal messages being transmitted through the network.

Other drugs, such as amphetamine or cocaine, can cause the nerve cells to release abnormally large amounts of natural neurotransmitters or prevent the normal recycling of these brain chemicals. This disruption produces a greatly amplified message, ultimately disrupting communication channels. The difference in effect can be described as the difference between someone whispering into your ear and someone shouting into a microphone.

How Do Drugs Work in the Brain to Produce Pleasure?

All drugs of abuse directly or indirectly target the brain's reward system by flooding the circuit with dopamine. Dopamine is a neurotransmitter present in regions of the brain that regulate movement, emotion, cognition, motivation, and feelings of pleasure. The overstimulation of this system, which rewards our natural behaviors, produces the euphoric effects sought by people who abuse drugs and teaches them to repeat the behavior.

How Does Stimulation of the Brain's Pleasure Circuit Teach Us to Keep Taking Drugs?

Our brains are wired to ensure that we will repeat life-sustaining activities by associating those activities with pleasure or reward. Whenever this reward circuit is activated, the brain notes that something important is happening that needs to be remembered, and teaches us to do it again and again, without thinking about it. Because drugs of abuse stimulate the same circuit, we learn to abuse drugs in the same way.

Why Are Drugs More Addictive Than Natural Rewards?

When some drugs of abuse are taken, they can release 2 to 10 times the amount of dopamine that natural rewards do. In some cases, this occurs almost immediately (as when drugs are smoked or injected), and the effects can last much longer than those produced by natural rewards. The resulting effects on the brain's pleasure circuit dwarfs those produced by naturally rewarding behaviors such as eating and sex. The effect of such a powerful reward strongly motivates people to take drugs again and again. This is why scientists sometimes say that drug abuse is something we learn to do very, very well.

What Happens to Your Brain If You Keep Taking Drugs?

Just as we turn down the volume on a radio that is too loud, the brain adjusts to the overwhelming surges in dopamine (and other neurotransmitters) by producing less dopamine or by reducing the number of receptors that can receive and transmit signals. As a result, dopamine's impact on the reward circuit of a drug abuser's brain can become abnormally low, and the ability to experience any pleasure is reduced. This is why the abuser eventually feels flat, lifeless, and depressed, and is unable to enjoy things that previously brought them pleasure. Now, they need to take drugs just to bring their dopamine function back up to normal. And, they must take larger amounts of the drug than they first did to create the dopamine high—an effect known as tolerance.

How Does Long-Term Drug Taking Affect Brain Circuits?

We know that the same sort of mechanisms involved in the development of tolerance can eventually lead to profound changes in neurons and brain circuits, with the potential to severely compromise the long-term health of the brain. For example, glutamate is another neurotransmitter that influences the reward circuit and the ability to learn. When the optimal concentration of glutamate is altered by drug abuse, the brain attempts to compensate for this change, which can cause impairment in cognitive function. Similarly, long-term drug abuse can trigger adaptations in habit or nonconscious memory systems. Conditioning is one example of this type of learning, whereby environmental cues become associated with the drug experience and can trigger uncontrollable cravings if the individual is later exposed to these cues, even without the drug itself being available. This learned "reflex" is extremely robust and can emerge even after many years of abstinence.

What Other Brain Changes Occur with Abuse?

Chronic exposure to drugs of abuse disrupts the way critical brain structures interact to control behavior—behavior specifically related to drug abuse. Just as continued abuse may lead to tolerance or the need for higher drug dosages to produce an effect, it may also lead to addiction, which can drive an abuser to seek out and take drugs compulsively. Drug addiction erodes a person's self-control and ability to make sound decisions, while sending intense impulses to take drugs.

THE NATIONAL INSTITUTE ON DRUG ABUSE, part of the United States' National Institute of Health, is an organization with a mission "to advance science on the causes and consequences of drug use and addiction and to apply that knowledge to improve individual and public health." NIDA supports most of the world's research on the health aspects of drug abuse and addiction.

Peter Hitchens    **NO**

The Fantasy of Addiction

I never meant to start an argument about addiction. I had carried my private doubts on the subject around in my head for years, in the "heresy" section where I keep my really risky thoughts. And I don't recommend disagreeing in public with Hollywood royalty, either, which is how it happened. In such a clash, most people will think you are wrong and Hollywood is right, especially if your opponent is Chandler Bing, the beloved character from *Friends*. Of course, he wasn't really Chandler Bing, just an actor called Matthew Perry—but an actor with an entourage so big it filled an entire elevator at the BBC's new studios in central London where we quarreled.

Our debate wasn't even supposed to be about addiction. I'd been asked onto the corporation's grand but faded late-night current affairs show *Newsnight* to talk about drug courts, one of many stupid ideas suggested by the idea of addiction. I reckoned my main opponent would be the other guest, Baroness (Molly) Meacher, whose name sounds like something out of *The Beggar's Opera*. While she looks like the sort of harmless, kindly housewife who knits next to you on the bus, she is in fact a campaigner for the wilder sorts of drug liberalization. If this Chandler Perry wanted to horn in, well and good. Who cared? Yet when I began to sense sarcasm mingled with unearned superiority oozing from the character from *Friends*, I decided to let my impatience show.

Hence my rash, irreversible plunge into an argument which has been going on ever since, consuming billions of electrons on social media, and which will probably still be going on when I die. I heard myself using the words "the fantasy of addiction." There, I'd done it. Let the heavens fall.

Chandler Bing called me various names and was even more sarcastic than before. He is extremely good at sarcasm, even if he understands very little about the drug problem. I have never heard the words "your book" pronounced with such eloquent contempt. The final "k" seemed to contain two whole syllables. Is this a Canadian thing? He was referring to my modest volume on the topic *The War We Never Fought*, so energetically ignored by

reviewers and booksellers that it is known among London publishers as *The Book They Never Bought*.

I took a while to realize what I had done. Only for a moment did I feel that chill in the innards which always follows any sort of dangerous speech. The more I thought about it, the more pleased I became. It was a bit like the long-ago days when I had begun to change my mind about revolutionary socialism. I was wholly liberated. I had found the courage to say what I really thought, and so was more fully human than before.

Words are congealed thought—in some cases, very congealed indeed. Some words are congealed *lack* of thought. When we use words badly, it is because we are too lazy, or too hurried, to think about what they mean. This is most of the time, which is George Orwell's greatest point in his matchless essay on "Politics and the English Language." If the words that come out of your mouth or your keyboard do not make a picture in your mind, then they will certainly be dull and will probably be wrong.

But if we pause to let words unfold and grow, then we understand and use them better—or abandon them, as we abandon clichés and exploded theories.

The chief difficulty with the word "addiction" is the idea that it describes a power greater than the will. If it exists in the way we use it and in the way our legal and medical systems assume it exists, then free will has been abolished. I know there are people who think and argue this is so. But this is not one of those things that can be demonstrated by falsifiable experiment. In the end, the idea that humans do not really have free will is a contentious opinion, not an objective fact.

So to use the word "addiction" is to embrace one side in one of those ancient unresolved debates that cannot be settled this side of the grave. To decline to use it, by contrast, is to accept that all kinds of influences, inheritances, and misfortunes may well operate on us, and propel us toward mistaken, foolish, wrong, and dangerous actions or habits. It is to leave open the question whether we can resist these forces. I am convinced that declining the word "addiction" is both the only honest thing to do, and the

Hitchens, Peter, "The Fantasy of Addictions" *First Things*, February 2017. pp 37–41. Institute on Religion and Public Life.

only kind and wise thing to do, when we are faced with fellow creatures struggling with harmful habits and desires. It is all very well to relieve someone of the responsibility for such actions, by telling him his body is to blame. But what is that solace worth if he takes it as permission to carry on as before? Once or twice I have managed to explain to a few of my critics that this is what I am saying. But generally they are too furious, or astonished by my sheer nerve, to listen.

So let us approach it another way. The English language belongs to no state or government. It is not ruled by academies or even defined by dictionaries, however good. It operates on a sort of linguistic version of common law, by usage and precedent. And the expression "addiction" is very widely and variously used. There are people who claim, seriously, to be "addicted" to sex or to gambling.

It is now impolite to refer to habitual drunkards. They are "alcoholics," supposedly suffering from a complaint that is not their fault. The curious variable ambiguity of Alcoholics Anonymous (AA) on this point has added to the confusion. AA, to begin with, asked its adherents to admit they had no control over themselves, as a preliminary to giving that power to God. Somehow I suspect that God plays less of a part in modern AA doctrine, but the idea of powerlessness remains. Members of the organization quietly moved from calling alcoholism an "illness" or a "malady" to describing it as a "disease," round about the time that the medical profession began to do the same thing.

We are ceaselessly told that cigarettes are "addictive." Most powerfully, most of us believe that the abusers of the illegal drug heroin are "addicted" to it. Once again, the public, the government, and the legal and medical systems are more or less ordered to believe that users of these things are involuntary sufferers. A British celebrity and alleged comedian, Russell Brand, wrote recently, "The mentality and behaviour of drug addicts and alcoholics is wholly irrational until you understand that they are *completely powerless* [my emphasis] over their addiction and, unless they have structured help, they have no hope."

Brand is a former heroin abuser who has by now rather famously given up the drug. But how can that be, if what he says about addiction is true? The phrase "wholly irrational" simply cannot withstand the facts of Brand's own life. It will have to be replaced by something much less emphatic—let us say, "partly irrational." The same thing happens to the phrase "completely powerless." Neither the adverb nor the adjective can survive. Nor can the word "addiction" itself, which is visibly evaporating. We have to say "they struggle over their compulsion."

Or you might turn to this definition of addiction from the American Society of Addiction Medicine:

> Addiction is a primary, chronic disease of brain reward, motivation, memory and related circuitry. Dysfunction in these circuits leads to characteristic biological, psychological, social and spiritual manifestations. This is reflected in an individual pathologically pursuing reward and/or relief by substance use and other behaviors.

This definition prompted one writer at Alternet, an influential pro-addiction website, to say:

> If you think addiction is all about booze, drugs, sex, gambling, food and other irresistible vices, think again. And if you believe that a person has a choice whether or not to indulge in an addictive behavior, get over it. . . . Fundamental impairment in the experience of pleasure literally compels the addict *to chase the chemical highs produced by substances like drugs and alcohol and obsessive behaviors like sex, food and gambling.*

In other words, conscious choice plays little or no role in the actual state of addiction; as a result, *a person cannot choose not to be addicted. The most an addict can do is choose not to use the substance or engage in the behavior that reinforces the entire self-destructive reward-circuitry loop.* So even if the supposed "addict" ceases (as many do) to be "addicted" in practice to the addictive substance or activity, he remains "addicted" in some spiritual, subjective way, which cannot actually be seen in his behavior.

The defender of the concept of "addiction," confronted with evidence that many "addicts" cease to be "addicted," will say that of course he didn't mean to suggest the phenomenon was wholly irresistible and could not be mastered by will. Oh no, he will say, reasonable people quite understand that it is not like that at all. In any normal argument, this would be the end of the matter. Anyone who confesses to using a word in one sense when it suits him, and in a wholly contradictory sense when it also suits him, has expelled himself from the company of all reasonable people and admitted that he respects neither truth nor logic.

And yet, though he has lost the point, according to the rules, a higher umpire grants him the victory. I am still pestered weekly by peeved and affronted correspondents, with demands that I "prove" that "addiction" does not exist. Like Kipling's Gods of the Copybook Headings, I limp up to explain it once more: It is the *proposer* of any such concept who has to provide a testable and falsifiable theorem. But because the existence of "addiction" is assumed, the rules of normal science and discourse are reversed.

The consequences of this usage, in medical practice and law, are huge. Actions once punished or scorned are sympathetically treated as if they arose from diseases rather than choices. Persons repeatedly caught in possession of illegal drugs (a crime that in theory attracts a prison sentence of several years) are not punished according to law, but supplied by the authorities with clean needles, put into the care of doctors, and, in some jurisdictions, given free substitute drugs at the expense of the taxpayer.

It is no longer acceptable to disapprove of certain selfish and inconsiderate actions, some of them illegal. Of these alleged "addictions," only the smoking of cigarettes is still disparaged by polite liberal-minded persons. This is probably because of its undoubted antisocial stink and foul mess, the huge shared cost of treating smokers for the diseases they voluntarily contract, and the alleged danger to nonsmokers exposed to its fumes.

As a result, huge numbers of supposed cigarette "addicts," forced out of workplaces and bars and compelled to stand outside in pathetic gaggles, and frowned and coughed at when they light up in the privacy of their homes, have in recent years overcome their "addiction" and stopped smoking altogether. I personally know many such people. Several have been glad of the pressure to stop. It is interesting that the habit (as it used to be called) now tends to be commonest among the hopelessly poor, the ill-educated, and young women driven by fashion into seeking those tricky gifts which cigarettes still offer them—sexual allure and a pleasure that does not make them less thin.

But the fundamental point should not be lost. Supposed "addicts" can and do give up their supposed addictions. It is not only smokers who do this. I also know several formerly very heavy drinkers who have done it, generally because of fears for their health or their professional standing. Even heroin abusers, and gamblers, can and do just stop. Reason has overcome desire. In which case the whole idea of "addiction," as a power greater than will, is overthrown. Once again, if "addiction" exists, these people cannot exist. If they exist, "addiction" cannot exist. Since we know that such people do exist, the riddle is solved.

Scan the drug abuser's brain as you will, you will not be able to demonstrate that any part of it has *forced* him to take his drug of choice, or is stopping him from giving it up. Recently, the psychologist and former "addict" Marc Lewis attacked this scientistic determinism in a book *The Biology of Desire*. Yes, the brain of the drug user changes

physically and observably (so, it might be noted, does the brain of the London taxi-driver who must learn by heart the streets of London before being given his license). But this is the sign of an organ adapting to conditions, not a disease. The same brain can go on to adapt to a life without the drug involved, or a life without taxi driving.

What sustains the continuing belief that "addiction" is a physical disease is presupposition, based upon conventional wisdom, allied with desire. People feel a near-superstitious terror that mere contact with the "addictive" substance is enough to bring ruin. This belief long predates the current era of drug abuse. A character in Somerset Maugham's *The Razor's Edge*, recently rescued from a dissolute life of servitude to substances, is lured back into alcohol-sodden doom by a bottle of Zubrowka bison-grass vodka purposely left on a table by a rival in love. It is absurd. But millions believe that some such process happens. They think, especially, that the merest brush with heroin will imprison its user for life, just as the reformed "alcoholic" will be sent flying down the chute of doom by a single sip of wine or even the whiff of it in a sauce. In the 1975 movie *French Connection II*, the American narcotics cop "Popeye" Doyle (played by Gene Hackman) is shown being turned into a junkie by repeated forced injections. In the 1996 movie *Trainspotting*, withdrawal from heroin is portrayed as a nightmarish struggle. Are these fictional arguments, which have left powerful impressions in many minds, truthful?

As for the power of heroin to enslave people against their will and afflict them with terrible withdrawal, I must turn to an author whose book on drugs (unlike mine, so disdained by Chandler Bing) has been a critical and commercial success. This is perhaps because he is largely on the side of decriminalization. Johann Hari's *Chasing the Scream* is devastating on the subject of "addiction," yet what he writes has not gotten him into any trouble at all.

Hari cites the complete blockade of the heroin supply in Vancouver during the 1970s, when supposed "addicts" carried on taking the inert powders that dealers continued to sell for several weeks. They suffered no "withdrawal symptoms." Hari goes on to quote the medical researchers John Ball and Carl Chambers, who, he says, studied medical literature from 1875 to 1968, and found that nobody had died from heroin withdrawal alone in that time. "The only people who are killed by withdrawal," Hari says, "are people who are already very weak." But the myth of addiction requires the myth of withdrawal, a logical consequence of the idea of physiological dependence.

The desire to maximize the effects of "withdrawal" and minimize the effects of long-term abuse also features in the parallel argument about alcohol. Modern medicine, for instance, likes to say that the terrible affliction called delirium tremens (DTs) is a symptom of "withdrawal" from alcohol. By "withdrawal," by the way, they do not mean total stoppage, just a reduced intake. But older reference books (the DTs were first described and defined in 1813) clearly attribute DTs to long-term alcohol abuse, not to withdrawal, partial or total, from it. No doubt a total or partial cessation of drinking can bring it on. I would be interested to see any research work showing that people who have *not* done serious long-term damage to themselves by drinking are susceptible to DTs under any circumstances.

According to research cited by Hari, from *The Archives of General Psychiatry*, some 20 percent of U.S. soldiers serving in Vietnam had "become addicted to" heroin while there. The study showed that 95 percent of these men had stopped using heroin within a year of returning home. "Treatment" and "rehabilitation" made no difference to this outcome. As Hari writes, "If you believe the theory that drugs hijack your brain and turn you into a chemical slave . . . then this makes no sense."

Indeed it doesn't. I could also cite the millions of hospital patients given medical morphine (effectively the same as heroin) during illness or recovery from injury, who do not become dependent upon it. Or I could note the view of Anthony Daniels, who often writes under the pseudonym Theodore Dalrymple. He was for many years a prison doctor and constantly encountered heroin abusers. He describes their withdrawal symptoms as being similar to a fairly bad bout of influenza.

But it makes little difference. The belief is implanted in the modern mind, taught to the young not by explanation, experiment, and example but by being repeatedly and universally assumed. First of all, it is conventional wisdom, built into thousands of sentences, newspaper articles, TV and radio programs, sermons, speeches, and private conversations. Secondly, it is what we desire. Which of us, indulging in some pleasure, is not secretly relieved to find that others are weaker than we are, have nastier and more selfish pleasures, and that these things are generally excused because of a vast, universal thing that we cannot control or influence? Indulgence, like misery, seeks company for reassurance. Unlike misery, it generally finds that company. Beliefs spread in this way cannot really be challenged. Jonathan Swift rightly observed that you cannot reason a man out of a position he was not reasoned into in the first place.

The mass abandonment of cigarettes by a generation of educated people demonstrates that, given responsibility for their actions and blamed for their outcomes, huge numbers of people will give up a bad habit even if it is difficult. Where we have adopted the opposite attitude, and assured abusers that they are not answerable for their actions, we have seen other bad habits grow or remain as common as before. Heroin abuse has not been defeated, the abuse of prescription drugs grows all the time, and heavy drinking is a sad and spreading problem in Britain.

Most of the people who read what I have written here, if they even get to the end, will be angry with me for expressing their own secret doubts, one of the cruelest things you can do to any fellow creature. For we all prefer the easy, comforting falsehood to the awkward truth. But at the same time, we all know exactly what we are doing, and seek with ever-greater zeal to conceal it from ourselves. Has it not been so since the beginning? And has not the greatest danger always been that those charged with the duty of preaching the steep and rugged pathway persuade themselves that weakness is compassion, and that sin can be cured at a clinic, or soothed with a pill? And so falsehood flourishes in great power, like the green bay tree.

Peter Hitchens is an English journalist and author. He has published six books and worked as a foreign correspondent in Moscow and Washington, DC. He was awarded an Orwell prize for journalism in 2010. He is known for his bold writing, particularly on politics and social issues. He studied politics at York University.

EXPLORING THE ISSUE

Is Addiction a Disease?

Critical Thinking and Reflection

1. Is there sufficient evidence for the disease model of addiction?
2. How does the National Institute on Drug Abuse article argue that compulsive behaviors are tied to neurobiology? How do you think Hitchens would respond to this argument?
3. What are parts of the brain change in addiction? How can these changes lead to compulsive and irrational behavior?
4. According to Hitchens, what is the problem with the definition of addiction? How does this affect free will?

Is There Common Ground?

Drug and alcohol addiction is a pervasive problem that affects thousands of people, and, as such, is worthy of detailed and careful study. Although the authors of both articles may disagree as to what the most useful conceptual approach to addiction is, they clearly agree that addiction is a pervasive social issue and that addicts need help in their rehabilitation. With this as a basis for common ground, it is likely that a more even stance between the issues could be successfully adopted. On the disease model side, the consequences of choices and the existence of spontaneous remission could be taken into consideration without ignoring the importance of the brain. Likewise, the free will side may continue to emphasize the importance of choices while also recognizing that a structurally and functionally intact brain may be necessary to make meaningful choices. The various effects that drugs can have on the brain may explain why some people find it incredibly difficult to quit their drug use, even when there is a strong and sincere desire to do so.

Another possible area in which researchers on opposite sides of this issue can perhaps find some common ground involves that mounting evidence that people already diagnosed with clear physical ailments (i.e., diseases) can actually experience improved health outcomes in light of some of the choices they make. For example, there is evidence to suggest that people diagnosed with cancer who routinely watch comedies, laugh more often, and work to maintain a positive attitude have better health outcomes than those who did not. Additionally, some research indicates that people with heart disease who have strong social support networks tend to have better health outcomes than those with weak or nonexistent social support networks. Thus, it would seem that even diseases that clearly fit the disease model can be affected by psychological factors. As such, there may be room for the disease model as an approach to conceptualizing addiction but not one in which the importance of the choices and reasoning of the individual is left out of research or treatment.

The deeper philosophical issue raised specifically by Hitchens—and in passing by the National Institute on Drug Abuse—concerns the centuries-long debate over whether human behavior is ultimately determined or in some way free. These arguments are diametrically opposed, and often difficult to meld in any meaningful way. While it is possible to take a more even stance, this philosophical issue and the consequence of either side must be taken into consideration when seeking common ground.

Additional Resources

Dunington, K. (2011). *Addiction and Virtue: Beyond the Models of Disease and Choice*. Westmont, IL: IVP Academic.

Heyman, G. M. (2009). *Addiction: A Disorder of Choice*. Cambridge, MA: Harvard University Press.

Lewis, M. (2015). *The Biology of Desire: Why Addiction is Not a Disease*. New York, NY: PublicAffairs.

Rastegar, D. A., Fingerhood, M. I. (2005). *Addiction Medicine: An Evidence-based Handbook*. Philadelphia, PA: LWW.

Internet References . . .

Addiction Recovery Guide

http://www.addictionrecoveryguide.org/articles/

National Institutes on Drug Abuse

https://www.nih.gov/about-nih/what-we-do/nih-alma-nac/national-institute-drug-abuse-nida

The Clean Slate Addiction Site

http://www.thecleanslate.org/myths/addiction-is-not-a-brain-disease-it-is-a-choice/

Selected, Edited, and with Issue Framing Material by:
Edwin E. Gantt, *Brigham Young University*

ISSUE

Are Psychiatric Medications Safe?

YES: Robert H. Howland, from "Do Psychiatric Medications Cause More Harm than Good?" *Journal of Psychosocial Nursing* (2015)

NO: Gary G. Kohls, from "Psychotropic Drugs, Are They Safe? Fourteen Lies That Our Psychiatry Professors in Medical School Taught Us," *Global Research* (2016)

Learning Outcomes

After reading this issue, you will be able to:

- Assess benefits and harms of psychiatric medications.
- Understand biases in research on psychotropic drugs.
- Discuss the role of pharmaceutical companies in drug promotion.
- Understand the history of treating mental illness through medication.

ISSUE SUMMARY

YES: Robert H. Howland argues that although medications may be dangerous in some situations, the history of psychiatric pharmacology has demonstrated that the actual benefits from the medications outweighs the potential harm.

NO: Gary G. Kohls, a retired physician, argues that many of the "facts" about psychiatric medications are myths and raises a number of questions regarding the effectiveness and safety of their use.

$\mathbf{Q}$uestions regarding the safety of psychiatric medications have been asked almost from the beginnings of their use in the mid-20th century. Many have been critical of the usefulness of such drugs beginning with the invention of chlorpromazine in the 1950s—a drug that went on to become a highly effective way of treating schizophrenia, as well as a number of other psychotic disorders. Indeed, by 1964, over 50 million people had used the drug. Since that time, numerous antipsychotic and antidepressant drugs have been developed and used widely. In light of growing concerns about the social and political, as well as personal, impact of these drugs, however, an antipsychiatry movement sprang up in the 1960s, led by R. D. Laing and others, that sought to raise awareness both in the medical profession and among the general public.

There has since been a continuous struggle between those who emphasize the successes of these medications in helping those suffering from mental illness and those who emphasize the negative side effects, which they argue can cause even more suffering. A dichotomy has formed between psychiatry and psychology, and while there are those who conclude that a combination of therapy and medication is usually the best treatment plan, there are those who strictly favor therapy over prescriptions and those who are quick to prescribe psychiatric medications without engaging in psychotherapy.

Specifically, in the YES article, "Do Psychiatric Medications Cause More Harm than Good?," Howland states that the progress that has been made in recent years, in terms of making medications available, has significantly improved the lives of those who suffer from mental disorders.

He explains that people are better off today with current treatment options then they would have been 60 years ago. He also addresses some of the criticisms of psychiatric medication use, including increased suicide and death rates, and provides a counter argument suggesting that those rates are not positively correlated with the increase in antipsychotic medication usage. Howland concedes that there may be issues with prescribing medications, as well as the research surrounding them, but as the title of his article suggests, the harms do not outweigh the benefits.

In contrast, in the NO article, "Psychotropic Drugs, Are They Safe? Fourteen Lies That Our Psychiatry Professors in Medical School Taught Us," Kohl argues against Howland's more optimistic conclusions. He discusses commonly taught truths about psychiatric medications and dispels them as myths and falsehoods spread primarily by the pharmaceutical industry. He refutes claims that drugs have been adequately tested, calling into question the validity and reliability of the research, as well as the integrity of the companies backing the research. He also makes the point that long-term effectiveness is not something that researchers have truly studied, nor can they, because the drugs in question are still relatively new. Kohl also suggests that mental illness isn't just brain chemical imbalance. In sum, he calls into question the effectiveness and safety of these medications.

YES ↵

Robert H. Howland

Do Psychiatric Medications Cause More Harm than Good?

Whether psychiatric drugs cause more harm than good is an important question to ask, but is difficult to answer because of the complexity of defining and measuring concepts of "harm" and "good" as they pertain to treating (or not treating) psychiatric disorders with medication. Even nondrug psychological therapies can cause harm.

What the research investigation is (e.g., observational study, clinical trial, and animal laboratory experiment) and who or what is included in the investigation (e.g., healthy or diseased individuals, administrative claims records, and type of animal) necessarily limits what can be learned and generalized from the study. Results must be interpreted in the context of inherent limitations of the study design and methodology. Whether this knowledge validly translates into the "real world" clinical setting can be debated, as it often is.

Ultimately, what is relevant to addressing the issue of psychiatric drug benefits and harms, and what is important to practicing nurses, physicians, and other healthcare providers, is the valid translation of preclinical and clinical research findings into clinical practice. Investigators who conduct clinical research as well as see patients in clinical settings understand what I mean. What is perceived by a "real world" patient to be beneficial or harmful by taking medication is not a mirror image experience of individuals who participate in a study.

Historical Aspects of Psychiatric Treatment

President Jimmy Carter and challenger Ronald Reagan debated just once in the U.S. presidential contest of 1980. At the end of the debate, in his final statement, Reagan delivered what ultimately was a knockout blow to Carter's reelection.

Next Tuesday is Election Day. Next Tuesday all of you will go to the polls, will stand there in the polling place and make a decision. I think when you make that decision, it might be well if you would ask yourself, are you better off than you were four years ago? Is it easier for you to go and buy things in the stores than it was four years ago? Is there more or less unemployment in the country than there was four years ago? Is America as respected throughout the world as it was? Do you feel that our security is as safe, that we're as strong as we were four years ago? And if you answer all of those questions yes, why then, I think your choice is very obvious as to whom you will vote for. If you don't agree, if you don't think that this course that we've been on for the last four years is what you would like to see us follow for the next four, then I could suggest another choice that you have.

I think of this quote because I would ask analogous questions about the use of drug treatments for psychiatric patients. Are psychiatric patients better off or worse off now than they were 60 years ago, when chlorpromazine (Thorazine®) was introduced? If you experienced a major mental illness, would you prefer being a psychiatric patient treated according to today's standards or as a patient treated according to the standards of the first half of the 20th century or the standards of the 19th century and even earlier?

Before 1955, the history of psychiatric therapeutics included, but was not limited to, the following treatments: trephination; exorcism and prayer; mesmerism; asylum treatment using isolation and physical restraints; instillation of "moral" discipline; psychoanalysis; cold water dunking or ice water baths; bleeding or purging using emetics, laxatives, leeches, and phlebotomy; malarial (fever) therapy; surgical excision of "infected" organs believed to cause mental illness; crudely performed frontal lobotomies; and insulin shock (coma) therapy.

In 1955, there were approximately 560,000 severely mentally ill patients in public psychiatric hospitals. By

Howland, Robert H. (2015) "Do Psychiatric Medications Cause More Harm Than Good?" *Journal of Psychosocial Nursing and Mental Health Services* 53(7), 15-18. Used with permission of Slack, Inc.

1994, this number had been reduced to less than 72,000 patients. The number is much less today. If private psychiatric hospitals and general hospital psychiatric beds are included, the proportion of psychiatric beds per 100,000 population has dropped from 264 in 1970 to 112 in 1998, and length of hospital stay has also declined. Deinstitutionalization occurred for three reasons: (a) the advent of psychotropic drugs, (b) the social–political movement in favor of community mental health services, and (c) financial cost-shifting from federal to state governments. Although adverse consequences of deinstitutionalization have been appropriately highlighted, it not rectified, the transition from inpatient to outpatient treatment, facilitated by the use of psychiatric drugs, has been beneficial for most patients and their families.

Mental Illness, Drug Therapy, and Mortality

Mental illness itself is associated with significant morbidity, mortality, and disability. In a systematic review of mortality among individuals with mental illness, Walker et al. (2015) determined that mortality was significantly higher among individuals with mental illness than among the comparison population. Moreover, 2/3 of deaths were due to natural causes, but less than 20 percent were due to unnatural causes (a category that includes suicide). They estimated that 8 million deaths worldwide annually can be attributed to mental illness. One might argue that psychotropic drugs are harmful and potentially lethal, perhaps contributing to these 8 million annual deaths. However, excess mortality and shortened life spans among mentally ill individuals, for natural and unnatural reasons, had been observed long before psychotropic drug treatments were introduced in the 1950s.

As recently as 1977, 64 percent of psychiatric visits were exclusively for psychotherapy with no prescription provided, but in 2002 this was true for less than 10 percent of visits to psychiatrists. Approximately 11 percent of Americans (more than 35 million individuals) take antidepressant medications, and the rate of antidepressant drug use increased 400 percent since fluoxetine (Prozac®) was marketed in 1988. Various atypical antipsychotic drugs were introduced between 1990 and 2002. From 1996 to 2003, an estimated 47.7 million adult ambulatory care visits involved mention of an antipsychotic drug. During these eight years, visits involving atypical antipsychotic drugs and combinations of antipsychotic drugs increased by 195 percent and 149 percent, respectively. More of the atypical antipsychotic drug visits also involved antidepressant drugs. Given the explosive rise in use of antidepressant, antipsychotic, and other psychotropic drugs, and the common practice of polypharmacy, why has there not been an explosive increase in suicide rates or nonsuicide mortality rates during the past half-century, as would be predicted if such drugs harbor especially lethal effects?

Limitations of Research Findings

I do not disagree with the premise that there is a tendency for psychotropic drugs to be overprescribed and that their benefits are often oversold or their harms underemphasized. But the magnitude of these tendencies simply does not rise to the level of harm that some would claim. Analysis of harms and benefits is largely based on observational studies and meta-analyses, without considering the limitations of these investigations. Causality cannot be established from observed associations or meta-analyses. Most reported associations in observational clinical research are false, and the minority of associations that are true are often exaggerated. Weak or small magnitude associations, even if statistically significant, are more likely to be attributable to bias than to causal association. All observational research has one or more types of bias, and bias is especially true of epidemiological research using administrative databases.

The conviction that meta-analysis provides the best level of evidence, because it includes mathematically combining a complete body of evidence from different studies, is flawed. Because of heterogeneity (variation in true effect sizes and in factors that may influence those effect sizes) and because of various methodological problems, meta-analysis should be considered as an observational study, such that the findings are interpreted as associations rather than as causal effects. Different approaches to including studies in a meta-analysis can lead to different estimates of effect sizes and different interpretations of the study findings.

Conclusion

To some, the harms and benefits of psychiatric drugs can be reduced to discrete quantifiable variables that can be measured, with certainty and precision, among a small subset of patients who agree to be participants in a research study or that can be gleaned from administrative databases. Collecting and statistically analyzing such data from as many studies as possible may form the basis for detailed research-based knowledge about psychiatric drugs. But this data-rich soup of knowledge is nutritionally deficient in wisdom—the wisdom that comes from an appreciation of the history of psychiatry; the wisdom gained from hands-on experience working with psychiatric patients and their families; and the wisdom to be aware of one's own limits and biases, not just the conflicts of interest and biases of others.

Antipathy to psychotropic drugs and his cynicism toward psychiatry is unfortunate. Such views are harmful not only to patients and families but also to nurses, physicians, and other professionals whose mission is to treat mental disorders safely, effectively, and compassionately.

Dr. Robert H. Howland is an associate professor of psychiatry at the University of Pittsburgh School of Medicine as well as an attending psychiatrist in the Mood Disorders Treatment and Research Program and the Western Psychiatric Institute and Clinic in Pittsburgh, Pennsylvania. His interests include psychopharmacology, psychotherapy, and neurostimulation therapies, particularly in the treatment of mood disorders. His emphasis is on the treatment of chronic and resistant forms of depression.

Gary G. Kohls

Psychotropic Drugs, Are They Safe?

Fourteen Lies That Our Psychiatry Professors in Medical School Taught Us

Myth # 1

"The US Food and Drug Administration (FDA) Tests All New Psychiatric Drugs"

False. Actually the FDA only reviews studies that were designed, administered, secretly performed, and paid for by the multinational profit-driven drug companies. The studies are frequently farmed out by the pharmaceutical companies by well-paid research firms, in whose interest it is to find positive results for their corporate employers. Unsurprisingly, such research policies virtually guarantee fraudulent results.

Myth # 2

"FDA Approval Means That a Psychotropic Drug Is Effective Long-term"

False. Actually, FDA approval doesn't even mean that psychiatric drugs have been proven to be safe—either short-term or long-term! The notion that FDA approval means that a psych drug has been proven to be effective is also a false one, for most such drugs are never tested—prior to marketing—for longer than a few months (and most psych patients take their drugs for years). The pharmaceutical industry pays many psychiatric "researchers"—often academic psychiatrists (with east access to compliant, chronic, already drugged-up patients) who have financial or professional conflicts of interest—some of them even sitting on FDA advisory committees who attempt to "fast track" psych drugs through the approval process. For each new drug application, the FDA only receives one or two of the "best" studies (out of many) that purport to show short-term effectiveness. The negative studies are shelved and not revealed to the FDA. In the case of the selective serotonin reuptake inhibitor (SSRI) drugs, animal lab studies typically lasted only hours, days, or weeks and the human clinical studies only lasted, on average, four to six weeks, far too short to draw any valid conclusions about long-term effectiveness or safety!

Hence, the FDA prescribing physicians and patient-victims should not have been "surprised" by the resulting epidemic of SSRI drug-induced adverse reactions that are silently plaguing the nation. Indeed, many SSRI trials have shown that those drugs are barely more effective than placebo (albeit statistically significant!) with unaffordable economic costs and serious health risks, some of which are life-threatening and known to be capable of causing brain damage.

Myth # 3

"FDA Approval Means That a Psychotropic Drug Is Safe Long-term"

False. Actually, the SSRIs and the "antipsychotic" drugs are usually tested in human trials for only a couple of months before being granted marketing approval by the FDA. And the drug companies are only required to report one or two studies (even if many other studies on the same drug showed negative, even disastrous, results). Drug companies obviously prefer that the black box and fine print warnings associated with their drugs are ignored by both consumers and prescribers. One only has to note how small the print is on the commercials.

In our fast-paced shop-until-you-drop consumer society, we super-busy prescribing physicians and physician assistants have never been fully aware of the multitude of dangerous, potentially fatal adverse psych drug effects that include addiction, mania, psychosis, suicidality, worsening depression, worsening anxiety, insomnia, akathisia, brain damage, dementia, homicidality, violence, and so on.

Kohls, Gary G., "Psychotropic Drugs, Are They Safe? Fourteen Lies That Our Psychiatry Professors in Medical School Taught Us" *Global Research*, January 2016, 1-5. Used with permission of the author.

Myth # 4

"Mental 'Illnesses' Are Caused by 'Brain Chemistry Imbalances'"

False. In actuality, brain chemical/neurotransmitter imbalances have never been proven to exist (except for cases of neurotransmitter depletions caused by psych drugs) despite vigorous examinations of lab animal or autopsied human brains and brain slices by neuroscientists who were employed by well-funded drug companies. Knowing that there are over 100 known neurotransmitter systems in the human brain, proposing a theoretical chemical "imbalance" is laughable and flies in the face of science. Not only that, but if there was an imbalance between any two of the 100 potential systems (impossible to prove), a drug—that has never been tested on more than a handful of them—could never be expected to rebalance it!

Such simplistic theories have been perpetrated by Big Pharma upon a gullible public and a gullible psychiatric industry because corporations that want to sell the public on their unnecessary products know that they have to resort to 20-s sound bite-type propaganda to convince patients and prescribing practitioners why they should be taking or prescribing synthetic, brain-altering drugs that haven't been adequately tested.

Myth # 5

"Antidepressant Drugs Work Like Insulin for Diabetics"

False. This laughingly simplistic—and very antiscientific—explanation for the use of dangerous and addictive synthetic drugs is patently absurd and physicians and patients who believe it should be ashamed of themselves for falling for it. There is such a thing as an insulin deficiency (but only in type 1 diabetes), but there is no such thing as a Prozac deficiency. The SSRIs (so-called selective serotonin reuptake inhibitors—an intentional misrepresentation because those drugs are NOT selective!) do not raise total brain serotonin. Rather, SSRIs actually deplete serotonin long-term while only "goosing" serotonin release at the synapse level while at the same time interfere with the storage, reuse, and recycling of serotonin (by its "serotonin reuptake inhibition" function).

Myth # 6

"SSRI 'Discontinuation Syndromes' Are Different than 'Withdrawal Syndromes'"

False. The SSRI "antidepressant" drugs are indeed dependency-inducing/addictive and the neurological and psychological symptoms that occur when these drugs are stopped or tapered down are not "relapses" into a previous "mental disorder"—as has been commonly asserted—but are actually new drug withdrawal symptoms that are different from those that prompted the original diagnosis.

The term "discontinuation syndrome" is part of a cunningly designed conspiracy that was plotted in secret by members of the psychopharmaceutical industry in order to deceive physicians into thinking that these drugs are not addictive. The deception has been shamelessly promoted to distract attention from the proven fact that most psych drugs are dependency-inducing and are therefore likely to cause "discontinuation/withdrawal symptoms" when they are stopped. The drug industry knows that most people do not want to swallow dependency-inducing drugs that are likely to cause painful, even lethal withdrawal symptoms when they cut down the dose of the drug.

Myth # 7

"Ritalin Is Safe for Children (or Adults)"

False. In actuality, methylphenidate (= Ritalin, Concerta, Daytrana, Metadate, and Methylin; also known as "kiddie cocaine"), a dopamine reuptake inhibitor drug, works exactly like cocaine on dopamine synapses, except that orally dosed methylphenidate reaches the brain more slowly than snortable or smoked cocaine does. Therefore, the oral form has less of an orgasmic "high" than cocaine. Cocaine addicts actually prefer Ritalin if they can get it in a relatively pure powder form. When snorted, the synthetic Ritalin (as opposed to the naturally occurring, and therefore more easily metabolically degraded cocaine) has the same onset of action but, predictably, has a longer lasting "high" and is thus preferred among addicted individuals. The molecular structures of Ritalin and cocaine both have amphetamine base structures with ring-shaped side chains which, when examined side by side, are remarkably similar. The dopamine synaptic organelles in the brain (and heart, blood vessels, lungs, and guts) are unlikely to sense any difference between the two drugs.

Myth # 8

"Psychoactive Drugs Are Totally Safe for Humans"

False. See Myth # 3 above. Actually, all five classes of psychotropic drugs have, with long-term use, been found to be neurotoxic (i.e., known to destroy or otherwise alter the physiology, chemistry, anatomy, and viability of vital energy-producing mitochondria in every brain cell and nerve). They are therefore all capable of contributing to dementia when used long-term.

Any synthetic chemical that is capable of crossing the blood-brain barrier into the brain can alter and disable the brain. Synthetic chemical drugs are NOT capable of healing brain dysfunction, curing malnutrition, or reversing brain damage. Rather than curing anything, psychiatric drugs are only capable of masking symptoms while the abnormal emotional, neurological or malnutritional processes that mimic "mental illnesses" continue unabated.

Myth # 9

"Mental 'Illnesses' Have No Known Cause"

False. The Diagnostic and Statistical Manual (DSM, published by the American Psychiatric Association, is pejoratively called "the psychiatric bible and billing book" for psychiatrists. Despite its name, it actually has no statistics in it, and of the 374 psychiatric diagnoses in the DSM-IV (there is now a fifth edition), there seem to be only two that emphasize known root causes. Those two diagnoses are post-traumatic stress disorder and acute stress disorder. The DSM-V has been roundly condemned as being just another book that laughingly pathologizes a few more normal human emotions and behaviors.

Myth # 10

"Psychotropic Drugs Have Nothing to Do with the Huge Increase in Disabled and Unemployable American Psychiatric Patients"

False. See Myths # 2 and # 3 above. In actuality, recent studies have shown that the major cause of permanent disability in the "mentally ill" is the long-term, high dosage, and/or use of multiple neurotoxic psych drugs—any combination of which, as noted above, has never been adequately tested for safety even in animal labs. Many commonly prescribed drugs are fully capable of causing brain-damage long-term, especially the antipsychotics (aka, "major tranquilizers") like Thorazine, Haldol, Prolixin, Clozapine, Abilify, Clozapine, Fanapt, Geodon, Invega, Risperdal, Saphris, Seroquel, and Zyprexa, all of which can cause brain shrinkage that is commonly seen on the MRI scans of antipsychotic drug-treated, so-called schizophrenics—commonly pointed out as "proof" that schizophrenia is an anatomic brain disorder that causes the brain to shrink! (Incidentally, patients who had been on antipsychotic drugs—for whatever reason—have been known to experience withdrawal hallucinations and acute psychotic symptoms even if they had never experienced such symptoms previously.)

Of course, highly addictive "minor" tranquilizers like the benzodiazepines (Valium, Ativan, Klonopin, Librium, Tranxene, and Xanax) can cause the same withdrawal syndromes. They are all dangerous and very difficult to withdraw from (withdrawal results in difficult-to-treat rebound insomnia, panic attacks, and seriously increased anxiety), and, when used long-term, they can all cause memory loss/dementia, the loss of IQ points and the high likelihood of being misdiagnosed as Alzheimer's disease (of unknown etiology).

Myth # 11

"So-called Bipolar Disorder Can Mysteriously 'Emerge' in Patients Who Have Been Taking Stimulating Antidepressants like the SSRIs"

False. In actuality, crazy-making behaviors like mania, agitation, and aggression are commonly caused by the SSRIs. That list includes a syndrome called akathisia, a severe, sometimes suicide-inducing internal restlessness—like having restless legs syndrome over one's entire body and brain. Akathisia was once understood to only occur as a long-term adverse effect of antipsychotic drugs (see Myth # 10). So it was a shock to many psychiatrists (after Prozac came to market in 1987) to have to admit that SSRIs could also cause that deadly problem. It has long been my considered opinion that SSRIs should more accurately be called "agitation-inducing" drugs rather than "antidepressant" drugs. The important point to make is that SSRI-induced psychosis, mania, agitation, aggression, and akathisia is NOT bipolar disorder nor is it schizophrenia!

Myth # 12

"Antidepressant Drugs Can Prevent Suicides"

False. In actuality, there is no psychiatric drug that is FDA-approved for the treatment of suicidality because these drugs, especially the so-called antidepressants, actually increase the incidence of suicidal thinking, suicide attempts, and completed suicides. Drug companies have spent billions of dollars futilely trying to prove the effectiveness of various psychiatric drugs in suicide prevention. Even the most corrupted drug company trials have failed! Indeed what has been discovered is that all the so-called "antidepressants" actually increase the incidence of suicidality.

The FDA has required black box warning labels about drug-induced suicidality on all SSRI marketing materials, but that was only accomplished after overcoming vigorous opposition from the drugmakers and marketers of the offending drugs, who feared that such truth-telling would hurt their profits (it hasn't). What can and does avert suicidality, of course, are not drugs, but rather interventions by caring, compassionate and thorough teams of caregivers that include family, faith communities, and friends as well as psychologists, counselors, social workers, relatives (especially wise grandmas!), and, obviously, the limited involvement of drug prescribers.

Myth # 13

"America's School Shooters and Other Mass Shooters Are 'Untreated' Schizophrenics Who Should Have Been Taking Psych Drugs"

False. In actuality, 90 percent or more of the infamous homicidal—and usually suicidal—school shooters have already been under the "care" of psychiatrists (or other psych drug prescribers) and therefore have typically been taking (or withdrawing from) one or more psychiatric drugs. The SSRIs (such as Prozac) and psychostimulants (such as Ritalin) have been the most common classes of drugs involved. Antipsychotics are too sedating, although an angry teen who is withdrawing from antipsychotics could easily become a school shooter if given access to lethal weapons.

The 10 percent of school shooters whose drug history is not known have typically had their medical files sealed by the authorities. The powerful drug industry and psychiatry lobby, with the willing help of the media that profits from being their handmaidens, repeatedly show us the photos of the shooters that look like zombies. They have successfully gotten the viewing public to buy the notion that these adolescent, white male school shooters were mentally ill rather than under the influence of their crazy-making, brain-altering drugs, or going through withdrawal.

A thorough study of the scores of American school shooters, starting with the University of Texas tower shooter in 1966 and (temporarily) stopping at Sandy Hook, reveals that the overwhelming majority of them (if not all of them) were taking brain-altering, mesmerizing, impulse-destroying, "don't give a damn" drugs that had been prescribed to them by well-meaning but too-busy psychiatrists, family physicians, or physician assistants who somehow were unaware of or were misinformed about the homicidal and suicidal risks to their equally unsuspecting patients (and therefore they had failed to warn the patient and/or the patient's loved ones about the potentially dire consequences).

Most practitioners who wrote the prescriptions for the mass shooters or for a patient who later suicided while under the influence of the drug will probably (and legitimately so) defend themselves against the charge of being an accomplice to mass murder or suicide by saying that they were ignorant about the dangers of these cavalierly prescribed psych drugs because they had been deceived by the drug companies that had convinced them of the benign nature of the drugs.

Myth # 14

"If Your Patient Hears Voices, It Means He's a Schizophrenic"

False. Auditory hallucinations are known to occur in up to 10 percent of normal people; and up to 75 percent of normal people have had the experience of someone that isn't there calling their name.

Nighttime dreams, nightmares, and flashbacks probably have similar origins to daytime visual, auditory, and olfactory hallucinations, but even psychiatrists don't think that they represent mental illnesses. Indeed, hallucinations are listed in the pharmaceutical literature as a potential side effect or withdrawal symptom of many drugs, especially psychiatric drugs. These syndromes are called substance-induced psychotic disorders, which are, by definition, neither mental illnesses nor schizophrenia. Rather, substance-induced or withdrawal-induced psychotic disorders are temporary and directly caused by the intoxicating effects of malnutrition or brain-altering drugs such as alcohol, medications, hallucinogenic drugs, and other toxins.

Psychotic symptoms, including hallucinations and delusions, can be caused by substances such as alcohol, marijuana, hallucinogens, sedatives, hypnotics, and anxiolytics, inhalants, opioids, PCP, and the many of the amphetamine-like drugs (like Phen-Fen, [fenfluramine]), cocaine, methamphetamine, Ecstasy, and agitation-inducing, psycho-stimulating drugs like the SSRIs).

Psychotic symptoms can also result from sleep deprivation, sensory deprivation and the withdrawal from certain drugs like alcohol, sedatives, hypnotics, anxiolytics and especially the many dopamine-suppressing, dependency-inducing, sedating, and zombifying antipsychotic drugs.

DR. GARY G. KOHLS is a now retired physician, who practiced holistic (nondrug) mental health care. He is specialized in Post-Traumatic Stress Disorder (PTSD), brain nutrition, neurotransmitter disorders, and problems with psychotropic drugs. He helped many of his patients to eliminate or reduce their psychiatric medication usage and succeed in safe drug withdrawal.

EXPLORING THE ISSUE

Are Psychiatric Medications Safe?

Critical Thinking and Reflection

1. Taking into account the relatively short existence of psychiatric medications, is it possible to test their long-term effectiveness? Why or why not?
2. Does the historical account of treating mentally ill patients with medications demonstrate the safety of Psychiatric drug use today?
3. What is the role that pharmaceutical companies play in testing new psychiatric drugs?
4. What does it mean for a psychiatric medication to be safe? Is there a difference in safety for children and safety for adults?

Is There Common Ground?

Both authors agree that the testing of psychiatric drugs is an important issue. While one argues that the current testing regime is adequate, and the other that it is not, it might be possible to develop new testing processes that would be appealing from both perspectives.

Likewise, both perspectives reinforce the seriousness of the need to respond appropriately to those who are suffering with mental illness. Even though they disagree on the adequacy of particular responses to mental health issues, both admit that there are better and worse ways of responding, and that simply doing nothing is not likely to be helpful at all.

Additional Resources

Eisenberg, L., & Guttmacher, L.B. (2010). Were we all asleep at the switch? A personal reminiscence of psychiatry from 1940 to 2010. *Acta Psychiatrica Scandinavica, 122*(2), 89–102. doi:10.1111/j.1600-0447.2010.01544.x

Gøtzsche, P.C. (2014). Why I think antidepressants cause more harm than good. *The Lancet Psychiatry, 1*(2), 104–106.

Healy, D. (2004). *Let them eat Prozac: The unhealthy relationship between the pharmaceutical industry and depression.* New York: New York University Press.

Valenstein, E.S. (1998). *Blaming the brain: The truth about drugs and mental health.* New York, NY: Free Press.

Whitaker, R. (2015). *Anatomy of an epidemic: Magic bullets, psychiatric drugs, and the astonishing rise of mental illness in America.* New York, NY: Broadway Books.

Internet References . . .

American Psychological Association

http://www.apa.org/monitor/2012/06/prescribing.aspx

CCHR International: The Mental Health Watchdog

https://www.cchrint.org/psychiatric-drugs/

National Institute of Mental Health Medications

https://www.nimh.nih.gov/health/topics/mental-health-medications/index.shtml

Unit 6

UNIT

Psychotherapy Issues

*M*any psychologists specialize in treating the mental, emotional, and behavioral difficulties of life and living. Yet there is considerable debate about what difficulties should be treated and how therapy should be conducted. Should difficulties in dealing with Facebook, for example, be treated, or is Facebook a primarily positive social influence? Also, are all types of therapy equally effective, or is there psychological evidence that some therapeutic techniques are more effective than others? What about therapist training? Should therapists specialize in particular approaches and theories of psychotherapy, or should they be more eclectic and train to be ready to administer all approaches and theories for the life problem at hand?

Selected, Edited, and with Issue Framing Material by:
Edwin E. Gantt, *Brigham Young University*

ISSUE

Are All Psychotherapies Equally Effective?

YES: Mark A. Hubble, Barry L. Duncan, and Scott D. Miller, from "Introduction" to *The Heart and Soul of Change: What Works in Therapy*, American Psychological Association (1999)

NO: Jedidiah Siev, Jonathan D. Huppert, and Dianne L. Chambless, from "The Dodo Bird, Treatment Technique, and Disseminating Empirically Supported Treatments," *Behavior Therapist* (April 2009)

Learning Outcomes

After reading this issue, you will be able to:

- Discuss the role "technique" plays in the successful outcome of therapy.
- Discuss whether the disorder dictates the treatment.
- Identify common factors to be found in all successful psychotherapies.

ISSUE SUMMARY

YES: Psychologists Mark Hubble, Barry Duncan, and Scott Miller argue that all effective therapies are essentially alike, while all ineffective therapies are ineffective in their own way. In addition, while many different psychotherapies are effective in relieving the suffering of patients, all of these therapies are effective because of the factors they all possess in common, not for any unique belief or procedure a therapy may possess.

NO: Psychologists Jedidiah Siev, Jonathan Huppert, and Dianne Chambless assert that outcomes among the various psychotherapies differ primarily because one technique or therapy is better than another.

Have you or a member of your family ever considered psychotherapy? If so, you may have wondered how you would select the best therapist. Are some therapists better than others? Are some techniques or theories better than others? Will just any therapist or technique do? These kinds of concerns have led psychologists to investigate the effectiveness of various elements of psychotherapy. They attempt to examine not only which of these elements—therapists, techniques, and even the clients themselves—are the most influential but also whether certain types of psychotherapy theories are more effective than other theories in relation to these elements.

Most researchers have concluded that the different elements of therapy do come together to prompt positive changes. However, some disagree on the specific features that make one therapy more effective than another.

One camp of researchers believes that all psychotherapy techniques are essentially equal in their effectiveness. This position is sometimes called the *Dodo hypothesis*, because the Dodo bird in *Alice's Adventures in Wonderland* arranged a race in which all the contestants won, and "all must have prizes." In other words, all the different therapy techniques "won" or are equally effective, so the differential effects of psychotherapy must be due to other factors (sometimes called "common factors"), such as client relationship and therapist skill. The other camp, by contrast, believes that therapeutic techniques are crucial to any effective therapy. In fact, for psychologists who oppose the Dodo hypothesis, technique is pivotal because it often interacts with common factors to produce therapeutic change.

In the YES article, Mark Hubble, Barry Duncan, and Scott Miller defend the first camp. They affirm that psychotherapy works—that mental health issues can and have been positively addressed to the benefit of mankind. They also affirm the many different types of therapy work to bring about positive results in clients. They argue, however, that there is plenty of evidence to support the idea that the many effective therapies all work for the same reasons, due to common factors that they all share—the differences are superfluous. Thus, without referring to it by name, they back the Dodo hypothesis. They believe that the obsession with varying techniques is the result of ideological and theoretical differences rather as opposed to any observed difference in patient outcomes. They believe that, in order best to improve the results of therapy, therapists should stop focusing on perfecting specific techniques and focus on what works—the common factors that all successful therapies share.

By contrast, in the NO article, Jedidiah Siev, Jonathan Huppert, and Dianne Chambless argue that research on the Dodo hypothesis conceals significant differences in treatment outcomes for therapies and techniques. From their perspective, such research is aggregated from so many different populations, disorders, and treatments that it cannot make comparisons on particular treatments for specific disorders. Yet this is what consumers and therapists most need—information about which therapy or technique is most effective for specific problems under certain circumstances. Siev, Huppert, and Chambless do not deny the significance of "common factors," but they also do not believe that this significance eliminates the importance of therapy strategies. Indeed, it is in the interaction of these factors and these techniques that the greatest effectiveness is achieved.

POINT

- Effects of psychotherapy are due to common factors rather than specific techniques.
- Meta-analyses provide evidence that particular treatments do not significantly differ.
- Therapies are equally effective because all forms share similar technical components.
- Because no one technique is better than another, more therapy options are available to treat distressed persons.

COUNTERPOINT

- Specific techniques interact with and influence common factors to produce the general effects of psychotherapy.
- Meta-analyses confound too many variables to discern specific treatment superiorities.
- Techniques among therapies differ enough to produce different results.
- The disorder should dictate what technique is used. No psychotherapy can be superior for all disorders and all contexts.

YES

**Mark A. Hubble, Barry L. Duncan, and
Scott D. Miller**

Introduction to *The Heart and Soul of Change: What Works in Therapy*

Although the mental health professions can rightly claim they have arrived—to the degree we know clinical services do make a difference in the lives of our clientele—we remain strangely adrift. The apparent contradiction is resolved when it is recognized that we have yet to agree on what enables our work to work. In short, if therapy is a mighty engine that helps convey clients to places they want to go, what provides the power? This question is central both to our identity and survival as we enter the next millennium.

The search for what works has contributed to the explosion of therapy models described above. With Freud, modern psychotherapy was born. Yet before he barely left a mark on the professional landscape, others rose to propose alternatives to his theory and methods. Setting aside discussion of the divisive, emotional tensions at play in Freud's small group of followers, Jung, Adler, Rank, and Ferenczi broke ranks. The former disciples proclaimed their theoretical differences, if not independence, promoting their own versions of mental life and therapy. Since those days, the divisions have multiplied. New schools of therapy arrive with the regularity of the Book-of-the-Month Club's main selection. Many claim to be the corrective for all that came before. In addition, most profess to have the inside line on human motivation, the causes of psychological dysfunction, and the best remedies.

Once therapists broke the early taboo against observing and researching therapy, they turned to proving empirically that their therapies were the best. A generation of investigators ushered in the age of comparative clinical trials. Winners and losers were to be had. As Bergin and Lambert described this time, "Presumably, the one shown to be most effective will prove that position to be correct and will serve as a demonstration that the 'losers' should be persuaded to give up their views." Thus, behavior, psychoanalytic, client-centered or humanistic, rational-emotive, cognitive, time-limited, time-unlimited, and other therapies were pitted against each other in a great battle of the brands.

Nonetheless, all this sound and fury produced an unexpected "bonfire of the vanities." Hubris and the pursuit of dominance flared as the results of these studies mounted. Put another way, reiterating Huxley's epigram introducing this section, science slew a beautiful hypothesis with an ugly fact.

As it turned out, the underlying premise of the comparative studies, that one (or more) therapy would prove superior to others, received virtually no support. Besides the occasional significant finding for a particular therapy, the critical mass of data revealed no differences in effectiveness among the various treatments for psychological distress. This finding of no difference was cleverly tagged the dodo bird verdict. Borrowed from *Alice in Wonderland* it says, "Everyone has won and so all must have prizes." Now, more than 20 years later and after many attempts to dismiss or overturn it, the dodo bird verdict still stands. Therapy works, but our understanding of what works in therapy is unlikely to be found in the insular explanations and a posteriori reasoning adopted by the different theoretical orientations.

Enter the Common Factors

Left with "little evidence to recommend the use of one type [of therapy] over another in the treatment of specific problems," psychotherapy observers and researchers redirected their attention. A less provincial or *metaview* of therapy was adopted. Breaking with the tradition of saying, "mine's better," efforts were made to identify the pantheoretical elements that made the various treatments effective. The organizing question became, if therapies work, but it has nothing to do with their bells and whistles, what are the common therapeutic factors?

Interestingly enough, this formulation is not new. The possibility that therapies have more in common

Hubble, M. A., Duncan, B. L., & Miller, S. D. (1999). Introduction. In M. A. Hubble, B. L. Duncan, & S. D. Miller (Eds.), *The Heart and Soul of Change: What Works in Therapy* (pp. 1–19). doi:10.1037/11132-014 than less was broached more than 60 years ago. In 1936, Saul Rosenzweig writing in the *Journal of Orthopsychiatry*, suggested that the effectiveness of different therapy approaches had more to do with their common elements than with the theoretical tenets on which they were based. Luborsky says that Rosenzweig's article "deserves a laurel in recognition of its being the first systematic presentation of the idea that common factors across diverse forms of psychotherapy are so omnipresent that comparative treatment studies *should* show nonsignificant differences in outcome." Without any way of knowing, Rosenzweig anticipated the recent interest in the therapeutic alliance as a critical pantheoretical factor. In particular, he mentioned that one of the most common factors across therapies was the relationship between the client and clinician. He also noted that all of the therapies of his day involved a system of explanation.

If Rosenzweig wrote the first note of the call to the common factors, Johns Hopkins University's Jerome Frank composed an entire symphony. In all three editions of *Persuasion and Healing: A Comparative Study of Psychotherapy*, Frank placed therapy within the larger family of projects designed to bring about healing. He (with his psychiatrist daughter, Julia, in the last edition) looked for the threads joining such different activities as traditional psychotherapy, group and family therapies, inpatient treatment, drug therapy, medicine, religiomagical healing in nonindustrialized societies, cults, and revivals.

In their analysis, Frank and Frank concluded that therapy in its various forms should be thought of as "a single entity." They proposed the following analogy:

> Two such apparently different psychotherapies as psychoanalysis and systematic desensitization could be like penicillin and digitalis—totally different pharmacological agents suitable for totally different conditions. On the other hand, the active therapeutic ingredient of both could be the same analogous to two aspirin-containing compounds marketed under different names. We believe the second alternative is closer to the truth.

They also identified four features shared by all effective therapies: (a) "an emotionally charged, confiding relationship with a helping person," (b) "a healing setting," (c) "a rationale, conceptual scheme, or myth that provides a plausible explanation for the patient's symtoms and prescribes a ritual or procedure for resolving them," and (d) "a ritual or procedure that requires the active participation of both patient and therapist and that is believed by both to be the means of restoring the patient's health."

Weinberger observed that after 1980, an outpouring of writing began to appear on the common factors. Until that time, Frank's work stood virtually alone. Now, a flood of "views on and lists of common factors' may be found; Weinberger noted, too, that a positive relationship exists between year of publication and the number of common factors proposals offered.

. . .

The Big Four

In 1992, Brigham Young University's Michael Lambert proposed four therapeutic factors—extratherapeutic, common factors, expectancy or placebo, and techniques—as the principal elements accounting for improvement in clients. Although not derived from a strict statistical analysis, he wrote that they embody what empirical studies suggest about psychotherapy outcome. Lambert added that the research base for this interpretation of the factors was extensive; spanned decades; dealt with a large number of adult disorders and a variety of research designs, including naturalistic observations, epidemiological studies, comparative clinical trials, and experimental analogues.

Inspired by this specification of a "big four," the editors of this volume turned to the literature with the purpose of selecting the major components or ingredients of therapy that provided the best bridge between the various schools. The result of this effort builds on Lambert's earlier work and, more important, significantly broadens the base of what has traditionally been called the common factors. . . .

Client/Extratherapeutic Factors

Without a client, therapy does not exist. These factors, unquestionably the most common and powerful of the common factors in therapy, are part of the client or the client's life circumstances that aid in recovery despite the client's formal participation in therapy. They consist of the client's strengths, supportive elements in the environment, and even chance events. In short, they are what clients bring to the therapy room and what influences their lives outside it. As examples of these factors, persistence, faith, a supportive grandmother, membership in a religious community, sense of personal responsibility, a new job, a good day at the tracks, a crisis successfully managed all may be included. Lambert estimated that the client/extratherapeutic factors account for 40% of outcome variance. This hefty percentage represents a departure from convention, considering, as Tallman and Bohart indicate, most of what is written about therapy celebrates the contribution of the therapist, therapist's model, or technique.

Relationship Factors

The next class of factors weighs in with 30% of the successful outcome variance and largely coincides with what has been typically called the common factors in the literature. These represent a wide range of relationship-mediated variables found among therapies no matter the therapist's theoretical persuasion. Caring, empathy, warmth, acceptance, mutual affirmation, and encouragement of risk taking and mastery are but a few. Except what the client brings to therapy, these variables are probably responsible for most of the gains resulting from psychotherapy interventions. True to the position of Rosenzweig and Frank and Frank, investigators have recently expended much time and energy in researching the therapeutic alliance as one of the more important relationship factors. Therapist-provided variables, especially the core conditions popularized by Carl Rogers, also have been closely examined.

Placebo, Hope, and Expectancy

Following extratherapeutic and relationship factors are placebo, hope, and expectancy. Lambert put their contribution to psychotherapy outcome at 15%. In part, this class of therapeutic factors refers to the portion of improvement deriving from clients' knowledge of being treated and assessment of the credibility of the therapy's rationale and related techniques. Expectancy parallels Frank and Frank's idea that in successful therapies both client and therapist believe in the restorative power of the treatment's procedures or rituals. These curative effects therefore are not thought to derive specifically from a given treatment procedure; they come from the positive and hopeful expectations that accompany the use and implementation of the method.

Model/Technique Factors

Models and techniques are the last of the four factors. Like expectancy, Lambert suggested that they account for 15% of improvement in therapy. In a narrow sense, model/technique factors may be regarded as beliefs and procedures unique to specific treatments. The miracle question in solution-focused brief therapy, the use of the genogram in Bowen-oriented family therapy, hypnosis, systematic desensitization, biofeedback, transference interpretations, and the respective theoretical premises attending these practices are exemplary.

In concert with Frank and Frank, the editors of this volume interpret model/techniques factors more broadly as therapeutic or healing rituals. They include a rationale, offer an explanation for the client's difficulties, and establish strategies or procedures to follow for resolving them. Depending on the clinician's theoretical orientation, different content is emphasized. Nevertheless, most therapeutic methods or tactics share the common quality of preparing clients to take some action to help themselves. In particular, therapists expect their clients to do something different—to develop new understandings, feel different emotions, face fears, or alter old patterns of behavior.

Staying with What Works

Unless revolutionary new findings emerge, a prospect in which we place little faith, we maintain that our knowledge of what makes therapy effective is already in the hands of mental health professionals. We know what works. More than 40 years of research points the way toward the defining role of common factors. As for EVTs, the latest manifestation of touting powerful main effects for specialized and preferred therapies, a step forward into the past is being made. It is a practice with faint support. At the same time, the historical and continuing courtesy extended to theoretical proliferation suggests a place in which both assertions, "The world is round" and "the world is flat," receive equal respect. This civility that extends forbearance to all in the end gives consideration to none.

Focusing on what unites the different therapies has the best promise of not only helping practicing clinicians do their job more effectively but also ensuring that mental health professions continue to have a viable role in health care. Unfortunately, except the dedicated efforts of some of the field's integrationists, the leadership for such an undertaking is not likely to be found within the various schools of therapy or at the highest levels of the professional organizations. Invoking the popular saying, the ship is sinking and all the gurus seem able to do is argue over which way to arrange the deck chairs.

In time, if current fashions continue (i.e., trumpeting one therapy as better than the rest or parroting the activities of whatever profession currently has the favor of third-party payers), the continued diminution of professional therapy looks assured. Unless clinicians come together, they may find themselves sharing the same status as the real dodo bird of Mauritius and Réunion—extinct. There is no doubt. Staying with whatever has not worked in the past does not promise to bring security in the future. Accordingly, the purpose of this book is to reverse the slide toward greater divisiveness and present the state of therapy's data and knowledge. In short, it is time to articulate clearly the effective elements of therapy, all therapy.

A Position Statement

If fact is defined as a straightforward presentation of what is now known, then this work is factual. It aims to explain what enables psychotherapy and practices in certain related fields to achieve their results. For this reason, we have attempted to put to rest the customary equivocation found in the writings of therapy researchers and clinicians. The profession has labored under the conventions of "it seems," "it appears," "it also could be" when describing therapy and its processes. Further, the discussion sections of research articles habitually bow to the need for further research; in effect, often trivializing whatever was found or not found in the report at hand. It is no wonder practicing clinicians do not read research. It is easy to derive the impression that nobody wants to say, "This is it. This is fact as close as we can come to it now, and here's what to do."

The facts contributing to the longstanding schism between practice and research are legion. What is even more compelling and troubling are the results. The recurrent finding that theories and their associated technical operations do not significantly contribute to outcome is very important news. It deserves much more notice. This discovery holds implications for professional specialization, the training and licensure of therapists, continuing education, reimbursement, research, clinical work, and above all, the public welfare. Accordingly, as unpopular as it may be among the separate therapy schools, the stand taken in this work is that the common factors require the helping professions' utmost attention. We are in complete agreement with Sol Garfield, who said that to overlook their significance is to limit our understanding of the therapeutic process and the possibility of improving our therapeutic effectiveness and efficiency. If this position puts this book outside the mainstream of current professional discourse, we welcome the chance to be outliers. The weight of the extant empirical literature suggests that to do less is to be out of step with the facts.

. . .

MARK A. HUBBLE is a psychologist and national consultant. He is a graduate of the postdoctoral fellowship in clinical psychology at the Menninger Clinic in Topeka, Kansas. He is also the founder and former director of the Brief Therapy Clinic at the University of Missouri—Kansas City and a former faculty member of the Dayton Institute for Family Therapy in Centerville, Ohio. Dr. Hubble is a cofounder of The Institute for the Study of Therapeutic Change. He has served as a contributing editor for *The Family Therapy Networker* and has published numerous scholarly articles in addition to four books with co-authors Scott Miller and Barry Duncan.

BARRY L. DUNCAN is a therapist, therapist trainer, and clinical researcher. Dr. Duncan is the director of the Heart and Soul of Change Project, a practice-driven, training and research initiative that focuses on what works in therapy and how to deliver it most effectively. Dr. Duncan has over 100 publications, including 15 books, many of which have been written with co-authors Scott Miller and Mark Hubble.

SCOTT D. MILLER is the founder of the International Center for Clinical Excellence, an international consortium of clinicians, researchers, and educators dedicated to promoting excellence in behavioral health services. Dr. Miller conducts workshops and training in the United States and abroad, helping hundreds of agencies and organizations, both public and private, to achieve superior results. Dr. Miller is the author of dozens of scholarly articles and several books concerning evidence-based psychotherapies and effective practice of psychotherapy.

Jedidiah Siev, Jonathan D. Huppert, and
Dianne L. Chambless

 **NO**

The Dodo Bird, Treatment Technique, and Disseminating Empirically Supported Treatments

In a recent presidential column in *the Behavior Therapist*, Raymond DiGiuseppe observed that efforts to disseminate empirically supported treatments (ESTs), and especially cognitive-behavioral treatments, have been limited by perceptions "that all psychotherapies are equally effective [the Dodo Bird verdict], and . . . that common factors, therapist, and relationship variables account for the majority of the variance in therapy outcome studies" (2007, p. 118). He called for dialogue with proponents of those views, in an effort to understand their perspective and convey the alternative. Ultimately, "either we rebut these conclusions, conduct new research to show they are wrong, or we accept them and change our message" (p. 119). The aim of this article is to provide some historical context in terms of previous attempts to respond to these contentions and to present an update on recent research bearing directly on the Dodo Bird verdict and the assertions regarding variance accounted for by active ingredients (e.g., technique).

Aggregation

Evidence for the claim that all psychotherapies are equally efficacious derives from meta-analyses that combine various treatments for various disorders (e.g., Luborsky et al., 2002; Wampold et al., 1997). At most, these meta-analyses yield small effect sizes for average between-condition comparisons (e.g., $d = 0.21$; Wampold et al.), and the authors infer that, overall, no two psychotherapies are differentially efficacious for treating a disorder. Such a conclusion, however, is based on the fallacious reasoning that because all treatments for all disorders do not differ on average, no particular treatment is superior to another for a specific disorder (see Beutler, 2002; Chambless, 2002; Crits-Christoph, 1997; Hunsley & Di Giulio, 2002; and many others who have argued this point). Even operating with this reasoning,

most meta-analyses have found differences between treatment orientations (Luborsky et al.; Shapiro & Shapiro, 1982; Smith & Glass, 1977; Wampold et al.), even when taking into account allegiance. Furthermore, in response to Wampold et al.'s meta-analysis, Crits-Christoph suggested that aggregating various populations, disorders, and treatments would likely obscure real differences in treatment outcomes. Moreover, half of the studies examined by Wampold and colleagues evaluated the treatment of anxiety, and nearly 70% compared cognitive to behavioral therapies, characteristics of the studies that may minimize the likelihood of finding substantial treatment differences. Crits-Christoph demonstrated that 14 of the 29 studies that Wampold and colleagues included that compared two treatments for specific disorders grounded in different orientations yielded large effect sizes. Similarly, Beutler, Chambless, and others (Chambless & Ollendick, 2001; Hunsley & Di Giulio, 2002) have cited multiple studies and reviews that question the Dodo Bird verdict.

As a further challenge to the Dodo Bird verdict, Siev and Chambless (2007) recently conducted meta-analyses comparing CBT and relaxation (two bona fide treatments for anxiety disorders) for panic disorder (PD) and generalized anxiety disorder (GAD). In so doing, we compared two specific cognitive-behavioral interventions in the treatment of two anxiety disorders. The results revealed that for PD, CBT outperformed relaxation at posttreatment on all panic-related measures and indices of clinically significant change. In contrast, for GAD, the two treatments were equivalent on all measures. Furthermore, therapists in all studies were crossed with treatment condition, and most authors assessed client expectations and ratings of treatment credibility, which were high and never differed by treatment group. These methodological strengths bolster the likelihood that treatment techniques affected treatment effects.

In addition to combining various treatments and disorders, many meta-analyses in which the Dodo Bird verdict is advanced do not distinguish between primary and secondary outcome measures (Wampold et al., 1997). Rather, they derive a single effect size for each between-condition comparison by averaging all outcome measures. Their logic for doing so is:

> Given the assumption that researchers choose outcome measures that are germane to the psychological functioning of the patients involved in the study, it is the effect of the treatment on the set of outcome measures that is important. . . . Focusing on a few of many outcome measures to establish superiority causes fishing and error rate problems (Cook & Campbell, 1979) and distracts the researcher from examining the set of outcome measures, which might have produced a negligible effect size. (Wampold et al., 1997, p. 210)

However, the average of all outcome measures does not accurately capture the efficacy of the treatment for individuals suffering from a specific disorder, and is likely artificially to attenuate the magnitude of the effect size. The extent to which a treatment for a disorder (e.g., PD) affects domains of common comorbidity (e.g., depression) is critical information, but is not of equal import in evaluating the treatment's efficacy as is the extent to which it affects core symptoms of the disorder (e.g., panic symptoms and diagnostic status). Although it is true that researchers should articulate a priori the primary dependent measures, reasonable concerns about post hoc reporting biases (e.g., selectively emphasizing significant findings from a large set of mostly nonsignificant findings) ought not preclude researchers from investigating secondary outcomes. Combining measures of primary and secondary outcomes forces can obscure or mask entirely meaningful differences in treatment effects (see Crits-Christoph, 1997).

Meta-analytic data comparing CBT and relaxation for PD and GAD that were not published in Siev and Chambless (2007) illustrate the importance of considering not only disorders separately, but primary and secondary outcome measures separately, as well. . . .

Rather, in conducting or interpreting these data, one must consider a fundamental issue: What is the question? It is our contention that rarely does the researcher, clinician, or consumer care whether, on average, treatments for all disorders across all domains do not differ. Rather, the consumer (to take one, for example) wishes to know what treatment will best alleviate the distress caused by his or her symptoms (cf. the fundamental psychotherapy question of Paul,

who articulated the importance of asking not only whether psychotherapy works, but "What treatment, by whom, is most effective for this individual with that specific problem, and under which set of circumstances?" [1967, p. 111; emphasis in the original]). When the presenting problem is PD, the best answer to that question (if the options are CBT and relaxation) is that CBT is likely to reduce primary panic-related symptoms by approximately half a standard deviation more than is relaxation. Cast as a binomial effect size display,[1] this represents an increase in the rate of success from 38% to 62%. The wise consumer suffering from PD will choose CBT.

Bona Fide Treatments

Even advocates of a common factors approach to psychotherapy acknowledge that not all conceivable interventions are efficacious. Instead, the Dodo Bird verdict extends only to bona fide treatments, meaning those "intended to be therapeutic" (Wampold et al., 1997, p. 205). This distinction between bona fide and sham treatments in evaluating the relative efficacy of different treatments, while having appeal, also introduces a number of theoretical and conceptual difficulties.

Wampold and colleagues (e.g., Ahn & Wampold, 2001; Messer & Wampold, 2002) conclude that treatment outcome studies are futile because comparisons between bona fide treatments yield clinically insignificant differences and those between bona fide treatments and controls yield uninteresting differences. This contention is somewhat circular, however, because categorization as a bona fide treatment is both a criterion for inclusion in, and an implication of, the results of clinical experience and treatment outcome research (and meta-analyses that synthesize multiple such studies). To illustrate, consider the history of behavioral treatments for obsessive-compulsive disorder (OCD). Forty years ago, behavioral therapists treated OCD with relaxation. As exposure and response prevention (ERP) was developed, clinicians discovered that it was far more efficacious than relaxation, which is now considered a placebo in the treatment of OCD. Does the discovery that one treatment outperforms a second render that very comparison invalid? In fact, in a recent survey of psychologists who treat anxiety disorders and who predominantly favor a CBT approach, more clinicians endorsed using relaxation to treat OCD, than endorsed using ERP (Freiheit, Vye, Swan, & Cady, 2004). Surely those clinicians consider relaxation to be a bona fide treatment. How can it then become something other than a bona fide treatment when a researcher uses it? Wampold and colleagues' concern that comparisons between bona fide treatments and shams are rigged and sometimes uninformative is well taken. Certainly treatments should be compared to real treatments and not trimmed down, three-legged horses. At the same time, to conduct component analyses that evaluate particular techniques often presented together as parts of a larger treatment package, certain treatment elements must be excluded. This is part of the bind.

A related complication stems from the study- or disorder-specific classification of a treatment as bona fide. Although Wampold et al. (1997) formulate an operational definition of bona fide to identify particular studies for inclusion in their meta-analysis, there is little conceptual justification for some resultant distinctions. For example, according to Wampold et al.'s guidelines, whereas relaxation is now considered a placebo for OCD, it is a bona fide treatment for GAD because studies have demonstrated that relaxation works as well as other treatments for GAD (and therefore therapists expect relaxation to be therapeutic), but not for OCD (and therefore [study] therapists now do not expect relaxation to be therapeutic). In other words, researchers expect some treatments to work because they have found them to do so, and others to work less well because they have found them to do so. Herein lies another difficulty with Wampold et al.'s classification of treatments as bona fide: It is circular to discount the superior efficacy of a treatment on the grounds that "I knew it would work better," if that assumption derived from observation of the same superior efficacy. Moreover, if this reasoning is correct, on what other grounds is relaxation a bona fide treatment for one anxiety disorder and not another? Considering that Wampold et al. aggregate across disorders and treatments, this poses a particular theoretical difficulty. Is it reasonable to include comparisons of CBT and relaxation for GAD (as they do), but not for OCD? Wampold et al. use the notion of bona fide treatment to ensure that the patient and the therapist have positive expectancies about outcomes, as expectancies are proposed to be an essential common factor related to outcome. However, if a therapist and a patient expect ERP to work better than relaxation for OCD, for example, then they are correct in their expectation, but it does not mean that expectancy is driving the treatment effect. Are the effects caused by expectancy, or do people expect more from treatments that work better? Finally, Wampold et al.'s criterion of bona fide treatment comparisons creates the potential trap that if consensus were reached that exposure-based CBT is the treatment of choice for OCD, then one could not establish its efficacy, as there could not be a bona fide treatment with which to compare exposure-based CBT.

Figure 1

Breakdown of Clark et al.'s (2006) Data by Technique, Therapist Effects, and Unknown

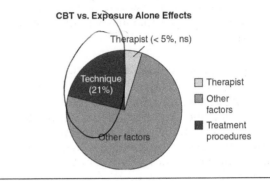

CBT vs. Exposure Alone Effects

Therapist (< 5%, ns)

Technique (21%)

Other factors

- Therapist
- Other factors
- Treatment procedures

Relationship and Therapist Variables, Common Factors, and Technique

The notion that the therapeutic relationship, therapist, and/or common factors contribute significantly more to treatment outcomes than do specific techniques has been stated by many (e.g., Levant, 2004; Messer & Wampold, 2002; Wampold, 2001), although with voices of opposition (Beutler, 2004; Huppert, Fabbro, & Barlow, 2006). The claim that technique accounts for approximately 10% to 15% of the variance of therapy outcome, whereas expectancy, relationship factors, and common factors account for closer to 40%, is frequently demonstrated in a pie chart (e.g., Lambert & Barley, 2001; 2002). However, the history of this chart may give the reader pause. Originally published in 1986 by Lambert, Shapiro, and Bergin in the *Handbook of Psychotherapy and Behavior Change* (3rd edition), the pie chart represented a summary of Lambert's reading of the literature from the previous 20+ years; it was not an empirical determination. One would hope that some progress has been made in the 20 years since, especially with regard to understanding mediators, moderators, and processes in therapy, and in CBT in particular. To take one study as exceptional in terms of such progress, Clark et al. (2006) showed that CBT targeting core cognitions and concerns of individuals with social anxiety disorder was more effective than exposure therapy (with a purely behavioral rationale of habituation) plus relaxation. Clark et al. report the effects of technique, alliance, and expectancy (see pie chart in Figure 1). Not only were therapist effects not large or significant, but there were no differences between the two treatment conditions in ratings of alliance ($p = .57$), credibility ($p = .26$), or expectancy ($p = .22$), suggesting that these mechanisms were not responsible for the differential treatment outcome between CBT and exposure. Similar data from another research group suggest that these CBT techniques for social anxiety disorder may be more effective than exposure alone (Huppert, Ledley, & Foa, 2007). At the same time, treatment technique did not account for 70% or 80% of the variance, and it is unlikely that any treatment will reach such a threshold.

How large are technique effects likely to be? Even Lambert's pie chart indicates that up to 15% of treatment effects may be due to technique, whereas Wampold (2001) suggests 8%. Before speculating about their magnitude, one needs to consider how best to determine technique effects. One method may be to compare active therapy to placebo. Overall, CBT for anxiety disorders has in fact shown significant superiority to placebo (cf. Hofmann & Smits, 2008), with an average effect size for the magnitude of the difference of 0.33 for intent-to-treat and 0.73 for completer analyses. However, there is variability in these effects, with the strongest evident in the treatment of acute stress disorder and OCD, and the weakest in the treatment of PD. Why might this be? It has been shown previously that OCD is less placebo responsive than is PD or social anxiety disorder (Huppert et al., 2004; Khan et al., 2005), and technique effects are most demonstrable in the disorders that have the smallest placebo effects. In fact, for some disorders (e.g., major depression), significant technique effects are somewhat difficult to demonstrate by comparing placebo to CBT (DeRubeis et al., 2005), although such effects are more prominent when examining follow-up data (e.g., Hollon et al., 2005). Similarly, in the case of PD, for which the magnitude of placebo response also appears to be high (Huppert et al.; Khan et al.), significant between-treatment effects are more evident at long-term follow-up (Barlow, Gorman, Shear, & Woods, 2000). In sum, it is difficult to determine the overall effect of technique without considering disorder and population, a conclusion reinforced by our discussion of the Dodo Bird verdict.

There are other methods by which one may examine technique effects. For example, Ablon and Jones (2002) showed that cognitive therapy techniques accounted for a significant amount of change in depressive symptoms in the NIMH Treatment of Depression Collaborative Research Program in both CBT and interpersonal psychotherapy treatment conditions. In addition, Cukrowicz et al. (2005) reported data suggesting that when a clinic changed its policy to conduct only ESTs, there was significant improvement in patient outcomes. Howard (1999) noted that individuals

in a managed care environment who had specialty training in CBT for anxiety disorders were more likely to retain their patients, and those patients were also less likely to receive further treatment 1 year later. It is important to note that studies that simply examine orientation are unlikely to find such effects, as many practitioners who identify their primary orientation as cognitive-behavioral continue to use relaxation as a treatment of choice for OCD and PD (e.g., Freiheit et al., 2004).

But what about the contribution of alliance, common factors, and therapist effects? On average, studies yield a correlation of .22 between measures of alliance and outcome (Martin, Garske, & Davis, 2000), demonstrating that the former accounts for 5% of the variance in the latter. Note that this effect size derives from data aggregated across studies of a range of therapies and treatments, similar to the effect sizes calculated by Wampold and colleagues, and Luborsky and colleagues. Again, looking at specific therapies and specific populations, the verdict is much less clear. For example, Lindsay, Crino, and Andrews (1997) showed that the alliance in ERP and the alliance in relaxation were equal for patients with OCD, but the differences in efficacy were substantial. Similarly, Carroll, Nich, and Rounsaville (1997) showed that alliance was correlated with outcome in a supportive therapy for substance abuse, but not CBT. In CBT for depression, the data from DeRubeis and colleagues' studies have consistently showed that the therapeutic alliance is better for patients whose symptoms and cognitions have already changed for the better (e.g., Tang & DeRubeis, 1999); that is, early improvement in treatment leads to a more positive alliance. However, in Cognitive Behavioral Analysis System of Psychotherapy, where the alliance is an explicit focus of treatment, alliance appears to be predictive of outcome (Klein et al., 2003). Overall, alliance may have the greatest relationship to outcome if the therapist makes it a central focus of treatment. However, in such treatments, the distinction between alliance and technique is blurred. As others have noted (Beutler, 2002; Crits-Christoph et al., 2006), if one addresses alliance directly in treatment sessions, the very focus on alliance becomes a treatment technique. There is only one pilot study to date that attempts to improve alliance by using specific alliance-enhancing techniques (Crits-Christoph et al.), and the results are equivocal. The effects of alliance-enhancing techniques in certain areas (e.g., change in alliance and improvement in quality of life) are large, but the impact on symptoms is small, and the results are difficult to interpret without a comparison group of new trainees who may have learned to improve alliance without additional techniques. However, the study is seminal in its attempt directly to improve alliance, and further such studies are needed to evaluate the causal impact of alliance on outcome.

Therapist effects have been discussed on and off for over 30 years. More recently, some have shown that differences between therapists in treatment outcome may be decreased with manualized treatments (Crits-Christoph et al., 1991), although not eliminated (e.g., Huppert et al., 2001). How large are therapist effects? Overall, they seem to range from 5% to 15% (see also Crits-Christoph & Gallop, 2006; Lutz, Leon, Martinovitch, Lyons, & Stiles, 2007). However, the question of what makes therapists different from each other remains, and one answer may be technique. Some therapists are likely more adept than others at using some techniques, formulating treatment plans, encouraging their patients to do difficult exposures, etc., even within CBT. Of course, therapists also differ on ability to form an alliance, but the therapist who is able to articulate a strong treatment rationale tailored to the patient's specific presentation and to explain why the treatment can help (or the therapist who is able to provide an example of an imaginal exposure that directly taps into an OCD patient's fears) will likely be experienced by the patient as empathic and understanding. Thus, techniques may be part of therapist effects (or vice versa), and not something that can be truly separated from them.

Just as alliance and therapist effects sometimes may be accounted for by technique, so may other putative common factors (consider, for example, how data on outcome provided during psychoeducation probably influence both therapist and patient expectancy). Indeed, the notion of common factors itself has broadened to the point that some would include the technique of exposure as a common factor (Lambert & Ogles, 2004). However, as Weinberger (1995) noted, common factors may not be so common after all. The extent of focus on alliance differs between treatments, and so does the amount, type, or quality of exposure. And if the goal of psychotherapy research is to determine the best ways to relieve suffering for the most people, researchers need to continue to focus on the areas that are most manipulable, such as technique. In fact, Lambert's latest research is an excellent example of high-quality research that integrates the arguments for the importance of technique, alliance, and therapist factors. In brief, Lambert has improved the quality of treatment outcome in therapy by providing therapists with feedback on patient progress and whether therapists are off track with their patients' predicted trajectories (Lambert, 2007). Notably, the feedback includes specific techniques that may help put them back on track. One may wonder aloud

whether use of other types of disorder-specific information could further enhance the efficacy of such interventions.

Overall, many researchers—ourselves included—attempt to quantify the relative contributions of technique and other effects. Frequently such data are presented so as to support the exclusive role of one of the aforementioned effects (e.g., alliance, therapist, common factors, technique) in influencing treatment outcome. It is equally important, however, to demonstrate how such partisan divisions are not reflected in the real world, where all of these effects meet in a complex series of interactions. In fact, the patient's contribution to outcome (including diagnosis, insight, motivation, severity, psychosocial background, etc.) is likely the greatest. One may conclude that effective techniques are likely to positively influence not only treatment outcomes, but also therapy relationships. Few would argue that one should conduct therapy in the context of a hostile or negative therapeutic relationship. However, techniques are ubiquitous and need to be studied in order to determine how to best improve them and, thereby, patient outcomes.

DiGiuseppe (2007) suggested that unless the Dodo Bird verdict and contentions regarding greater effects of therapist, alliance, and common factors are addressed empirically, psychologists who value scientific inquiry must accept the implications of those assertions. In fact, these notions have been argued against for years, and many continue to examine the data. In this review, we have attempted to convey the following. First, the Dodo Bird verdict is predicated on meta-analyses that aggregate data across treatments, disorders, and outcome measures, and such aggregation likely masks or attenuates treatment differences between particular treatments for particular disorders on primary outcomes, even though such differences have the most direct implications for treatment. Second, there are numerous logical difficulties with the classification of treatments as bona fide, a requisite criterion for inclusion in some of the aforementioned meta-analyses. Third, there is empirical evidence that technique effects are sometimes greater than effects of common factors. More generally, the magnitude of technique effects depends on disorder and population, bolstering the assertion that broad judgments about the relative importance of technique and common factors are insufficient and can be misleading. Instead, more nuanced accounts that do not aggregate across moderating variables are necessary to conduct and evaluate psychotherapy outcome research. Finally, putative common factors such as therapist skill, the therapeutic alliance, and treatment expectancy are likely influenced by technique. Hence, their effects are not easily separable from those of active ingredients, but instead are explained by series of complex interactions. Nevertheless, there will always be others who critique the analyses, draw different conclusions, and advocate for those stances, and efforts to disseminate ESTs are limited in part because opponents of ESTs have presented their perspective more aggressively to wide-spread audiences. We must continue to address their arguments with empirically based data and logic and make our voices heard in the broad court of professional opinion.

Note

1. The binomial effect size display is a means of depicting an effect size as a relative success rate. Based on the assumption that the rate of treatment success is 50% overall, the binomial effect size display is used to translate an association between treatment and outcome into the proportion of successes in one treatment group relative to another.

JEDIDIAH SIEV is a clinical fellow in psychology (psychiatry) at the Massachusetts General Hospital/Harvard Medical School. While completing his graduate studies at the University of Pennsylvania, he specialized in empirically supported treatments for obsessive-compulsive disorder and related disorders, as well as other anxiety and internalizing disorders. He is interested in cognitive factors that contribute to the development and maintenance of obsessive-compulsive disorder and related disorders. He also investigates the relationship between psychotherapy outcomes in regard to active ingredients and common factors.

JONATHAN D. HUPPERT is a professor of psychology at The Hebrew University of Jerusalem. His research efforts are aimed at developing the optimal psychosocial treatments for anxiety and related disorders. He conducts studies on the process and outcomes of cognitive-behavioral treatments for anxiety disorders. He also examines the impact of the co-occurrence for other types of psychopathology such as depression or psychosis on anxiety and their impact on treatment outcomes and processes.

DIANNE L. CHAMBLESS is a Merriam Term Professor of Psychology at the University of Pennsylvania. She is also the director of clinical training for the Department of Psychology. Her areas of research include anxiety disorders, expressed emotion, and empirically supported treatments.

EXPLORING THE ISSUE

Are All Psychotherapies Equally Effective?

Critical Thinking and Reflection

1. What is the difference between "technique" and the "common factors"? Could a common factors approach be considered a technique?
2. Assuming that the Dodo hypothesis is correct, would *any* technique—perhaps even a nonsensical or an evil technique—produce equivalent results? Why or why not?
3. How would you know if one technique was superior to another? How do you think the authors of the readings would know? What does it mean to be psychologically healthy?
4. From the perspective of the authors of the NO reading, why is it important to consider whether one technique or therapy is more effective than another?
5. Would the authors of the NO reading say that technique alone is sufficient to produce desired results in psychotherapy? What if the therapist is unskilled or inexperienced? Explain your answer.
6. Assuming that the Dodo hypothesis has been tested and found to be valid, how might it have advantages for the treatment of psychological disorders?

Is There Common Ground?

Psychotherapy is a multi-billion dollar industry. When we are mentally disordered, depressed, or anxious, we expect therapists to make us better. We trust them with the most intimate details of our lives in the hopes that they can help us to live fuller, happier lives for having counseled with and followed them. For all the faith that our society places in therapists, we should expect that the therapy they are giving us actually works.

Fortunately, there is a consensus that it does. All of our authors and the scientific community at large agree that therapy works. In the care of a properly-trained therapist, we may become mentally whole and it is not an illusion. Beyond that, there is further agreement that all successful therapies do in fact possess the "common factors" in common—they all invoke extra-therapeutic and relationship factors, hope and expectancy, and model/technique factors (healing rituals). The common factors provide a great deal of common ground on which to build.

Nonetheless, the question of whether "that is as good as it gets" persists. That is to say, is all therapy-specific technique irrelevant once the common factors are in place? Even here there may be some room for agreement and mutual understanding. While there is disagreement as to whether current evidence supports the notion that specific techniques work better for treating specific mental ailments, there is nothing to suggest that a specific technique cannot ever be found that is more beneficial than another. Therefore, so long as the common factors continue to be a respected foundation for therapeutic success, future exploration into improving specific techniques can only benefit our health—if the techniques are irrelevant, they cannot hurt us; but if we do find specific techniques to be better for specific ailments, then they can certainly help us.

Additional Resources

Hansen, B. (2005). The dodo manifesto. *Australian and New Zealand Journal of Family Therapy, 26*(4), 210–218.

Silverman, D. K. (2005). What works in psychotherapy and how do we know? What evidence-based practice has to offer. *Psychoanalytic Psychology, 22*(2), 306–312.

Wampold, B. E. (2006). *The Great Psychotherapy Debate.* PhD dissertation, University of Wisconsin—Madison. Retrieved December 2006.

Internet References . . .

APA Division 12: Society of Clinical
Psychology

> http://www.apa.org/about/division/div12.aspx

The National Council of Psychotherapists

> http://thencp.org/

SAMHSA's National Registry of Evidence-
Based Programs and Practices

> http://www.nrepp.samhsa.gov/Index.aspx

Scott D. Miller, PhD

> http://www.scottdmiller.com/

Selected, Edited, and with Issue Framing Material by:
Edwin E. Gantt, *Brigham Young University*

ISSUE

Should Therapists Be Eclectic?

YES: Jean A. Carter, from "Theoretical Pluralism and Technical Eclecticism," *American Psychological Association* (2006)

NO: Don MacDonald and Marcia Webb, from "Toward Conceptual Clarity with Psychotherapeutic Theories," *Journal of Psychology and Christianity* (2006)

Learning Outcomes
After reading this issue, you will be able to:
• Determine the potential benefits that could be derived from an eclectic approach to psychotherapy.
• Identify some detrimental effects an eclectic approach could have.

ISSUE SUMMARY

YES: Counseling psychologist Jean Carter insists that the continued improvement and effectiveness of psychotherapy requires that techniques and theories include the different approaches of psychological theory and practice through an eclectic approach.

NO: Professors of psychotherapy Don MacDonald and Marcia Webb contend that eclecticism creates an unsystematic theoretical center for psychological ideas and methods that ultimately limits overall therapeutic effectiveness.

Most psychotherapists acknowledge that they need a good theory or theories to help guide their treatment of clients. If you were a psychotherapist, how would you use these ideas? Would you try to find the *single* best or most favorite theory, or would you pick and choose various parts from among *all* the theories? Some psychotherapists choose the single-theory approach because it seems more systematic and less fragmented. Other psychotherapists choose to work with many theories, because they see it as a way to create comprehensive therapies that are capable of addressing a variety of client situations.

The second approach is usually considered *eclectic* because psychotherapists select or employ individual elements from a variety of sources, systems, and styles. The word "eclectic" is derived from the ancient Greek and literally means "to choose the best." For example, some eclectic psychotherapists choose to subscribe to theories

from humanistic psychology for their view of human nature, while practicing techniques derived from the cognitive psychology movement. Eclecticism is a popular way to resolve the varied problems of therapy. Surveys report that roughly two-thirds of all psychotherapists endorse some form of eclecticism. Still, its merit and validity as a guiding framework for psychological endeavors continues to generate debate.

Counselor Jean Carter is a prominent example of one side of this debate. In the YES selection, she argues that patients and their problems rarely fall into well-defined categories. As such, she believes that psychotherapists must embrace a variety of theories and associated techniques to overcome this challenge—eclecticism. She contends that real-world applications of an eclectic approach is a better treatment model, especially in comparison to single-theory approaches, because it is tailored for each patient and therefore adaptive and flexible across various scenarios. For this reason, she maintains that therapists should add diverse perspectives to their theoretical framework and avoid committing to any one conceptual approach.

Psychotherapists Don MacDonald and Marcia Webb oppose eclectic approaches because they sacrifice clarity in the process of psychotherapy. They argue that many psychotherapists opt for an eclectic approach just to avoid the difficult task of finding a single theory to guide their therapy. However, by sidestepping the process of committing to and thus understanding thoroughly a particular theory, eclectics unknowingly run the risk of understanding very little about the theories they employ. Indeed, this course of action eventually leads to a type of eclectic approach that is called *syncretism*. Syncretism occurs when psychotherapists try to unite aspects of theories and methods that are often contrary to one another. Don MacDonald and Marcia Webb conclude that a return to traditional single-theory approaches is required to achieve better clarity and effectiveness within psychotherapeutic practice.

POINT

- Therapy based on eclectic theories and techniques can manage diversion situations more readily.
- Eclectic systems allow therapists to choose the best methods and ideas for use.
- Therapy becomes more practical because therapists have all the theories and techniques they need.
- Therapists are better able to focus on therapeutic relationship because they do not have to focus on rigid single-theory concepts.

COUNTERPOINT

- Eclectic approaches have weak conceptual bases that fail to create a cogent rationale for clients to understand and trust.
- Without a guiding framework, therapists are less knowledgeable about theories overall.
- Access to a wide variety of theories and techniques does not necessarily ensure that the best option is selected.
- Single-theory therapists are well versed in the techniques and conceptual basis that guide how they form the therapeutic relationship.

YES ⤹

Jean A. Carter

Theoretical Pluralism and Technical Eclecticism

The real world of psychotherapy practice is complex, requiring moment-by-moment decisions about the treatment plan, the techniques being used, the working diagnosis, and even the goals. Patients rarely can be put into neat diagnostic boxes, and there is a great deal about their lives that psychotherapists cannot control. Clinicians know that psychotherapy occurs within a relationship that is personal and interpersonal, deeply textured, and responsive to the patient. Psychologists are trained in both the science and the practice of psychology, and they firmly believe in the value of evidence and the science base for their practice. The integration of these factors in recent calls for greater accountability and quality improvement in health care practice creates important challenges for both the scientists and the practitioners within psychology. Although the two groups share the goals of improving the effectiveness of psychotherapy and enhancing outcomes for patients, the tools and methods each uses to approach these goals may reflect quite different viewpoints. Like the blind men exploring an elephant, the part of psychotherapy one touches shapes how one understands the nature of the endeavor.

Although psychology has been committed to the integration of science and practice throughout its history, current initiatives to articulate and implement evidence-based practice principles highlight both that commitment and the difficulties inherent in integrating disparate views (American Psychological Association [APA], 2005). From a scientific perspective, psychologists seek greater control of variables, clarity of questions and methods, and general principles that are valid and reliable. From a practice perspective, they are committed to enhancing the lives of patients, drawing on general psychological principles, treatment-oriented research, and their experience in the multilayered world of practice.

Inevitably, divergent perspectives result in conflicts as psychologists attempt to bring together different approaches to the same shared goal of more effective practice. The significance of these conflicts, and the tension surrounding them, rises as funding and policy implications are increasingly based on demonstrable effectiveness and its evidence base. Practitioners are concerned about the limitations required by scientific methodologies and the direct application of research findings to any particular individual or treatment, as well as funding and treatment constraints arising out of misapplications of methodologies and results. . . .

Clinicians know the impact of psychotherapy; they experience it as they sit with their patients hour after hour, struggling with the anguish and difficulties patients bring into their offices. A long history of evidence supports the effectiveness and durability of psychotherapy (Ahn & Wampold, 2001; Barlow, 2004; Elkin et al., 1989; Lambert & Barley, 2002; Lambert & Bergin, 1994; Lipsey & Wilson, 1993; Roth & Fonagy, 1996; Sloane, Staples, Cristol, Yorkston, & Whipple, 1975; Smith, Glass, & Miller, 1980; Wampold et al., 1997). These reports include psychotherapy studies, literature reviews, and meta-analyses and represent many theoretical perspectives, patient and treatment types, and a variety of outcome measures. The picture is clear—psychotherapy works, and works well, much of the time.

At the same time, no particular form or model of therapy has been found to consistently work better than others (Wampold, 2001). In recent research designed to evaluate psychological interventions to relieve specific target problems in well-defined treatment populations using controlled treatment protocols (Barlow, 2004), the data support the efficacy of specific treatments but do not clearly support differential treatment effects (Wampold, 2001; Westen, Novotny, & Thompson-Brenner, 2004). In addition, questions about the applicability of the results of these studies to the general treatment population and therapeutic realities abound. One cannot conclude that particular treatments are clearly better than other treatments or clearly better than treatment as usual in the community. The research literature thus supports clinicians' experiential knowledge that psychotherapy works but does not offer them specific information about what to do when or with whom to provide effective psychotherapy.

Practitioners value the grounding of practice within evidence, including the evidence that they collect and draw on as they engage in a version of science within the hour (Carter, 2002; Strieker & Trierweiler, 1995). They continually ask questions about what is or is not working and why, and they attempt to understand how to enhance the multilayered practice that occurs within a specific interpersonal context (Samstag, 2002) and with its own unique demands. . . . Within this continually changing world of practice, clinicians rely on the therapeutic relationship; a broad knowledge of individual differences, psychological principles, and change processes; a theoretical grounding that offers cogent explanations; and techniques that provide the necessary tools for change.

This chapter offers a perspective on the importance of maintaining multiple theoretical formulations for effective psychological practice and on the role of related techniques in the psychotherapy process. Evidence-based practice in psychology has as its background the complex factors that affect the psychotherapy process and the history of research demonstrating the effectiveness of psychotherapy. It reflects an understanding of the contextual model of psychotherapy with its emphasis on common factors. I propose the essential integration of theoretical pluralism and technical eclecticism as significant components of real-world applications of evidence-based practice in psychology.

The Multilayered Real World of Psychotherapy

Psychotherapy is complex and requires continual responsiveness. Many factors operate at any given moment, all of which may call for the clinician's attention, and many of which are not within his or her control. Clinicians look for ways to understand psychological distress and to effect change in a way that takes into account this complexity. Although this chapter does not primarily address the wide range of presentations and problem types or specific treatments designed to be effective with the variety of clients clinicians face, it is important that the reader understand the psychotherapy process as an ongoing complex interplay of factors in which the clinician makes frequent decisions within an uncertain context, using their own clinical expertise and probabilistic research evidence to guide them in the moment. . . .

[P]atients present dramatically different pictures, even those who meet the same diagnostic criteria from the *Diagnostic and Statistical Manual of Mental Disorders* (American Psychiatric Association, 1994). Clinicians attend to disorder-related issues, including presenting problem, level of distress, level of function, co-occurring problems, and attachment style (see Norcross, 2002). They attend to life circumstances (e.g., available resources and support systems, medical concerns, social skills), individual and group characteristics (APA, 2002, 2003; Sue, 2003; Sue & Lam, 2002), and values. These factors are what patients bring into treatment and what influences their lives outside of treatment as well as the treatment itself (see Miller, Duncan, & Hubble, 1997). In addition, these patient factors do not remain static and do not follow neat lines of development or change and may be affected by happenstance, or things that occur in people's lives that may not be under their control but that significantly affect their lives and the treatment.

In addition to patient factors, there are a number of factors related specifically to the therapist that operate throughout treatment (see Norcross, 2002, for a discussion of clinician factors). Clinicians vary in interpersonal skills and abilities, experience, training, values, personal characteristics, knowledge base, and worldview, as well as other factors. Just as no two patients are exactly the same, clinicians are not interchangeable.

Structural aspects of the clinical situation affect what can or does occur within treatment. These factors may include the resources available and costs related to engaging in treatment (Yates, 1994, 1995, 2000). The payer or agency may impose session or treatment limits. Moves, job changes, and other life events may affect the length or nature of treatment independent of patient preference or clinician recommendation.

Theoretical models also play a significant role in psychotherapy. Clinicians may rely on theory to explain change processes, and in the contextual model (Wampold, 2001) theories are valuable because they provide rationales for treatment, help organize it, and guide appropriate therapeutic goals for the particular clinical context. Clinicians also rely on a range of techniques drawn from multiple theoretical perspectives that research has found to be effective for particular symptom pictures or particular patient types and that the clinicians have found to be effective through their own experience and expertise (e.g., Arnkoff, Glass, & Shapiro, 2002; Beutler, Alomohamed, Moleiro, & Romanelli, 2002; Norcross, 2002).

The Contextual Model of Psychotherapy

Psychotherapy practice is inextricable from the context in which it occurs. Psychotherapy is an interpersonal experience, with a patient who is in distress and a treatment based on psychological principles and offered by a therapist. Wampold (2001), in *The Great Psychotherapy Debate*, presented a compelling differentiation between the medical model of psychotherapy and the contextual model of psychotherapy and described the research foundation on which the contextual model rests. Although not all clinicians or researchers see this model as a more accurate fit for psychotherapy process and outcomes data, the presentation closely matches the lived experience of many clinicians. It also provides the foundation for the remainder of this chapter. . . .

The Therapeutic Relationship

The therapeutic relationship is foundational to the psychotherapy endeavor. Just as psychotherapy cannot proceed without patients, it cannot proceed without a clinician,[1] and the therapeutic relationship is built by the two participants. The therapeutic relationship accounts for 30% of the variance in outcome in psychotherapy, second only to patient factors, which represent 40% of the variance (Assay & Lambert, 1999; Lambert, 1992; Lambert & Barley, 2002). . . .

The Working Alliance

The *therapeutic relationship* and the *working alliance* are often referred to synonymously, particularly in the research literature. The working alliance (originally conceptualized by Bordin, 1975) includes a bond between patient and therapist, agreement on goals, and consensus on therapeutic tasks. The alliance has repeatedly been found to be significantly related to outcome; Wampold (2001) and Horvath and Bedi (2002) provided summaries of this research. Given the large proportion of variance in outcome accounted for by the alliance, it is clearly important for clinicians and researchers to be continually attentive to the role and impact of the alliance and to the ways in which the alliance as a relationship can be enhanced.

The agreement on tasks and consensus on goals that are components of the alliance are significant in any consideration of the role of theory in evidence-based practice in psychology. Although well-designed research supports the effectiveness of psychotherapy, it does not offer clear support for relative effectiveness—that is, of one form of treatment over another, including treatment as usual in the community (Westen et al., 2004). . . .

The working alliance includes clinician and patient agreement on goals and tasks as major components of a successful alliance, and positive working alliance is related to better outcomes. The question may arise, however, about which goals and tasks the clinician and patient may agree on and how they come to the definition and the agreement. There are many possible goals and expected or desirable outcomes from psychotherapy, and it sometimes appears that there are as many measures of goals and outcomes as there are possible outcomes. Some examples included in studies of outcomes are self-esteem, premature termination, global change, symptom severity, interpersonal functioning, addiction severity, change in distress, drug use, alleviation of depressive symptoms, social adjustment, specific symptoms, social relationships, indecision, personal growth, relations with others, social or sexual adjustment, interpersonal problems, defense style, employment status, legal status, self-concept, anxiety symptoms, medication compliance, quality of life, hospitalization, productivity, and satisfaction with treatment (Horvath & Bedi, 2002). It is clear that the range of possible outcomes is huge. At the same time, the clinician and patient must identify outcomes they believe to be desirable and goals to be achieved and must reach agreement on these goals as an essential part of the alliance. The definition of outcomes arises from a shared perspective held by the clinician and patient.

Typically, the desirable goals for any particular psychotherapy are derived from patient need and problem type and patient and clinician worldviews. They are consistent with the theoretical framework from which the treatment was developed. Thus, agreement on goals implies agreement (whether implicit or explicit) on the theoretical framework (cogent and coherent explanation or rationale) from which the clinician operates. Therefore, the theoretical framework provides an important structure within which psychotherapy occurs and is significantly related to one of the components of psychotherapy outcome (agreement on goals as part of the alliance).

Patient Belief in the Treatment

According to Frank (1973; Frank & Frank, 1991) and Wampold (2001), the patient's belief in the treatment, its context, and the clinician is a component shared by all psychotherapy approaches. Indeed, it is hard to imagine how a patient without some belief and hope in the effectiveness of treatment could be an active participant in psychotherapy or could share an agreement on goals or outcome with the clinician. The participation of patients is essential, of course. Duncan (2002) described patients as the heroes of the treatment; it is the patient's therapy, and he or she makes whatever changes are to be made. Successful collaboration between clinician and patient (Tryon & Winograd, 2002) and lower levels of resistance (Beutler, Moleiro, & Talebi, 2002) are related to positive outcomes. Patient factors such as positive expectation, motivation, and openness to treatment (Grencavage & Norcross, 1990) account for 40% of the variance (Assay & Lambert, 1999). These factors, which are central to the patient's belief in the treatment, make patient characteristics and values the most potent component of successful treatment. These findings support the importance of agreement on goals and consensus on tasks, which are part of the alliance and part of the patient's belief in the healing benefit of psychotherapy. When there are difficulties in collaboration and resistance to the treatment is high (both reflect difficulties in the alliance), existing evidence suggests that acknowledging the patient's concerns, attending to the relationship, and renegotiating goals and roles may be effective in ameliorating problems in the alliance (Beutler & Harwood, 2002; Beutler, Moleiro, et al., 2002; Safran & Muran, 2002).

The Value of Flexible Theoretical Frameworks

Effective treatment clearly needs a cogent rationale, and clinician and patient need to agree on goals and tasks based on that rationale. At the same time, the complexity of psychotherapy may require renegotiating goals and roles to better align patient and clinician and to better match patient characteristics and worldview. Renegotiation and realignment call for flexibility in the theoretical framework guiding the treatment designed for the specific patient and his or her situation, as well as flexibility in the use of techniques derived from various theoretical approaches. The clinician needs to be adaptive and conversant with multiple theoretical perspectives that may guide his or her ability to integrate clinician worldview and patient worldview to match the particular patient. The clinician must be prepared to incorporate additional or different theoretical components to achieve better fit for the patient. In other words, the clinician's effectiveness rests in part on maintaining theoretical pluralism and the ability to be integrative in those theories.

A Conceptual Scheme

Rosenzweig (1936/2002) and Frank (Frank & Frank, 1991) supported the importance of an ideology or rationale provided by the clinician that presents a cogent, coherent, and plausible explanation for both the patient's distress and the approach the clinician will take to help the patient. This ideology engages the patient. It offers the patient hope and expectation (remoralization through positive expectation) in the treatment, as well as a way to understand the goals and tasks of treatment, which in turn enhance outcomes. Ideology, rationale, and coherent and cogent explanation are all different words for the *theoretical formulation* that guides the clinician in the treatment.

Patient Expectancy

Patient expectancy and hope are potent contributors to positive outcomes. Assay and Lambert (1999) suggested that the accumulation of research puts the contribution of patient expectancy for outcomes at about 15% of the variance. Expectation is typically cast as a placebo effect in medical model approaches, but the contextual model includes it as a central component of effective treatment. Placebo effects are essentially psychological effects and thus are undesirable in a model that attempts to minimize extrinsic factors through tight control and adherence to the treatment as defined. However, increased psychological effects as a result of psychological treatments seem desirable—not undesirable—outcomes and should be supported, and factors that increase positive expectations should be promoted. For example, a patient who moves into a hopeful state and no longer exhibits hopelessness (one of the primary symptoms of depression) because of his or her belief in the treatment demonstrates the effectiveness of nonspecific psychological factors in the treatment. The clinician wants to enhance the patient's belief in what he or she is offering to enhance expectancy effects. Therefore, the clinician would promote the importance of the theoretical framework to engage and encourage patients and heighten expectancy effects, as well as to take advantage of the positive contribution theory makes to agreement on goals and tasks.

Allegiance

Trust is a significant part of therapy; patient belief in and openness to treatment and the patient-clinician bond component of the alliance rely on trust (Horvath & Bedi, 2002). Clinicians' belief in their therapeutic models or theories is related to outcomes through its impact on clinician–patient agreement on goals and desirable outcomes and the extent to which it engages the patient. Therefore, the clinician must believe in his or her own treatment model, just as the patient does. The theoretical framework must therefore be cogent, coherent, and explanatory for the clinician as well as for the patient.

Theory also provides the clinician with an underlying organization for the large amounts of information that are relevant to psychotherapy and that must be available for the clinician's use in the treatment.

To the extent that the clinician believes the theory to be explanatory for the patient's distress and to provide a rationale for the treatment plan and its implementation, one would expect the clinician to have considerable allegiance to the theoretical model he or she is using. Wampold (2001) offered extensive evidence regarding clinician allegiance to an espoused theoretical model and its strong positive relationship to outcomes.

It is important to note that the relationship between allegiance and outcomes appears to hold regardless of the truth value of the theory. One might think that this would lead to rampant development of a vast array of untested and untestable theoretical models. Despite frequent counts of theoretical models that number several hundred (e.g., Bergin & Garfield, 1994), the major models remain largely consistent categories.[2] At the same time, consistent with the importance of the theoretical model to both clinician and patient, clinicians would be expected to do one of two things: either endorse one of the existing general theoretical models or endorse an approach that draws from more than one model. Both seem to occur simultaneously, however. Clinicians choose one model as primary (often with a secondary choice when that is an alternative) and may also espouse an integrative perspective (drawing on multiple models) or eclecticism as their theoretical perspective (Garfield & Bergin, 1994; Jensen & Bergin, 1990; Norcross, Prochaska, & Farber, 1993; Wampold, 2001). Typically, *eclectic* draws the largest endorsement as a single category. Norcross et al. (1993) found that 40% of the members of the Division of Psychotherapy of the APA who responded to a survey of theoretical orientation chose *eclectic*, reflecting individualized versions based on experience, training in multiple models, and alterations in response to patient need. Clinicians' choice of eclectic as a theoretical perspective needs attention to understand its meaning, impact, and role as an explanatory system and the extent to which it is a well-developed individualized model versus a process for integrating multiple models (Carter, 2002).

Currently, theoretical integration, technical eclecticism, and common factors are receiving considerable attention, reflecting dissatisfaction with individual theoretical approaches and attempts to develop more flexible approaches. Theoretical integration is problematic if it becomes its own model, because it then has all of the problems that are associated with a single theoretical model (Feixas & Botella, 2004; O'Brien, 2004). However, it provides a useful framework if it provides procedures for integrating diverse perspectives into a system that is applicable for the particular clinician-patient pair, to the particular patient problems, and in the particular context (Feixas & Botella, 2004).

Technical eclecticism alone as a response to the poor fit of theoretical models is limited, because it takes only interventions into account and ignores the relevance and role of theoretical models. From an integrative or theoretically eclectic perspective, however, it is important for clinicians to be skilled in techniques drawn from the multiple theories from which their own theoretical perspective is derived. Because allegiance to a cogent rationale is important and clinicians and patients rely on theories to organize and guide their work, clinicians are expected to modify models as needed to be responsive to patients. Thus, psychologists must continue to develop and teach multiple models, to understand the components of the theories as explanatory tools, and to understand and effectively implement the techniques derived from the models.

Rituals and Procedures (Otherwise Known as Techniques)

Frank and Frank (1991), drawing on Rosenzweig's formulation (1936/2002), focused on the importance of rituals and procedures that are consistent with the rationale given for the treatment. The rituals and procedures that Frank and Frank suggested may best be understood as the interventions or techniques that are logically derived from the theoretical formulation of the causes of the patient's distress and the approach to ameliorating the dysfunction. Clinicians design techniques, then, to have a specific impact on symptoms, behaviors, or other components as defined by the theory from which they arise and with which they are consistent. Rosenzweig believed that an impact on any subsystem (or aspect) of personality affects all of the personality, suggesting that effective treatment may occur with any one of multiple symptoms as the target of interventions. If Rosenzweig was correct, techniques should have a positive impact on outcomes, but the impact should account for a relatively small portion of the variance. According to Assay and Lambert (1999), techniques overall account for only 15% of the variance, and specific techniques appear to make little additive difference in outcome (Wampold, 2001). Valuable research using designs that offer well-controlled and targeted interventions for specific symptom pictures demonstrates their effectiveness in both absolute and relative terms (Barlow, 2004). Although application of these results may call for adaptation to the particular treatment picture, these are useful tools for the clinician to have readily available. It is interesting to note that Westen et al. (2004), in a review of the current status of what have been known as empirically supported treatments, offered a hypothesis on the role of negative diatheses as an underlying principle that may be common to all psychological disorders and explanatory for varied presentations and comorbidity. The relationship between specific techniques for specific symptoms and the complex symptom picture in a typical clinical practice offers great opportunities for collaboration between research and practice.

Nevertheless, techniques do matter. Interventions are the tools through which psychotherapy occurs within the context previously described. They are the expression of the belief system arising from theoretical models. They operationalize the therapeutic tasks that are part of the alliance. They are the medium by which the relationship is developed and maintained. They build hope in the patient through active engagement in the tasks of therapy. They effectively alter specific symptoms. Hence, it is essential for clinicians to be technically eclectic and prepared with a wide range of tools to address the needs of patients in the continually changing world of psychotherapy. The contextual model, which reflects the deeply complex interpersonal world of psychotherapy, supports the importance of techniques as tools in trade (Wampold, 2001), with clinicians having the ability to apply multiple techniques in the service of an individually tailored psychotherapy.

Conclusion

Most clinicians strongly support models of psychotherapy that are context centered, that place a strong value on the relationship and alliance, and that are embedded in theoretical models. At the same time, clinicians rely on eclectic or integrative models, and their work reflects theoretical pluralism. In addition, experienced clinicians from different theoretical perspectives are more similar than different within the psychotherapy hour, using techniques drawn from a variety of theoretical approaches and reflecting technical eclecticism in the application of psychotherapy.

Psychological scientists and psychological practitioners have a number of areas of agreement about the evidence base underlying practice. The therapeutic relationship, a central component to practice, has strong evidentiary support as an essential factor in successful outcomes. Therefore, clinicians should devote considerable attention to building and maintaining a strong therapeutic relationship in the implementation of evidence-based practice. Evidence drawn from research on psychotherapy supports

the importance of coherent and cogent explanations for distress, dysfunction, and treatment to positive outcomes. Therefore, clinicians who engage in evidence-based practice should devote time, energy, and attention to strengthening the cogency and clarity of their theoretical formulations, including both the major theoretical perspectives and the variants that are consistent with their own worldviews and psychology's scientific base. Theoretical pluralism is an important part of evidence-based practice.

The therapeutic alliance (which is part of the relationship) rests on agreement on goals and tasks and is positively related to outcomes. Agreement on goals and tasks is drawn from agreement on and belief in the explanations for and implementation of the treatment (the theoretical model the clinician uses and the techniques drawn from that model). The alliance necessarily takes into account the therapist's role, the patient's role, and the relationship between them. Clinicians who integrate principles of evidence-based practice devote energy to learning techniques that emanate from their own theoretical model. In addition, they should maintain openness to techniques that may complement or supplement those derived from their model, that may enhance the relationship, and that may fit the patient's desired goals, problems, and characteristics.

Placebo or expectancy effects are essentially belief in or hope for the treatment that rests on the patient's and the therapist's belief that the explanation is valid and that it will work—again, the important role of theory. Clinicians demonstrating evidence-based practice should support patients' hopes and beliefs, as well as their own, which requires a somewhat different approach to the evidence foundation for psychotherapy that draws on a context of discovery rather than a context of justification for the scientific thinking occurring within the hour.

Skill with a range of techniques is important as an expression of the theory (agreement on tasks), as a way to effectively manage the alliance and relationship, as rituals, and as ways to accommodate multiple problems, worldviews, and expected outcomes. Technical eclecticism is an important component of evidence-based practice in psychology.

Psychological research underlying evidence-based practice in psychology

- supports the use of theoretical pluralism and technical eclecticism to enhance the alliance and strengthen the therapeutic relationship;
- supports a coherent, cogent, and organized explanation for patient distress and its amelioration;
- fosters patient hope; and
- uses a range of techniques to maximize effectiveness.

Evidence-based practice in psychology has at its core an effort to enhance patient involvement and choice, as well as participation in his or her own health care. Implementing evidence-based practice requires the continuous and deliberate incorporation of both a scientific attitude and empirical research into an understanding and appreciation for the unique demands of psychotherapy practice. Commitment to evidence-based practice continues a strong belief in the integration of science and practice in psychology. Embracing it reflects psychology's past and supports its future.

Notes

1. Some computer models of intervention do not require the active participation of a clinician. However, psychotherapy is commonly understood to be an interpersonal process between a patient and a therapist.
2. The major models are behavioral and cognitive-behavioral, psychodynamic, humanistic or experiential, systems theory, and feminist theory. All of them have multiple variants that reflect shifts in perspective or incorporation of new knowledge drawn from general psychological principles or research on the treatment model itself.

JEAN A. CARTER is currently a member of the board of directors of the American Psychological Association. She began a psychotherapy practice in Washington, D.C., after receiving her PhD in counseling psychology from the University of Maryland in 1980 and continues her practice. At the Washington Psychological Center, she focuses on psychotherapy with individuals and couples, emphasizing aspects of serious trauma, relationship issues, depression, and work stress/vocational adjustment. Other areas of interest for her include grief and loss and issues related to sexual orientation for both individuals and couples. She also serves as an adjunct faculty member at the University of Maryland in counseling psychology.

Don MacDonald and Marcia Webb  **NO**

Toward Conceptual Clarity with Psychotherapeutic Theories

The proliferation of theories for conducting psychotherapy makes it easy for a therapist to become lost in the welter of ideas. In particular, clarity about the criteria for and the evaluation of theories lags. The present article discriminates between syncretism and eclecticism. As part of the discrimination, it provides 14 interrelated criteria by which to assess a theory. It also distinguishes between theories and treatment models. Finally, it presents a proposal for the reciprocal development of both. These 14 criteria come from a broad array of professional literature, and provide an approximation of a holistic perspective of humanity. They also describe theories in a complex and comprehensive manner, and offer therapists the opportunity to make indepth attempts toward the integration of one's personal faith commitments and one's professional identity. Even with responsible efforts toward conceptual clarity, the authors describe the high potential for syncretism, due to the multitude of theories, models, and criteria currently available to psychotherapists. The authors further propose strategies to prevent the conceptual compromises associated with a syncretistic approach to the conceptualization and conduct of psychotherapy.

Psychotherapists look to theories to help them develop treatment goals, assessments, methods, and evaluations of processes and outcomes. Theory is a map and, as such, is an indispensable tool. Cherry, Messenger, and Jacoby (2000) and Striker (2002) identified psychotherapy as an important professional function, regardless of the preparation orientation of the therapist, viz., clinical scientist, scientist-practitioner, and practitioner-evaluator. Psychotherapeutic theories as maps, however, are only as helpful as their clarity permits. This article explores major sources of compromise for theoretical clarity and discusses means for fostering clarity. It makes no claims for achieving clarity. Rather the article proposes criteria that will hopefully stimulate discussion about the intentional development of theory. Thus, it is meant to be heuristic.

Theories of psychotherapy abound. Literally hundreds of theories exist and the number is growing (Corsini, 2000; Miller, Duncan, & Hubble, 1997). Naturally, it is impossible for a psychotherapist to know all or even most of them. Given that meta-analyses on the comparative effectiveness of many different therapeutic approaches indicate most are similar in being generally helpful (Shadish, Matt, Navarro, & Phillips, 2000; Smith & Glass, 1977; Wampold et al., 1997), it is unnecessary for psychotherapists to know multiple theories in order to work effectively. Rather, it seems that the therapist must be thoroughly grounded in the concepts and methods that he or she uses.

While knowledge of multiple theories may be unnecessary, it is nevertheless essential for effective psychotherapists to understand at least one theory well in order to apply it. On a continuum for comprehension of theory (McBride & Martin, 1990), one end entails understanding one or more theories thoroughly while the opposite end of the continuum entails understanding very little about even one theory. Limited understanding of even one theory relegates psychotherapists to adding a method here and an idea there, without a systematic conceptual basis to hold those methods and ideas together; this is conceptual *syncretism*. In the worst cases, psychotherapists operate out of syncretism, wherein they unsuccessfully attempt to synthesize different, perhaps contradictory, ideas and methods, with little or no awareness of their inherent incongruities. A cogent conceptual system, though, would solve this difficulty. . . .

The conceptual formation that psychotherapists go through is tantamount to the development of philosophies of science and practice. It may be a personal philosophy or one shared by colleagues in a department, school, or professional organization. It is nevertheless a conceptual guide to conducting and understanding research as well as clinical practice (Kendall, Butcher, & Holmbeck, 1999; Polkinghorne, 1986).

Arriving at a place of conceptual clarity vis-à-vis psychotherapeutic theories and a Christianity-theories relationship is far from an exact or predictable process. However, the process need not be hopeless or haphazard. We propose three broad approaches to intentionally enhance conceptual clarity. One, a common factors approach, is well established. The second, a rubric for theoretical criteria, is a proposal to establish descriptive criteria for theories of psychotherapy. Third, discriminating between theories and treatment models, is an established issue that is still seldom addressed. Admittedly all are exploratory efforts and will hopefully be heuristic. All are meant to stimulate discussion around how Christian psychotherapists and psychotherapy students can develop clear understandings of the profession and of themselves as persons and professionals.

Common Factors

Some researchers have suggested that common factors across all therapeutic modalities are responsible for treatment effectiveness, more than effects of any particular therapeutic approach (Carkhuff & Berenson, 1967; Corrigan, Dell, Lewis, & Schmidt, 1980; Hubble, Duncan, & Miller, 1999; Weinberger, 2002). Multiple studies confirm, for example, that a psychotherapist's warmth, regardless of the treatment modality employed in sessions, is associated with positive client outcomes. A placebo effect of treatment, or the client's simple expectation of progress, has also been demonstrated to be a catalyst of positive change in therapy, again regardless of the specific treatment approach.

Given the proliferation of multiple treatment modalities from which to choose for positive therapeutic outcomes and the evidence for common factors across various modalities, it is perhaps not surprising that in the last 40 years, movements for psychotherapeutic eclecticism or integration, have developed. Writers proposing the integration[1] of psychotherapies argue that no single theoretical system can account for, and meet, all therapeutic needs. They suggest instead that the use of flexible, varied treatment approaches is necessary to accommodate the multifaceted nature of human experience, rather than strict adherence to one narrowly defined, limited psychotherapeutic modality (Brammer, Shostrom, & Abrego, 1993; Carter, 2002; Prochaska & Norcross, 1999).

The prevalence of these ideas is evident in surveys of psychotherapists. Norcross and his colleagues undertook surveys in 1981, 1991, and 2001 (Norcross, Hedges, & Castle, 2002). Across the three surveys, more than one-third of the psychotherapists who practiced psychotherapy described themselves as eclectic; eclecticism was by far the largest group. Jensen, Bergin, and Greaves (1990) obtained a broad sampling of psychotherapists, including psychologists and psychiatrists. Jensen et al. found that 59% (psychiatrists) to 70% (clinical psychologists) of the groups sampled regarded themselves as eclectic. While the figures vary, it is clear that a substantial number of psychotherapists, including psychologists, draw upon multiple theories to inform their clinical practices. Such a strategy, however, is no solution for syncretism; indeed, it may increase the risk of syncretism.

Eclecticism need not be de facto syncretistic. One of the more widely respected attempts at a form of eclecticism, known as Therapeutic Integration, is found in the writing of Paul Wachtel (1977). Wachtel provides a model for the harmonious interaction among diverse theories of treatment. His efforts toward integration of psychotherapeutic theories helped establish the potential and validity of the integration movement (Prochaska & Norcross, 1999). More recently, he reworked his original formulation to include further developments in psychotherapy, such as general system theory (Wachtel, 1997).

Even with prototypes such as Wachtel (1977, 1997), the task of psychotherapeutic integration is not for the faint of heart; it is more complex than assumed by perhaps too many psychotherapists. Given that the pluralistic praxis of daily experiences for psychotherapists is often complicated and challenging, conceptual clarity is a sine qua non. Unfortunately, more than one observer has noted that attempts at theoretical integration are often haphazard, unsystematic, internally conflicted, and arbitrary (Ginter, 1988; Norcross, 1986; Patterson, 1990). In other words, many psychotherapists function in a syncretistic manner.

The worst results of syncretism are conceptual confusion and ineffectiveness in treatment (McBride & Martin, 1990; Smith, 1982; Travis, 2003). In syncretism, the psychotherapist lacks overall organizing principles to guide treatment—the map is flawed or incomplete. As the descriptions of mental health and goals of therapy can vary across theories of psychotherapy, the syncretistic psychotherapist may unknowingly drift amidst competing, and potentially contradictory, notions of treatment plans and methods.

Understanding theoretical constructs is often difficult. Yet application of theory is even more difficult. Psychotherapy students often complain it is hard to put a theory into practice, as it ideally appears in a text or video. Even an experienced psychotherapist may have trouble clearly describing the theory drawn upon and its appearance in clinical situations. Conceptual clarity is essential, though, if psychotherapy is to fulfill its claim and potential to provide scientifically based services (Deegear & Lawson, 2003; McPherson, 1992; Striker, 2002). . . .

Figure 1

Major Pieces in the Development of Theories and Models

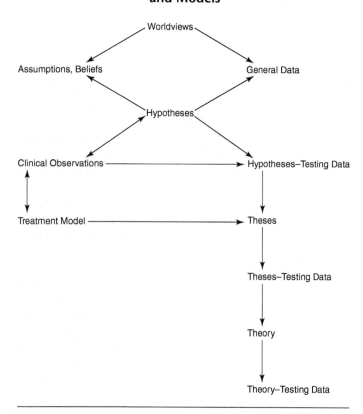

Distinctions Between Theories and Models

A major detraction from theoretical clarity exists around use of the term "theory." It is typically used inaccurately, with vague definitions and criteria (Blocher, 1987). As applied here, a theory is a formally organized collection of facts, definitions, constructs, and testable propositions that are meaningfully interrelated (Kendall et al., 1999; Mullins, 1971; Wallsten et al, 2000).

Few of the hundreds of "theories" meet most of the rubric's fourteen criteria. Probably none fulfill all of the criteria. Most of what are called theories are more accurately called treatment models. They develop in a process parallel to theories and share some features with theories (see Figure 1). A treatment model usually identifies therapy goals, processes, and methods thought to be helpful, but lack clarity about specific, foundational theses and hypotheses that support the use of certain treatment strategies. Instead, the assessment of helpfulness usually follows from clinical experiences of the person(s) who developed

the model. While possibly useful and immediately applicable, a treatment model lacks the formal organization and verification of a theory (Blocher, 1987). It is possible for a treatment model to develop into a theory (Figure 1), however few do so.

Figure 1 traces major pieces in the development of theories and models. While a two-dimensional illustration suggests this development is linear and sequential, the actual process is more like a hologram: a three-dimensional sphere with worldviews . . . in the center and the other pieces arranged around the center, linked to each other through reciprocal feedback loops. Ideally, the process is open to new information on a selective basis (i.e., based on theory construction criteria), which balances change with organization and stability (Bertalanffy, 1968; Keeney & Ross, 1985).

Worldviews pervade all other theory development processes, as discussed in the section on theory development criteria. These cognitions directly affect the assumptions and beliefs a psychotherapist applies to creating, interpreting, and applying a theory or model. Insofar as they influence all aspects of theory, conceptual neutrality is impossible (MacDonald, 1991; Sue & Sue, 2003). A psychotherapist, for example, who holds the belief that the world is basically a safe place may tend to draw attention to instances of safety in the life of a client who was physically abused as a child and overlook the client's own view of the world as essentially a dangerous place.

Worldviews relate reciprocally with general life data. Worldviews are influenced by learning experiences and, in turn, affect what people perceive and how they interpret their perceptions. While genetically transmitted temperaments provide broad parameters for worldviews, daily life experiences affect the particular manifestations of these temperaments (Kristal, 2005). Say, for instance, both the psychotherapist and client in the previous paragraph are born with a temperament of approach to human relations or sociability. The psychotherapist's overall life experiences of trust and security in relationships, . . . builds on this inherent tendency. The client's experiences of pain and betrayal in significant relationships, however, prompt an approach-avoidance conflict around relationships (i.e., temperament plus positive experiences prompt formation of relationships, while potent negative experiences signal danger in human relations).

Assumptions and beliefs and general life data, with their worldviews substrate, combine to foster hypotheses about psychotherapy in general and about specific clients (Figure 1). Thus, the personal life of the psychotherapist is an active participant in the conceptualization and execution of treatment processes (Corey, Corey, & Callanan, 2003; Tjeltveit, 1986). Hypotheses, then, have a recursive relationship with clinical observations, wherein the psychotherapist notes how clients act vis-à-vis their personalities, therapeutic issues, and the therapeutic setting (including the psychotherapist), while the personalities, issues, and setting influence the psychotherapist.

Psychotherapy hypotheses are also tested as to their veracity. That is, the psychotherapist checks the validity and reliability of conceptualizations about an individual or a group of clients (e.g., those diagnosed with bulimia). The psychotherapist systematically collects and tests data pertinent to therapeutic hypotheses. This is where the criteria of the rubric may be especially useful. Testing usually involves a few clients and may consist of parametric, nonparametric, or qualitative research designs and statistics (Beutler, 2000; Striker, 2002).

The hypothesis-testing of therapeutic data demarcates the divergence of theory development from treatment model development (Figure 1). With the latter, clinical observations and inferences from them remain the primary data. The treatment model might be a valid and reliable representation of clients and psychotherapy, but subjectivity precludes such determinations (Campbell & Stanley, 1966). Data that are systematically collected and analyzed, plus clinical observations and inferences, afford a broader platform upon which to build theoretical constructs (Kendall et al., 1999). . . .

Well developed and tested hypotheses allow for thesis construction. Theses, of course, guide formal data collection and analyses. From theses-testing, the psychotherapist has a clear data-based foundation for theory building. Theoretical constructions, in turn, are tested, retained, rejected, or modified (Carter, 2002; Mullins, 1971; Persons, 1991). Theory development through theses-testing does not guarantee unambiguous results, eliminate subjectivity, or partition out worldviews, but effects of these factors are easier to identify and explain when referenced to specific data.

Discussion in this section summarized general conceptual development of psychotherapeutic treatment models and theories. Even though most psychotherapists do not develop a formal theory or model, they either adopt an existing approach to psychotherapy or create a personal one (Corsini, 2000). This process yields optimal conceptual clarity when the psychotherapist manages it in the intentional, explicit manner of theory development.

Choosing a Theory or Model

At some point the psychotherapist chooses one or more theories or models as a means to work with people. This choice typically occurs in a preparation program (Capuzzi & Gross, 1995), although it is not limited to this period of time and the psychotherapist may subsequently add to the choice or even change entirely. Regardless of the timing, psychotherapists often experience direct or de facto pressure to make one of three choices: (a) align with one theory or model, (b) take an intentional eclectic or integration stance, or (c) do not think about it, thereby opening the door to syncretism. The preferred professional route, as discussed shortly, is either aligning with one theory or taking an intentionally eclectic stance. Both of these preferred choices are deliberate, systematic, and have their respective benefits and limitations. Unfortunately, some research suggests that psychotherapists who choose the third option of not thinking about it can be unaware of the degree to which they have adopted a de facto syncretistic approach to treatment.

Researchers have distinguished, for example, between those practitioners who are *explicitly eclectic*, who are aware of and intentional regarding their modalities of preference, and those who do not endorse an eclectic approach, but who nevertheless employ terminology and techniques from a variety of theories. This latter group has been described as *implicitly eclectic* (Hollanders, 1999). Findings surrounding the phenomenon of implicit eclecticism suggest that some practitioners in the process of theory adoption opt for the not-think-about-it stance, as listed above, or invest so little intellectual energy in a single theory or in an eclectic stance that it is almost the same as not thinking about the process altogether (Omer & Dar, 1992). It is this choice that fosters syncretism.

Selecting and staying with one theory or model has a number of benefits. Psychotherapists who commit themselves to the study and application of one theory or model have the potential to achieve a type of professional integrity in their practice of psychotherapy. They may be less prone to alteration by vacillations within the profession arising from, for example, treatment fads or pressures from external sources, such as insurance companies or public opinion (Prochaska & Norcross, 1999). These psychotherapists may be more likely to offer a consistent, balanced vision of treatment via their given modalities of intervention. In addition, adherence to a single theory or model allows for an enriched dialogue among similarly committed professionals who share the common knowledge of its language, ideas and history. This shared dialogue further augments the possibilities for development of the theory or model within professional societies over time. Finally, commitment to one theory or model may foster an appreciation not only of its unique advantages and limitations in psychotherapy, but also of its differences from other theories and models.

Syncretism, with its hodge-podge of multiple treatment elements, increases the possibility for the distinctiveness and organization of each theory or model, with its particular terminology and application, to be lost. This may result, paradoxically, in the lack of appreciation for, or even awareness of, the genuine diversity that exists across conceptual and treatment approaches.

Part of the difficulty in selecting and employing "theories," however, is that many of them are actually treatment models (ref. Figure 1), which are often less articulated than many psychotherapists find useful. The less articulated a model is, of course, the harder a psychotherapist must work to make sense of the model and to apply it. The assumption here is that no treatment strategy optimally coheres outside of the more comprehensive, schematic system afforded by a theory (Kendall et al., 1999). Perhaps the psychotherapist works out a personal resolution to the unexplained parts of a treatment model, creating individual theses and hypotheses where none have been formally articulated by proponents of the model. It is also possible, though, that the psychotherapist remains unclear about what the model means and how to implement it.

While this lack of comprehensiveness in models is problematic for psychotherapists, the adoption of a personal resolution surrounding the missing elements of a model may create other difficulties. This strategy unwittingly encourages the formation by multiple psychotherapists of idiosyncratic conceptualizations around a single model, each of which is tailor-made for and by the therapist in question, yet each of which bears the same name, and is promoted as reflecting the original model upon which it was based. This in itself may serve as a catalyst for some degree of confusion, rather than clear communication, among psychotherapists and consumers of therapeutic services.

Despite these difficulties, going the route of a treatment model has definite appeal. For one, it has fewer steps and is a faster route than theory-building (Omer & Dar, 1992) (Figure 1). Second, the usual datum of proof, "clinical observations," has a way of supporting existing hypotheses (Travis, 2003). That is, the subjectivity and arbitrariness of these observations makes it very difficult to validate their accuracy between observers. The observations are what Campbell and Stanley (1966) called case studies or crude correlations. Case studies or crude correlations may provide nominal data that are helpful in stimulating further research, but neither is sufficient in the long-term for inferring causality or systemic relational patterns.

Research in cognition identifies a tendency to focus upon and recall selectively that information which supports original ideas, a reasoning fallacy known as *confirmation bias. Belief perseverance,* a reasoning fallacy similar to confirmation bias, further complicates the problem. According to research examining belief perseverance, people tend to adhere to their original ideas, regardless of the presence of disconfirming evidence. While these studies in cognition considered the problematic reasoning of the average individual in everyday situations, anecdotal evidence also exists to support the existence of these fallacies in academic and scientific reasoning as well (Eysenck & Keane, 2000; Howard, 1985; Reisberg, 1997). As Tjeltveit (1986) demonstrated, psychotherapists also succumb to reasoning fallacies in their practical, daily work with clients and in how they think about working with clients. Theories, with their inherent processes of verification that are involved in their establishment and development, allow for greater challenges to reasoning fallacies such as confirmation bias and belief perseverance.

Knowing What to Believe: Strategies Toward the Prevention of Syncretism

Unfortunately, preparation programs may inadvertently encourage the development of syncretism among students. This implicit encouragement comes about when programs feel appropriately obligated to present students with the widest possible exposure to various treatment theories and models. The syncretistic effect compounds where faculty teach no differentiation between theories and models. At the same time, constraints on programs (e.g., administrative budget, faculty experience) may make it impossible to teach each of these approaches at sufficient depth or breadth to foster conceptual sophistication. Given this challenge, how might preparation programs provide opportunities for students both to grasp the diversity of theories and models available to psychotherapists today, while steering clear of the conceptual compromises accompanying syncretism?

Many programs offer at least one survey course in multiple therapeutic modalities (APA, 2003). In addition to its presentation of various approaches to treatment, this course could also include sections examining the broad distinctions between theories and models, and the relative benefits and challenges of each. Examining and applying the 14 criteria for a theory may help students comprehend significant issues involved when selecting a theory or model, or when considering some form of eclecticism or integration (MacDonald, 1991). Current research on common factors might be included as a topic for this course, allowing the student as well to consider the importance of factors beyond modality that impact treatment efficacy. In addition, this course might examine the movement for therapeutic integration, with its more sophisticated exemplars (e.g., Watchel, 1977, 1997). Finally, explicit discussion regarding the problems of syncretism might be included in a survey course covering multiple approaches to treatment. Faculty could describe examples of syncretistic analyses in class as an effort to illuminate their limitations.

It might be essential to cover philosophies of science and practice in a preparation program. These broad topics would provide students general worldviews through which they could evaluate theories and models. . . . Inasmuch as psychology and allied professions prematurely truncated the close relationship with its parent discipline, philosophy (MacDonald, 1991, 1996; Miller, 2005), the helping professions have unknowingly suffered from a lack of conceptual breadth and perspective. Addressing philosophy of science in a course or courses should help speak to this lack. . . .

Philosophies of science and practice in psychotherapy courses might consider the strengths and the limitations of the scientific enterprise in general, as well as the many variables which impact the development and application of psychotherapy over time. Such perspectives may allow the Christian therapist greater understanding when examining various psychotherapeutic theories or models. . . .

Following a preliminary course introducing several theories and models, students might be encouraged to focus upon one or two for the remainder of their preparation. This choice would hopefully impact the focus and themes of various papers they construct in classes. . . .

Supervision of therapy is another opportunity for preparation to focus upon one modality (Matarozzo & Garner, 1992). For individual supervision, programs could intentionally assign students to supervisors based on that supervisor's preferred treatment theory or model, allowing the student an extended opportunity to observe the elements of that approach in a mentoring relationship. Supervisors might also assign to supervisees readings composed by the major contributors to the theory or model under consideration. Supervisees could be taught to prepare in their client progress notes a written summary of the components of sessions, specifically utilizing the language and ideas of the specific model, to bring each time to supervision. In group supervision, supervisors might distribute information about one case to supervisees, with each supervisee assigned to describe that case from the perspective of a distinct theory or model before the group.

Fundamental to each of these suggestions is the need to be more intentional with the preparation of psychotherapists in order to foster greater conceptual clarity and to reduce the likelihood of syncretistism. The rapid proliferation of new therapies has created a situation in which the explicit discussion of the choice for therapeutic stance becomes all the more important. A student's eventual clinical efficacy as a psychotherapist, and thus even the future direction of psychotherapy as a valid resource for the community, necessitates clarity about communication and choices regarding therapeutic modalities.

Note

1. We realize that some authors distinguish between eclecticism and the more recent term of integration. To complicate matters further, the term integration has been used for several decades to denote efforts to bring Christian faith and psychology together. It is beyond the scope of our article to discern between eclecticism and integration. Since the terms overlap substantially, we use them interchangeably. We also assume that most psychotherapists who are Christians wish to integrate their faith and their craft, understanding that some differ on this point.

Don MacDonald is a professor of marriage and family therapy in the psychology department at Seattle Pacific University. He received his PhD in counseling psychology at Michigan State University in 1984. His interests include the theological, philosophical, and historical influences of Christianity and psychology.

Marcia Webb is an associate professor in the Department of Clinical Psychology at Seattle Pacific University. She is involved in the Living Well Initiative, a multidisciplinary program providing education and conducting research about severe and persistent mental illnesses. Her research emphasizes forgiveness, the self-conscious emotions of shame and guilt, the integration of psychology and theology, and the psychology of religion.

EXPLORING THE ISSUE

Should Therapists Be Eclectic?

Critical Thinking and Reflection

1. What are the advantages and disadvantages inherent in an eclectic approach and a single-theory approach?
2. Consider how you would go about selecting a theoretical orientation. What factors would be most important in deciding whether to adhere to one theory over another and why?
3. What hidden biases motivate the authors of the YES and NO selections to promote either an eclectic or a single-theory approach?
4. Are eclectic approaches ever truly capable of being systematic if they are created from diverse theories and techniques? State your own position on this issue and describe your justification for endorsing it.
5. Are there instances where a single-theory approach can draw from ideas and techniques that are not traditionally a part of that system?

Is There Common Ground?

The two positions reflected in these articles are not nearly so far apart as it may at first seem. In neither instance is there to be found any direct condemnation of eclecticism as a viable perspective in therapy. What is condemned is syncretism—the adoption of a garbled mess of inconsistent and mutually exclusive ideas and practices in the hopes of just finding something that works. Each of the authors agree that such a state of affairs would be a bad thing for therapy.

In addition to condemning syncretism, each of the authors agree in a few other fundamental ways. For example, there is agreement that psychotherapy is something that can genuinely help people. There is also agreement that the common factors of successful psychotherapy form a good foundation for the creation and evaluation of various therapeutic models and techniques. Furthermore, there is agreement that even "eclectic" therapists must convey an internally consistent and sensible explanation of illness and its remedies to a patient in order for successful therapy to take place.

Finally, there is agreement that eclectic therapeutic models carry the inherent risk of syncretism if careful thought is not given to the matter by therapists, researchers, and theorists. Indeed, for many psychotherapists and

therapy researchers, careful reflection on the nature of therapy and therapeutic change is thought to be one of the most important things to which time and effort can be devoted. Certainly, a given psychologist can believe that subscribing to a single theory is wise because it is inherently true. Similarly, another psychologist can believe that the truth value of a given theory is irrelevant so long as it is consistent and produces the desired results. Either way, therapists must take upon themselves the burden of their clients' mental well-being, and they owe it to their clients to give careful thought to the issue of why they are doing what they are doing.

Additional Resources

Brooks-Harris, J. E. (2008). *Integrative Multitheoretical Psychotherapy*. Boston, MA: Houghton-Mifflin.

Lazarus, A. A. (2005). Multimodal therapy. In *Handbook of Psychotherapy Integration* (2nd ed., pp. 105–120), J. C. Norcross and M. R. Goldfried (Eds.). New York, NY: Oxford.

Good, G. E., and Beitman, B. D. (2006). *Counseling and Psychotherapy Essentials: Integrating Theories, Skills, and Practices*. New York, NY: W. W. Norton.

Internet References . . .

Integrated Psychotherapy

http://www.integratedpsychotherapy.com/

Psych Central

http://psychcentral.com/therapy.htm

Unit 7

UNIT

Social Issues

*S*ocial psychology is the study of humans in their social environments. For example, a social psychologist might ask how the social environment of torture affects a prisoner. Is coercive interrogation (possibly torture) a good method of gaining important information, or is it a waste of time that only does psychological harm? What can psychologists contribute to these questions? How much are social environments responsible for female mating preferences? Might mating preferences be more influenced by innate genetic and thus evolutionary factors? What about the relatively recent changes in our social environment? Some psychologists have pointed to the recent upsurge of sexually explicit "societal and cultural messages" on the Internet and other media. Could this upsurge lead to problems, such as pornography and sexual addictions in general? Do such addictions even exist?

Selected, Edited, and with Issue Framing Material by:
Edwin E. Gantt, *Brigham Young University*

ISSUE

Can Psychotherapy Change Sexual Orientation?

YES: Joseph Nicolosi, A. Dean Byrd, and Richard W. Potts, from "Retrospective Self-Reports of Changes in Homosexual Orientation: A Consumer Survey of Conversion Therapy Clients," *Psychological Reports* (2000)

NO: Pan American Health Organization, from "'Cures' for An Illness That Does Not Exist," PAHO (2012)

Learning Outcomes

After reading this issue, you will be able to:

- Understand some of the major ways in which encouraging or demanding that an individual change his or her sexual orientation might affect them.
- Determine if psychotherapy is ever an effective means of changing sexual orientation.
- Discuss whether being able to freely choose therapy to change one's sexual orientation or being forced into it could affect the outcomes for and experiences of clients.

ISSUE SUMMARY

YES: Nicolosi, Byrd, and Potts surveyed a large number of individuals who self-identified as homosexual—both before and after receiving conversion therapy—to determine whether the therapy was an effective means of changing sexual orientation.

NO: PAHO asserts that there is no scientific evidence for the effectiveness of sexual reorientation efforts, and that efforts aimed at changing non-heterosexual orientations lack medical justification. The PAHO statement views "conversion therapies" as threats to personal autonomy and to personal integrity.

Few contemporary social and political issues are more controversial than those relating to sexual orientation and homosexuality. Opinions on this topic run strong and vary widely based on differing social, political, moral, and religious views. While the debate in today's political landscape often centers on the legality of homosexual marriage, topics relating to homosexuality have a complicated history with psychology and psychiatry. A few decades ago the Diagnostic and Statistical Manual of Mental Disorders listed homosexuality as a mental disorder in the category of sexual deviations. In 1973, social norms, the views of some experts, and an active gay community in the United States led the American Psychiatric Association to remove homosexuality from the DSM, despite the fact that some

psychiatrists strongly opposed this change. Today, however, the American Psychological Association states quite straightforwardly that lesbian, gay, and bisexual orientations "represent normal forms of human experience." Yet some aspects of homosexuality still elicit differing professional opinions, in particular the notion of sexual orientation change efforts (SOCE).

SOCE, also known as "reparative therapies" or "conversion therapies," involve individuals seeking help from distress caused by an unwanted sexual orientation and are typically administered in faith-based ministries and clinics. While proponents see these treatments as a valuable option available to those seeking relief from a burden defined within personal moral guidelines, opponents take offense at the notion that homosexuality could or should be treated at all. Conflicting research findings have further complicated the issue. The APA has attempted to clarify the issues by expressing concern over the safety of any therapy "promoted to modify sexual orientation." A recently enacted California law bars the application of SOCE techniques to minors. On the other hand, supporters of SOCE treatments argue that some research supports the effectiveness and safety of efforts to alter an unwanted sexual orientation.

Psychologists Joseph Nicolosi, A. Dean Byrd, and Richard W. Potts, three prominent SOCE researchers, present research that they say demonstrates the possibility of sexual orientation change among those individuals who desire it. In this research, they report the results of an extensive survey of 882 homosexual individuals dissatisfied with their sexual attraction regarding their beliefs about conversion therapy and the possibility of change in sexual orientation. Nicolosi, Byrd, and

Potts report that as a group the participants reported large and statistically significant reductions in the frequency of their homosexual thoughts and fantasies, which they attributed primarily to conversion therapy or self-help. The individuals surveyed also reported large improvement in their psychological, interpersonal, and spiritual well-being. The authors cite this evidence to support the possibility that homosexual orientation is changeable.

The Pan American Health Organization, on the other hand, argues that SOCE does not have sufficient scientific evidence to support the claim that a person's sexual orientation can change. The organization argues that for non-heterosexual people to be treated with respect, their LGBT identities must be accepted. To try and change a person's sexual orientation is to take away some of their autonomy and that governments, therapists, the media, etc. should refrain from supporting reparative therapies.

POINT

- SOCE patients have reported significant changes in sexual orientation.
- The specific subjects involved in this research were highly motivated to seek a change and demonstrate the realm of what is possible.
- Clients who desire to change their sexual orientation should be given the opportunity to access the tools to do so.

- Those seeking change reported no negative effects of treatment.

COUNTERPOINT

- Some former SOCE clients report going back to a homosexual orientation after treatment.
- The samples used at religious ministries do not represent a normal population from which to draw conclusions.

- SOCE misrepresents the possibility of successful change, giving false hope of changing what is likely a permanent feature of sexuality.
- Self-report measures are unreliable from those who are religiously motivated and seeking change in sexual orientation.

YES

Joseph Nicolosi, A. Dean Byrd, and Richard W. Potts

Retrospective Self-Reports of Changes in Homosexual Orientation: A Consumer Survey of Conversion Therapy Clients

The treatment of homosexuality has a long history in the psychiatric and psychological professions. Beginning with Sigmund Freud at the turn of the 20th century, many clinicians since then have attempted to help homosexual clients. Psychoanalysis, psychoanalytically oriented psychotherapy, a wide variety of behavioral therapies, and a variety of group psychotherapy approaches have all been utilized to help homosexual clients. Reviews of the literature on the outcome of such therapies indicate that therapists reported considerable success at helping homosexual people minimize and overcome their homosexual behaviors and attractions.

Despite these reports of dierapeutic success, during the late 1970s the treatment of homosexuality and research evaluating its efficacy came to a virtual halt. The major reason for this is that on December 14, 1973, the Board of Trustees of the American Psychiatric Association voted to remove homosexuality as an abnormal diagnostic category from the association's Diagnostic and Statistical Manual (DSM). In January 1975 the governing body of the American Psychological Association voted to support the American Psychiatric Association's decision. With the removal of homosexuality from the DSM, many mental health professionals felt it was no longer necessary to treat homosexuality, and most researchers lost interest in investigating whether homosexual orientation could be changed.

. . .

In response to requests for assistance from dissatisfied homosexually oriented people; that is, from people who do not value the gay lifestyle and culture and who desire assistance in controlling and changing their homosexual attractions and behavior, some mental health professionals and pastoral counselors have persisted in providing sexual reorientation or conversion therapies.

All conversion therapy approaches have in common the goal of attempting to help dissatisfied homosexually oriented people learn to resist and minimize their homosexual behaviors, thoughts, and feelings so that they can live more happily within the mainstream heterosexual culture which they value. The approaches differ in terms of their theoretical orientation, techniques, and view of the origins of homosexuality. There are several contemporary approaches to conversion therapy, including psychoanalytic, psychodynamic, and Christian or pastoral approaches. Some therapists also use an integrative approach that combines elements from psychodynamic, cognitive-behavioral, family systems, and spiritual therapy perspectives.

During the past several years, a number of professionals have provided a theoretical and ethical defense of why conversion therapies are needed in contemporary society. Essentially, they have argued that all homosexual people have the right to choose and pursue their own values and lifestyle. It people wish to affirm their homosexuality and pursue a gay lifestyle, they have the right to seek gay affirmative therapy. If they wish to minimize their homosexual tendencies and pursue a heterosexual lifestyle, dissatisfied homosexually oriented people have the right to seek conversion therapy. Theoretical rationales which articulate why conversion therapies are effective and clinical guidelines describing how to do it have been provided. There is also some clinical evidence which supports the efficacy of conversion therapies.

During the past two decades, conversion therapists have sometimes been criticized as being unenlightened, prejudiced, homophobic, and unethical. Some professionals have argued that the only ethical treatment option for all homosexual people is gay affirmative therapy. Some gay activists within the American Psychological Association have publicly acknowledged that it is their desire to have the APA Council of Representatives declare conversion therapies as unethical on the grounds that such therapies are harmful to homosexually oriented people.

. . .

In the on-going professional debate about the ethical appropriateness and effectiveness of conversion therapies, it is crucial for additional research to be done with these approaches. As mentioned above, some clinical and antidotal evidence already indicates that conversion therapies are helpful to some people. However, in light of continuing allegations that conversion therapies are harmful, and that no evidence exists to support their efficacy, additional studies are needed that investigate and document what types of people have been helped by such therapies, and in what way they have been helped. Such studies may help therapists sort out "fact from fiction" in this controversial area.

The purpose of this article is to report the results of a survey in which we asked a large sample of dissatisfied homosexually oriented people who have attempted to change their sexual orientation about their experience with conversion therapy. We asked participants to share their experiences about a variety of issues, including (1) whether conversion therapy has been helpful to them, (2) what types of changes have they experienced in their sexual orientation, (3) what types of emotional and psychological changes have they experienced since making efforts lo change their sexual orientation, and (4) what influences were most helpful in their efforts to change. By surveying a large number of people who have made efforts to change their sexual orientation, the present survey allowed us to examine the ways people who have actually experienced conversion therapy believe that they have been helped or harmed.

Method

Survey Description

The first page of the survey explained that the purpose of the survey was to "explore the experiences of individuals who have struggled with homosexuality during a time in their lives, were dissatisfied with that orientation, and have since sought and experienced some degree of change." It also explained that "participation in this study is completely voluntary and anonymous. You may choose not to participate, and you have the right to refuse to answer any question." The survey participants were also instructed to mail the completed survey directly to the first author.

There were 70 questions on the survey. Participants were asked to provide (1) basic background and demographic information, (2) information about their past and current sexual orientation, behaviors, and experiences, (3) information about their experiences with conversion therapy, (4) information about self-help change efforts they had made, and (5) information about their past and current psychological functioning. In making the ratings about their past functioning, participants were asked to recall the time in life when they were most strongly experiencing homosexual thoughts, feelings, or behaviors and to rate how they perceived their sexual and psychological functioning at that time. They were then asked to rate their current sexual and psychological functioning. These ratings were all made on 7-point Likert type scales, which gave participants the opportunity to provide a full range of responses (very poor to very good, very little to very much, very much to none). Thus, the items and responses were worded so as not to bias participants' responses in a positive or negative direction. There were also five open-ended questions that asked participants to share their perceptions about the therapy they had received, e.g., what about it was helpful, the self-help change efforts they had engaged in, and the changes they had experienced.

. . .

Statistical Analysis

Basic descriptive statistics, i.e., means, medians, frequencies, percentages, were computed to describe the characteristics of the participants. Chi-square tests and paired t tests were used to assess whether the frequency of the participants' homosexual behaviors and their perceptions of their psychological, interpersonal and spiritual well-being changed.

As a measure of clients' deterioration, all participants who indicated that they were doing more poorly after conversion therapy than before treatment on three or more of the well-being items were identified (even if they indicated they were doing better after treatment on the rest of the well-being items). Given that critics say conversion therapy harms clients, we felt it was important to examine the data carefully for evidence of possible harm or deterioration; hence, our rather stringent criteria of clients' deterioration.

We also qualitatively analyzed the participants' written responses to the open-ended questions using the constant comparison method. First, each written response was typed and coded. This yielded 280 pages of responses. We then printed two copies of all participants' responses. One remained intact, while the third author cut up the other one with scissors into meaningful units. The second step was emergent category designation. During this step, the third author took the units of data from Step 1 and sorted them into categories or themes. He followed this procedure until all units had been assigned to a category, one of which was a miscellaneous category. In this study, we considered major themes those in which the majority (at least 60%) of the participants provided relevant comments.

Participants

Eight hundred and eighty-two people returned the survey.[1] Six hundred and eighty-nine (78%) were men and 193 (22%) were women. The average age of the participants was 37.6 yr. and the median age was 37. Seven hundred and fifty-nine (86%) participants were Caucasian (probably mostly Euro-American) and 122 (14%) were of some other racial or ethnic background, e.g., African-American ($n = 17$), Asian ($n = 32$), Hispanic ($n = 31$), Native American ($n = 16$).

Of the participants 530 (60%) were Protestant, 103 (12%) Catholic, 79 (9%) Mormon, 8 (1%) Jewish, and 159 (18%) were some other religious faith. Eight hundred and forty-three (96%) participants said that religion or spirituality was very important to them, 35 (4%) said it was somewhat important, and 4 said it was not important. In light of this demographic finding, it is clear that the results of our survey cannot be generalized to *nonreligious* dissatisfied homosexually oriented people.

Dissatisfied homosexually oriented people from throughout the United States responded to the survey. The largest number of participants, 93 (12%), lived in California, 82 (11%) were from Texas, 44 (6%) were from New York, 43 were from Washington (6%), and 34 (5%) were from Florida. One to four percent of the rest of the participants were distributed throughout the other states. The participants were well educated as a group: 236 (27%) of the participants had a graduate degree, 95 (11%) had some graduate school training. 261 (30%) had completed a bachelor's degree, and 185 (21%) had some college education. Two hundred and eighty-one (32%) participants were married, 65 (7%) divorced, 12 (1%) separated, and 509 (59%) said they had never been married.

. . .

Two hundred and sixteen participants said they had participated in conversion therapy *only* with a professional therapist, 229 said they had participated in conversion therapy with *both* a professional therapist and a pastoral counselor; 223 said they had received treatment *only* from pastoral counselor. Another 156 said they had never received conversion therapy from a therapist or counselor but had made efforts to change on their own by doing things such as reading self-help literature, talking to friends and family, and attending conferences and meetings provided by Exodus, Evergreen International, and ex-gay ministries.[2] One hundred and eighty-eight participants said that their most helpful therapist was a pastoral counselor, 134 said a psychologist, 78 said a marriage and family therapist, 63 said a licensed clinical social worker, 25 said a psychiatrist, 13 said a psychoanalyst, and 155 did not know the training. Participants were not asked to speculate about their therapists' theoretical orientation.

. . .

Results

Table 1 indicates that as a group the participants reported retrospectively that they had experienced major changes in their sexual orientation, thoughts, and behaviors. Over 67% of the participants indicated they were exclusively homosexual or almost entirely homosexual at one time in their lives, whereas only 12.8% of them indicated that they now perceived themselves in this manner. Before treatment or change, only 2.2% of the participants perceived themselves as exclusively or almost entirely heterosexual, whereas after treatment or change 34.3% perceived themselves as exclusively or almost entirely heterosexual. As a group, the participants also reported statistically significant decreases in the frequency of their homosexual behavior with a partner from before to after treatment or change.

Of the 318 participants who viewed themselves as exclusively homosexual in their orientation before treatment or change, 56 (17.6%) reported that they now view themselves as exclusively heterosexual in their orientation, 53 (16.7%) now view themselves as almost entirely heterosexual, and 35 (11.1%) of them view themselves as more heterosexual than homosexual. Thus, 45.4% of the exclusively homosexual participants retrospectively reported having made major shifts in their sexual orientation. The exclusively homosexual participants also reported large and statistically significant decreases in the frequency of their homosexual behavior with a partner from before to after treatment or change.

---

[1]The numbers do not always add up to 882 because not all participants responded to every question.

[2]These numbers do not add to 882 because some participants reported that they have received therapy from both professional and nonprofessional therapists/counselors.

Table 1

Retrospective Self-reported Sexual Orientation and Behavior Change Data for Total Sample and Exclusively Homosexual Participants

Variable	Before[a]		Current[a]		χ^2	p
	n	%	*n*	%		
Total Sample						
Homosexual Orientation					201.3	<.00001
1. Exclusively homosexual	318	36.6	40	4.6		
2. Almost entirely homosexual	269	31.0	71	8.2		
3. More homosexual than heterosexual	192	22.1	194	22.3		
4. Equally homosexual and heterosexual	39	4.5	95	10.9		
5. More heterosexual than homosexual	32	3.7	171	19.7		
6. Almost entirely heterosexual	8	0.9	15	18.1		
7. Exclusively heterosexual	11	1.3	141	16.2		
Frequency of Homosexual Behavior with a Partner					84.1	<.00001
1. Very Often	253	29.6	8	0.9		
2.	127	14.8	11	1.3		
3.	144	16.8	19	2.2		
4.	84	9.8	23	2.7		
5.	53	6.2	44	5.1		
6.	80	9.3	125	14.6		
7. Never	115	13.4	626	73.1		
Exclusively Homosexual						
Homosexual Orientation						
1. Exclusively homosexual	318	100.0	37	11.6		
2. Almost entirely homosexual			36	11.3		
3. More homosexual than heterosexual			77	24.2		
4. Equally homosexual and heterosexual			22	6.9		
5. More heterosexual than homosexual			37	11.6		
6. Almost entirely heterosexual			53	16.7		
7. Exclusively heterosexual			56	17.6		
Frequency of Homosexual Behavior with a Partner					34.7	<.001
1. Very Often	117	37.1	1	0.3		
2.	44	14.0	3	1.0		
3.	56	17.8	4	1.3		
4.	30	9.5	6	1.9		
5.	13	4.1	16	5.1		
6.	23	7.3	35	11.1		
7. Never	32	10.2	250	79.4		

[a]Participants retrospectively rated their sexual orientation and behavior at a time in their lives *before* they had entered therapy or sought to change, and then rated their perceptions of their *current* sexual orientation and behavior.

There was evidence that the changes in sexual orientation reported by many of the participants were long lasting. The average length of time that had elapsed since the participants reported the changes in their sexual orientation was 6.7 yr. (*Mdn* = 5.0; range = less than 1 year to 40 years). Twenty-three percent of the participants said that it had been 10 or more years since they had experienced the changes in their orientation.

Table 2 documents the participants' self-reported perceptions of their psychological, interpersonal, and sexual status before and after treatment or change. The magnitude of retrospective change reported by the participants was large, ranging from 1 to 3 standard deviation units. Higher numbers indicate better functioning and so the participants reported that they were doing much better psychologically, interpersonally, and sexually after treatment or change. The magnitude of the change reported by the exclusively homosexual participants also ranged from 1 to 3 standard deviation units, again suggesting both statistically and clinically significant retrospective change and improvement.

Table 2

Retrospective Self-reported Sexual, Psychological, and Interpersonal Changes for Total Sample and Exclusively Homosexual Participants

Variable	N	Before[a]		Current[a]		t
		M	SD	M	SD	
Total Sample						
Self-acceptance	870	2.1	1.3	5.2	1.2	56.4
Self-understanding	873	2.0	1.1	5.6	1.1	72.1
Trust of opposite sex	873	2.9	1.8	4.8	1.5	30.2
Personal power	852	2.3	1.5	5.0	1.3	40.4
Self-esteem	865	2.0	1.3	5.0	1.3	56.1
Satisfying relationships	869	2.7	1.6	5.0	1.4	40.2
Emotional stability	867	2.3	1.4	5.1	1.3	48.3
Spirituality	867	2.8	1.6	5.6	1.2	42.0
Relationship with church	851	3.0	1.9	5.5	1.5	31.1
Relationship with God	863	2.8	1.7	5.7	1.3	41.9
Relationship with family	858	3.2	1.5	4.8	1.4	29.2
Depression	865	2.6	1.6	5.2	1.3	40.7
Frequency of homosexual thoughts	873	6.4	1.1	3.4	1.5	48.5
Intensity of homosexual thoughts	868	6.4	1.0	3.2	1.5	52.4
Frequency of masturbation (with homosexual fantasies)	865	5.6	1.7	2.6	1.5	43.3
Interest in heterosexual dating	756	2.4	1.7	4.4	2.1	22.5
Belief in the possibility of heterosexual marriage	751	2.9	2.1	5.3	1.9	27.4
Exclusively Homosexual						
Self-acceptance	319	2.0	1.3	5.2	1.1	36.0
Self-understanding	321	1.9	1.1	5.6	1.0	42.0
Trust of opposite sex	321	2.8	1.9	4.8	1.5	18.5
Personal power	315	2.1	1.4	5.0	1.3	27.4
Self-esteem	321	1.8	1.2	5.0	1.3	36.1
Satisfying relationships	319	2.4	1.6	5.0	1.5	25.7
Emotional stability	317	2.0	1.3	5.1	1.3	33.6
Spirituality	319	2.5	1.5	5.7	1.3	30.7
Relationship with church	308	2.5	1.8	5.7	1.5	24.3
Relationship with God	317	2.5	1.6	5.8	1.3	30.6
Relationship with family	313	2.9	1.5	4.7	1.5	19.6
Depression	318	5.6	1.5	1.7	1.2	29.5
Frequency of homosexual thoughts	321	6.7	0.7	3.4	1.5	35.3
Intensity of homosexual thoughts	319	6.7	0.7	3.1	1.5	38.9
Frequency of masturbation (with homosexual fantasies)	318	6.0	1.4	2.5	1.6	31.3
Interest in heterosexual dating	289	1.7	1.4	4.1	2.1	15.3
Belief in the possibility of heterosexual marriage	290	2.0	1.7	4.9	2.1	19.4

Note.—All comparisons were significant at *p.*<.001. "Participants retrospectively rated their sexual, psychological, and interpersonal functioning at a time in their lives *before* they had entered therapy or sought to change their sexual orientation and then rated their perceptions of their *current* sexual, psychological, and interpersonal functioning. Rating scale was a 7-point Likert scale.

A case by case analysis indicated that 34 (7.1%) of those participants who had received conversion therapy or both conversion therapy and pastoral counseling reported that they were doing worse on three or more of the psychological, interpersonal, and spiritual well-being items after treatment than before treatment. Thus, we concluded that these participants had deteriorated in some ways, at least, during their participation in conversion therapy.

Our qualitative analysis of the participants' responses to the open-ended questions yielded three major themes (at least 60% of the participants commented on each of these themes). We labeled Theme 1, *"Participants' views of homosexuality."* Within this theme, participants shared a variety of their beliefs about homosexuality: (1) homosexuality is wrong (sinful); (2) homosexuality is not in-born; (3) homosexuality is a learned or acquired behavior; (4) homosexuality is caused in part, at least, by a poor relationship with one's same-sex parent; (5) sexual abuse may contribute to the development of homosexual tendencies; (6) persons who struggle with homosexual thoughts and attractions are not perverted, evil, or defective; (7) homosexual behaviors are addictive and extremely difficult to overcome; and (8) persons who are strongly motivated can minimize and sometimes completely overcome their homosexual tendencies.

We labeled Theme 2, *"Perceived benefits of conversion therapies."* Within this theme, participants described specific ways they felt they had been helped by conversion therapies: (1) therapy helped them grow in self-esteem, self-understanding, and self-acceptance; (2) therapy helped free them from feelings of shame, guilt, self-condemnation, and unworthiness; (3) therapy helped them feel more accepted and loved; (4) therapy helped them feel more intimate—physically and emotionally—with their spouse; (5) therapy helped them decrease their homosexual thoughts and behaviors to varying extents (from "some reduction" in homosexual thoughts and behavior to "completely free" from such thoughts and behaviors); (6) therapy helped men feel more masculine and women more feminine; and (7) therapy helped them enjoy healthier relationships with others.

We labeled Theme 3, *"Mechanisms of change."* Within this theme, participants identified a number of specific influences that helped them heal and change: (1) support they received in group therapy; (2) individual counseling (professional and/or pastoral); (3) their personal spirituality and faith, e.g., scripture study, confession to spiritual leader, faith in God, prayer, experiencing God's love, acceptance, and forgiveness; (4) being accountable for one's behavior to friends, support groups, pastors; (5) understanding better the causes of their homosexuality and their emotional needs and issues; (6) developing nonsexual relationships with same-sex peers, mentors, family members, friends; (7) learning to maintain appropriate boundaries; (8) reading books, tapes, and conferences about homosexuality and change; (9) participating in organizations such as Evergreen and Exodus International; and (10) having a desire to change.

Finally, although we did not ask about this and it did not emerge as a major theme, approximately 3% or 4% of the participants expressed their frustration with previous psychotherapists who had devalued and ignored their wish to overcome their homosexual tendencies and who had attempted to impose gay affirmative therapy on them.

Discussion

This study was of self-reported data, which places some limitations on the conclusions that can be drawn. It is possible that the participants may have exaggerated the magnitude of the changes they have experienced due to social desirability or seeking approval. However, the anonymous nature of the survey may have helped minimize this possibility.

Due to the retrospective design, some participants may also have had difficulty accurately remembering how they were functioning before seeking treatment and change which could also have caused to them overestimate the benefits of conversion therapy or self-help. The nonrandom sample also limits our ability to generalize the findings of the survey. We cannot safely generalize our findings to all dissatisfied homosexually oriented people or to all people who have experienced conversion therapy. We can only safely draw conclusions about responses of the 882 participants whom we surveyed.

We also cannot draw any conclusions about what types of conversion therapy may be most helpful, e.g., psychoanalytic, reparative, cognitive-behavioral, spiritually oriented, etc. This question was beyond the scope and purpose of this survey, which was simply to document whether or not there are *any* dissatisfied homosexually oriented people who believe they have been helped by conversion therapy and to gain some insight into what ways they perceive that they have been helped.

The limitations acknowledged above do not mean that this survey has no scientific value. For most surveys given to clients in psychotherapy the sample of clients is nonrandom; the results have limited generalizability. Such surveys are still valuable, however, because they allow researchers to learn more about the attitudes of at least some clients and provide documentation about whether and how the clients believe a particular therapy was helpful to them. Such surveys allow researchers to assess whether there are *any* clients who believe that a specific type of therapy has helped them. It also allows researchers to gain some insight into what types of people are helped by the therapy and in what ways they believe it has benefited them. Over time, as numerous nonrandom studies such as this are done, a data base accumulates that collectively begins to give researchers and clinicians a clearer picture about the effectiveness and limitations of a given therapy approach.

Thus, despite the fact that we cannot safely generalize beyond our specific sample, this study is important because it documents the existence of a group of dissatisfied homosexually oriented people who experienced conversion therapy from professional therapists and pastoral counselors and perceived that they benefited. It provides clear *prima facie* evidence that conversion therapies and pastoral counseling do help at least *some* dissatisfied homosexually oriented people. Given the fact that 96% of the participants in our sample indicated that religion or spirituality was very important to them, we can only confidently conclude that some *religiously or spiritually devout* dissatisfied homosexually oriented people perceive that they have been helped by conversion therapy. We cannot say much about the question of whether nonreligious dissatisfied homosexually oriented people have been helped by such therapies. Research must address this question.

Our finding that approximately 20% to 30% of the participants said they shifted from a homosexual orientation to an exclusively or almost exclusively heterosexual orientation is consistent with numerous studies done in the 1960s and 1970s in which changes in homosexual orientation were reported as possible. It is also consistent with a more recent survey of 285 psychoanalysts who reported that 23% of the 1,215 homosexual patients they had treated made the transition to heterosexuality. Additional evidence that people can change their sexual orientation is underscored by a recent national survey on sexuality which indicated that some people change their sexual orientation even without psychotherapy and by our finding that some of the respondents to our survey perceived that they had changed through self-help efforts alone.

. . .

Not only did many participants report that they made significant changes in their sexual orientation and improvements in their interpersonal and psychological functioning, many reported that these changes were long lasting. The average reported length of time since the changes in sexual orientation and psychosocial growth had occurred was 6.7 yr., with many participants reporting that the changes had lasted much longer. This finding conflicts with the claims of critics who say that conversion therapies lift self-esteem and psychological well-being only superficially and temporarily by fostering conformity with social norms rather than psychological integration.

Our findings suggest that conversion therapies may be psychologically harmful for some people, which is of course true of all forms of psychotherapy. The finding that a small percentage (7.1%) of the participants we surveyed reported that they were doing worse in some ways after receiving conversion therapy underscores this point. Conversion therapy is not appropriate for all clients. Clients

who have decided they wish to affirm a gay identity and lifestyle could feel shamed and emotionally hurt if therapists attempted to impose conversion therapy on them. Conversion therapy is also inappropriate for clients who are ambivalent about their homosexual tendencies and who have not yet made a decision whether to affirm or overcome them. Gay affirmative therapy is also inappropriate for such clients. As with all forms of psychological and medical treatment, therapists must carefully assess whether a treatment is indicated or contraindicated for a given client at the beginning of treatment and over time as treatment progresses.

The finding that approximately 30% to 40% of the participants we surveyed reported that they continue to struggle to some extent with unwanted homosexual behaviors and thoughts, despite treatment and efforts to change, highlights the often reported clinical observation that overcoming homosexuality is not easy for many people. Our finding that the average length the participants had received therapy was 3.4 years further underscores this point. The change process is often difficult and lengthy, but many of the participants in our survey and in other studies have reported that to them it is worth it. As part of informed consent procedures, we think therapists need to tell prospective conversion therapy clients that the change process may be difficult and lengthy.

. . .

Some people have criticized dissatisfied homosexually oriented people's rejection of the gay lifestyle by arguing that they do so because they have internalized society's homophobia and that therapists who assist them in their efforts to change are only fostering this homophobia. Such critics, however, do not acknowledge the possibility that many people with unwanted homosexual tendencies reject the gay lifestyle, not because they are "homophobic" but because they have decided that they do not value it, and because they believe that God does not want them to pursue such a lifestyle. They have made an autonomous and difficult choice to let their religious beliefs and values take priority over their sexual urges and desires, often after failing in their efforts to accept a gay identity and find fulfillment in the gay lifestyle.

The American Psychological Association's ethical guidelines explicitly include religion as one type of diversity that psychologists are obligated to respect. If clients decide to reject the gay lifestyle and seek conversion therapy for religious or spiritual reasons, psychotherapists must respect their value choice rather than labeling such beliefs as homophobic and attempting to impose an alien value framework upon them. Trying to coerce dissatisfied homosexually oriented people who desire assistance in coping with and minimizing their homosexual tendencies into gay affirmative therapy is a violation of one of the mental health profession's most widely agreed upon ethical guidelines: respect for people's self-determination and autonomy.

Implications for Practice of Psychotherapy

In light of our finding that some dissatisfied homosexually oriented people believe that conversion therapy has helped them sexually, psychologically, socially, and spiritually, we think conversion therapy should remain a treatment option for clients who desire it. Psychotherapists should not impose gay affirmative or conversion therapy on their clients, but rather they should do their best to provide a professionally noncoercive environment that gives clients maximum freedom to express, explore, and clarify their values and beliefs about homosexuality.

When clients acknowledge that they have homosexual tendencies, we think that therapists should carefully assess their clients' beliefs and values about homosexuality to assess whether gay affirmative or conversion therapy is indicated. Clients who have made a decision that they would like to affirm and pursue a gay identity and lifestyle are probably most suitable for a gay affirmative therapy approach. Clients who for religious, spiritual, or other personal reasons have made a decision that they do not value the gay lifestyle and would like help in minimizing and overcoming their homosexual tendencies may benefit from a conversion therapy approach. When clients are ambivalent or uncertain about their sexual orientation, therapists should be especially careful not to assume or dictate what type of treatment would be best for them, but help them, if they wish, to explore and clarify their beliefs and values until they can decide for themselves what treatment option they would prefer.

We also think that therapists should openly and honestly discuss available treatment options with dissatisfied homosexually oriented clients. They should inform clients that many professionals believe that homosexuality cannot be changed and that the best treatment option is gay affirmative therapy. They should also inform clients that many other professionals believe that homosexuality can be minimized and overcome and that the best treatment option is conversion therapy. Therapists can also inform their clients that research is needed to demonstrate more convincingly the effectiveness of both gay affirmative and conversion therapy, and caution clients that not all people who participate in either gay affirmative or conversion therapy benefit from it. Therapists explain to their clients that there are no guarantees and that probably the best

criteria clients can use for deciding which type of therapy they would prefer is to select the approach that is most consistent with their values and goals.

Therapists should adhere to the American Psychological Association's ethical guideline to obtain "training, experience, consultation, or supervision necessary to ensure the competence of their services" when they encounter "differences of age, gender, race, ethnicity, national origin, religion, sexual orientation, disability, language, or socioeconomic status" that "significantly affect" their work. Psychotherapists should not only "ensure the competence of their services, or . . . make appropriate referrals" for gay people but should also do so for religious and other dissatisfied homosexually oriented people. In addition to receiving education and training in gay affirmative therapy and assumptions, we think therapists should also seek out education and training in conversion therapy. At the least, they should be prepared to refer sensitively and appropriately dissatisfied homosexually oriented clients to conversion therapists.

During the past couple of decades, mental health professionals have made great strides in becoming more sensitive to the needs and concerns of members of the gay community. Gay affirmative therapy was and is needed to protect the rights of homosexual people who have made the decision to affirm a gay identity and live the gay lifestyle. Conversion therapy is needed to protect the rights of dissatisfied homosexually oriented people who wish assistance in coping with and minimizing their unwanted homosexual tendencies. We think that it is time for mental health professionals to preserve the rights of *all* homosexually oriented people, gay or dissatisfied, religious or nonreligious, to choose and pursue their own values and lifestyle.

Joseph Nicolosi is the founder and former president of the National Association for Research and Therapy of Homosexuality, as well as the founder and director of the Thomas Aquinas Psychological Clinic in Encino, California. He is a licensed psychologist in California.

A. Dean Byrd was on faculty at the University of Utah School of Medicine, with appointments in the Department of Family Medicine and the Department of Psychiatry. He served as president of the National Association for Research and Therapy of Homosexuality. He passed away in April 2012.

Richard W. Potts received his post-doctoral training at Brigham Young University and currently works in the Utah Valley Psychiatry and Counseling Clinic.

Pan American Health Organization

"Cures" for an Illness That Does Not Exist: Purported therapies aimed at changing sexual orientation lack medical justification and are ethically unacceptable

Introduction

Countless human beings live their lives surrounded by rejection, maltreatment, and violence for being perceived as "different." Among them, millions are victims of attitudes of mistrust, disdain and hatred because of their sexual orientation. These expressions of homophobia are based on intolerance resulting from blind fanaticism as well as pseudo-scientific views that regard non-heterosexual and non-procreative sexual behavior as "deviation" or the result of a "developmental defect."

Whatever its origins and manifestations, any form of homophobia has negative effects on the affected people, their families and friends, and society at large. There is an abundance of accounts and testimonies of suffering; feelings of guilt and shame; social exclusion; threats and injuries; and persons who have been brutalized and tortured to the point of causing injuries, permanent scars and even death. As a consequence, homophobia represents a public health problem that needs to be addressed energetically.

While every expression of homophobia is regrettable, harms caused by health professionals as a result of ignorance, prejudice, or intolerance are absolutely unacceptable and must be avoided by all means. Not only is it fundamentally important that every person who uses health services be treated with dignity and respect; it is also critical to prevent the application of theories and models that view homosexuality as a "deviation" or a choice that can be modified through "will power" or supposed "therapeutic support".

In several countries of the Americas, there has been evidence of the continued promotion, through supposed "clinics" or individual "therapists," of services aimed at "curing" non-heterosexual orientation, an approach known as "reparative" or "conversion therapy."[1] Worryingly, these services are often provided not just outside the sphere of public attention but in a clandestine manner. From the perspective of professional ethics and human rights protected by regional and universal treaties and conventions such as the American Convention on Human Rights and its Additional Protocol ("Protocol of San Salvador")[2], they represent unjustifiable practices that should be denounced and subject to corresponding sanctions.

Homosexuality as a Natural and Non-Pathological Variation

Efforts aimed at changing non-heterosexual sexual orientations lack medical justification since homosexuality cannot be considered a pathological condition.[3] There is a professional consensus that homosexuality represents a natural variation of human sexuality without any intrinsically harmful effect on the health of those concerned or those close to them. In none of its individual manifestations does homosexuality constitute a disorder or an illness, and therefore it requires no cure. For this reason homosexuality was removed from the relevant systems of classification of diseases several decades ago.[4]

The Ineffectiveness and Harmfulness of "Conversion Therapies"

Besides the lack of medical indication, there is no scientific evidence for the effectiveness of sexual re-orientation efforts. While some persons manage to limit the expression of their sexual orientation in terms of conduct, the orientation itself generally appears as an integral personal characteristic that cannot be changed. At the same time, testimonies abound about harms to mental and physical health resulting from the repression of a person's sexual orientation. In 2009, the American Psychological Association conducted a review of 83 cases of people who had been subject to "conversion" interventions.[5] Not only was it impossible to demonstrate changes in subjects' sexual orientation, in addition the study found that the intention to change sexual orientation was linked to depression, anxiety, insomnia, feelings of guilt and shame, and even suicidal ideation and behaviors. In light of this evidence, suggesting to patients that they suffer from a "defect" and that they ought to change constitutes a violation of the first principle of medical ethics: "first, do no harm." It affects the right to personal integrity as well as the right to health, especially in its psychological and moral dimensions.

Reported Violations of Personal Integrity and Other Human Rights

As an aggravating factor, "conversion therapies" have to be considered threats to the right to personal autonomy and to personal integrity. There are several testimonies from adolescents who have been subject to "reparative" interventions against their will, many times at their families' initiative. In some cases, the victims were interned and deprived of their liberty, sometimes to the extent of being kept in isolation during several months.[6] The testimonies provide accounts of degrading treatment, extreme humiliation, physical violence, aversive conditioning through electric shock or emetic substances, and even sexual harassment and attempts of "reparative rape," especially in the case of lesbian women. Such interventions violate the dignity and human rights of the affected persons, independently of the fact that their "therapeutic" effect is nil or even counterproductive. In these cases, the right to health has not been protected as demanded by the regional and international obligations established through the Protocol of San Salvador and the International Covenant on Economic, Social, and Cultural Rights.

Conclusion

Health professionals who offer "reparative therapies" align themselves with social prejudices and reflect a stark ignorance in matters of sexuality and sexual health. Contrary to what many people believe or assume, there is no reason—with the exception of the stigma resulting from those very prejudices—why homosexual persons should be unable to enjoy a full and satisfying life. The task of health professionals is to not cause harm and to offer support to

patients to alleviate their complaints and problems, not to make these more severe. A therapist who classifies non-heterosexual patients as "deviant" not only offends them but also contributes to the aggravation of their problems. "Reparative" or "conversion therapies" have no medical indication and represent a severe threat to the health and human rights of the affected persons. They constitute unjustifiable practices that should be denounced and subject to adequate sanctions and penalties.

The Long History of Psychopathologization

For centuries, left-handed persons suffered because the use of the left hand ("sinister" in Latin) was thought to be associated with disaster. These people were regarded as carriers of misfortune and as having a "constitutional defect." Until relatively recently, there were attempts to "treat" and "correct" this supposed defect, causing suffering, humiliation, learning difficulties and difficulties in adapting to daily life in the affected persons.

Recommendations

To Governments:

Homophobic ill-treatment on the part of health professionals or other members of health care teams violates human rights obligations established through universal and regional treaties. Such treatment is unacceptable and should not be tolerated.

"Reparative" or "conversion therapies" and the clinics offering them should be reported and subject to adequate sanctions.

Institutions offering such "treatment" at the margin of the health sector should be viewed as infringing the right to health by assuming a role properly pertaining to the health sector and by causing harm to individual and community well-being.[7]

Victims of homophobic ill-treatment must be treated in accordance with protocols that support them in the recovery of their dignity and self-esteem. This includes providing them treatment for physical and emotional harm and protecting their human rights, especially the right to life, personal integrity, health, and equality before the law.

To Academic Institutions:

Public institutions responsible for training health professionals should include courses on human sexuality and sexual health in their curricula, with a particular focus on respect for diversity and the elimination of attitudes of pathologization, rejection, and hate toward non-heterosexual persons. The participation of the latter in teaching activities contributes to the development of positive role models and to the elimination of common stereotypes about non-heterosexual communities and persons.

The formation of support groups among faculty and within the student community contributes to reducing isolation and promoting solidarity and relationships of friendship and respect between members of these groups. Better still is the formation of sexual diversity alliances that include heterosexual persons.

Homophobic harassment or maltreatment on the part of members of the faculty or students is unacceptable and should not be tolerated.

To Professional Associations:

Professional associations should disseminate documents and resolutions by national and international institutions and agencies that call for the de-psychopathologization of sexual diversity and the prevention of interventions aimed at changing sexual orientation.

Professional associations should adopt clear and defined positions regarding the protection of human dignity and should define necessary actions for the prevention and control of homophobia as a public health problem that negatively impacts the enjoyment of civil, political, economic, social, and cultural rights.

The application of so-called "reparative" or "conversion therapies" should be considered fraudulent and as violating the basic principles of medical ethics. Individuals or institutions offering these treatments should be subject to adequate sanctions.

To the Media:

The representation of non-heterosexual groups, populations, or individuals in the media should be based on personal respect, avoiding stereotypes or humor based on mockery, ill-treatment, or violations of dignity or individual or collective well-being.

Homophobia, in any of its manifestations and expressed by any person, should be exposed as a public health problem and a threat to human dignity and human rights.

The use of positive images of non-heterosexual persons or groups, far from promoting homosexuality (in virtue of the fact that sexual orientation cannot be changed), contributes to creating a more humane and diversity-friendly outlook, dispelling unfounded fears and promoting feelings of solidarity.

Publicity that incites homophobic intolerance should be denounced for contributing to the aggravation of a public health problem and threats to the right to life, particularly as it contributes to chronic emotional suffering, physical violence, and hate crimes.

Advertising by "therapists," "care centers," or any other agent offering services aimed at changing sexual orientation should be considered illegal and should be reported to the relevant authorities.

To Civil Society Organizations:

Civil society organizations can develop mechanisms of civil vigilance to detect violations of the human rights of non-heterosexual persons and report them to the relevant authorities. They can also help to identify and report persons and institutions involved in the administration of so-called "reparative" or "conversion therapies."

Existing or emerging self-help groups of relatives or friends of non-heterosexual persons can facilitate the connection to health and social services with the goal of protecting the physical and emotional integrity of ill-treated individuals, in addition to reporting abuse and violence.

Fostering respectful daily interactions between persons of different sexual orientations is enriching for everyone and promotes harmonic, constructive, salutary, and peaceful ways of living together.

Notes

1. Human Rights Committee (2008). Concluding Observations on Ecuador (CCPR/C/ECU/CO/5), paragraph 12. <http://www2.ohchr.org/english/bodies/hrc/docs/co/CCPR.C.ECU.CO.5.doc>

   Human Rights Council (2011). Discriminatory Laws and Practices and Acts of Violence Against Individuals Based on Their Sexual Orientation and Gender Identity (A/HRC/19/41), paragraph 56. <http://www.ohchr.org/Documents/HRBodies/HRCouncil/RegularSession/Session19/A-HRC-19-41_en.pdf>

   Human Rights Council (2011). Report of the Special Rapporteur on the Right of Everyone to the Enjoyment of the Highest Attainable Standard of Physical and Mental Health (A/HRC/14/20), paragraph 23. <http://www2.ohchr.org/english/bodies/hrcouncil/docs/14session/A.HRC.14.20.pdf>

   United Nations General Assembly (2001). Note by the Secretary-General on the Question of Torture and Other Cruel, Inhuman or Degrading Treatment or Punishment (A/56/156), paragraph 24. <http://www.un.org/documents/ga/docs/56/a56156.pdf>

2. The human rights that can be affected by these practices include, among others, the right to life, to personal integrity, to privacy, to equality before the law, to personal liberty, to health, and to benefit from scientific progress.

3. American Psychiatric Association (2000). Therapies Focused on Attempts to Change Sexual Orientation (Reparative or Conversion Therapies): Position Statement. <http://www.psych.org/Departments/EDU/Library/APAOfficialDocumentsandRelated/PositionStatements/200001.aspx>

   Anton, B. S. (2010). "Proceedings of the American Psychological Association for the Legislative Year 2009: Minutes of the Annual Meeting of the Council of Representatives and Minutes of the Meetings of the Board of Directors". American Psychologist, 65, 385–475. <http://www.apa.org/about/governance/council/policy/sexual-orientation.pdf>

   Just the Facts Coalition (2008). Just the Facts about Sexual Orientation and Youth: A Primer for Principals, Educators, and School Personnel. Washington, DC. <http://www.apa.org/pi/lgbc/publications/justthefacts.html>

4. World Health Organization (1994). International Statistical Classification of Diseases and Related Health Problems (10th Revision). Geneva, Switzerland.

   American Psychiatric Association (2000). Diagnostic and Statistical Manual of Mental Disorders (4th ed., text revision). Washington, DC.

5. APA Task Force on Appropriate Therapeutic Responses to Sexual Orientation (2009). Report of the Task Force on Appropriate Therapeutic Responses to Sexual Orientation. Washington, DC. <http://www.apa.org/pi/lgbt/resources/therapeutic-response.pdf>

6. Taller de Comunicación Mujer (2008). Pacto Internacional de Derechos Civiles y Políticos: Informe Sombra. <http://www.tcmujer.org/pdfs/Informe%20Sombra%202009%20LBT.pdf>

   Centro de Derechos Económicos y Sociales (2005). Tribunal por los Derechos Económicos, Sociales y Culturales de las Mujeres. <http://www.tcmujer.org/pdfs/TRIBUNAL%20DESC%20ECUADOR%20MUJERES.pdf>

7. See General Comment No. 14 by the Committee on Economic, Social, and Cultural Rights with regards to the obligation to respect, protect and comply with human rights obligations on the part of States parties to the International Covenant on Economic, Social, and Cultural Rights.

THE PAN AMERICAN HEALTH ORGANIZATION (PAHO), founded in 1902, is the world's oldest international public health agency. It provides technical cooperation and mobilizes partnerships to improve health and quality of life in the countries of the Americas. PAHO is the specialized health agency of the Inter-American System and serves as the Regional Office for the Americas of the World Health Organization (WHO). Together with WHO, PAHO is a member of the United Nations system.

EXPLORING THE ISSUE

Can Psychotherapy Change Sexual Orientation?

Critical Thinking and Reflection

1. Nicolosi, Byrd, and Potts describe in detail their efforts to perform an extensive study according to standardized research procedures, while Beckstead cites the flaws of general SOCE research as one of SOCE's major limitations. Why are methods so important in determining the worth of psychological research?

2. Much of the SOCE research supporting the possibility of a changeable sexual orientation is conducted at institutions espousing religious values. Do you believe that such values may be a hindrance to scientific research? Why or why not?

3. Imagine a therapist with two clients, both teenage males attracted to men. One client desires to cope with persecution he is feeling at school, while the other finds his attraction to men unwelcome and wants to change it. How do the personal views of the therapist affect the treatment he or she will give to each of these males?

4. Over the years, the APA has changed its stance on homosexuality. What is the role of national psychological organizations such as APA in influencing public opinion? What is the role of the scientific establishment in informing the public?

5. As PAHO discusses, changing a person's sexual orientation is partly a matter of autonomy. Should laws and standards regarding gay conversion therapy differ when involving minors versus adults? Is changing a minor's sexual orientation a matter of parental rights or the minor's right?

Is There Common Ground?

The degree of change a client may experience in the course of psychotherapy is influenced by a wide variety of factors, such as the client's attendance at therapy being by choice or mandate, the congruence of the client's and psychotherapist's values and style of therapy, and even the cause of the issue at hand. As such, a simple answer to the question of whether or not psychotherapy can consistently or effectively change sexual orientation is really not possible to give. Aside from that, SOCE may impede a person's autonomy. A client who is experiencing same-sex attraction and is forced to attend psychotherapy by his/her parents is much less likely to genuinely consider or accept the things that their therapist might happen to suggest. Conversely, a client who believes in the efficacy of a specific therapeutic approach, and who freely opts to participate in therapy, is much more likely to learn from their therapist – even if the therapists in both cases employ essentially the same therapeutic approaches. This, of course, is not something that

is restricted to conversion therapies, but is a common feature of nearly all forms of therapy. For example, individuals who undergo therapy because they have been required to do so by a criminal or civil court ruling often show less benefit from therapy than do those who willingly seek out therapy for whatever problems they may be facing.

Although the causes of homosexuality are still very much open to debate, as is the matter of how best to approach therapy with those experiencing same-sex attraction, one thing upon which both proponent and critics of sexual orientation change efforts in therapy can agree is that therapy should always be about helping individuals to live fuller and more meaningful lives. How exactly psychologists might go about balancing the individual's own desires in dealing with feelings of same-sex attraction and the social and scientific understandings of the nature and causes of such feelings is, of course, a very difficult and challenging question. It is, nonetheless, one that deserves our most careful and thoughtful consideration for psychologists, religious organizations, and society at large.

Additional Resources

The APA's report on "Appropriate Therapeutic Responses to Sexual Orientation," to which A. Lee Beckstead contributed. Retrieved from http://www.apa.org/pi/lgbt/resources/therapeutic-response.pdf

Bailey, J. M. (2003). Biological perspectives on sexual orientation. In *Psychological Perspectives on Lesbian, Gay,* and *Bisexual Experiences* (pp. 50–79). New York, NY: Columbia University Press.

Flentje, A., Heck, N. C., & Cochran, B. N. (2014). Experiences of ex-ex-gay individuals in sexual reorientation therapy: Reasons for seeking treatment, perceived helpfulness and harmfulness of treatment, and post-treatment identification. *Journal of Homosexuality*, 61(9), 1242–1268. doi:10.1080/00918369.2014.926763

Spitzer, R. L. (2003). Can some gay men and lesbians change their sexual orientation? 200 Participants reporting a change from homosexual to heterosexual orientation. *Archives of Sexual Behavior*, 32(5), 403–417.

Internet References . . .

National Association for Research and Therapy of Homosexuality

http://www.narth.com

Report of the APA Task Force on Appropriate Therapeutic Responses to Sexual Orientation

http://www.apa.org/pi/lgbt/resources/sexual-orientation.aspx

Sexual Orientation and Homosexuality

http://www.apa.org/helpcenter/sexual-orientation.aspx

Selected, Edited, and with Issue Framing Material by:
Edwin E. Gantt, *Brigham Young University*

ISSUE

Is Gender Identity Biological?

YES: Aruna Saraswat, Jamie D. Weinand, and Joshua D. Safer, from "Evidence Supporting the Biological Nature of Gender Identity," *Endocrine Practice* (2015)

NO: Michael J. Carter, from "Gender Socialization and Identity Theory," *Social Sciences* (2014)

Learning Outcomes

After reading this issue, you will be able to:

- Understand some of the theories and empirical evidence that support gender identity as societally constructed or biologically based.
- Identify some of the limitations in the current research surrounding gender formation.
- Understand the underlying implications of each article in regard to gender formation and the current gender binary in society today.
- Formulate an adequate argument for gender having or not having a biological basis.

ISSUE SUMMARY

YES: Saraswat, Weinand, and Safer review empirical studies that suggest gender as biologically caused. They discuss congenital adrenal hyperplasia (CAH), gray and white matter studies, and twin case studies as evidence for their argument is that gender has a biological basis.

NO: Michael J. Carter explores a review of the literature that emphasizes gender identity as being based in learned roles. He discusses how gender is learned over time in the family environment and how gender can be a person identity, role identity, or social identity in gender identity theory. He argues that gender comes from learned roles in society.

The relationship between sex and gender is a very controversial topic these days. Whether it is a news story on transgender people using different public restrooms or a feminist cry for equality in the workplace, the issue is almost impossible to avoid. One of the most heated debates revolves around the etiology of gender: Is gender biologically based or does it stem purely from society?

Much of the recent research and theorizing about the origins of gender and identity have focused on gender as a learned. Right after a baby is born, his or her parents start to treat the baby as a girl if the baby is biologically female, or as a boy if the baby is biologically male. The child then creates a gender identity based off what he or

she has learned from family and society. Most children's gender identity lines up with their sex, but that is not always the case.

The Oscar-winning movie The Danish Girl famously, although not entirely accurately, depicts the true and tragic story of Einar Wegener/Lili Elbe, one of the first people to undergo sex-reassignment surgery. This movie increased international awareness of the transgender community and added to the discussion on gender. To be transgender is to have a gender identity that does not match your biology. For example, somebody born male (i.e., with XY chromosomes and testicles) may identify as a woman and live life conforming to women's gender roles in being more feminine (such as wearing dresses or using makeup). This person may then identify as a transwoman and may or may not seek medical means to become more female. Conversely, someone whose sex matches their gender is cisgender.

The two articles presented in this section represent opposing views on the etiology of gender. The first article by Saraswat, Weinand, and Safer presents a biological account of gender by reviewing the research of transgender individuals. Some of the studies they discuss show that people being raised as a gender opposite than their sex (many received sex reassignment surgery as infants due to abnormalities) often do not identify as the gender they are raised as but rather as the gender that matches their chromosomes. The authors of this article attempt to show that gender formed from biological mechanisms such as brain structure or chromosomes.

In contrast, the article by Carter argues that gender ultimately arises out of learned social and gender roles taught and reinforced by family and society. He draws on identity theory to explain how gender identity may be formed from different aspects of identity (i.e., personal, social roles, and/or social–cultural expectations). He claims that gender identity is learned early in youth and then becomes strengthened throughout development.

**Aruna Saraswat, Jamie D. Weinand,
and Joshua D. Safer**

Evidence Supporting the Biologic Nature of Gender Identity

Abbreviations

BDNF = brain-derived neurotrophic factor; **BSTc** = bed [nucleus] of the stria terminalis; **CAH** = congenital adrenal hyperplasia; **DES** = diethylstilbestrol; **DSD** = disorder of sex development; **MTF** = male-to-female; **FTM** = female-to-male.

Introduction

Gender identity is a fundamental human attribute that has a profound impact on personal well-being. Transgender individuals are those whose lived and identified gender identity differs from their natal sex. Various etiologies for transgender identity have been proposed, but misconceptions that gender identity can be altered persist. However, clinical experience with treatment of transgender persons has clearly demonstrated that the best outcomes for these individuals are achieved with their requested hormone therapy and surgical sexual transition as opposed to psychiatric intervention alone. In this review, we will discuss the data in support of a fixed, biologic basis for gender identity.

Methods

This traditional literature review was conducted using a search of PubMed and Google Scholar for the following key terms: gender identity, gender dysphoria, transsexual, transgender, transmen, and transwomen.

Results

Disorders (or Differences) of Sex Development (DSDs)

A seminal study by Meyer-Bahlburg et al. involving outcomes of XY individuals raised as females due to severe nonhormonal, anatomic abnormalities of sex development provided the most convincing evidence that gender identity is fixed. These congenital abnormalities include penile agenesis, cloacal exstrophy, and penile ablation. For many years, female gender assignment along with surgical feminization was the dominant approach for these patients. In this study, 78 percent of all female-assigned 46 XY patients were living as females. While the majority of these patients did not initiate a gender change to male, none of the 15 male-raised 46 XY patients initiated a gender change to female. Thus, the risk of questioning gender identity was higher in those 46 XY subjects raised as females than in those raised as males. The same group examined the degree of satisfaction with surgical intervention reported by patients with 46 XY genotypes and found that those subjects raised as boys were considerably more comfortable with their gender identity.

Another seminal study relevant to this topic was by Reiner and Gearhart. In their review of 16 XY genotype subjects with cloacal exstrophy who underwent female gender reassignment surgery, four of the 14 individuals raised as girls announced they were male, and four later chose to live as boys when they became aware of their genotype. The two individuals who were raised as males identified as males throughout life. The sexual behavior and attitudes of all 16 subjects ultimately reflected strong masculine characteristics regardless of gender assignment. Thus, children who were born genetically and hormonally male identified as males despite being raised as females and undergoing feminizing genitoplasty at birth. Although the cohort sizes in these studies were small, the data provide the strongest evidence for the biologic underpinnings of gender identity.

In congenital adrenal hyperplasia (CAH), the adrenal glands produce excessive amounts of androgens, causing genital virilization with a spectrum of different phenotypes in 46 XX neonates. Dessens et al. reported that the prevalence of male gender identity in 46 XX female-raised subjects with CAH was higher than the prevalence of female-to-male (FTM) transgender individuals in the general population of chromosomal females. In this study, the large majority (95 percent) of 250 female-raised patients later maintained a female gender identity. However, 13 (5.2 percent) had serious problems with their gender identity.

Saraswat, Aruna; Weinand, Jamie D.; Safer, Joshua D., "Evidence Supporting the Biological Nature of Gender Identity" *Endocrine Practice* 21(2) February 2015. 199–202 American Association of Clinical Endocrinologists, Inc. Used with permission.

Deficiencies of 5 alpha-reductase-2 and 17-beta-hydroxy-steroid dehyrogenase-3 are similar conditions in which the synthesis and conversion of testosterone to dihydrotestosterone is inhibited, preventing the development of external male genitalia and resulting in potential genital ambiguity. As with CAH, affected individuals are often raised as females. In a study of affected subjects, gender role changes were reported in 56 percent to 63 percent of cases with 5 alpha-reductase-2 deficiency and 39 to 64 percent of cases with 17-beta-hydroxysteroid dehydrogenase-3 deficiency who were raised as girls. These data support the concept that gender identity might be attributed to hormone milieu during intrauterine development.

Data from DSDs highlight the potential influence of abnormal hormone exposure on the development of transgender identity in some individuals. However, it is important to note that most transgender individuals develop a gender identity that cannot be explained by atypical sexual differentiation. It is possible for individuals with normal sexual differentiation to develop transgender identity later in life.

Neuroanatomical Differences

Many of the current hypotheses for the biologic origin of transgender identity are based on atypical sexual differentiation of the brain. The perception of one's own gender is linked to sexual differentiation of the brain, which differs from the body phenotype in transgender individuals. Swaab et al. have proposed that this discrepancy could be due to the fact that sexual differentiation of the brain takes place only after sexual differentiation of the gonads in early fetal life. Along these lines, the degree of genital masculinization may not reflect that of the brain.

The notion of transgender-specific cerebral phenotypes is further supported by postmortem brain studies investigating the underlying neuroanatomical correlates of gender identity. The vast majority of these studies have compared particular regions of interest only in male-to-female (MTF) transgender individuals. These studies support the hypothesis that atypical cerebral networks in transgender individuals have a neuroanatomical basis.

Gray Matter Studies

Studies of cerebral gray matter in transgender individuals have provided the strongest neuroanatomical case for transgender gender identity. Postmortem brain studies suggest that some subcortical structures are feminized in MTF individuals. One of the earliest and most influential studies in this area investigated the bed nucleus of the stria terminalis (BSTc), which was reported to be a sexually dimorphic nucleus in humans with a larger volume in males than in females. In 1995, Zhou et al. reported that the size and number of neurons in the BSTc of six MTF estrogen-treated transgender individuals was typical for the size and neuron numbers generally found in control females. The authors further reported that these findings could not be explained by differences in adult sex hormone levels.

A similar study by Kruijver et al. provided further data supporting the role of the BSTc in transgender identity. They examined tissue from the same six MTF estrogen-treated transgender persons studied by Zhou et al. and found that the number of neurons in the BSTc was more similar to genetic XX female controls. BSTc neuron number was also in the male range in the one FTM androgen-treated transgender individual studied.

Most transgender individuals experience feelings of gender dysphoria that begin in childhood. However, in a study of BSTc volume in postmortem brains of 50 control subjects, Chung et al. reported that sexual dimorphism in the BSTc did not develop until adulthood. Yet, the same group remarked that changes in fetal hormone levels could have delayed effects on BSTc volume and neurons in adulthood, thereby suggesting a role for BSTc as a marker for gender identity. Still, delayed development of sexual dimorphism in the BSTc would not explain childhood development of gender dysphoria or gender identity discrepancy.

In 2008, Garcia-Falgueras and Swaab were the first to report a sex reversal in the uncinate nucleus. They examined the third interstitial nucleus of the anterior hypothalamus (INAH 3), which is a sexually dimorphic component of the uncinate nucleus, in relation to the brains of transgender individuals. They reported that the mean INAH3 volume and neuron number in 11 MTF transgender subjects were in the female ranges.

The above studies are limited by the fact that they involved postmortem examinations of a small number of brains from MTF individuals, some of whom had either received hormone treatment or surgery. Therefore, the study findings may represent confounding effects from exogenous hormones in a small group of transgender individuals. Despite their small sample size, these studies provide valuable evidence that gender identity is linked to neuroanatomy.

Studies by Luders et al. provided further evidence that transgender identity is associated with distinct cerebral patterns. In 2009, the group analyzed magnetic resonance imaging (MRI) data of 24 MTF transgender individuals who had not yet begun hormone treatment. These subjects were shown to have a pattern that was more similar to control males. However, they also observed a significantly larger, more "feminized" volume of regional gray matter in the right putamen in these subjects. In

2012, the same group observed thicker cortices in 24 MTF transgender individuals who had not yet received exogenous hormones compared with 24 age-matched control males in a number of regions across the lateral and medial cortical surfaces. The data supported a dichotomy between MTF transgender individuals and gender congruent males with regard to brain structure.

Differences in brain volume and cerebral activation patterns have been proposed as potential explanations for transgender identity. In 2011, Savic et al. examined brains of 24 living MTF transgender individuals and found significant volume reductions of the putamen in MTF transgender individuals and significant increases in gray matter volumes compared with male and female controls. Although these findings differ from the findings of smaller, "feminized," putamens in MTF transgender individuals, they still indicate that certain brain areas in the transgender group have characteristic structural features compared with controls.

The same group investigated 12 living MTF transgender individuals who smelled two steroidal compounds: the progesterone derivative 4,16-androstadien3-one (AND) and the estrogen-like compound estra-1,3,5, 16-tetraen-3-ol. These compounds have been reported to activate the hypothalamic networks in a sex-differentiated way. MTF transgender individuals who had not received hormone treatment were found to respond similarly to female controls, with AND activating the anterior hypothalamus. Another study by Gizewski et al. showed a similar cerebral activation in MTF transgender individuals relative to female controls while they viewed erotic stimuli. While the above studies only involved MTF transgender individuals, they nonetheless provided evidence of neuroanatomical pathway alteration as an explanation for transgender identity.

The following two studies were unique from the aforementioned ones because they included both MTF and FTM transgender individuals who had not received hormone treatment. Zubiaurre et al. reported that FTM transgender individuals showed evidence of subcortical gray matter masculinization in the right putamen, while MTF transgender individuals had feminized cortical thickness. In 2013, Simon et al. reported differences in gray matter in 17 living transgender subjects compared with controls. Differences were seen in transgender patients in the cerebellum, angular gyrus, and parietal lobe compared with controls, independent of their biologic gender.

White Matter Studies

Although an early study by Emory et al. found no difference in the whole corpus callosum or splenium region between MTF and FTM transgender individuals, the following MRI studies of white matter brain characteristics of transgender individuals suggested a strong neuroanatomical explanation for transgender identity. Yokota et al. reported that the pattern of corpus callosum shape in both FTM and MTF transgender individuals was closer to subjects with shared gender identities than to subjects who shared the same natal sex. Among FTM transgender individuals who had not received hormone treatment, certain white matter fasciculi involved in higher cognitive functions were closer to the pattern of control males than to control females. Among MTF transgender individuals who had not received treatment, diffusion tensor imaging revealed an intermediate white matter pattern that was between those of male and female controls.

Genetic Factors and Exposures

Although limited in size and scope, the role of genetic factors in transgender identity is supported by small studies of gene abnormalities associated with steroid hormones, twin case studies, neuroproteins, and prenatal exposures.

Steroid Hormone Genetics

Select genes have been associated with transgender identity. Although these studies have been small, they are most convincing findings to date linking atypical genes with transgender identity in both MTF and FTM transgender individuals. The CYP17 gene encodes the 17-alpha hydroxylase enzyme and is associated with elevated serum levels of estradiol, progesterone, and testosterone. In a case-control study of 151 transgender individuals, Bentz et al. reported a significant association between the CYP17 gene and FTM transgender individuals but not in MTF transgender individuals. Another study by the same group examined a polymorphism in the gene coding for 5-alpha reductase and found no association in a sample of both MTF and FTM transgender individuals.

Various groups have investigated steroid hormone receptor gene variants to determine if they confer risk of developing transgender identity. Steroid hormones exert profound influences on fetal sexual development and act via specific receptors. It is therefore plausible that abnormal sex hormone receptor function may predispose to transgender identity. However, the existing studies on this topic have been contradictory and require replication. Henningson et al. found an association between MTF transgender individuals and a dinucleotide CA polymorphism in the estrogen receptor beta gene (ERb). However, two subsequent studies by separate groups reported different results. Hare et al. performed a larger study of MTF transgender individuals and found no relationship with the ERb, but they did find a significant association with an androgen receptor repeat. In a similar study of 242 MTF and FTM transgender individuals, Ujike et al. examined sex steroid receptor genes and found no association with transgender identity.

There have been several small case reports of atypical sex chromosomes in transgender individuals. The most common association reported was with disomy-Y (47, XXY); however, no statistically significant association between particular genes has been described. Two recent studies of MTF and FTM transgender individuals reported that [aneuploidies] are slightly more common in transgender individuals than in the general population, but neither was controlled. In the first, karyotype abnormalities were found in 2.5 percent of the 368 transgender individuals studied. A second study of 302 transgender individuals also showed a low overall incidence (1.5 percent) of chromosomal abnormalities.

Twin Studies

Twin literature supports the potential contribution of genetic factors to the development of transgender identity. In two separate retrospective studies of twin pairs, Bailey et al. and Coolidge et al. demonstrated a strong heritable component among twins with transgender identity. Hylens et al. performed a similar study of 23 monozygotic twin pairs and showed that nine were concordant for transgender identity compared to no concordance among dizygotic twin pairs. Two small studies also demonstrated a higher concordance for transgender identity among monozygotic twins versus dizygotic twins. Nevertheless, the overall prevalence of monozygotic twins discordant for transgender identity still outnumbers those who are concordant.

Neuroproteins

Brain-derived neurotrophic factor (BDNF) is a member of the growth factor family involved in synaptic plasticity and neuronal development. Altered BDNF signaling is thought to be a contributor to psychiatric conditions. Fontanari et al. reported that serum BDNF levels were 15 percent lower in an uncontrolled study of 45 MTF transgender individuals. However, all study subjects were treated with hormones, and no female subjects were included.

Neurokinin B (NKB) is a potent regulator of gonadotropin-releasing hormone secretion, which is essential for reproductive function. A postmortem brain study of four MTF transgender individuals by Taziaux et al. showed a mean infundibular NKB volume similar to control females. The observed feminization may have been explained either by medical estrogen therapy or lack of androgens due to orchiectomy.

Prenatal Exposures

Dessens et al. reported that three prenatally anticonvulsant-exposed subjects were transgender individuals. For many years, researchers have been assessing the impact of prenatal exposure to the estrogenic antimiscarriage drug diethylstilbestrol (DES) on the development of gender dysphoria in affected offspring. While the vast majority of DES-exposed children have not developed transgender identity, a five-year online study of DES-exposed sons by Kerlin et al. reported at least 150 cases of moderate-to-severe gender dysphoria among 500 sons with confirmed or suspected prenatal DES exposure.

Although no studies to date demonstrate mechanism, multiple studies have reported associations with gender identity that support it being a biologic phenomenon.

Conclusion

Current data suggest a biologic etiology for transgender identity. Studies of DSD patients and neuroanatomical studies provide the strongest evidence for the organic basis of transgender identity. Because the sample sizes of most studies on this subject were small, the conclusions must be interpreted with caution. Further, research is required to assign specific biologic mechanisms for gender identity.

Aruna Saraswat is an endocrinologist and an assistant professor at Tufts University, School of Medicine in Massachusetts. In 2007, she received the prestigious Paul Brand International Medicine Scholarship. She received her MD in 2008 from the University of Texas Medical School at San Antonio and specializes in endocrinology, diabetes, and metabolism.

Jamie D. Weinand is a Rosen Goertz Point scholar and currently attends the Boston University School of Medicine to receive an MD. He has a bachelor's from Duke in both Spanish and Biology and while there started an LGBTQ magazine. While at medical school, he came out as FTM transgender and is interested in transgender health advocacy and research.

Joshua D. Safer received his MD from the University of Wisconsin School of Medicine in Madison. He is currently an associate professor of medicine and molecular medicine at Boston University School of Medicine where he is also the director of the Endocrinology Fellowship Training Program. His research interests include studying how thyroid hormones can aid in healing and transgender medicine.

Michael J. Carter

 **NO**

Gender Socialization and Identity Theory

Introduction

The idea that gender is learned through socialization is ubiquitous in sociological literature on gender; the prevalent sociological viewpoint generally rejects biologically deterministic explanations for differences in gender and gendered behavior. This article examines sociological facets of gender and gender socialization by applying identity theory and identity control theory to explain how gender stereotypes emerge and perpetuate throughout the human life course. While the etiology of gender and the causes of gendered behavior are difficult to study, these two variants of identity theory offer a sound theoretical framework that describes why gender ideals and stereotypes perpetuate, as well as how the socialization process operates internally. By employing identity theory and identity control theory to the study of gender, we can better conceive why gender identities seem to be so important for individuals, and why gender identities generally perpetuate across the life course after they are formed.

Gender socialization and the family have a broad and varied literature. Research on gender in childhood, adolescence, and adulthood consider different stages that are unique to human development. The focus for this discussion is based on how males and females *learn* masculinity and femininity through family/primary group interactions and how they are *socialized* into dichotomous, "traditional" gender roles. Specifically, the idea that males learn masculinity and masculine impressions in *opposition* to femininity and feminine behavior is examined. These mechanisms of socialization are examined as identity processes that the family and other primary groups help to create and maintain.

Gender Socialization and Families: A Review of the Literature

Before examining the socialization literature on gender and families, a definition for "family" is needed. Following literature that has documented the diverse nature of contemporary families, family here is understood as *any primary group of people who share an obligatory relationship with one another*, rather than the traditional, legal conception which limits the definition to married couples with children. This more inclusive definition is provided so as to broaden the scope of what a family truly is; it is also provided to emphasize that socialization occurs for *every* actor in society, regardless of their type of familial surrounding. Indeed, a benefit of the variants of identity theory regards their inclusiveness in that any agents of socialization—whether legally bound or otherwise—have similar effects and influences on children. What is important for understanding identity processes is not how the structure of society views authority figures or official familial members *per se*, but rather how proximal agents nurture and socialize children. Families are the most proximate agents of identity socialization; both identity theory and identity control theory can explain the socialization process regardless if these agents fall within the traditional boundaries of "family," or if they are qualitatively different.

Family and the Construction of Gender

The socialization of children in the family unit has been examined in various ways. Research has generally focused on four traditions: the *parent effect perspective*, the *child effects perspective*, the *reciprocal socialization perspective*, and the *systemic-ecological perspective*; each perspective provides a unique understanding to child socialization. The parent effect perspective addresses how the different styles, behaviors, and dispositions of parents socialize traits and behavior in children. This perspective is the most common area of inquiry in literature on gender socialization. The child effects perspective reverses the order of operations in family socialization, focusing on how children socialize parents. A common area of inquiry in the child effects perspective examines how the presence of a child forces mothers/fathers to enter the workplace to support the added economic stress a child brings, hence influencing parents to develop additional, new identities. The reciprocal effects perspective examines how both children and parents socialize one another reflexively; the impact of gender and family socialization are mutually tied to both entities. The systemic-ecological perspective considers that gender and family socialization is neither a parent-to-child nor child-to-parent process, but that all family socialization is embedded in an *environment* or *context* that can have great impact. This perspective treats family socialization as a social system in which multiple sources of socialization simultaneously impact both parents and children.

The parent effect perspective is the oldest in the tradition of socialization theories and provides the basis for the proceeding discussion on socialization. This is primarily due to the fact that while identity construction is a reflexive process, more cues are provided to children *from* parents (especially in infancy and youth) than the other way around. This is an important aspect to understanding how identity theory serves as a control mechanism for actors (as will be examined shortly); parental definitions of acceptable behavior—which is usually gendered—is internalized by children early on and serves as a foundation for all subsequent interactions. Regardless of the application or analysis of the family, the family is usually the first unit with which children have continuous contact and the first context in which socialization patterns develop.

Doing Gender

Another perspective on gender socialization is influenced by ethnomethodology and provided by West and Zimmerman (and others). In this perspective, gender is understood as created and maintained while actors assume and play out roles in society. Here, emphasis is placed on the fact that many roles and tasks in society tend to be gendered. Doing yard work, cooking in the kitchen, caring for children, working on a presentation for one's boss—activities such as these often carry some form of gendered meaning, both for actors performing these tasks and for others observing them. When actors fulfill the expectations and scripts for these "gendered" tasks they are actually "doing gender." Gender thus is something created and maintained in *practice*; doing a task associated with a specific gender creates and perpetuates meanings that define who one is and what it means to be a man or woman, or masculine or feminine. In the "doing gender" perspective, gender is a routine, methodical, and recurring accomplishment. Fenstermaker and West elaborate on this perspective:

> When we view gender as an accomplishment, an achieved property of situated conduct, our

attention shifts from matters internal to the individual and focuses on interactional and, ultimately, institutional arenas. In one sense, of course, it is individuals who do gender. But it is a situated doing, carried out in the virtual or real presence of others who are presumed to be oriented to its production. Rather than as a property of individuals, we conceive of gender as an emergent feature of social situations: both as an outcome of and a rationale for various social arrangements and as a means of legitimating one of the most fundamental divisions of society.

The "doing gender" perspective helps us understand the social constructionist aspect to gender and how gender identities are not static but rather fluid entities that are continually formed in social interactions. Gender may be fundamental, institutionalized, and enduring, but because actors "do gender" as a process in social settings gender meanings and identities are always capable of and ripe for change. This perspective aligns with identity theory's idea of gender identity commitment and salience, which will be discussed shortly. The more one "does gender" among others in interactions, the more likely ones gender identity will become more committed, and thus salient within the self.

Variants of Identity Theory and Gender: Nascent Stages of Inquiry

The idea that gender is learned differently by the sexes is prevalent in much of the literature on gender and socialization. This phenomenon is specifically examined to show how identities that are formed by the family become internalized. Research on gender or gender socialization in literature on identity theory often examines how internalized socialization processes are maintained by a control mechanism (known as an *identity control loop*, explained shortly) which compares internalized standards (i.e., for appropriate gender behavior) to perceptions of others (i.e., how others react and respond to behavior) and, through emotion, regulates interaction between individuals.

Work within identity theory and identity control theory examines how and why such identities perpetuate, and why they do not often change even when in situations that persuade altering patterns of behavior. When applied to gender, identity theory's treatment of gendered identity construction is fascinating for many reasons. One of the most intriguing elements to gender is why human beings (who are supposedly rational creatures or at least capable of rational thought and behavior) *continue* to operate according to gender expectations and stereotypes. Identity theory explains why such (sometimes) irrational behavior perpetuates, and also why both men and women adhere to the identities they learn early on that are acquired from the messages and cultural influences of family and society.

Of particular interest in this article is how gender is influenced by families and how family shapes and molds a child's self-concept. This theme is common in the family literature, but treatment within the identity theory literature has not been as extensive. Indeed, one of the prime reasons for undertaking this project of applying the derivations of identity theory to socialization and family influence is to address the vacant areas within identity theory. While there is a dearth of research that deals directly with families and identity theory (especially identity control theory), there is work that addresses how children assimilate and internalize messages by primary caretakers.

Identity theory is used in such work as an underpinning to describing how identities emerge by family socialization, which generally occurs through the following three ways: (1) by ascription, (2) by identification (i.e., when children claim or cultivate similarity to a parent), and (3) by discovery of resemblances between oneself and a parent. Identity theory offers a framework that shows how the ascribed, identified, and discovered elements to socialization develop. Research in this area examines the attachments children have to others (such as parents) and how gender ideals are transferred from generation to generation.

While there has been a glut of exploratory and descriptive research concerning gender socialization, much of it is not theoretical. I use identity theory to show why gendered behavior emerges and perpetuates. Identities that are forged by individuals, families, and social structures can be explained by applying the phenomenon to the identity framework. The following discussion provides an explanation to how and why actors internalize gender, and why once they are internalized they are slow to change. In order to apply identity theory to family socialization and gender, the theory needs to be systematically developed. The following section briefly examines identity theory and its evolved subtheory, identity control theory.

Using Identity Theories to Understand Gender

To understand how families socialize gender roles and construct identities, it is necessary to review the components of identity theory. Identity theory is social psychological theory that emerged from structural symbolic interactionism. Similar to other structural symbolic interactionist theories, identity theory assumes that society is a patterned, stable social structure. Identity theory has mostly addressed role engagements, specifically how individuals create and maintain meanings in the multiple roles they play. Once actors develop identity meanings, they are motivational toward behavior. In identity theory, the self is a reflexive process that is revealed in social interaction and portrayed to others through identities that fit specific situations.

Variants of identity theory have three main emphases. One emphasis addresses the relationship among social structures, identities, and behavior, and how actors' many role identities are organized in a *salience hierarchy*. A second emphasis addresses how *internal dynamics* within the self-influence behavior. The third area also specifically examines role identities, but conceives identities arranged not only in a salience hierarchy, but also in a *prominence hierarchy*. In this variant of identity theory, identities are high in one's prominence hierarchy when they are seen as an *important* facet of the self. All three variants are important and add to the general understanding of identity within structural symbolic interactionism; however, most research has developed from the first two emphases and focused on the ideas of Stryker and Burke. Therefore, the discussion below focuses on the two most prevalent variants of identity theory that have established empirical research programs.

Identity Forms: Person, Role, and Social Identities

Identity theory assumes that the self is comprised of multiple identities. Based on the work of James, identity theory posits that there are as many different selves as there are different positions one holds in the social structure (and also as many selves as there are individuals to whom one is connected). These identities determine how an actor behaves when *alone*, while playing a *role*, or when attached to a *group*. Thus, identities are commonly classified in three ways: *person identities*, *role identities*, and *group identities*. *Person identities* refer to the self-meanings that allow an actor to realize a sense of individuality. Person identities are self-meanings such as being *dominant, competitive, caring*, or *honest*.

These identities are often activated because they are not generally unique to any specific circumstance; they rather apply across many situations. *Role identities* (e.g., athlete, worker, student, etc.) are defined by the meanings one attributes to the self while performing a role. These meanings emerge from socialization and through culture, as well as by the unique, individual assessment of what a role means for an actor. Role identities are a combination of *shared* and *idiosyncratic* meanings which are developed over time and played out by an actor during interactions. *Social identities* describe identity meanings actors have when they identify with groups or categories (e.g., Mexican, American, Muslim, NRA member, etc.). When one has a social identity others are categorized as either *similar* or *different*, depending on whether others are classified as part of the in-group or out-group. Social identities allow actors to create a sense of unity with others and share common bonds, and provide mutual reinforcement to act in various ways. Social identities also allow actors to feel good about themselves (i.e., social identities have a self-enhancement dimension), as well as reduce uncertainty about their environment. All three types of identities can operate simultaneously, indeed in many situations actors have multiple identities activated—including role, social, and personal identities.

Gender as a Person, Role, and Social Identity: Perpetuating Gendered Behavior

Identity theory helps to explain why gendered behavior and gender stereotypes that are learned through family socialization perpetuate over the life course. In brief, gender identities are *diffuse* identities can assume *any* of the three types of identities. One's masculinity or femininity can be engaged and triggered by various situations and are not specific to person, role, or social identities.

The interactions that occur while occupying any (or all) of these roles is often based on internalized beliefs about gender and appropriate behavior of one's gender, and these interactions sustain the gender system as a whole; even when social structural conditions change, gender cues that are internalized by families and in youth serve to maintain the stability of human behavior (and behavior that is gendered). Identities based on gender affect the basic rules that people use to frame interaction; the fact that gender can emerge in person, role, and social (or group) identities shows how powerful perceptions of gender are.

Gender as a "Person" Identity

To review, person identities describe the set of meanings that are tied to and sustain the self as an *individual* rather than sustaining a role or group. Culture, and most importantly, socialization impacts the dimensions of meanings which form the basis for one's "person" identity. For example, these identities may take the form of being *dominant*

or *submissive*; these are traits that are not usually internalized equally between boys and girls while socialized by the family, and subsequently they are also not traits that equally resemble men and women as adults. Males tend to learn that dominance, autonomy, and aggression are linked to their gender; females grow up in surroundings that promote being collectivistic, expressive, and connected. Socialization along these tracts begins as soon as babies are born, and families help to cultivate person identities for their kin according to gender.

Person identities are generally *salient* identities; they are triggered in many situations and figure into many interactions, relationships, and behaviors. For example, a wife who's has a person identity of being compassionate is likely to exhibit compassionate behavior in many situations. Or, a father who is highly controlling is likely to attempt to control many facets of his surroundings. Since person identities are activated across many situations, they are especially powerful agents of socialization for children. Because the family is a primary source of learning behavior and norms, these person identities are internalized and eventually emulated by observing adults and others. Coupled with the fact that many characteristics of person identities tend to vary according to gender, it is in the family setting that gender differentiation is first learned and internalized. Since person identities are often activated, they perpetuate and solidify over time. Boys who are encouraged to be assertive become men who are defined by the same characteristics. Girls that learn compassion, caring, and expressivity become women with the same internalized identity standards. Person identities are salient, individually characteristic identities that encompass many of the traits associated with gendered behavior. This typology of identity especially shows how individuals, while unique entities, still internalize personal mannerisms and identities that are in line with expected gender behaviors. These expected behaviors emerge from various sources, but initially from the family.

Gender as a "Role" Identity

Considering that role identities include the meanings that a person attaches to themselves while performing roles, it is easy to understand how gender expectations, behavior, and stereotypes perpetuate when engaged in role taking. Role identities are socialized identities; the meanings of specific roles are learned by considering the context of the role and the social surroundings in which it is played. Role identities thus are learned early on, and many of the different roles actors learn and play are based on *differentiated* expectations for behavior; this differentiation is often gendered.

For example, the family is especially defined by role identities. The role of mother, father, son, daughter, grandmother, grandfather, husband, wife, and so on are all role identities that are based within the family. These roles also share a common theme: they are based on *sex*, and sex is highly correlated with gender. It is also interesting how role identities share many characteristics of person and social identities; gender, being a diffuse characteristic, defines *all* types of identities.

For example, the role identity of "mother" may involve meanings of being *nurturing* and *caring*; the performance of mothering matches these meanings as in feeding and bathing a child or engaging in warm and intimate interactions. The role identity of husband may include meanings of *powerfulness* and *control*, and the behavior of husband should match these meanings by being the one who makes the major decisions in the family.

The oppositional characteristic of role identities is also privy to gender. Role identities are based on a self/other dichotomy; roles cannot exist alone—rather they are defined as *alternatives* to other roles. For example, one cannot be a student without the existence of an alternate other who is a teacher, and vice versa; one cannot be a medical doctor without there being patients. In line with the previous discussion of psychoanalytic theories of gender and families, one learns what it means to be male or female in reference (and against) to the alternate gender. Learning behavior then is a form of role taking. Boys that identify with the roles of their fathers are likely to also learn that many of those roles are defined by what behavior is prevalent and acceptable; this socialization operates similarly for girls. Of course, boys and girls can interpret roles of the opposite-sex parent, but gender is likely to be salient here as well. For example, the roles of parent and child are abstract categories, but the ways in which these roles are played is contingent on what sex the parent and children are. Treatment of the "child" by the "parent" is likely to vary according to whether the child is a boy or a girl; role taking thus involves gender. Here identity theory shows how gender is socialized across many situations, in families and throughout the life course. Gender is socialized into person identities, and gender operates while assuming roles as well.

Gender as a "Social" Identity

Social identities represent an individual's group memberships and concern an individual's participation in such collective categories as political affiliation, religion, or nationality. Libertarian, Jew, and American are examples of social identities that a person can assume. Culture and especially socialization influence the meanings of different group memberships and provide cues for what behavior is expected from such memberships. While many social categories refer to identities that are assumed in adulthood (i.e., being a republican likely is a function of age), the family is often the primary group that nudges individuals toward the groups in which one eventually becomes attached. Some group memberships are based on gender, and many groups are defined by gendered behavioral norms and expectations.

One's gender identity is socialized early on in one's life, and it is in the nascent stages of development where individuals learn how being a boy or girl means more than simply assuming a role; it also means sharing similar viewpoints and behavioral expectations with a larger group of similar gendered individuals. For example, parents who place their children in gendered organizations (such as girl scouts and boy scouts) contribute to the creation of a gendered social identity. Girl scouts are what girls "do"; boy scouts are what boys "do." Here children learn norms and expectations that come to be labeled as masculine or feminine. Little girls may accompany mothers to gatherings with other women; little boys may go to sporting events with fathers. Each of these activities instills a sense of the things females and males commonly do in opposition to one another, and in these activities a sense of social identification with one's particular gender emerges.

It is easy to see why gender can be conceived as a social identity when considering that individuals often refer to others of same or different gender as part of one's in-group or out-group. For example, a woman who proclaims, "We are women, hear us roar!" is referencing gender as a social category, that is, as a *group* in which she belongs, not as a role or idiosyncratic personal characteristic. Notions of gender being a group are commonly found in feminist literature, and many social organizations center on gender differences for inclusion (e.g., the National Organization for Women and Mothers against Drunk Driving).

This type of gender socialization certainly occurs in the family, but it is particularly evident in such socializing agents as schools. For example, the idea that boys learn what it means to be masculine by attempting to do that which is "not feminine" is evident in the patterns and characteristics of schoolyard play. Research has shown that boys tend to play in large groups (i.e., by playing sports that have multiple member teams, etc.) while girls tend to form smaller, more intimate relationships. This phenomenon is potentially prevalent more in school settings than in the family as there are more opportunities for tactics of inclusion and exclusion for children at school (i.e., there is simply a larger congregation of individuals at school than there is at home). The social identities that boys form are likely to be different than the social identities formed by girls. Since social (or group-based) identities are defined by their uniformity of perception and action among group members, it might be posited that boys learn to incorporate social identities earlier than do girls. If this is so, it is aligned with the idea that boys are socialized to be leaders and to be competitive while girls are socialized to be caretakers and supportive, and also with the fact that men tend to have more powerful positions within social networks than do women.

Social identities are not universally developed by all individuals. They rather are similar to person identities and role identities in that gender socialization (whether from the family or otherwise) greatly determines how identities are formed and maintained. The socialization that children receive by parents or significant authority figures (uncles, grandparents, etc.) within the family align children into separate tracts that are dependent on gender.

The previous discussion has shown that while there are different types of identities that are either constantly, usually, or occasionally activated, these identities are greatly predicated on gendered behavioral expectations that are socialized during the early stages of development. Identity theory's triadic typology of identity (person, role, and social) is greatly defined by gender; families socialize children to be individuals, assume roles, and eventually determine group membership. All such forms of identity involve gender and all have varying levels of expectations for how males and females should act according to traditional gender ideals.

Conclusions

This article has examined the ways in which family socialization can be applied and explained by an identity framework. While the locus of gender, gendered stereotypes, and gendered behavior remains relatively obscure, identity theory and identity control theory can identify how and why such phenomena perpetuate. The aim of this endeavor was to further the understanding of the socialization process, especially the mechanisms of how gender ideals are maintained and replicated. This was attempted by incorporating a theoretical structure that is yet to be fully fused and incorporated with the existent literature on family and socialization. Identity theory's explanation for how role typologies are defined by gender and how gender is salient across multiple situations, as well as identity control theory's use of emotion as a control system both serve to provide a better understanding of why males and females experience the world in different ways.

Further, research is needed to test the generalizations made in this article. This is especially true for work concerning the family setting and child socialization. Much of the current research in identity theory that examines the family addresses such themes as marriage and the division of household labor; the socialization process (especially in the earliest stages of socialization) is a relatively vacant area that needs to be explored. It is hoped that the conceptual application of identity theory and identity control theory that is presented here will provide an impetus toward testing how and to what degree such claims are empirically verifiable. Many aspects of identity theory and its derivatives are still in their relative infancy as theories; the application of these theories to gender, socialization, and the family is a logical step to make the theories more robust and sociologically viable.

References

Fenstermaker, Sarah, and Candace West. 2002. *Doing Gender, Doing Difference: Inequality, Power, and Institutional Change.* New York: Routledge.

James, William. 1890. *Principles of Psychology.* New York: Holt Rinehart and Winston.

Stryker, Sheldon, and Peter J. Burke. 2000. "The Past, Present, and Future of an Identity Theory." *Social Psychology Quarterly* 63:284–294.

West, Candace, and Don H. Zimmerman. 1987. "Doing Gender." *Gender and Society*, 1:125–151.

MICHAEL J. CARTER received his PhD in sociology from the University of California-Riverside and currently teaches sociology courses at California State University, Northridge. He has also taught courses at San Diego State University and the University of California-Riverside. His research interests include social psychology and microsocial psychological theory, particularly focusing on studying the areas of self and identity. He also studies identity processes in the deaf community.

EXPLORING THE ISSUE

Is Gender Identity Biological?

Critical Thinking and Reflection

1. What could be the goals behind each author's position in the gender controversy? Knowing that some of the authors have a history of working in transgender medicine, how might this affect their perspective on the etiology of gender? How might being transgender affect someone's position versus being cisgender?
2. Do you agree with the perspective that we are actors acting out gender roles? Look at your own life and count the things you do that could be labeled as "feminine" and those that could be labeled "masculine." What happens when people want to change their role? What would a world look like without gender?
3. Carter discusses person, role, and group identities. What are your own person, role, and group identities and how might they be influenced by your gender?
4. Carter's article relies more on theory than empirical evidence while the Saraswat et al. article references many empirical studies as evidence for gender as being biologically based. How do these two methods affect your opinion on the credibility of the authors' research? Which is the best way to study gender in your opinion?
5. While many of the cloacal exstrophy males with sex reassignment surgery (i.e., their exterior biology became more that of a female even though their chromosomes remained XY) in the Saraswat et al. article felt more male than female, how might the four individuals who kept a female identity undermine the supposition that gender is based purely on biology? How strong is the authors' evidence in supporting their claim?

Is There Common Ground?

While gender identity formation is arguably one of the more heated and controversial topics in society today, Saraswat et al. and Carter each take an academic, rather than simply a political, approach in exploring this issue. Saraswat et al. argue for the biological basis of gender while Carter argues for a societal etiology to explain why gender identity persists the way it does.

But while they have distinct differences, the two articles do reach some common ground. Neither article gives a definite cause for gender identity, but rather focus on how identity is either socially or biologically learned. Both articles focus on the formation of gender identity as being an individual experience, whether one is accepting a learned gender role or building an identity based on his or her biology. Each article also agrees that gender is an important attribute in a person's life that affects an individual's view their established roles in society.

One limitation of the articles is that each side seems deadlocked into distancing themselves from the other position to cement their own argument. Rather than looking at only one cause of gender from one specific field, perhaps we should be looking at gender's etiology from a multifaceted perspective from multiple disciplines; one that treats society, biology, and so on as potential causes working together that produce one's gender identity.

Additional Resources

Martin, C. L., Andrews, N. Z., England, D. E., Zosuls, K., & Ruble, D. N. (2017). A dual identity approach for conceptualizing and measuring children's gender identity. *Child Development, 88*(1), 167–182. doi:10.1111/cdev.12568

Shainess, N. (1969). The formation of gender identity. *The Journal of Sex Research, 5*(2), 75–85. Retrieved from http://www.jstor.org/stable/3811598

Viloria, H. (2017). *Born both: An intersex life.* New York: Hachette Books.

Westbrook, L., & Schilt, K. (2014). Doing gender, determining gender: Transgender people, gender panics, and the maintenance of the sex/gender/sexuality system. *Gender & Society, 28*(1), 32–57. doi:10.1177/0891243213503203

Internet References . . .

12 Causes of Gender Dysphoria

http://www.patheos.com/blogs/
catholicauthenticity/2015/07/12-causes-of-gender-
dysphoria/

Between the (Gender) Lines: The Science of Transgender Identity

http://sitn.hms.harvard.edu/flash/2016/gender-lines-
science-transgender-identity/

David Reimer, 38; After Botched Surgery, He Was Raised as a Girl in Gender Experiment

http://articles.latimes.com/2004/may/13/local/me-
reimer13

Dr. Money and the Boy with No Penis (Documentary)

https://www.youtube.com/watch?v=MUTcwqR4Q4Y

Gender Dysphoria

https://www.psychologytoday.com/conditions/gen-
der-dysphoria

The Gender Unicorn

http://www.transstudent.org/gender

Selected, Edited, and with Issue Framing Material by:
Edwin E. Gantt, *Brigham Young University*

ISSUE

Is Marriage Uniquely Important?

YES: Galena Rhoades, from "Sliding versus Deciding: How Cohabitation Changes Marriage," *The Family in America* (2016)

NO: Brienna Perelli-Harris and Marta Styrc, from "Re-evaluating the Link between Marriage and Mental Well-being: How Do Early Life Conditions Attenuate Differences between Cohabitation and Marriage?" *ESRC Center for Population Change, Working Paper 75* (2016)

Learning Outcomes

After reading this issue, you will be able to:

- Identify differences between dedication and constraint forms of commitment and the potential impact this has on marital quality and endurance.
- Recognize how timing of children (before or after marriage), prior relationship experience, and relationship history can affect marital quality.
- Understand the potential gender differences in regard to what childhood characteristics affect the benefits of marriage.
- Understand in what context, according to Perelli-Harris and Styrc, marriage is more beneficial than cohabiting, and what major variables confound this relationship.

ISSUE SUMMARY

YES: Rhoades summarizes research findings that indicate that stronger and more enduring marital relationships, and better mental health outcomes, occur when people make conscious decisions to commit to another person in a marital relationship rather than "sliding into" a marriage as the result of a progressive development of cohabiting.

NO: Perelli-Harris and Styrc argue that marriage affords no benefits over cohabitation in most circumstances. Their results indicate that when controlling for childhood characteristics, living with a partner increases well-being, but the type of relationship (marriage vs. cohabitation) does not matter.

Marriage between a man and a woman has been a strong and pervasive tradition in the Western civilization for centuries. The traditional union between a man and woman was believed to be the foundation and building block of the family, as well as a major cornerstone of society. It has been a widely held belief that marriage leads to the best allocation of resources, the happiest and most productive couples, and children with the highest chance of success in life. In Western society, there are also many religious reasons given in regard to marriage. The role of marriage has also implied much about the expected boundaries for sexual relationships, with abstinence before and fidelity within marriage traditionally touted as vital to the moral and social health of society. Advocates of traditional marriage often point to the many challenging social consequences that result from sexual relations and childbearing outside the bonds of marriage as evidence of the importance of marriage to a well-functioning society.

Recently, however, there has been a large movement taking aim at, or at least deemphasizing, the role of marriage. Much of this response has revolved around what is seen as sexual repression and an overly religious and unrealistic devotion to abstinence. Many claim that sex only within marriage is unhealthy, both physiologically and psychologically, and can later lead to sexual compatibility issues within a marriage. Skyrocketing divorce rates have also been cited as evidence that marriage has become outdated. Additionally, increasing pressure to marry for love, ensure the correct spouse, and be financially and emotionally prepared has led many individuals to opt to marry later in life, or even forgo marriage altogether. In fact, rates of cohabitation before marriage have steadily increased as traditional marriage paths have decreased, with people choosing to live together to ensure compatibility before getting married.

Galena Rhoades, the author of the YES articles, believes that dedication is the most important aspect of marriage, rather than love, compatibility, or preparation. Rhoades cites the dangers of "sliding" into a marriage, meaning cohabitation before marriage to ensure compatibility. She states that although this manner of cohabitation is agreed to be preparatory by both parties, decisions are frequently made that tie their lives together without the initial dedication and understanding of fidelity that the construct of marriage brings. Examples of such decisions include having a child, adopting a pet, or buying a home. When these decisions are made during the preparatory stage of cohabitation, it vastly complicates the situation if the couple decides that they want to split up rather than be married, leading to far worse situations. Rhoades' data suggest that the commitment to be married before these steps are taken can lead to healthier marriages and better mental health outcomes.

On the other hand, Perelli-Harris and Styrc, the authors of the NO article, state that marriage itself is not uniquely important, but rather the aspects of close human relationship and contact. In other words, it is not important whether or not the couple is married, but rather whether they are together and love each other. They make the argument that most of the data regarding marriage and mental health/happiness levels are misleading and do not account for many important confounding variables. For example, they cite childhood characteristics as a variable that, when taken into consideration, drastically changes the statistical outcomes of marital versus cohabitation rates of mental health/happiness levels. According to their data, marital advantages over cohabitation disappear for females when education plans and scores are accounted for and for males when adolescent mental well-being is accounted for. Across the board, however, living with a partner regardless of marital status was beneficial. Thus, according to the authors, marriage itself is not beneficial, but rather living with a partner in a committed relationship.

YES

Galena Rhoades

Sliding versus Deciding: How Cohabitation Changes Marriage

My colleague Scott Stanley and I put out a report in the summer of 2014 that was called "Before I Do," sponsored by the National Marriage Project at the University of Virginia; that report is the foundation for this article. A generation or two ago, people formed relationships and made commitments differently than they do now. We were interested in looking at the ways dating and commitment sequences have changed over the years, and how those sequences might be related to later marital quality.

One of the perspectives Scott Stanley and I have been working on is what we call "sliding versus deciding." This concept refers, in part, to the number of choices young people have today. This variety of choices might be one of the biggest differences between dating today and dating a generation or two ago; now people have many more options, not just in the partners that they choose, but also in the paths that might or might not lead them to marriage. Our general premise is that we can expect better outcomes if people make conscious decisions rather than sliding into new circumstances.

"Sliding versus deciding" summarizes the distinction between "dedication" and "constraint" commitment. "Commitment" usually implies the idea of a relationship having a long-term future, and that is what we call "dedication." It is a sense that the couple is working together as a team; there is the expectation of a future together and of planning for the future. The flip side of dedication commitment is "constraint" commitment. Constraint commitment comes from things that build up and make it harder to leave the relationship. Some examples of constraints are buying a home together, having a child together (that one does not happen to be predictive of whether or not couples stay together if they are unmarried, interestingly), or adopting a pet together—things that might make it harder to end a relationship regardless of how committed or dedicated you feel to that relationship. In simpler terms, constraint commitment is sliding; dedication is deciding.

A generation or two ago, deciding was the norm. You felt love toward another person, you felt attracted to another person, you decided to be more committed to another person, commitment built, and then you built constraints. It was after you made a commitment that you moved in together, had a child together, changed your career, moved across the country, bought a house together, and adopted pets. In that case, it did not really matter that you had taken on those extra constraints because you already felt dedicated to this person. But when you slide through new circumstances or relationship transitions like moving in together or having sex in a relationship, you break up that traditional sequence. For example, you might feel attracted to someone, you might feel like you love someone, and then you start building constraints without really developing a sense of dedication to the relationship. You are still on this track toward staying together, however, because of those constraints. We think what happens when people slide into relationship transitions is that they may start building constraints before they have a chance to think about whether they want to be committed or dedicated to this person and this relationship; and this constraint before commitment could cause problems later on.

To look at some of these questions about experiences and sequences before marriage, Scott and I used a study that we had conducted with our colleague Howard Markman at the University of Denver, a study that was initially funded by the National Institute of Child Health and Human Development. We call it the relationship development study. About 1,300 people started this study. They were recruited nationally, all of them unmarried English-speaking people in the United States. They completed surveys 30–35 pages long in 11 waves four to six months apart. We were interested in looking at these unmarried couples and following them over time to see what happened. (I am very grateful that these participants stuck with us long enough to complete this study because it was

Rhoades, Galena, "Sliding vs. Deciding: How Cohabitation Changes Marriage" *The Family in America*, Spring 2016. The Howard Center for Family, Religion & Society. Used with permission.

fairly time-consuming and a little intrusive.) We focused only on people in opposite-sex relationships in this study. When the study started, about ⊠ of participants were dating, and the other third had already moved in with their partners. For this report, we chose people who got married during the course of the study so that we could examine the histories of those relationships and those individuals, maybe even before they got into the relationship that turned into marriage, and then we could look at their marital quality after marriage.

Here are some of the results in basically a $y = mx + b$ kind of equation. We used multilevel modeling so that we could aggregate the information that people had given us about themselves over these 11 waves of data to predict marital quality. We measured marital quality with a brief version of a widely used instrument called the Dyadic Adjustments Scale. This instrument asks people to rate their marital happiness, how often they confide in one another, how often they think things are going well, and how often they have thought of breaking up or getting a divorce. In this sample, people were relatively happy, reporting fairly high marital quality, which makes sense, since most of them had just gotten married. In order to continue with the study, they had to get married during the study period; and usually newlyweds have the highest level of marital quality they will ever experience. Marital quality tends to decline after marriage, but why wouldn't it? You are not going to get married if you are not pretty sure you are happy in the relationship.

We analyzed a number of background characteristics before we started looking at the main questions about different relationship experiences and transitions. Most of our findings did not vary much when control variables were added. Often, the association was a little weaker with controls, but there were very few instances when a finding became nonsignificant. One of the messages from our results is that not many background characteristics were related to marital quality, at least in these first couple of years into marriage. What we do see are associations between factors that are significant, significance that has been well replicated. For example, we know that people who have higher levels of education tend to report higher marital quality, and they are less likely to get a divorce. We know that people who were living with both of their biological parents when they were 14-years old also report higher marital quality later on. (There is nothing magical about the number 14; it is just the age that was used in other research.) We know that people who come from more stable families tend to have more stability in their own relationships later on. Unfortunately, we also see

some important gaps between African Americans and Caucasians in terms of stability and quality of relationships. In this study, we do not see that religiousness was associated with marital quality. That contradicts a number of findings in this field, however, and merits some explanation. I think the reason we do not see an association between religion and marital quality in this study is because we are looking at such an early segment of marital quality; the effects of religiousness might show up later in marriage, especially when couples are having children together. Similarly, we did not find that income was associated with marital quality in this study and that also contradicts other findings, especially about the way income is related to the risk for divorce. Here again, I think that is likely because we were looking at marital quality right after marriage.

In terms of the main findings, we focused on two broad categories of experiences people might have before getting married. One category is experiences from prior relationships. The other category is experiences with the person whom they eventually marry, the couple's history before marriage. Based partly on the findings discussed earlier regarding background characteristics but also on the general literature, we controlled for a number of variables related to marital quality. We also looked at some moderators, factors that might make the findings different for different people. We wanted to know if any of those associations might be different for men and women or if they might be different for people with and without a college level of education.

Regarding individuals' prior relationship experiences, here is what we have found. Most of the people in the study were entering a first marriage. People who were entering a first marriage reported higher marital quality than people who were entering a second or third or even fourth (there was ¼ marriage in this sample). Couples with children from prior relationships had lower marital quality later on. We also looked at their experiences with past sexual partners. People who had sex only with their future spouse and no one else reported higher marital quality later on. About 23 percent of this sample had sex only with the person they married. (Unfortunately, we did not ask this question quite correctly to discern if they had sex before they got married or not. There has not been much research on that in a number of years; the timing of sex in relationships and what that might mean for marital quality later on is still a very important question.) Almost 40 percent of the sample had lived with a prior partner before they got together with the person they married; having had other cohabiting partners was associated with lower marital quality later on.

One of the most interesting things about these findings, which in many ways were new to this field, is that prior relationship experience really matters, but in a somewhat counterintuitive way. If you are hiring an architect, you want to hire someone who has a lot of experience. If you are going to see a doctor, you probably want a doctor who has a lot of experience in your illness. But in terms of relationships, we are seeing that the opposite is true. People with more experience might end up having more trouble later on in their marriages. There are a couple of potential explanations for this. One is that, if you have a lot of experience, you also have a greater sense of what the alternatives are, and you have more comparisons to make to other people. It is also true that the more experience you have in relationships, the more experience you have in breaking up. That experience with breaking up might make it seem easier to break up later in a marriage or it may make you think about breaking up more and question the quality of the relationship more. We also see that more experience means you are more likely to have children before you get married, and we saw the effect of that earlier.

More than 40 percent of babies born in the United States today are born to unmarried parents. We used to say they were born to single mothers, but they are not "single" mothers, for the most part. The mothers are often partnered with the baby's father or with someone else when the baby is born. We also know that those families tend to be quite fragile, and we are seeing some of that fragility carried over in these findings about marriage as well: children from prior relationships tend to be difficult on a marriage. Having children is hard, and it is especially hard to start a marriage already having children.

It is interesting to think about the messages young people hear today about relationship experience, messages like, "Don't settle down too soon." "Make sure you get everything out of your system." "Your 20s are a time for great exploration." "What happens in Vegas stays in Vegas." "Those things won't affect your future marital quality or outcomes." In fact, what we are seeing here seems to be the opposite. Those experiences do impact us in some important ways and may lead us to having a more difficult time later on in marriage. Scott Stanley talks about the "duct-tape hypothesis," which is the idea that, if you have a piece of duct tape and you keep sticking it to things, it gets less sticky over time. Applied to relationships, the idea is that the more relationships you have, the harder it may be to really commit to another partner going forward.

We asked people if their relationship started with "hooking up," and we let them self-define what "hooking up" meant. About 32 percent of the sample did start that way, and we found that those couples had lower marital quality later on.

Couples who had children together already or who were pregnant before they got married also had lower marital quality. This finding may reflect the fact that having kids is hard, but it may also be a result of sliding into marriage. Hooking up, having sex before getting into a relationship, before feeling committed in a relationship, and having children or becoming pregnant before getting married may also reflect that sliding mentality to some degree.

However, education level was also related to how strongly being pregnant before marriage was associated with later marital quality. People who had a college degree were much less likely to be in the top marital quality group if they had a child together before they got married. For people who did not have a college degree, we hardly saw any difference at all in their marital quality based on whether they had a child before they got married. That difference is important for us to think about in future work and in public policy as well. In part, what this reflects are the norms. People who do not graduate from high school are much more likely to have a child outside of marriage than people who graduate from college. It is really quite outside the norm for people who do graduate from college to have a baby or become pregnant, or to let anyone know about that before getting married. Those social norms might affect later marital quality.

We also tried to look at some potential red flags in a relationship before getting married. We asked people in the study whether they had ever had a sexual relationship with someone other than their partner while they were dating that person; in other words, had this person ever cheated on their partner before getting married. In our sample, 16 percent said yes, but this was only very weakly related to marital quality later on. Again, this is not a great message for us to be telling young people. Many dating relationships where there is infidelity end long before they would turn into marriage. About ten percent of our sample knew that their partner had had a sexual relationship with someone else while the two of them were dating and that was related to lower marital quality later on.

We asked a number of questions about commitment and cohabitation. We asked people about the timing of moving in together and whether they had committed to marriage before they moved in together. About 70 percent of this sample had lived together before they got married. We found that people who had lived together before they were committed to marriage together, before they had a mutual and clear plan to get married, reported lower marital quality later on. About 70 percent to 75 percent of people now live together before they get married. The most common answer to the question "Why did you move in together?" is "It just kind of happened." And that it was more convenient. What we are seeing here is that, if a couple has already made the commitment to marry, if they are already dedicated to one another, moving in together is not associated with lower marital quality. However, moving in is associated with lower marital quality among those couples that slide into living together but then maybe build a number of those constraints. For some of them, it may be the constraints that lead them to get married, when they otherwise maybe would not have married this partner after all. That is also an important finding to consider, because a lot of young people today really like the idea of collecting lots of data before making the big decision of getting married. What better way to do that than by moving in with this person? You want to know if this person is going to leave the toilet seat up, or you want to know how she handles money. You want to find out all these things about this person. This desire may come from a really good place, but the problem is that moving in together may put couples on a track toward getting married that is hard to get off. It is harder to end a relationship once you have moved in together, even if the relationship fails that test, essentially.

We asked people who did live with their partners before they got married how it happened. Was it a slide, or did you make the decision together? We found that people who said they made a decision together reported higher marital quality, which supports the idea that deciding is generally associated with better outcomes. We also asked people at every wave to rate their own commitment on a one to seven scale, and then immediately afterward to rate their partner's commitment on the same one to seven scale. Interestingly, across those waves, before they got married, if they ever thought they were more committed than their partner was, they had lower marital quality later on. The results reflect the idea that, if there are major differences between a couple in how they like to make decisions and what commitment means to them, those differences may continue to cause problems.

We asked about the wedding and whether people got any kind of premarital education. An amazing 43 percent of people said that they got some kind of premarital education together. That education could range from something like meeting with the pastor at the church one time to talk about wedding plans to something much more intensive, like a 30-hr workshop on relationships. There

is good evidence that premarital education—especially the kind that teaches couples communication skills and gets them talking about differences and expectations—is associated with a lower risk for divorce later on. We asked if people had a wedding, and about 90 percent said yes. Those who were in the minority on that question reported lower marital quality later on. We also asked how many people attended the wedding. The mean number of people was 116 in this sample, and the more people you had at your wedding, the higher your marital quality later on.

Further, research that has come out recently has looked at this question of wedding attendance more carefully, and they also find that the more people who attend your wedding, the higher your marital quality and the lower your risk for divorce—and it is not related to how much money you spend on the wedding. There are some really good theoretical reasons to think that the number of people who attend might actually be important. One reason is that the more public your commitment is, the more likely you are to follow through on that. If you stand up and tell 100 or 200 people that you are promising to spend the rest of your life with this person in sickness and in health, it is going to be a little harder for you to break that promise because it has been such a public commitment. The other reason is that the large group likely reflects a greater social system and social network that supports your marriage. It may be that people who have more wedding attendees simply also have greater social networks. There may also be a causal relationship there as well, because it means that this entire audience of people has also committed to you to help protect your marriage and support you in this marriage. We were a little nervous about the implications of these findings at first, and I think this is a great area to do more research to really understand what these dynamics mean before we start sending the message, "Go have a big wedding and make your parents spend lots of money on it." This is, however, an interesting finding to think about in terms of sliding versus deciding, of commitment and what it means.

So what does this all mean for educating people about relationships? One thing is clear: there are some experiences and background characteristics people have that they cannot change. We cannot go back and change whether we were living with both our biological parents at age 14, but there may be some ways we can change the dynamics that those kinds of background characteristics initiate. We also see that there are many things young people have some control over that may be related to later marital quality and outcomes. We really need to start thinking about ways that we can impact people and help them make good relationship decisions earlier. The field of relationship education has focused on couples and pre-marital couples. It seems important to teach people how to communicate better, but I think we could have a much greater impact if we helped people think about their relationship experiences before they have them—when they are teenagers, when they are young adults, and when they are in the middle of making some of these decisions or sliding through things. These are the times to think about whether they should hook up with somebody, whether they should get pregnant, and whether they should move in with someone. There is a great amount of education that we could be doing long before a couple is about to walk down the aisle.

GALENA RHOADES, PhD, is a research associate professor in the Psychology Department at the University of Denver. Her research focus investigates romantic relationship development and functioning and the related implications for children and adults.

Brienna Perelli-Harris and Marta Styrc,

Re-evaluating the Link between Marriage and Mental Well-being

How Do Early Life Conditions Attenuate Differences between Cohabitation and Marriage?

Introduction

Numerous studies have found that marriage benefits health and well-being. The strength and persistence of these findings have led some policy makers to call for programs that encourage marriage. For example, pro-marriage policy initiatives were pushed during the George W. Bush administration in the United States, and the current conservative UK government led by David Cameron has recently legislated tax breaks for married couples and plans to extend them further in the next few years. Much of the research underlying these initiatives, however, has compared the married and unmarried, without distinguishing between those who were in cohabiting partnerships or single. In addition, the majority of previous research was conducted in the United States during a period when cohabitation was relatively rare or practiced by a select few; less is known about marriage and mental well-being in other contexts. Given the recent increase in cohabitation and its changing meaning as it becomes more widespread, it is important to revisit whether partnerships in general, and marriage in particular, continue to provide distinct benefits to well-being, especially for those who are less likely to marry.

Here, we examine to what extent being in a partnership and the type of the partnership—marriage or cohabitation—increases well-being. We analyze recent data from the United Kingdom, which has experienced a rapid increase in cohabitation over the past few decades. In the United Kingdom, cohabitation has become the normative pathway to union formation: in 2004–2007, 80 percent of all marriages started with premarital cohabitation. The duration of cohabiting unions has also been steadily increasing. In addition, cohabitation has become common for childbearing: in 2012, 30 percent of all births were born to cohabiting mothers. The increase and pervasiveness of cohabitation suggests that cohabitation may be taking on much of the form and function of marriage. Because two people live together in an intimate relationship, cohabitation may provide many of the same benefits to well-being that marriage does, including sexual intimacy, emotional and social support, and social control. Thus, the act of marriage per se may not matter for well-being; instead, simply forming a stable partnership may be what is important.

Background

While numerous studies have established a positive link between marriage and well-being, few have compared cohabitation and marriage. Note, however, that cohabitation and marriage are usually not either–or statuses; couples who are currently married in midlife may have previously cohabited, and those who are currently cohabiting may have plans to marry. In our study, 75 percent of current unions that started as cohabiting relationships converted to marriage. This fluidity of partnership status indicates that it is usually incorrect to simply label people as "cohabitors" or "married people." In this study, we consider marriage a "treatment," in that couples must officially decide to marry and act on that decision, but we recognize the fluidity of relationships and that cohabiting couples may marry later in life.

Below, we focus on several conceptualizations of partnership that may result in benefits to well-being. First, we examine whether simply living with a partner at age 42, regardless of being married or cohabiting, provides a boost to well-being.

Then, we consider current partnership type (at age 42); marriage may provide an additional benefit to well-being above and beyond simply living with a partner. However, examining current status is insufficient; mar-

Perelli-Harris, Brienna; Styrc, Marta (2016) "Re-evaluating the Link Between Marriage and Mental Well-Being: How do Early Life Conditions Attenuate Differences Between Cohabitation and Marriage?" ESRC Centre for Population Change Working Papers, 75.

riages are often of longer duration, and cohabiting unions are more likely to dissolve. The length of a union may be related to the partners' commitment, and the experience of union dissolution can have long-lasting effects on well-being. Thus, we compare union status for individuals in increasingly committed relationships: those in partnerships lasting longer than three years and first relationships which never dissolved. Finally, we examine whether the partners have children, as they may signal an important investment in the relationship.

Current Relationship Status

An individuals' current partnership status, regardless of whether married or cohabiting, is potentially the most relevant to current well-being. Living in a partnership usually provides sexual and emotional intimacy, companionship, and daily interaction, which can promote well-being. An intimate partner can provide care and social and emotional support and encourage healthy behaviors. In addition, partners often link each other to greater friendship and kin networks that can provide social support. Living together and sharing a household can lead to economies of scale. The savings incurred may be particularly important for low-income couples, who in qualitative interviews in the United Kingdom have mentioned that the decision to move in together was motivated by housing costs.

Beyond simply living with a partner, however, living in a marital union may provide unique benefits to well-being. Marriage is often a social sign of commitment, also known as "enforceable trust." The symbolic promise of marriage may provide couples with a long-term perspective that the future of their relationship is secure. Because marriages are legally harder to dissolve, couples may be more motivated to work through their disagreements, thereby maintaining union stability and with its general life stability. The long-term perspective may also benefit personal and social control, meaning spouses deliberately influence each other's personal behavior, because they want them to be healthy and live longer. The reduction in life uncertainty and increased care could enhance well-being and even result in psychological or cognitive changes that promote mental well-being. These benefits may be enhanced further through personal networks, such as in-laws, which provide extra support to married couples, because the relationships are more defined. In addition, the UK legal system continues to favor marriage in terms of inheritance tax and access to the courts when unions dissolve. Although general social disapproval of cohabitation is low in Britain, the social expectation to marry is still pervasive.

Thus, although living with someone may result in many of the same benefits to mental well-being, in today's Britain, marriage may still be a sign of a more committed relationship and confer additional social and legal benefits, which would in turn enhance well-being.

Unions with Children

Having shared children can be an important sign of investment in a relationship. Previous studies have considered childbearing to be an indicator of the similarity between cohabitation and marriage. Like married parents, cohabiting parents have a shared interest in their children, can provide care and other resources, and may work harder to maintain their relationship to ensure stability.

Unmarried fathers in the United Kingdom have the same rights as married fathers and face little social disapproval for not marrying their child's mother. Nonetheless, studies show that cohabiting parents continue to be different from married parents; for example, in the United Kingdom, cohabiting parents are more likely to separate and have lower second birth rates than their married counterparts. Hence, cohabiting parents with shared children may continue to have different well-being than married parents.

Selection Characteristics from Childhood

The benefits of partnerships and marriage may not be causal, but instead the result of social selection, which suggests that differences in well-being are due to the characteristics of the people who choose to be in a particular type of partnership. In our study, we focus on childhood characteristics that occur before the "treatment," or entering into an adult partnership. Parental influences and characteristics that have developed in childhood are very important for determining later life outcomes.

Health and mortality research suggests that the "long arm of childhood" extends into adulthood and is a significant predictor of adult health outcomes. In this paper, we consider three types of interrelated background characteristics: parents' socioeconomic status and family structure, child's cognitive development and educational aspirations, and psychological attributes.

Parental socioeconomic status is one of the most significant predictors of future life outcomes. The intergenerational transmission of conditions and behaviors is extremely important for educational trajectories, social mobility, and future employment, all of which can have implications for both partnerships and mental well-being. Parents' socioeconomic position influences childhood development and adult outcomes through a complex set of transmission mechanisms, including values and attitudes, resources, behaviors, social interactions, and genetic endowments. Some of the characteristics of the parents seem to directly influence cohabitation and marriage, for example, in Britain, the mother's age at birth and father's social class have been associated with entrance into cohabitation. Parents' marital status and divorce in childhood can also hinder the development of interpersonal and relationship skills, cognitive growth, and educational achievement, which again may influence both partnership formation and mental health. Parental divorce often leads children to reject the institution of marriage and adopt more favorable attitudes toward cohabitation and divorce, as well as choose cohabitation for their own relationships.

Despite the strong influence of the parental home, however, children usually develop their own independent personalities, dispositions, and abilities throughout childhood and adolescence. Many different factors can influence this independent development; for example, during adolescence, peers can be more important for personal development and individual behavioral choices than parents. The children's cognitive development and educational aspirations in childhood usually influence future educational attainment, which can in turn influence mental well-being and partnership formation. In many countries, marriage is associated with higher education, which may also influence well-being, suggesting that childhood cognitive abilities and educational aspirations may be key predictors for both partnership formation and mental well-being.

Finally, an individual's psychological and behavioral attributes in childhood can have major influences on both partnership formation and mental well-being. Psychological attributes, for example, depression, self-esteem, locus of control, and behavioral problems, are usually predictors of future mental health, or even an alternative way of measuring the baseline of mental health. Previous studies demonstrate that childhood psychological problems have a long-term effect on adult family income and other noneconomic outcomes. Psychological attributes in childhood may be influenced by genetic predispositions that lead to mental health problems such as depression. An individual's capacity to mobilize available resources, develop coping mechanisms, and become resilient to adversity can shape behavior and psychological outlook. Hence, examining the contribution of childhood mental health on future mental health helps us to better understand the relationship between partnership formation and mental well-being.

Discussion

This study provides insights into the role of marriage and cohabitation, and relationships in general, on mental well-being in midlife. As in previous studies, we see significant benefits to marriage when comparing raw differences in well-being scores between cohabiting and married people, even when comparing increasingly committed relationship types. However, the benefits to marriage versus cohabitation disappear completely when we compare the effects of marriage among people who have similar childhood characteristics. This is also the case for people who have a low propensity to marry: marriage would not improve their well-being. The benefits to currently being in any type of relationship, on the other hand, do not disappear when matching people on childhood characteristics; people who do not live with a partner have on average well-being scores that are lower than those who live with a partner.

First, we see the importance of currently being in a coresidential relationship for mental well-being in midlife, regardless of relationship type. The raw differences in well-being scores were relatively large, and numerous selection mechanisms in childhood, many of which would have predicted future behavior and well-being, were unable to eliminate these differences. These results suggest that living with an intimate partner is likely to boost well-being, possibly by providing emotional support, social networks, sexual intimacy, companionship, and social meaning—all of which are good for mental health. Nonetheless, we did not control for developments in adulthood or current factors which may impact well-being, such as income or friends, and we cannot say the models completely isolated causal effects. Additional research, for example, using weighted regression, could be used to control for contemporaneous effects, but because the main focus of this paper is cohabitation and marriage, we have not conducted these analyses.

Our main finding that cohabitation and marriage have similar long-term implications for well-being after matching is particularly interesting, given the rapid increase in cohabitation in Britain. For the 1970 cohort, 81 percent of current marriages started with cohabitation. Hence, cohabitation is becoming an acceptable and common partnership form, especially as a way to enter a union. Nonetheless, by age 42, relatively few are still in first unions which have lasted for at least three years, have not married, and have had children (only about five percent of all people, and 12 percent of those still in a first long-lasting union). This small percentage suggests that staying in a long-term cohabiting union into midlife is still a marginal behavior in Britain. Also note that the positive association between marriage and well-being only disappears when matching on early childhood characteristics, implying that while marriage may not have a causal effect on well-being, the people who choose to enter cohabitation are still different on average from those who marry.

Although the analyses provide evidence that a range of background characteristics eliminates the differences between cohabitation and marriage for both men and women, we also found variation according to specific sources of selection. Surprisingly, the large range of parental background characteristics was unable to remove differences between cohabitation and marriage, except for men currently in a partnership with shared children. These results suggest that marriage would still be beneficial, if the only source of selection was socioeconomic status. Childhood test scores and educational plans, on the other hand, resulted in an interesting gender distinction. For women, matching on educational aspirations eliminated differences in well-being for cohabitors and married women, except for those currently in a union. These results imply that once women are selected based on education (i.e., lower education), marriage no longer matters. For men, however, educational aspirations do not completely diminish the benefits of marriage; for low educated men, those who were married still had higher well-being, except for those currently married with children. Hence, marriage may still provide an advantage to men who are more disadvantaged, potentially indicating that marriage is an indicator of social control, commitment, and enforceable trust.

Finally, the results demonstrate that the role of childhood psychological attributes differs somewhat between men and women. Men who have low psychological well-being at age 16 are more likely to cohabit at age 42, but marriage is unlikely to boost their mental well-being if they are in long-term cohabiting relationships with the mother of their children. Among women who are less likely to marry, however, marriage would boost well-being, except for women in first, long-term unions with children. These results imply that women with mental health issues may benefit from marriage, potentially because marriage signals greater stability and long-term social support.

This study has demonstrated the importance of early childhood conditions for understanding the relationship between cohabitation, marriage, and mental well-being. While previous studies comparing outcomes between cohabitation and marriage have generally controlled for contemporaneous selection effects or unobserved heterogeneity, to our knowledge none has specifically examined how selection mechanisms dating back to childhood explain the differential effects of marriage. Our study provides further evidence that early childhood conditions are important for understanding later life well-being. While we found that all of the childhood characteristics together eliminate differences between cohabitation and marriage, we also found some interesting differences between the three domains of childhood selection factors and gender, as described above. Of course, the three domains are interrelated, and it is impossible to know to what extent parental socioeconomic background and family structure explain educational attainment or psychological attributes; in addition, the effects may be reciprocal, that is, childhood behavioral difficulties could strain the parents' marriage and lead to divorce. Nonetheless, taken together, these background characteristics all play strong role in eliminating differences between cohabitation and marriage. Hence, in order to improve mental well-being, policy makers should focus on reducing the adverse effects of disadvantage in childhood and improving mental well-being in adolescence, rather than legislating incentives to marry in adulthood.

BRIENNA PERELLI-HARRIS is an associate professor at the University of Southampton. Previously, she was a research scientist at the Max Planck Institute for Demographic Research in Rostock, Germany and a postdoc at the University of Wisconsin.

MARTA STYRC is a visiting research fellow in the field of demography at the University of Southampton. Previously, she was a research fellow for CPC working within the fertility and family change strand.

EXPLORING THE ISSUE

Is Marriage Uniquely Important?

Critical Thinking and Reflection

1. Do married couples have significantly higher rates of well-being than cohabiting couples? What variables can potentially affect the answer to this question?
2. Why might educational scores eliminate differences in cohabiting and marriage for women, while adolescent mental well-being eliminates differences for men? What are possible explanations for these gender differences?
3. Why might prior relationships affect marital quality? Why would those entering a second marriage report lower qualities of marital satisfaction than those entering a first marriage?
4. Why might those who began a relationship through "hooking-up" report lower marital quality?

Is There Common Ground?

While these two different parties disagree on the benefits of marriage itself, they would agree that close human contact and relationships are critical to human health and well-being. Traits of a good relationship such as dedication, commitment, compatibility, and love are considered essential to mental health and happiness for both parties. It is conceivable that those in the "marriage" camp would agree that a loving and committed cohabitation relationship is an improvement over an abusive and violent marriage relationship, while those in the "cohabitation" camp would likely agree that marriage is not inherently evil, but rather that traditional marriage guidelines are overly restrictive.

A common thread of those criticizing cohabitation is a seeming lack of commitment and dedication, while a common thread of those criticizing traditional marriage is a fear of rushing a commitment before a beneficial matching can be ensured. There seems to be evidence for and against both of these claims. An understanding of individual differences versus general (and often weak and confounded) statistical patterns can potentially lead to common ground, as individual circumstances for each couple are taken into consideration in which one path makes more sense than the other. In other words, a potential common ground could be in understanding the needs of individual couples, and what will lead to greatest well-being for them.

Additional Resources

Esolen, A. (2014). *Defending Marriage: Twelve Arguments for Sanity*. Charlotte, NC: Saint Benedict Press.

Peters, H. E., & Kamp Dush, C. M. (2009). *Marriage and Family: Perspectives and Complexities*. New York, NY: Columbia University Press.

Stanton, G. T. (2011). *The Ring Makes All the Difference: The Hidden Consequences of Cohabitation—and the Strong Benefits of Marriage*. Chicago, IL: Moody.

Thornton, A., Axinn, W. G., & Xie, Y. (2007). *Marriage and Cohabitation*. Chicago, IL: The University of Chicago Press.

Internet References . . .

Cohabitating Couples Are Happier than Wedded Ones. Cornell Chronicle, 2012

http://www.news.cornell.edu/stories/2012/01/cohabiting-couples-are-happier-wedded-ones

Family Life

http://www.familylife.com/articles/topics/marriage

Marriage versus Cohabitation

http://family.findlaw.com/living-together/marriage-vs-cohabitation.html

The Knot Yet Report: The Benefits and Costs of Delayed Marriage in America

http://twentysomethingmarriage.org/

Selected, Edited, and with Issue Framing Material by:
Edwin E. Gantt, *Brigham Young University*

ISSUE

Is Excessive Use of Social Media a Form of Narcissism?

YES: Soraya Mehdizadeh, from "Self-Presentation 2.0: Narcissism and Self-Esteem on Facebook," *Cyberpsychology, Behavior, and Social Networking* (2010)

NO: Alex Lambert, from "Discovering Intimacy on Facebook," *Macmillan* (2013)

Learning Outcomes

After reading this issue, you will be able to:

- Decide if Facebook is a tool more frequently used by individuals with narcissistic personalities than other personality types.
- Discuss alternative explanations for why people might use Facebook, including its use as a tool to increase bonds of friendship and intimacy.
- Decide if there really is persuasive empirical evidence to support the contention that there is a causal relationship between Facebook use and narcissism.

ISSUE SUMMARY

YES: Soraya Mehdizadeh examines how narcissism and self-esteem are manifest on Facebook. Her study reveals that individuals who rate higher in narcissism and lower in self-esteem tend to use Facebook significantly more often than those who score lower in narcissism and higher in self-esteem.

NO: Alex Lambert, a researcher of new media at University of Melbourne, reviews the arguments against the narcissism hypothesis. He claims that Facebook use is primarily about seeking intimacy with other people and not about fulfilling narcissistic desires.

It seems that everybody has a Facebook account these days. Facebook has become so commonplace in our society that people are often considered strange for *not* having an account or not using it regularly. Still, Facebook use has become increasingly controversial in recent years (Anderson, Fagan, Woodnutt, & Chamorro-Premuzic, 2012). Common concerns include the prevalence of inappropriate behaviors, verbal abuse, cyber-bullying, interpersonal conflict, and breaches of privacy (Anderson, Fagan, Woodnutt, & Chamorro-Premuzic, 2012; Aydin, 2012). Though some of these concerns are similar to those regarding Internet use generally, the controversial nature of Facebook is unique insofar as Facebook use is just as much about the cultivation

and presentation of one's own self-image as it is about interacting with other people.

Some recent research suggests that Facebook's uniqueness is positive. Its format—which encourages expanding one's social network (or "audience") as well as encouraging emotional self-disclosure—may facilitate both the development of new friendships and the preservation of old friendships (Manago, Taylor, & Greenfield, 2012). For this reason, many psychologists regard Facebook as a welcome technological development, a tool for developing and maintaining social relationships in a rapidly evolving world. However, is it possible that *excessive* use of Facebook—with its inherent emphasis on cultivating and presenting one's self to others—is associated with *narcissism*? Psychologists consider narcissism to be a personality disorder in which people have an inflated sense of self-importance as well as extreme preoccupation with themselves. Needless to say, this consequence would not be a positive outcome of Facebook use.

The author of the YES selection, Soraya Mehdizadeh, agrees that Facebook can have negative consequences. She believes that Facebook is a fertile environment for people to express narcissistic tendencies. Because Facebook provides people with a means to develop and maintain a network of friends and acquaintances, with the express purpose of sharing personal information with that network, it can become an ideal setting for people with narcissistic personalities to feed their self-gratifying desires and to boost their low self-esteem. In order to support this claim, Mehdizadeh had 100 college students take a survey designed to determine if how they rated in regards to their narcissistic personality traits and self-esteem. According to Mehdizadeh, the results of the study suggest that those with higher narcissistic personality traits and lower self-esteem are more likely to use Facebook. Therefore, Facebook is a means by which narcissistic personalities can achieve a measure of self-gratification.

The author of the NO selection argues a much different point of view. Alex Lambert believes that self-gratification is unrelated to the end-goal of Facebook use. Though it is likely that narcissism may influence *some* people's behavior on Facebook, Lambert believes that the majority of young adults use Facebook merely as a tool to increase the intensity of intimacy with others—independent of narcissistic personality traits. As such, he contends that the frequency of Facebook use by those rated high on narcissistic traits *is not* indicative of narcissism. To support this claim, Lambert refers to various studies that have been administered to show how Facebook is primarily a tool of communication between individuals. According to Lambert, narcissism is unrelated to the frequency of Facebook use by narcissistic users but because of the relational nature of Facebook, it must be used to increase intimacy between individuals and communities.

YES ⤹

Soraya Mehdizadeh

Self-Presentation 2.0: Narcissism and Self-Esteem on Facebook

Introduction

The Internet officially gained public face in the early 1990s; since then, it has completely changed the way information is broadcasted to the world.[1] By means of the World Wide Web, any user with minimal knowledge of the Internet is able to relay information to a vast audience through personal blogging, videos, and photos via interactive Internet sites known as Web 2.0 applications.[1] By means of these specific Web communities, individuals can post self-relevant information, link to other members, and interact with other members. Most notably, these Web sites offer a gateway for online identity constructions.[2]

While the impact of the Internet on identity production has been under investigation for over a decade, most of these studies have focused on anonymous online environments, including chat rooms and bulletin boards.[3] More recently, researchers are shifting their attention to self-presentation in less anonymous online communities, known as social networking Web sites. These virtual settings cater to a specific population in which people of similar interest gather to communicate, share, and discuss ideas. In the early phase of this research, some studies examined the effect of Internet dating sites.[3] A study of this phenomenon by Ellison et al.[4] found that people act differently in social networking environments when compared to those interacting in anonymous settings. This finding had enormous implications in identity formation in the online world, as it indicated that online self-presentation varied according to the nature of the setting.

Along with dating sites, friend-networking sites such as MySpace and Facebook have become extremely popular among college and university students.[5] These sites offer a highly controlled environment for self-presentational behavior, which provides an ideal setting for impression management.[1]

. . .

Narcissism and Online Self-Presentation

Narcissism is a pervasive pattern of grandiosity, need for admiration, and an exaggerated sense of self-importance.[6] It is associated with positive self-views of agentic traits, including intelligence, physical attractiveness, and power. Central to most theoretical models of narcissism, the use of social relationships is employed in order to regulate narcissistic esteem. However, narcissists do not focus on interpersonal intimacy, warmth, or other positive aspects of relational outcomes. Instead, they use relationships to appear popular and successful, and they seek attractive, high status individuals as romantic partners.[7] Despite their tendency to seek out many superficial, empty relationships, narcissists rarely pursue these commitments for long periods of time. Relationships are solely pursued when an opportunity for public glory presents itself.[7]

Recently, there has been a tremendous amount of media attention surrounding the issue of narcissism and social-networking Web sites.[2] These online communities have been targeted as a particularly fertile ground for narcissists to self-regulate for a number of reasons. First, this setting offers a gateway for hundreds of shallow relationships (i.e., virtual friends), and emotionally detached communication (i.e., wall posts, comments). While these sites do indeed serve a communicative purpose among friends, colleagues, and family, other registered users can initiate requests to be friends, and one's social network often snowballs rapidly across institutions in this fashion.[8] Second, social-networking Web pages are highly controlled environments that allow owners complete power over self-presentations.[2] Users can convey desirable information about themselves (via features such as About Me, Notes, and Status Updates routinely found on social-networking sites) and can select attractive, self-promoting photographs. This type of virtual arena allows narcissists to pursue an infinite number of trivial friendships and further enables them to boast self-views of positive agentic traits.[2]

These effects may be even more evident in nonymous Web sites, such as Facebook, where users can make public "identity statements" that they may not normally do offline. These statements can take both explicit (i.e., autobiographic descriptions) and implicit (i.e., photos) forms and ultimately enable people to stage a public display of their hoped-for possible selves.[3] In accordance with this notion, research by Buffardi and Campbell[2] confirmed that narcissism predicted higher levels of social activity in the online community and more self-promoting content in several aspects of the social networking Web pages.[2]

Self-Esteem and Online Self-Presentation

In psychology, self-esteem is defined as a person's overall self-evaluation of his or her worth.[9] Implicit and explicit self-esteem are subtypes of self-esteem. Implicit self-esteem is an automatic, unconscious self-evaluation; explicit self-esteem is a more conscious, reflective self-evaluation.[9] Regardless of the type of self-esteem, one of the most pervasive facts about this construct is that all humans have a vital need to maintain and/or raise it.[1] Parallel to this line of thought, it can be expected that individuals will strive for positive self-presentations in both online and offline social settings. It is also likely that people with low self-esteem will be even more eager to engage in online activities that may raise their self-esteem.[1] By doing so, it may provide an outlet for the hoped-for possible self to be expressed.[1] However, with regard to online impression management, Krämer and Winter did not find any differences between self-presentation and low and high self-esteem users.[1] These contradictory results warrant further research within the emerging field of online self-presentation.

Overview of the Present Study

The present study extends the existing research on self-presentation in online friend-networking Web pages. Although there are many online venues appropriate for this type of research (e.g., MySpace), Facebook was used in this investigation for two reasons. First, Facebook is the most commonly used site by individuals in our sample—university students.[6] When this site was first created, a university e-mail address was required to set up an account. Although virtually anyone can now sign up for Facebook, this online community remains a popular site for college and university students. Second, Facebook profile pages have a structured, fixed format. This consistency allows for a controlled comparison among Web page users. This study examines the effects of narcissism and self-esteem on online social activity and their associations

with online self-promotional content. Gender differences are explored as moderators of types of self-promotional content presented on personal Web pages. The following hypotheses are tested:

> H1: Individuals with high narcissism scores will be correlated with a greater amount of Facebook activity.

> H2: Individuals with high narcissism scores will use more self-promoting content on Facebook.

> H3: Males with high narcissism scores will display descriptive self-promotion, while females with high narcissism scores will display superficial self-promotion.

> H4: Individuals with low self-esteem will be correlated with a greater amount of Facebook activity.

> H5: Individuals with low self-esteem scores will use more self-promoting content on Facebook.

Note that descriptive self-promotion is conveyed by text (e.g., via About Me, Status Updates, and Notes features), and superficial self-promotion involves images (e.g., photos posted as "Main Photo" or in Web page photo albums).

Method

Participants

One hundred Facebook owners (50 male, 50 female) were randomly recruited at York University. They ranged in age from 18 to 25 years ($M = 22.21$, $SD = 1.98$). All participants gave permission to be added to Facebook and agreed to have their pages coded for the present research.

Rater

The rater of the participants' Facebook page was the author of this study, a 22-year-old female undergraduate student at York University.

Materials

After agreeing to participate in this research study, Facebook owners were administered a brief four-part questionnaire. The first section required demographic information, including the participant's age and gender. The second section addressed Facebook activity; it required respondents to indicate the number of times they check their Facebook page per day and the time spent on Facebook per session. The remaining sections assessed two psychological constructs: self-esteem and narcissism.

The Rosenberg Self-Esteem Scale was used to measure participant self-esteem. This 10-item test measured self-esteem using a 4-point Likert scale, ranging from strongly disagree to strongly agree. Example items include "On the whole, I am satisfied with myself" and "I take a positive attitude toward myself." The original reliability of this scale is 0.72. This measure has gained acceptable internal consistency and test-retest reliability, as well as convergent and discriminant validity.[1]

Narcissism was assessed using the Narcissism Personality Inventory (NPI)-16. The NPI-16 is a shorter, unidimensional measure of the NPI-40. While the 40-item measure revealed an $\alpha = 0.84$, the NPI-16 has an $\alpha = 0.72$. Despite this discrepancy, the two measures are correlated at $r = 0.90$ ($p < 0.001$). This 16-item forced-choice format personality questionnaire also has notable face, internal, discriminant, and predictive validity.[10] Example items include "I am more capable than other people" versus "There is a lot that I can learn from other people," and higher scores on the NPI indicate more narcissistic personality. Overall, the NPI-16 is both a valid and reliable way to capture a range of different facets of this construct, particularly in situations where the use of a longer measure would be impractical.[10]

Procedure

Undergraduate students were randomly recruited on campus and asked to participate in a study exploring the use of Facebook. Participants were selected on the basis of whether or not they had an active Facebook account. Upon agreeing to participate in this research study, participants were presented with a waiver form to sign if they consented to being added to Facebook to have their page rated. Participants were also assured that all identifying information would be kept anonymous. Following their consent, participants were administered the four-part questionnaire. Upon completion, participants were immediately added to Facebook and were then fully debriefed.

Five features of the Facebook page were coded for the extent to which they were self-promoting; (a) the About Me section, (b) the Main Photo, (c) the first 20 pictures on the View Photos of Me section, (d) the Notes section, and (e) the Status Updates section. For the purpose of this study, self-promotion was distinguished as any descriptive or visual information that appeared to attempt to persuade others about one's own positive qualities. For example, facial expression (e.g., striking a pose or making a face) and

picture enhancement (e.g., using photo editing software) were coded in the Main Photo and View Photos of Me sections. The use of positive adjectives (e.g., nice, sexy, funny), self-promoting mottos (e.g., "I'm so glamorous I bleed glitter"), and metaphorical quotes (e.g., "A girl should always be two things: classy and fabulous—Coco Chanel") were coded in the About Me section. Self-promotion in the Notes section could include posting results from Facebook applications including "My Celebrity Look-alikes," which compares a photo of the user to celebrities, or vain online-quiz results, which often provide shallow descriptions of the user (e.g., You are very mysterious and sexy). Status Updates were also coded on the basis of self-promoting information provided by the user. Each section was rated on a 5-point Likert scale ranging from 1, *not at all*, to 5, *very much*. In cases where Facebook users kept these features private, the corresponding feature was not rated.

Results

A Pearson correlation addressed the relationship between narcissism ($M = 8.21$, $SD = 4.81$) and Facebook activity. As predicted, higher scores on the NPI-16 were positively correlated with the number of times Facebook was checked per day, $r = 0.462$, $p < 0.01$; and with the time spent on Facebook per session, $r = 0.614$, $p < 0.01$. Similarly, a Pearson correlation was used to test the relationship between self-esteem ($M = 17.05$, $SD = 4.96$) and Facebook activity. Results indicated a significant negative correlation between self-esteem and the number of times Facebook was checked per day, $r = -0.458$, $p < 0.01$; and with time spent on Facebook per session, $r = -0.432$, $P < 0.01$.

A series of Pearson correlation analyses were also used to assess the relation between owners' self-esteem scores and self-promotional Facebook page content. Results showed a sole significant negative correlation between self-esteem and self-promotion in the Main Photo section, $r = -0.374$, $P < 0.01$. The results are summarized in Table 1. Similarly, the relation between owners' narcissism

Table 1

Self-Promoting Facebook Correlates with Owners' Self-Esteem Scores

Facebook Content	Pearson Correlation
About Me	−0.139
Main Photo	−0.374**
View Photos (20)	0.097
Status Updates	−0.103
Notes	0.007

**$p < 0.01$.

Table 2

Self-Promoting Facebook Correlates with Owners' Narcissism Scores

Facebook Content	Pearson Correlation
About Me	0.136
Main Photo	0.493**
View Photos (20)	0.408**
Status Updates	0.200*
Notes	0.315**

*$p < 0.05$; **$p < 0.01$.

scores and self-promotional Facebook page content was assessed using Pearson correlations. Results indicated significant positive correlations between narcissism and self-promotional content in the following areas: Main Photo, View Photos (20), Status Updates, and Notes. The results are shown in Table 2.

Using this information, a univariate analysis of variance was conducted to determine any gender differences that existed in the types of self-promotional behavior presented by narcissistic Facebook page owners. Unexpectedly,

there were no significant interactions between narcissism, gender, and any of the coded self-promotional content. However, results indicated a main effect for gender and self-promotional information in the About Me section, $F(1, 96) = 6.367$, $p = 0.013$; the Notes section $F(1, 96) = 17.074$, $p < 0.001$; and the Main Photos section $F(1, 96) = 5.731$, $p = 0.019$. Specifically, males displayed more self-promotional content in About Me and Notes; see Figures 1 and 2. Females displayed more self-promotion in the Main Photo section; see Figure 3. No main effects were found for gender and self-promotional content in View Photos (20) or Status Updates. Results are presented in Table 3.

Discussion

Based on the literature review, it was postulated that online communities offer a gateway for identity construction and self-presentation. The goal of this exploratory study was to examine how particular offline personality traits manifested in nonymous online social environments. Building on the limited existing research within this relatively new field, one of the focuses of this study was to examine the

Figure 1

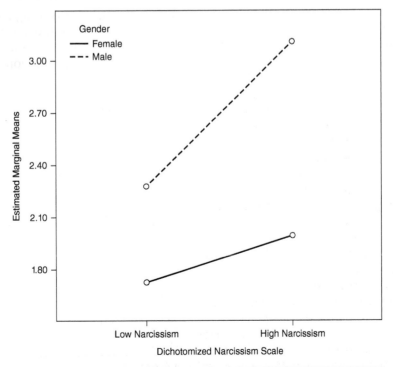

Estimated marginal means of About Me self-promotion.

Figure 2

Estimated marginal means of Notes self-promotion.

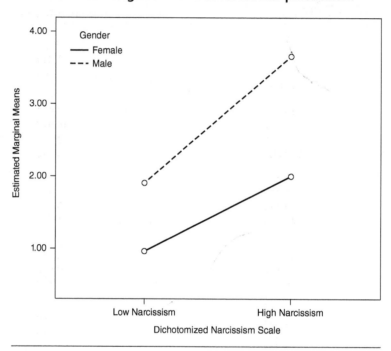

Figure 3

Estimated marginal means of Main Photo self-promotion.

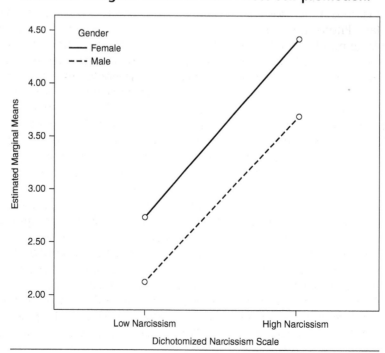

Table 3

The Effects of Gender On Self-Promotional Facebook Content

	Type III Sum of Squares	df	Mean Square	F	Sig.
About Me					
Gender	16.539	1	16.539	6.367	0.013
Narcissism	7.236	1	7.236	2.786	0.098
Gender & narcissism	1.883	1	1.883	0.725	0.397
Error	249.362	96	2.598		
Notes					
Gender	40.850	1	40.850	17.074	0.000
Narcissism	46.927	1	46.927	19.614	0.000
Gender & narcissism	3.122	1	3.122	1.305	0.256
Error	229.680	96	2.393		
Main Photo					
Gender	11.011	1	11.011	5.731	0.019
Narcissism	62.403	1	62.403	32.479	0.000
Gender & narcissism	0.125	1	0.125	0.065	0.800
Error	184.449	96	1.921		
View Photos (20)					
Gender	0.695	1	0.695	0.308	0.058
Narcissism	40.400	1	40.400	17.920	0.000
Gender & narcissism	0.637	1	0.637	0.283	0.596
Error	216.430	96	2.254		
Status Updates					
Gender	6.158	1	6.158	2.899	0.092
Narcissism	12.259	1	12.259	5.771	0.018
Gender & narcissism	3.496	1	3.496	1.645	0.203
Error	203.944	96	2.124		

effects of offline narcissism on Facebook activity. Given that this Web site offers various outlets for self-promotion (e.g., via About Me, Main Photo) and also presents the opportunity to display large numbers of shallow relationships (friends are counted and sometimes reach the thousands), it was hypothesized that narcissists would engage in more Facebook activity.

As predicted, there was a significant positive correlation between individuals who scored higher on the NPI-16, the number of times Facebook was checked per day, and the time spent on Facebook per session. This result is consistent with the findings presented in another study that examined narcissism and Facebook activity.[2]

While the nonymity of this environment places constraints on the freedom of individual identity claims,[3] this setting also enables users to control the information projected about themselves. In particular, users can select attractive photographs and write self-descriptions that are self-promoting in an effort to project an enhanced sense of self. Furthermore, Facebook users can receive public feedback on profile features from other users, which can act as a positive regulator of narcissistic esteem. Past research shows that narcissists, for example, are boastful and eager to talk about themselves,[11] gain esteem from public glory,[12] and are prevalent on reality television.[13] Given these findings, it was hypothesized that narcissists would present a similar opportunity for self-promotion on Facebook. Results partially supported this hypothesis. Significant positive correlations were found between scores on the NPI-16 and self-promotion in the following areas: Main Photo, View Photos (20), Status Updates, and Notes. However, a Pearson correlation analysis failed to show a significant correlation between narcissism and About Me self-promotion. A study by Zhao et al.[3] examining identity construction on Facebook also found that users were less likely to make positive self-descriptions in the About Me section yet were more apt to showcase themselves through photos. This preference for "show" versus "tell" can be attributed to the college sample, as the campus setting set the stage for offline socializing and thus a greater need to conceal socially undesirable narcissistic tendencies. Similarly, a study by Collins and Stukas[14] found that college students who rated higher on the NPI-40 were more apt to present themselves in a self-enhancing manner through an external domain (e.g., physical attractiveness) than through an internal domain (e.g., intelligence). Although, these studies support the findings in the About Me, Main Picture, and View Photos (20) sections, they are also paradoxical to the relation between narcissism and self-promotion in other implicit domains: Status Updates and Notes. This can be attributed to the distinctiveness of the Facebook environment and features. Status Updates are generally used to broadcast current states, and in this context, it is both acceptable and the norm to use this feature to boast. It should also be distinguished that the Notes feature of Facebook can include other information besides written text, such as images of My Celebrity Look-alikes. This application was common among this sample and was noted as self-promotional behavior.

Based on these findings, additional tests were also conducted to assess whether gender differences existed with regards to the types of self-promotional features that narcissists were apt to include in their Facebook profiles. It was hypothesized that male narcissists would include more descriptive self-promotion, while female narcissists would include more superficial self-promotion. Although no significant interactions were found among narcissism, gender, and self-promotional content, there were some main effects between gender and self-promotional content. Males displayed more self-promotional information in the About Me and Notes sections than women. Conversely, women displayed more self-promotional Main Photos.

Although there has been no research examining gender differences in types of self-promotional domains, particularly in online settings, this premise supports simple socialization processes. Specifically, it is probable that gender roles influenced narcissistic females' tendencies to include revealing, flashy, and adorned photos of their physical appearance and trends in narcissistic males to highlight descriptive self-promotion reflecting intelligence or wit in the About Me section.

Despite this notion, gender differences were not significant in the View Photos (20) or Status Updates sections. Although there is no empirical reasoning behind this finding, several hypotheses can be made to explain this result. First, self-promotional Status Updates are more widely accepted as normative behavior on Facebook. Thus, both males and females may be equally as likely to use it as a means of self-promotion. Second, View Photos (20) include photos of the user from other individuals' albums. For this reason, there is less control of what pictures are being displayed and thus a lesser likelihood for self-promotional differences among males and females. However, given the exploratory nature of this study, future research is needed to explore gender differences in Web page self-promotional content and interactions between narcissism and gender in an online environment.

A popular view on the etiology of narcissism, rooted initially in psychoanalytic theory, proposes that narcissism is deep-seated in fragile self-esteem or vulnerability to shame.[15] Although this hypothesis is widely accepted in clinical psychology, empirical evidence presents both equivocal and inverse findings with regards to this relationship.[15] Despite this uncertainty, this association was used to hypothesize that individuals with low self-esteem would be correlated with a greater amount of Facebook activity.

As predicted, results indicated a significant negative correlation between self-esteem and Facebook activity. Specifically, individuals who rated lower on the Rosenberg Self-Esteem Scale were correlated with a greater amount of time spent of Facebook per session and a greater number of Facebook logins per day. These results are contradictory to those presented by Krämer and Winter,[1] which found that self-esteem was unrelated to StudiVZ (a German Web 2.0 site) activity. Nevertheless, given the limited nature of research in this particular field, these results should not be viewed as conclusive.

The association between narcissism and self-esteem was also used to predict that individuals with low self-esteem would be correlated with a greater amount of self-promotional content on their Facebook pages. According to Markus and Nurius,[8] the actualization of the hoped-for possible self can be blocked by the presence of physical gating features, such as an unattractive appearance or shyness.[3] Using this theory, Zhao et al. suggested that nonymous online environments provide a fertile ground for these "gated" individuals to actualize the identities they hope to establish but are unable to achieve in face-to-face situations.[3]

In accordance with this notion, a significant negative correlation was found between participant self-esteem and Main Photo self-promotion. In this case, Main Photos could have been selected or enhanced to cover up undesirable features by individuals with low self-esteem in order to enable the actualization of their hoped-for possible selves. However, results failed to show any significant correlations between self-esteem and self-promotional content in View Photos (20), About Me, Status Updates, or Notes. These results can be explained by the context of the Facebook environment. The nonymity of the environment, especially the anticipation of subsequent face-to-face encounters with Facebook friends, has been hypothesized to narrow the discrepancy between the actual selves and the ideal selves in people's online self-presentations. Alternatively, a fully anonymous online environment might create a less inhibited environment for the fantasized ideal self to be projected (e.g., via About Me, Notes).[3] In this case, self-enhanced written descriptions are less likely, while self-promoting Main Photos are normative and thus accepted in this particular online community.

. . .

References

1. Krämer CN, Winter S. Impression management 2.0: the relationship of self-esteem, extraversion, self-efficacy, and self-presentation within social networking sites. Journal of Media Psychology 2008; 20:106–16.

2. Buffardi EL, Campbell WK. Narcissism and social networking web sites. Personality & Social Psychology Bulletin 2008; 34:1303–14.

3. Zhao S, Grasmuck S, Martin J. Identity construction on Facebook: digital empowerment in anchored relationships. Computers in Human Behavior 2008; 24:1816–36.

4. Ellison N, Heino R, Gibbs J. Managing impressions online: self-presentation processes in the online dating environment. Journal of Computer Mediated Communication 2006; 11:415–41.

5. Raacke J, Bonds-Raacke J. MySpace and Facebook: applying the uses and gratifications theory to exploring friend-networking sites. CyberPsychology & Behavior 2008; 11:169–74.

6. Oltmanns FT, Emery ER, Taylor S (2006) *Abnormal psychology*. Toronto: Pearson Education Canada.

7. Campbell WK. Narcissism and romantic attraction. Journal of Personality & Social Psychology 1999; 77:1254–70.

8. Walther BJ, Van Der Heide B, Yeon SK, et al. The role of friends' appearance and behavior on evaluations of individuals on Facebook: Are we known by the company we keep? Human Communication Research 2008; 34:28–49.

9. Weiten W. (2004) *Psychology themes and variations*. Belmont, CA: Wadsworth/Thomson Learning.

10. Ames RD, Rose P, Anderson PC. The NPI-16 as a short measure of narcissism. Journal of Research in Personality 2006; 40:440–50.

11. Buss DM, Chiodo LM. Narcissistic acts in everyday life. Journal of Personality 1991; 59:179–215.

12. Wallace HM, Baumeister RF. The performance of narcissists rises and falls with perceived opportunity for glory. Journal of Personality & Social Psychology 2002; 82:819–34.

13. Young SM, Pinsky D. Narcissism and celebrity. Journal of Research in Personality 2006; 40:463–71.

14. Collins RD, Stukas AA. Narcissism and self-presentation: the moderating effects of accountability and contingencies on self-worth. Journal of Research in Psychology 2008; 42:1629–34.

15. Lima NE. The association between narcissism and implicit self-esteem: a test of the fragile self-esteem hypothesis. PhD dissertation. Florida State University, 2007 In *Dissertations & Theses*, Full Text [database on the Internet]. Available from www.proquest.com. ezproxy.library.yorku.ca. Publication AAT 3282639.

SORAYA MEHDIZADEH was an undergraduate psychology student-researcher at York University when her study was conducted.

Alex Lambert

NO

Discovering Intimacy on Facebook

Positioning Facebook

Fundamentally, SNSs are online worlds which facilitate the creation of personal profiles capable of connecting people with other users. Profiles often afford forms of social interaction and the expression of personal information such as tastes, interests, political views, sexual orientation, and so forth. They also afford the articulation of one's connections, commonly displayed as a 'friends list'.

. . .

People use Facebook and like SNSs to socialise with their connections, gather information on these people, increase their self-esteem and popularity, express their identities through novel forms of content and association, and entertain themselves through interactive applications such as social games.

Scholars find that certain SNSs, Facebook in particular, are deeply embedded in everyday life, weaving through online and offline experience. Facebook has been referred to as a 'pervasive technology', 'deeply ingrained in [peoples'] daily routines'. . . .

Intimate Disclosures

Contemporary social psychology emphasises the importance of self-disclosure in the establishment of intimate relationships. Intimacy is constructed when one reveals one's inner self and perceives the validation and support of another. Likewise, sociologists such as Anthony Giddens view self-disclosure as an essential ingredient in the kinds of relationships which can endure the risky milieus of modern like. Jamieson refers to today's personal relationships as constructed around a regime of 'intimate disclosure'. Rather than viewing this as an essential aspect of intimacy, Jamieson locates this regime within historical processes which involve the dissemination of therapeutic discourses, the privileging of egalitarian relationships, and the individualisation of self-concepts.

These ideas help frame SNS scholarship, which heavily focuses on self-disclosures. Drawing on a survey of Canadian users, Christofides and colleagues discover that people are more likely to disclose personal information on Facebook than in general. They hypothesise that norms of self-disclosure are more permissive on Facebook. Certainly, researchers have noticed the preponderance of self-disclosures one encounters when navigating Facebook. Some of these constitute people's day-to-day trivialities and ephemeral thoughts. Some of these are of a more emotional and intimate nature. For example, based on a year-long observation of Facebook profiles, Enli and Thumin distinguish among three primary ways in which users 'practice' status updating: 'reluctance practice', whereby people post infrequently and refrain from disclosing intimate information; 'promoting practice', whereby people only post when they can paint themselves in a positive light; and 'sharing practice', whereby they liberally disclose aspects of themselves, including intimate information. Describing the last of these, they write: 'People might use their status updates to inform about their private life, including personal weaknesses and mistakes, and thus invite their online friends to engage in a more private and personal conversation'.

. . .

Critics . . . express deep worry about public intimacy online. Rather than expressing genuine concern for others, SNS users are only concerned with themselves, with their own intimate problems and therapeutic needs. Rather than seeking interpersonal fulfilment from social connections, they leverage these ties as an audience to hear their confessions and mirror their vanities. Rather than seeking 'I–thou' relationships, they seek 'I–it' connections. A friend is an 'it', a mirror, a means to an end. These are not authentic identities, but rather they are empty and ersatz.

In this vein, Facebook and like services seem emblematic of a 'culture of narcissism'. This phrase finds its popular origin in the work of Christopher Lasch. Looking at American culture, Lasch argues that a pathological form of narcissism has become normalised, one of weak ego requiring constant validation. According to Lasch, the incursion of therapy culture into family life causes the enervation of oedipal processes responsible for the formation of a strong super-ego. Simultaneously, the rise of individualism and consumer culture isolates people from meaningful relations and habitual, role oriented identities. The resultant psyche has little self-esteem or strong social bonds and, hence, must solicit from weak ties what can only be shallow recognition. Lack of fulfilment is inevitable, perpetuating a hopeless, continual desire for attention. It is important to emphasise the social deskilling which is implied here, because turning inward accommodates the degradation of social skills and conventions which facilitate 'other-concerned' sociality.

Lasch has been critiqued for failing to produce empirical evidence, for misreading 1960s emancipatory movements as symptomatic of narcissism, and for superimposing clinical dispositions on American culture proper without regard to the heterogeneous cultural groups constitutive of this broader space. Nevertheless, his ideas have taken hold and seem relevant to how SNS users supposedly beseech recognition from weak ties through public, intimate disclosures.

Sherry Turkle continues her ongoing and influential critique of cyberculture in *Alone Together*, in which she turns her attention to SNSs and narcissism. Like Lasch, she considers this narcissism does not reveal 'people who love themselves, but a personality so fragile that it needs constant support'. Services such as Facebook, argues Turkle, encourage this phenomenon by providing, on the one hand, the ability to judiciously control and broadcast self-presentations, and on the other, an immediately accessible audience from which to garner self-validation. With these options at hand, users neglect a much more mercurial but ultimately more rewarding source of self-discovery, namely, interpersonal experience. For Turkle, this is an experience defined by proximate, face-to-face sociality. Turkle's fondness for the non-mediated can be traced back to *Life on the Screen*, in which she critiques the self-invention which occurs on Multi User Domains because it allows people to sidestep processes of social mastery which allow mature, capable, psychically stable identities to form. Likewise, she believes Facebook provides a kind of false mastery, as it negates the necessary development of social skills that are based in genuine interpersonal engagement. Hence, users fail to grasp what this engagement involves and, hence, turn to publicising their intimacies with the hope this will yield social fruit and self-validation.

Again firmly routed in psychotherapy, Aboujaoude's reflections on Facebook echo Turkle's. Social networking bestows excessive control over how we present ourselves, hence, encouraging our vain and self-gratifying traits. It seduces us with the instantaneous gratification of sound-bite sociality, while we neglect rewarding interpersonal bonds. Aboujaoude laments how this erodes social mastery:

> Why put up with some character weaknesses when we can pretend to be omnipotent? Why struggle to advance at our job if we can be the reigning boss of our little corner of the blogosphere? Why work hard to socially integrate if we can count five hundred friends between MySpace and Facebook?

Once more, a kind of false mastery is evinced, a seductive omnipotence which Aboujaoude calls 'god mode'. Interpersonal intimacy is dead. Signed, God.

Rosen delivers a particularly potent critique of narcissism online, taking her cues from adolescent MySpace users. According to Rosen, MySpace suggests no more than a search for 'parochial celebrity'. She mourns the transformation of intimacy from an interpersonal aspect of friendships into a tool for garnering attention.

> '[F]riendship' in these virtual spaces is thoroughly different from real-world friendship. In its traditional sense, friendship is a relationship which, broadly speaking, involves the sharing of mutual interests, reciprocity, trust, and the revelation of intimate details over time and within specific social (and cultural) contexts. Because friendship depends on mutual revelations that are concealed from the rest of the world, it can only flourish within the boundaries of privacy; the idea of public friendship is an oxymoron.

. . .

Rosen closely parallels Frohne, who explores the way in which post-modern media collapse private boundaries and encourage the public theatricalisation of private life. Frohne deftly combines an analysis of how both media content and *form* determine a narcissistic condition. 'Medial self-realisation' has come to dominate cultural narratives which advocate modes of being. For example, reality television's focus on 'nobodies' convinces people who 'do not embody exceptional stories or careers that they can achieve this form of celebrity'. Also, these *vérité* psychodramas use intimacy to code reality and interpolate their viewers. They suggest that public audiences—rather than, say, a good friend or an actual psychiatrist—can act as a therapeutic mirror through which a person can come to know himself or herself.

. . .

Unfortunately, cultural critics offer little empirical evidence when seeking to connect 'SNS culture' with narcissism. Other, more empirically grounded, scholars have investigated Facebook narcissism from a clinical perspective. This research is grounded in trait psychology, which views narcissism as 'a highly inflated, positive but unrealistic self-concept, a lack of interest in forming strong interpersonal relationships, and an engagement in self-regulatory strategies to affirm . . . positive self-views'. These studies, however, merely ask how narcissists make use of SNSs and correlate behavioural questions with items that measure traits. Narcissism is not linked to technological, social, or cultural structures. In fact, with no causal elements at play, these studies say nothing about SNSs. Essentially, they discover that narcissists behave narcissistically, a tautology which could have permitted any case study: say, narcissism in Saharan poaching subcultures.

Moreover, empirical research cautions against an overt acceptance of the narcissism thesis. For example, in their investigation into the relationship between publicity and self-disclosure on a hypothetical SNS, Bateman and colleagues find that perceived publicity limits the amount and intimacy of self-disclosures. Similarly, a host of privacy-related research discerns that users do not always willingly accept the invisible gaze and take steps to curtail their levels of exposure. This literature . . . suggests that users are concerned with interpersonal life, and that the relationship between self and others online involves the development of a whole set of new social skills. Again, this points toward social life becoming more laborious, toward *intensive intimacy*. What are the socio-cultural dimensions of this intensive intimacy? How can we grasp an everyday, qualitative understanding of this phenomenon?

I think the critics mentioned above are fastened to a constrictive assumption which curtails an understanding of intimacy on Facebook. For instance, both Giddens and Bauman, although disagreeing on certain things, assume that privacy and intimacy are inseparable and, hence, public intimacy is inauthentic. 'Intimacy is the other face of privacy, or at least only becomes possible (or desired) given substantial privacy'. This assumption demands a definition of privacy, which is itself a slippery concept. The above critics imply a dyadic, rigidly bounded privacy, and this will be questioned throughout this book. More importantly, however, I believe the public intimacy

'contradiction' requires deconstruction, such that an analysis of intimacy on Facebook does not circumscribe its conclusions *a priori*.

Arguably, modern intimacy was produced through the 'privatisation' of personal relationships. Jamieson critically explores this process. Though sceptical of sharp historical divides, Jamieson proposes an analytic distinction between pre-modern and modern personal relationships. Existing up until the onset of industrial capitalism and urbanisation, 'pre-modern' bonds centred on obligatory relationships with kin and family. These lacked privacy, being relatively open to the closely knit communities they depended on. Communities were stratified, and marriage and children were often the product of economic contracts. The church demonised sexuality, and daily struggles for survival restricted autonomy. Intimacy based on private self-disclosure, moral and sexual equality, love, and freedom were in short supply.

Through the latter part of the Enlightenment, and culminating in the nineteenth and early twentieth centuries, industrialisation and urbanisation significantly changed the nature of social life, fracturing community bonds. In his seminal work, Tönnies portrays the death of traditional community (*Gemeinschaft*) at the hands of a society of cities (*Gesellschaft*). In this drama, intimate private life forms in reaction to the anomie of the industrial metropolis. Likewise, Sennett explores how successive market booms and busts ravaged the newly industrialised centres of nineteenth-century Europe. Provoked by this insecurity, people sought safe haven in the home. Bellah and colleagues trace similar connections, looking specifically at the onset of industrial urbanisation in America. As with Europe, people sought to escape into the solace of private life. Believing that the separation of a sentimental private sphere from a rationalised sphere of work would maximise productivity, industry assisted in the privatisation of personal relationships. 'Domesticity, love and intimacy increasingly became "havens" against the competitive culture of work'. This determined the evolution of polar human traits, of public utilitarian and private *expressive* individualism. Hence, the privatised home bore the germ of emotional self-disclosure. Giddens is likewise adamant that intimacy is born out of the mutual construction of private and public realms, and from this dichotomy our expressive capabilities are generated.

Bellah and colleagues also argue that friendships have undergone a process of privatisation. That is, friendships came to be influenced by the same 'expressive individualism' fostered in the home. This echoes Giddens' view of friendship as a form of pure relationship, a private, emotionally expressive bond. However, Allan argues that 'private' friendships were, for most of the twentieth century, enjoyed solely by the middle classes. Working class people constructed friendships in particular public spaces, such as pubs and sporting clubs, which were ritualistically separated from private life. Likewise, it is important to recognise that friendship formation was constricted by gender divisions. Through much of the last century the kinds of voluntary associations open to men were closed to women, who were constrained by a division of labour within the home. In more recent works, though, Allan recognises the way in which voluntary, mobile, and emotionally expressive relationships have cross-cut these structures.

Overall, the reality of the 'privatisation thesis' has been questioned because it provides too general a concept for understanding complex processes having to do with domesticity and social structure (Pahl & Wallace 1988), and because it neglects how leisure pursuits between friends often happen publicly outside the home and, hence, cannot be adequately considered 'privatised'. However, I argue that those who detect narcissism online are implicitly influenced by this privatised concept of personal relationships. This perpetuates a false dichotomy. Private, intimate life is juxtaposed against public life, which is viewed in terms of 'community'. That is, in terms of sociology's great tragedy, the loss of community and, hence, its great goal, the regeneration of community. This image of community is rooted in classical ethics and makes little room for intimacy. It can be traced back to Aristotle, who, in the *Nicomachean Ethics*, distinguishes between virtuous friendships, friendships based on utility, and friendships based on pleasure. Aristotle favours the virtuous kind, in which each party altruistically wishes good for the other. He imagines that, from this moral attribute, moral societies can form. That is, from virtuous friendships come virtuous communities: from the interpersonal 'good' comes the common good. Hence, virtuous friendships are central to Aristotle's ethical conception of civics and the polis.

In contemporary times, private intimacy is set against this civic ideal. Giddens views intimacy as the opposite of community, as taking shape against civics. Hence, intimate and virtuous friendships are at odds. Other writers

attempt to reconcile this divide, to understand how private relationships can take on virtuous aspects and transition into the community. For example, reflecting on Aristotle's tripartite definition of friendship, Bellah and colleagues write: 'In a culture dominated by expressive and utilitarian individualism, it is easy for us to understand the components of pleasure and usefulness, but we have difficulty seeing the point of considering friendship in terms of common moral commitments'. These writers wish to connect with a 'traditional view' of friendship, in which 'friendship and its virtues are not merely private: They are public, even political, because a civic order, a "city", is above all a network of friends. Without civic friendship, a city will degenerate into a struggle of contending interest groups unmediated by any public solidarity'. A similar concern is present in Putnam's influential work, Bowling Alone, in which he imagines how social capital may be used to regenerate community life.

If friendships are to be public, is this their only course? Is it either private intimacy, or public community? No in-between? Can we discover more nuanced, contextual, multifaceted understandings of public sociality which move beyond this limited dichotomy? These questions, I argue, should guide an analysis of Facebook. The cultural critiques of public intimacy discussed above are limited by this privacy/community dichotomy, a limitation best expressed when Rosen declares public friendship an oxymoron. Rather than accepting this limitation, I begin by being open and sensitised to the possibility of public intimacy which remains interpersonal and socially skilled. SNS research suggests that these attributes exist, albeit in a problematic state. This, in turn, suggests they are changing, and this change is significant. Hence, intimacy online should be considered *virtual* rather than virtuous. That is, as something *becoming*.

Alex Lambert is a researcher of new media at University of Melbourne. His research interests include social, mobile, and location-based media. His doctoral dissertation examines the influence of Facebook on cultural constructions of intimacy and friendship and the way Facebook users negotiate interpersonal intimacy both online and offline.

EXPLORING THE ISSUE

Is Excessive Use of Social Media a Form of Narcissism?

Critical Thinking and Reflection

1. Mehdizadeh's study shows only the correlations between those who have been classified as having a narcissistic personality and low self-esteem and their use of Facebook. What are some possible weaknesses in using a correlational study to justify the claim that social media is a form of narcissism? Come up with three points to support your claim.
2. Lambert suggests some alternative explanations for excessive social media use by individuals. Provide two of your own plausible alternative explanations to the narcissism hypothesis that might be considered.
3. Mehdizadeh's findings seem to suggest that individuals with lower self-esteem use Facebook more often than other individuals, and do so in order to boost their self-image. In your own opinion, could someone be justified in making this claim based on this study? Why or why not?
4. As Lambert claims, Facebook may possibly be used to increase the strength and intimacy of interpersonal relationships. Do you agree with this claim? What evidence might suggest otherwise? Come up with at least three reasons to support your claim.

Is There Common Ground?

Since the Internet began to increase in popularity in the 1990s it has come to be utilized in a variety of ways, including as a primary form of interpersonal communication. Social networking sites have provided individuals with opportunities to present themselves to the world, offering a gateway for online identity construction. Indeed, many individuals now use websites such as Facebook, Twitter, and MySpace to interact with others and to spotlight their own accomplishments. However, there is still much debate as to whether or not this use of social media is excessive in nature, whether it is a direct result of self-gratifying narcissism or if its use is the result of other motives.

Both articles agree that social media use is goal-oriented, though each views the primary goal of social media use quite differently. One of the central problems besetting both perspectives, however, is the difficulty of determining exactly how to most accurately define and measure the psychological concepts at issue. Indisputable empirical evidence is lacking when it comes to supporting either argument—thus the continuing debate. This state of affairs can't help but invite one to consider whether the evidence being presented in the various perspectives is really suggesting what the authors believe it is. In other words, just because individuals with narcissistic personalities may tend to use Facebook more than others, does that mean that Facebook is (or must be) primarily a tool of self-gratification? In other words, just because some (even many) social media users use Facebook to connect with other individuals, does that necessarily mean that achieving greater intimacy is their primary motive in doing so? Can either theory really be validated by current research findings and methods? Is the matter at hand in reality an "either/or" issue in which the two perspectives necessarily cancel one another out?

Additional Resources

Carpenter, C. J. (2012). Narcissism on Facebook: Self-promotional and anti-social behavior. *Personality and Individual Differences, 52*(4), 482–486.

McKinney, B. C., Kelly, L., & Duran, R. L. (2012). Narcissism or openness? College students' use of Facebook and Twitter. *Communication and Research Reports, 29*(2), 108–118.

Nadkarni, A., & Hofmann, S. (2001). Why do people use Facebook? (English). *Personality and Individual Differences, 52*(3), 243–249.

Urista, M. A., Dong, Q., & Day, K. D. (2009). Explaining why young adults use MySpace and Facebook through Uses and Gratifications Theory. *Human Communication, 12,* 215–229.

Wilson, K., Fornasier, S., & White, K. M. (2010). Psychological predictors of young adults' use of social networking sites. *Cyberpsychology, Behavior, and Social Networking, 13,* 173–176. doi: 10.1089/cyber.2009.0094

Internet References . . .

Facebook and Twitter Are Magnets for Narcissists

http://www.cbc.ca/news/technology/story/2013/06/11/tech-facebook-narcissism.html

How to Spot a Narcissist Online

http://www.theatlantic.com/health/archive/2014/01/how-to-spot-a-narcissist-online/283099/

Narcissism and Personality Inventory: Narcissism Test

http://personality-testing.info/tests/NPI.php